The Upland

AND

Webless Migratory Game Birds of Texas

Perspectives on South Texas

Sponsored by Texas A&M University–Kingsville

Timothy E. Fulbright, General Editor

The Upland

AND

Webless Migratory Game Birds of Texas

Leonard A. Brennan, Damon L. Williford, Bart M. Ballard,
William P. Kuvlesky Jr., Eric D. Grahmann, and Stephen J. DeMaso

Foreword by Fred C. Bryant

■ ■ ■

TEXAS A&M UNIVERSITY PRESS
COLLEGE STATION

This paper meets the requirements of ANSI/NISO Z39.48–1992 (Permanence of Paper).
Binding materials have been chosen for durability.
Manufactured in China by Everbest Printing Co., through FCI Print Group

Library of Congress Cataloging-in-Publication Data

Names: Brennan, Leonard A. (Leonard Alfred), author. | Williford, Damon L.,
    author. | Ballard, Bart M., author. | Kuvlesky, William P., Jr., author. |
    Grahmann, Eric D., author. | DeMaso, Stephen J., author.
Title: The upland and webless migratory game birds of Texas / Leonard A.
    Brennan, Damon L. Williford, Bart M. Ballard, William P. Kuvlesky Jr.,
    Eric D. Grahmann, and Stephen J. DeMaso.
Other titles: Perspectives on south Texas.
Description: First edition. | College Station : Texas A&M University Press,
    [2017] | Series: Perspectives on south Texas | Includes bibliographical
    references and index.
Identifiers: LCCN 2016027292 (print) | LCCN 2016028314 (ebook) |
    ISBN 9781623494988 (hardcover : alk. paper) | ISBN 9781623494995 (ebook)
Subjects: LCSH: Upland game birds—Texas. | Migratory birds—Texas. | Game
    protection—Texas.
Classification: LCC QL684.T4 B74 2017 (print) | LCC QL684.T4 (ebook) | DDC
    598.16/3—dc23
LC record available at https://lccn.loc.gov/2016027292

A list of titles in this series is available at the end of the book.

To all of the hunters who have supported the conservation of these birds, as well as the agency and private-lands biologists who have worked to conserve them.

Contents

Foreword

WHEN HUNTERS TODAY think of game birds, they logically and rightfully think first of quail, turkeys, and doves. They also might think about ducks and geese. But this book isn't about ducks. It is about migratory and nonmigratory game birds, only not the ones with webbed feet.

The webless migratory birds we are permitted by law to hunt include rails, gallinules, woodcocks, coots, snipes, and Sandhill Cranes. Oh yes, and don't forget a South Texas upland bird, the chachalaca. The only Texas game bird not native to North America is the Ring-necked Pheasant. This book is about these species too.

The reason for this set of essays, written exclusively by scientists and a former scientist at the Caesar Kleberg Wildlife Research Institute, is to bring to light the biology, ecology, and life history of these important birds. It was a daunting undertaking and a passionate attempt to impart knowledge about this group of birds at a level of detail that has never been accomplished before for Texas wildlife and Texas wildlife enthusiasts. I applaud the authors for their tireless effort, their thoughtful approach, and their diligent research into this topic.

We are blessed at the Institute to have assembled some of the nation's finest wildlife scientists. It is my hope that you appreciate them as much as I do. More important, it is my wish for all of us that these game birds are conserved for my grandkids to enjoy as future wildlife enthusiasts. If upland and webless migratory game birds are around for that generation, it will be the hunters who conserved them.

Fred C. Bryant
Leroy G. Denman Jr. Endowed Director of Wildlife Research
Caesar Kleberg Wildlife Research Institute
January 4, 2016

Preface

THIS IS A BOOK ABOUT some of the most well-known and cherished game birds in Texas. It is also about many lesser-known species of game birds that are hunted only by diehard individuals in Texas. Regardless of the species, this book is about the biology, ecology, and conservation of all the game birds in Texas, except the waterfowl.

This book is primarily a set of chapters that cover 21 species of upland and webless migratory game birds in Texas. At first mention, nearly every wildlife enthusiast knows exactly what an upland game bird is. An image of a quail or turkey or grouse instantly comes to mind. The term "webless migratory game bird," however, is a bit more obscure. Basically, it means all of the "other" migratory game birds, except for waterfowl. The Mourning Dove, which is a webless migratory game bird, is the most widely hunted wild bird in both Texas and the United States. Other webless migratory game birds, such as the rails, are hunted by only a handful of individuals. But they are still game birds, nonetheless.

We begin with a chapter that sketches out how the definition of what a game bird is has changed over the years. How human societies and culture have defined what is—and is not—a game bird has changed dramatically over time and still varies geographically. Again, if we use the Mourning Dove as an example, most states in the southern and western regions of the United States have considered it a game bird for decades. However, discussing the Mourning Dove as a game bird in the Northeast is anathema. It is simply not part of the hunting culture in that region.

The second chapter addresses the taxonomy and evolution of the 21 species covered in the core of the book. As wildlife scientists, we believe that both bird hunters and game bird biologists need to have an appreciation of the evolutionary history of the animals we are trying to manage and conserve. If nothing else, this chapter will give the reader background on how these species ended up where they are today, as well as on who their closest bird relatives are.

The species account chapters have some common threads that run throughout most of them. One is the range maps that show where each species can be found in Texas. The color scheme of the maps is similar to that in many field guides in that blue shading shows where certain nonbreeding species are found, green shading shows year-round geographic ranges, and yellow shading shows breeding-only areas. Several variations on this theme are present that show historical and current ranges as well as different hunting zones for certain species. Another common thread for many—but not all—species is the use of population trend graphs built from Christmas Bird Count data collected and compiled by the National Audubon Society. These data do not provide information on how many birds of each of these species are present in Texas. That is pretty much an impossible undertaking. What the Christmas Bird Count data do is indicate how populations of each species are trending over time. That is, are populations decreasing, such as Northern Bobwhites and Scaled Quail, or increasing and expanding, such as the White-winged Dove? We generally used the span of time from the early 1960s to around 2013 to select the data for these graphs. Prior to the early 1960s, count circle coverage for many parts of Texas was spotty. When we started compiling information for this book in 2015, the 2014 data were not yet available. In any event, simple visual inspection of each graph should give the reader clear information about whether the population of a species in Texas has declined, increased, or remained stable over the past four decades or so.

We conclude the book with an overview of two cooperative conservation initiatives—Joint Ventures, and Landscape Conservation Cooperatives—that have become prominent with respect to bird conservation in Texas today. These initiatives consist of public-private partnerships as well as cooperation and coordination among state and federal resource agencies and nongovernmental organizations. The conservation of the upland and webless migratory game birds of Texas is a monumental task that is far beyond the scope of any single program or organization. However, because such a task is daunting, it is an important conservation priority. Every victory in conservation is, unfortunately, temporary. But extinction is forever.

Acknowledgments

First AND FOREMOST, the productive and flexible work environment at the Caesar Kleberg Wildlife Research Institute made this book possible. The C. C. Winn Endowed Chair for Quail Research supported Brennan's efforts, and the C. Berdon and Rolanette Lawrence Endowed Chair in Waterfowl Research supported Ballard's efforts. Support from the South Texas Chapter of the Quail Coalition, and the Texas chapters of Quail Forever made Grahmann's participation possible. We appreciate having access to the stunning bird photographs by Larry Ditto and Greg Lasley. Dan Thomas of the Academy of Sciences VIREO collection provided the final photo of an American Woodcock at the eleventh hour. Barry Wilson of the Gulf Coast Joint Venture supported DeMaso's participation in this project; we are proud to have such support from the US Fish and Wildlife Service. Shannon Davies, director of Texas A&M University Press, has been an enthusiastic supporter of this project from the very beginning. Finally, we thank Tim Fulbright, editor of Perspectives on South Texas, for his support in including this book in that series.

Stephen J. DeMaso is employed by the US Fish and Wildlife Service, and the findings and conclusions in this book are those of the author(s) and do not necessarily represent the views of the US Fish and Wildlife Service.

The Upland

AND

Webless Migratory Game Birds of Texas

1

Historical and Cultural Importance of Upland and Webless Migratory Game Birds in Texas

Early markets carried general merchandise, agricultural products, home furnishings, and food staples requisite to life in 1800s Texas. Featured migratory game birds were mainly passenger pigeon, doves and woodcocks, while resident game birds included wild turkeys, prairie chickens and quail. Other offered birds commonly included robins, flickers, meadowlarks and blackbirds.—SAWYER (2013, 29)

Introduction

The term "game bird" typically refers to any bird that is hunted for food but also has not been domesticated. Over the years, classification of which species are, or are not, considered game birds has changed a great deal. Today, the range of species that people consider to be game birds is considerably narrower than what it was historically. Consider, for example, the line "four and twenty blackbirds baked in a pie" from the nursery rhyme "Sing a Song of Sixpence." More recently, at least back in the nineteenth and early twentieth centuries, "robin gumbo" was a common dish in the southern United States. Federal protection of robins and other migratory songbirds put an end to such gastronomical delicacies.

Native Peoples of Texas

The literature on aboriginal uses of game birds in Texas, while limited, contains a number of interesting anecdotes. First, it is important to understand that no single animal species in this region—bird or otherwise—was abundant enough to provide a reliable food supply. Bison in the plains may have been an exception, but otherwise, most native peoples endured with what they could capture opportunistically. Newcomb (1961) documented a variety of circumstances in which game birds were part of the cuisine and culture of Native Americans in what is now Texas.

Members of the Caddo tribe were known to consume a large assortment of small birds, while they also hunted turkeys and prairie-chickens. Curiously, the Lipan also hunted turkeys, but they considered "water birds" unfit for consumption for some mysterious reason. The Kiowa Apache apparently did not eat birds, bears, or fish, and they regarded owls and other nocturnal birds as reservoirs for the souls of their dead. The Jumano wove and tied crane feathers in their hair for decoration, and apparently Karankawa women created body-art decorations in the shape of birds. Both the Karankawa and their inland counterparts, the Coahuiltecan, were known to consume birds, probably on an opportunistic basis. It is not known whether they hunted migratory waterfowl.

These anecdotes from Newcomb (1961) certainly provide more than a hint that game birds, however the term is defined, played a significant role in the aboriginal cultures of the region that eventually became Texas.

Settlers from Europe

The arrival of Europeans in Texas had huge impacts on bird populations, and most of these impacts were not good. First subsistence hunting and then, even more importantly, market hunting (Sawyer 2013) resulted in extinction or near extinction of species that are closely related to species covered in this book. The Passenger Pigeon (*Ectopistes migratorius*) is a classic example of how such forces combined to create a perfect storm of events that brought what was once probably the most abundant species of bird in the world to extinction in less than half a century. Although it was probably never exceptionally abundant, the huge size and conspicuous nature of the Whooping Crane (*Grus americana*) no doubt made it a prized meal for many pioneering Texans who settled along the coast. Nearly all of the Greater Prairie-Chickens (*Tympanuchus cupido*) were extirpated from Texas by about 1850 (Oberholser 1974), except for the Attwater's subspecies (*T. c. attwateri*), which, while still extant, is maintained by annual releases of captive-reared stock. Recently, the Lesser Prairie-Chicken (*T. pallidicinctus*) was removed from the list of game birds in Texas and, at the time of this writing (May 2015), has been federally listed as threatened.

The Twentieth Century

The advent of the Migratory Bird Treaty Act of 1918 no doubt brought organization and structure to the conservation of many species of migratory birds, especially those that were hunted. It is interesting to note, however, that even during the early part of the twentieth century, the definition of a game bird was far more liberal than it is today. This is because many, many species of shorebirds (primarily members of the Scolopacidae) were hunted at this time. It was not unusual at all for people to hunt plovers, turnstones, oystercatchers, yellowlegs, and curlews, all of which are still found along the Texas coast today (Reed 1912; Forbush 1917). Today, only two species from this group, the American Woodcock (*Scolopax minor*) and Wilson's Snipe (*Gallinago delicate*), are hunted.

During the early 1960s, biologists and administrators in the US Fish and Wildlife Service (USFWS) realized that the scientific basis for conservation and management of the webless migratory game bird species lagged far behind the body of knowledge that had accumulated for both migratory waterfowl and several species of resident upland game birds. To remedy this situation, the USFWS, in cooperation with numerous state wildlife agencies, organized what became known as the Accelerated Research Program (Sanderson 1977), which ran from 1967 to 1982 and resulted in at least 340 scientific publications (Babcock 1994). The landmark book by Sanderson (1977), which described many of the early accomplishments of the Accelerated Research Program, was updated 17 years later by Tacha and Braun (1994). The original information from Sanderson and the update by Tacha and Braun became the scientific foundation for the conservation and management of the webless migratory game bird species described in this book.

In Texas, bird hunting is big business. More than 300,000 hunters spend more than one million hunter-days in pursuit of Mourning Doves. These metrics are far greater than for any other game bird in Texas. Thousands of youths are introduced to bird hunting by spending time on dove fields, usually first as "retrievers," before they are allowed to shoot. Millions of dollars in revenue are generated both directly (hunting licenses and excise taxes on firearms and ammunition) and indirectly (travel to and from hunting sites, overnight lodging, restaurant meals, and vehicle fuel, to name just a few commodities and services) and represent an important industry in Texas. A ranch near Mathis, Texas, for example, charges $650 per person for two days of dove hunting and $750 for a day of turkey hunting. South Texas bobwhite hunters often pay up to $15 per acre (nearly $40 per hectare) per year to lease hunting access on private ranches. These quail hunters and their operations are also often associated with "camps" (an understatement of the word if there ever was one) that make significant contributions to rangeland wildlife habitat improvement as well (Howard 2007).

IMPORTANT · AMERICAN · GAME · BIRDS
LYNN BOGUE HUNT
GREATER YELLOW-LEGS
See page 37
GOLDEN PLOVER
See page 41
BLACK-BELLIED PLOVER
See page 41

IMPORTANT · AMERICAN · GAME · BIRDS
UPLAND PLOVER
See page 39
HUDSONIAN CURLEW OR JACK CURLEW
See page 39

Figure 1.1. Some former webless migratory game birds that could be found on the Texas coast in the early twentieth century. (*Top left*), yellow-legs and plovers; (*top right*), Upland Plover and Hudsonian Curlew; (*right*), recommended shot-shell loads for game birds, early twentieth century; note the inclusion of plovers, yellow-legs, and curlew. Du Pont de Nemours and Company, the publisher of this booklet, was a leading manufacturer of gunpowder in the early 1900s; hence the motivation for producing this book was largely economic. From Forbush (1917).

IMPORTANT · AMERICAN · GAME · BIRDS

SUGGESTED HUNTING LOADS

The loads here tabulated are for 12-gauge guns, and are necessarily general. Allowances cannot be made for individualities in guns or shooters in the space available.

The powder charge given will be found sufficient when properly loaded to throw the size of shot mentioned *through* the birds at practical gunshot ranges.

Where there is more than one size shot given, allowance has been made for change during open season or differences in the manner of hunting the birds.

	DU PONT Drams	BALLISTITE Grains	SHOT Chilled	SIZE No.	PAGE
Mallard	3½	28	1⅛ oz.	6	6
Black Duck	3½	28	1⅛ oz.	6	6
Bald-pate or Widgeon	3¼	26	1⅛ oz.	7	10
Pintail, or Sprig	3¼	26	1⅛ oz.	6–7	14
Blue-winged Teal	3¼	26	1⅛ oz.	7	12
Green-winged Teal	3¼	26	1⅛ oz.	7	10
Wood Duck	3¼	26	1⅛ oz.	7	16
Wilson's Snipe	3⅛	25	1⅛ oz.	8–9	35
Greater Yellow-legs	3¼	26	1⅛ oz.	7	37
Black-bellied Plover	3⅛	25	1⅛ oz.	8	41
Golden Plover	3⅛	25	1⅛ oz.	8	41
Hudsonian or Jack Curlew	3¼	26	1⅛ oz.	7	39
Upland Plover	3⅛	25	1⅛ oz.	8	39
Bob-White	3	24	1 oz.	8–9	43
California Quail	3⅛	25	1⅛ oz.	8	45
Mountain Quail	3⅛	25	1⅛ oz.	7½	45
Dusky or Blue Grouse	3¼	26	1⅛ oz.	7–6	47
Ruffed Grouse	3¼	26	1⅛ oz.	7	47
Prairie Chicken	3¼	26	1⅛ oz.	7–6	50
Woodcock	3⅛	25	1⅛ oz.	8	33
Clapper Rail	3⅛	25	1⅛ oz.	7½	30
King Rail	3⅛	25	1⅛ oz.	7½	30

	DU PONT Drams	BALLISTITE Grains	SHOT Chilled	SIZE No.	PAGE
Virginia Rail	3	24	1 oz.	9	30
Sora Rail	3	24	1 oz.	9	31
Coot	3¼	26	1⅛ oz.	7	33
Broad-Bill	3¼	26	1⅛ oz.	6–7	20
Canvas-Back	3½	28	1⅛ oz.	6	18
Redhead	3½	28	1⅛ oz.	6	16
Canada Goose	3½	28	1¼ oz.	4	26
Greater Snow Goose	3½	28	1⅛ oz.	6	24
White-Fronted Goose	3½	28	1⅛ oz	6	24
Sharp-Tailed Grouse	3¼	26	1⅛ oz.	7–6	51
Wild Turkey	3½	26	1¼ oz.	4	52
Ring-necked Pheasant	3¼	26	1⅛ oz.	7–6	53
Black Brant	3½	28	1⅛ oz.	2 to 6	27
Common Brant	3½	28	1⅛ oz.	6	27
Shoveller or Spoon-bill	3¼	26	1⅛ oz.	7	12
Gadwall	3¼	26	1⅛ oz.	6–7	8
Golden-eye or Whistler	3¼	26	1⅛ oz.	7	20
White-winged Scoter or Coot	3½	28	1⅛ oz.	6	22
Mourning Dove	3⅛	25	1⅛ oz.	8	54
White-tailed Ptarmigan or Snow Grouse	3¼	26	1⅛ oz.	7–6	49
Band-Tailed Pigeon	3¼	26	1⅛ oz.	7	54

56

WILSON PLOVER (*Ochthodromus wilsonius*). This species differs from the "Ringneck" most noticeably in the large size of the wholly black bill and the broader black band across the breast. It is also slightly larger, measuring a little under 8 in. in length.

They breed along the South Atlantic and Gulf coasts from Virginia to Texas and casually wander to New England and also to southern California. Their notes are quite different from those of other closely allied species, the call note being more of a chirp than a whistle, and their notes of anger, delivered freely when one is in the vicinity of their nests, are excited chippering whistles. They match the color of their surrounding almost perfectly and, as might be expected, usually trust to their plumage to escape detection as they sit upon their eggs in slight depressions in the sand.

MOUNTAIN PLOVER (*Podasocys montanus*). These birds can be regarded as "mountain" only in that they are often found at high altitudes, but on arid plains they are often known as "Prairie Plover," a name that is in reality better suited to them, for they spend most of their time on the prairies picking up grasshoppers and other insects. In summer they are to be found distributed in scattered pairs, but in fall they unite in flocks of some size. They breed in western United States from Montana and Nebraska south to Texas and New Mexico and winter from the southwestern states through Mexico.

SURF BIRD (*Aphriza virgata*). This comparatively rare and little known bird, called the "Plover-billed Turnstone" wanders along the Pacific coast from Alaska to Chile. Its nest and eggs have not as yet been definitely reported, but it is believed to breed in the interior of northwestern Alaska.

WILSON PLOVER
MOUNTAIN PLOVER

Black Turnstone   Surf Bird

44

RUDDY TURNSTONE (*Arenaria interpres morinella*). Turnstones are unusual in form, in that the bill is quite stout, pointed and has an upturned appearance since the top of the upper mandible is perfectly straight. The present handsome species breeds on the Arctic coast and migrates abundantly along both coasts, wintering from southern United States southward. The common Turnstone, a grayer variety, is an Old World species, a few of which breed in western Alaska and migrate through Japan. The Turnstone is commonly known among sportsmen as "Calico-back," "Horse-foot Snipe" and "Beach Snipe."

BLACK-TURNSTONE (*Arenaria melanocephala*). Of the same size as the last, measuring about 9 in. in length. Found on the Pacific coast, breeding in Alaska and wintering south from British Columbia.

OYSTER-CATCHER (*Hæmatopus palliatus*). A very large shore bird, measuring about 19 in. in length, breeding on the South Atlantic and Gulf coasts from Virginia to Texas and wandering to New Brunswick.

BLACK OYSTER-CATCHER (*Hæmatopus bachmani*), shown in the pen sketch, is chiefly sooty black and white. This species, found along the whole Pacific coast of North America, is wholly blackish-brown in plumage; the bill is bright red and the feet flesh color.

MEXICAN JACANA (*Jacana spinosa*) is a most remarkable species common in Mexico and reaching our borders in southern Florida and Texas. The plumage is black, chestnut and yellowish-green; a scaly leaf-like shield protects the top of the head; the shoulders are armed with sharp horny points; and the toes and nails are of exceeding length, enabling them to walk over floating vegetation with ease.

Black Oyster-catcher   Jacana

RUDDY TURNSTONE
OYSTER-CATCHER

45

Figure 1.2. More former webless migratory game birds from Texas in the early twentieth century. *(Left)*, plovers and surfbird; *(right)*, turnstones and oystercatcher. From Reed (1912).

About This Book

This book represents an eclectic but ecologically and culturally significant group of 21 species of birds that range from the well known to the relatively obscure. The common thread that ties these species together, of course, is that they are (or were in the case of the two species of prairie-chicken) hunted. Even so, the nonconsumptive value of these species generated by birders, photographers, winter Texans, and others will no doubt continue to grow.

Their annual life cycles, habitat needs, management priorities, and other aspects of their life history are complex and diverse. This is why it is helpful to organize these species along familial lines such as cranes, rails, shorebirds, doves, and so forth and emphasize the common biological and ecological traits within each group.

This book is organized in three sections, beginning with an emphasis on the evolutionary and taxonomic relationships of the four orders and nine families represented by these groups of birds. Detailed accounts for 21 species of resident upland and webless (those without webbed feet) migratory species of game birds make up the core of the book. We conclude with a forward-looking perspective of some important emerging national trends in wildlife conservation that we believe have important implications for game bird conservation in Texas.

Much has changed with respect to how people have used and valued these game birds over the years. As noted previously, during the nineteenth and early twentieth centuries, numerous species were considered game birds that are no longer hunted today. We are sure that change will continue to be one of the few things that remain constant as we move forward. However, what also needs to remain constant is the presence of these birds on the Texas landscape.

Literature Cited

Babcock, K. M. 1994. Introduction to *Migratory Shore and Upland Game Bird Management in North America*, edited by T. C. Tacha and C. E. Braun, 1–2. Washington, DC: International Association of Fish and Wildlife Agencies.

Forbush, E. H. 1917. *Important American Game Birds: Their Ranges, Habits and the Hunting*. Wilmington, DE: E. I. du Pont de Nemours.

Howard, R. 2007. Operating a South Texas quail hunting camp. In *Texas Quails: Ecology and Management*, edited by L. A. Brennan, 336–62. College Station: Texas A&M University Press.

Newcomb, W. W., Jr. 1961. The Indians of Texas: From Prehistoric to Modern Times. Austin: University of Texas Press.

Oberholser, H. C. 1974. *The Bird Life of Texas*. Austin: University of Texas Press.

Reed, C. A. 1912. *American Game Birds*. Worcester, MA: Charles K. Reed.

Sanderson, G. C., ed. 1977. *Management of Migratory Shore and Upland Game Birds in North America*. Washington, DC: International Association of Fish and Wildlife Agencies.

Sawyer, R. K. 2013. *Texas Market Hunting: Stories of Waterfowl, Game Laws and Outlaws*. College Station: Texas A&M University Press.

Tacha, T. C., and C. E. Braun, eds. 1994. *Migratory Shore and Upland Game Bird Management in North America*. Washington, DC: International Association of Fish and Wildlife Agencies.

2

Evolutionary and Taxonomic Relationships

The first feathered creature we might call a bird lived at least 140 million years ago.—ROSENE (1969, 9)

The Importance of Evolution and Taxonomy to Wildlife Science, Conservation, and Management

Are evolution and taxonomy important to wildlife science? In an essay published in the *Wildlife Society Bulletin*, Thomas Gavin (1989) bemoaned the fact that many wildlife biologists did not see any use in applying evolutionary theory to their research. Gavin (1989, 1991) argued that wildlife biologists tended to focus on proximate causes (asking how something happens) rather than ultimate causes (asking why something happens) in their research. Gavin further argued that incorporating an evolutionary perspective into wildlife research would encourage scientists to search for ultimate causes while helping advance wildlife biology and management. Any aspect of a species (geographic distribution, diet, morphology, embryonic development, reproduction, behavior, etc.) is the result of interrelated sets of ultimate and proximate causes, and these can be understood only if the species' evolutionary history is also understood (E. Mayr 1961). Geneticist Theodosius Dobzhansky (1973) pointed out that nothing about the living world makes sense except in the light of evolution, because without it, one is left with a collection of disparate facts and data for each species. Although facts and data are

important, by themselves they do not explain why something is one way and not another. Only theories have explanatory power, and evolution is the unifying theory of biology (E. Mayr 1961; Dobzhansky 1973).

Gavin (1989, 348) argued that no wildlife species can be properly managed unless researchers and managers understand what "an organism evolved to do." He used a study of intraspecific brood parasitism by female Wood Ducks (*Aix sponsa*) in relation to visibility and spacing of nest boxes (Semel and Sherman 1986; Semel, Sherman, and Byers 1988) as an example of how an evolutionary perspective is useful in wildlife biology and management. Adaptation can occur over contemporary timescales (several decades or a few centuries); therefore, it is necessary that wildlife scientists and managers understand modern evolutionary theory and incorporate an evolutionary perspective in research and conservation strategies (Stockwell, Hendry, and Kinnison 2003). Darwinian reasoning and evolutionary theory have provided a deeper understanding of ecological traps (Schlaepfer, Runge, and Sherman 1998; Battin 2004); changes in behavior in captive-bred populations (McDougall et al. 2006); effects of harvest on phenotypic traits of targeted species (Law 2000; Olsen et al. 2004; Allendorf and Hard 2009); adaptation or failure to adapt to climate change and habitat alteration (Parmesan 2006; Gienapp et al. 2008); and the success of invasive species and how native species respond (Lee 2002; Strauss, Lau, and Carroll 2006; Sax et al. 2007).

Taxonomy is often viewed by nonspecialists as an arbitrary classification system, but modern cladistic taxonomy attempts to construct a classification system that reflects and conveys evolutionary relationships of hierarchically nested taxa. Taxonomic relationships "inevitably shape our basic perceptions of the biological world, influencing choice of research topics and interpretation of results," which in turn influences decisions and conservation policy (Avise and Nelson 1989). Subspecies are often used as proxies for management units under the assumption that morphology-based subspecies reflect adaptive variation within a species (Crandall et al. 2000); however, valuable conservation resources may be wasted in efforts to preserve ill-defined subspecies or species (Avise 2004; Zink 2004). For example, attempts to preserve the Dusky Seaside Sparrow (*Ammodramus maritimus nigrescens*) of Brevard County, Florida, were based on the assumption that this subspecies represented a unique phylogenetic lineage within the Seaside Sparrow. Mitochondrial DNA, in contrast, revealed that the Seaside Sparrow was divided into two distinct Atlantic and Gulf Coast groups and that the Dusky Seaside Sparrow was indistinct from other Atlantic Coast populations (Avise and Nelson 1989).

Large numbers of species and subspecies were described based on morphology and geographic distributions during the premolecular era (late nineteenth and early twentieth centuries) of biology. Unfortunately, many subspecies (and in some cases, species as well) were based on small sample sizes (sometimes $n = 1$), nonrigorous descriptions, and, in the case of birds, specimens that were collected outside the breeding season (Rising 2007). The growing acceptance of the biological species concept in the mid-twentieth century led many taxonomists to reclassify populations formerly regarded as distinct species as subspecies. The unfortunate decline of taxonomy as a major area of study in universities further compounds taxonomic confusion because the incorrect taxonomy will "stay on the books" for a species until someone takes the time to conduct a thorough study of a particular taxon (Winker 2010).

The growth of molecular biology has given biologists new tools to test species and subspecies designations originally based on phenotypic data. Genetic assays of many North American bird species have revealed that many named subspecies are not well differentiated, and the geographic patterns of genetic variation are often incongruent with intraspecific taxonomy (Zink 1996, 2004). In some cases, long-accepted species have been shown to be artificial groupings, as in the King–Clapper Rail (*Rallus elegans–R. longirostris*; Maley and Brumfield 2013) and Yellow–Citrine Wagtail (*Motacilla flava–M. citreola*; Voelker 2002; Pavlova et al. 2003) complexes, and the former lumping of Baltimore and Bullock's Orioles (*Icterus galbula* and *I. bullockii*) as a single species (Freeman and Zink 1995). In other cases, many avian subspecies were revealed to be distinct species (for examples see Zink and Blackwell 1998a; Friesen et al. 2002; Zink et al. 2002; Burbridge et al. 2003; Barrowclough et al. 2004; Li et al. 2006). One of the goals of conservation is the preservation of evolutionary processes that allow for adaptation (Soulé 1985); therefore, it is necessary to ascertain levels of genetic diversity and determine how that diversity is partitioned among populations.

Finally, genetic data give us a window into the past. Phylogeography is the science that studies the principles and processes that lead to geographic patterns of genetic variation (Avise 2000). Multiple phylogeographic studies have shown that temperate and tropical species exhibit evidence of range fragmentation and contraction as a result of Pleistocene glacial oscillations (Hewitt 2000, 2004). Many of those same species also exhibit genetic evidence of population and range expansions that coincide with the termination of the last glaciation. Cautious approaches to fossil calibration of molecular phylogenies allow researchers to determine when species, genera, and families diverged and relate those phylogenetic splits to past major geological or climatic events. These prehistorical approaches are necessary if we are to understand how life on earth has responded to past ecological changes, and how living species will respond to a warmer global climate and human-induced global change.

Evolution, origin, and phylogenetics of modern birds

The origin of birds extends back some 170 million years. The oldest fossil remains of a bird are those of *Archaeopteryx lithographica*. Ten specimens have been recovered from Late Jurassic (150 MYA) limestone deposits in Solnhofen, Bavaria, Germany. Although the phylogenetic position of *Archaeopteryx* relative to modern birds remains inconclusive (Holtz 2012; Naish 2012), evidence such as skeletal morphology, bone histology, embryology, gene expression, egg structure, integument, behavioral patterns, and phylogenetic analyses of amino acid sequences clearly established that the origin of birds lies within the dinosaur family tree (Vargas and Fallon 2005; Organ et al. 2008; Schweitzer et al. 2008; for thorough reviews see Prum 2002; Chiappe 2009; O'Connor, Chiappe, and Bell 2011). Birds are nested within Theropoda, a clade of bipedal, mostly carnivorous dinosaurs, including familiar behemoths such as *Tyrannosaurus* and *Allosaurus*, as well as many smaller, fleet-footed genera such as *Velociraptor* (now as familiar as *Tyrannosaurus* because of the success of the *Jurassic Park* movie franchise). Specifically, birds and their immediate ancestors (Avialae) are part of the clade Eumaniraptora ("true hand snatchers"). Eumaniraptora encompasses two other subclades in addition to Avialae: Dromaeosauridae (e.g., *Velociraptor*, *Deinonychus*, *Utahraptor*, and *Dromaeosaurus*) and Troodontidae (e.g., *Troodon*, *Saurornithoides*, and *Sinornithoides*; O'Connor, Chiappe, and Bell 2011; Naish 2012).

Birds diversified rapidly and invaded an array of ecological niches during the Early Cretaceous (Witmer and Chiappe 2002; Zhou, Barrett, and Hilton 2003; Zhou 2004; Zhonghe 2006; Naish 2012). Early birds were represented mostly by small-bodied and terrestrial forms, but Early Cretaceous (146–100 MYA) avifauna were represented by ecologically diverse taxa such as the seed-eating *Jeholornis*, herbivorous *Sapeornis*, sap-eating *Enantiophoenix*, fish-eating *Yanornis*, kingfisher-like *Longipteryx*, sandpiper-like *Longirostravis*, and loon-like *Gansus* (Zonghe 2006; Naish 2012; J. Mitchell and Makovicky 2014; Zheng et al. 2014). The Enantiornithes ("opposite birds,"

so named because the articulation of the scapula and coracoid is opposite that of modern birds) were the most abundant and diverse birds throughout most of the Cretaceous. However, the Ornithurae, which includes modern birds (Neornithes) as well as the aquatic Cretaceous taxa *Gansus*, gull-like *Ichthyornis*, and flightless loon-like *Hesperornis*, also made their appearance during the Early Cretaceous (Naish 2012). Birds, like many other taxonomic groups, suffered a mass extinction at the end of the Cretaceous (65 MYA), during which enantiornithines and archaic ornithurines disappeared (Longrich, Tokaryk, and Field 2011).

The timing of the origin of neornithine birds is unresolved and controversial. Molecular clock analyses of DNA sequences support a Late Cretaceous divergence for Neornithes, and Late Cretaceous divergence for several modern lineages, including ratites, gallinaceous birds (Galliformes), waterfowl (Anseriformes), doves (Columbiformes), shorebirds (Charadriiformes), and parrots (Psittaciformes) (Cooper and Penny 1997; van Tuinen and Dyke 2004; Crowe et al. 2006; Baker, Pereira, and Paton 2007; Pereira et al. 2007; Brown et al. 2008; Wright et al. 2008; Jiang et al. 2010; Haddrath and Baker 2012). In contrast, the fossil record suggests that most extant orders of birds appeared and diversified after the Cretaceous. Cretaceous-age fossils assigned to Neornithes are based mostly on fragmentary and poor-quality material, and the earliest avian remains confidently assigned to extant orders are mostly from Paleogene deposits (G. Mayr 2009). The exception to this is *Vegavis iaai*, a fossil neornithine recovered from terminal Cretaceous deposits (66–68 MYA) of Vega Island, western Antarctica (Clarke et al. 2005). Morphological phylogenetic analysis resulted in the placement of *V. iaai* within Anseriformes.

The discrepancy between fossil and molecular data may be due, in part, to gaps in the fossil record of many avian lineages (Ksepka, Ware, and Lamm 2014). The small body sizes and fragile skeletons of early neornithines may have decreased the likelihood of fossilization. However, fossils of other small-bodied vertebrate groups with fragile skeletons, such as amphibians, lizards, snakes, basal birds, and early mammals, are more frequent in Cretaceous rocks, which indicates that fossilization of early neornithines was not impossible (Benton 2004). Fossilization takes place only under special conditions, and it is possible that the earliest members of modern avian lineages may have lived in habitats where fossilization was not likely to occur. Brocklehurst et al. (2014) found that Mesozoic avian taxa that inhabited riverine and lacustrine habitats were more likely to be fossilized than those inhabiting marine or terrestrial environments. Unequal geographic distribution of paleontological studies may also contribute to gaps. The avian fossil record has improved dramatically since the 1970s thanks to new discoveries and the restudy and phylogenetic revision of previously described fossils (Ksepka and Boyd 2012). However, most avian fossils are from North America and Eurasia, and additional research in southern continents is needed to assess the completeness of the avian fossil record (Brocklehurst et al. 2014). The divergence times of many neornithine lineages may be overestimated by molecular clock studies using mitochondrial DNA, which tends to produce older dates than nuclear DNA (Ksepka, Ware, and Lamm 2014). The results of many molecular clock studies have been criticized because of the use of incorrectly identified fossil taxa to calibrate divergence times (G. Mayr 2005, 2008; Ksepka 2009) as well as the failure to provide adequate estimates of calibration errors (Graur and Martin 2004; Pulquério and Nichols 2007).

Recent molecular clock analyses using conservative fossil calibrations indicate that major divisions among modern birds took place during the Late Cretaceous, including the divergence of ratites and tinamous from neognathous birds and the divergence of Galloanserae (landfowl and waterfowl) from Neoaves (all other neognaths; Ericson et al. 2006; Phillips et al. 2010; Jarvis et al. 2014). Some basal splits within Galloanserae and Neoaves may have been initiated during the Late Cretaceous (Dyke and van Tuinen 2004; Clarke et al. 2005; Ericson et al. 2006; Ericson, Anderson, and Mayr 2007; Brown et al. 2008; Haddrath and Baker 2012), but divergence dating based on whole genomes indicates that most of the major divergences within Galloanserae and Neoaves began 65 MYA and continued over a period of 10–15 million years, with divergence of most orders complete by 50 MYA (Jarvis et al. 2014). Late Cretaceous and early Paleogene (65–40 MYA) fossils of extant avian orders usually represent basal or stem lineages. Fossils that can be confidently identified as belonging to modern avian families and genera are restricted largely to younger rock strata, which suggests that extant families and genera diverged during the late Eocene, Oligocene, and Miocene (G. Mayr 2005, 2009, 2014). Most extant avian species probably diverged during the Pliocene and the late to mid-Pleistocene (5.3–0.13 MYA), whereas late Pleistocene (126,000 to 10,000 years ago) glacial cycles were largely responsible for the geographic patterns of intraspecific genetic variation observed in avian species (Avise and Walker 1998; Klicka and Zink 1997, 1999; but see N. Johnson and Cicero 2004; Lovette 2005). Major exceptions to this pattern include taxa endemic to boreal forests of North America and Eurasia and the neotropical highlands, many of which underwent rapid speciation in response to habitat fragmentation caused by advancing glaciers (Weir and Schluter 2004; Weir 2006).

Higher-level phylogenetics and taxonomy of modern birds

Advances in DNA sequencing and molecular phylogenetics have helped resolve the evolutionary relationships within the avian tree of life. Neornithes is composed of two major lineages: Palaeognathae, which includes ratites and tinamous, and Neognathae, to which all other living birds belong. Genetic data revealed that Neognathae is itself composed of two clades, Galloanserae and Neoaves. Galloanserae is composed of two outwardly and ecologically dissimilar avian lineages: Anseriformes and Galliformes. Anseriformes includes ducks, swans, and geese (Anatidae), the magpie goose (Anseranatidae), and the pheasant-like South American screamers (Anhimidae). Galliformes contains mound-builders and brush turkeys (Megapodiidae), chachalacas, guans, and curassows (Cracidae), guineafowl (Numididae), jungle fowl, pheasants, Old World quail, francolins, partridges, grouse (Phasianidae), and the New World quail (Odontophoridae). A sister relationship between these two orders had previously been proposed (Beddard 1898; Simonetta 1963; Livezey and Zusi 2007); however, molecular data were required for the concept to gain universal acceptance among ornithologists (Ericson et al. 2006; Hackett et al. 2008).

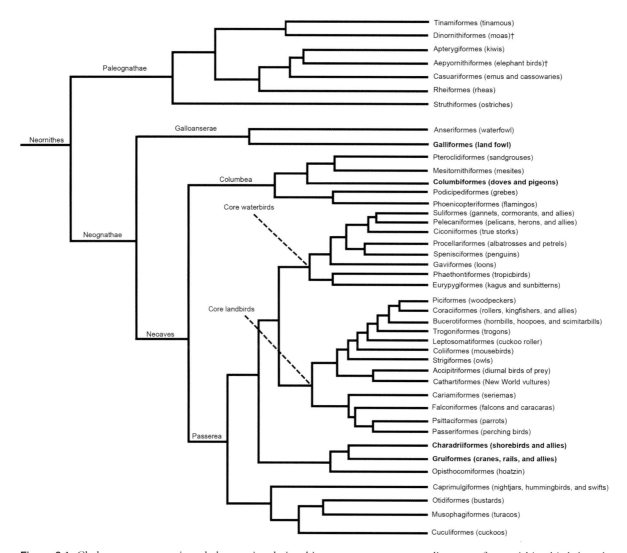

Figure 2.1. Cladogram representing phylogenetic relationships among crown group lineages of neornithine birds based on the results of recent studies utilizing molecular and morphological data (Cooper et al. 2001; Ericson et al. 2006; Hackett et al. 2008; Phillips et al. 2010; Mayr 2011a, 2014; Kimball et al. 1999; McCormack et al. 2013; Yuri et al. 2013; K. Mitchell et al. 2014; Jarvis et al. 2014). Orders that contain species that are covered by this book are in boldface. Recently extinct lineages are indicated by a dagger symbol (†).

All other neognathous birds belong to Neoaves. Phylogenetic relationships among the various lineages of Neoaves are still not fully resolved, but molecular phylogenetic studies indicate the existence of several major clades (fig. 2.1; Fain and Houde 2004; Ericson et al. 2006; Hackett et al. 2008; Ericson 2008; Jarvis et al. 2014), including the following:

Cypselomorphae (or Caprimulgimorphae): Caprimulgiformes (nightjars, potoos, oilbirds, owlet-nightjars, frogmouths, hummingbirds, and swifts).

Telluraves, landbird assemblage: Accipitriformes (hawks, eagles, kites, New and Old World vultures, ospreys, and secretary birds), Coraciiformes (rollers, ground-rollers, bee-eaters, todies, and kingfishers), Bucerotiformes (hornbills, hoopoes, wood hoopoes, and scimitar-bills), Leptosomatiformes (cuckoo roller), Trogoniformes (trogons), Coliiformes (mousebirds), Strigiformes (owls), Piciformes (woodpeckers, barbets, honeyguides, puffbirds, jacamars, and toucans), Cariamiformes (seriemas), Falconiformes (falcons and caracaras),

Psittaciformes (parrots), and Passeriformes (perching birds).

Aequornithia, waterbird assemblage: Gaviiformes (loons), Sphensciformes (penguins), Procellariiformes (albatrosses, shearwaters, and petrels), Ciconiiformes (true storks), Suliformes (cormorants, anhingas, boobies, and gannets), and Pelecaniformes (pelicans, hammerhead and shoebill storks, ibises, spoonbills, herons, egrets, and bitterns). Also part of this clade or closely related to it may be the Gruiformes (cranes, limpkins, trumpeters, finfoots, and rails), Otidiformes (bustards), Cuculiformes (cuckoos), and Musophagiformes (turacos); however, the positions of these taxa relative to other lineages vary depending on the type and number of loci examined (G. Mayr 2011a).

Charadriiformes (shorebirds and allies).

The remaining avian orders form a heterogeneous assemblage: Metaves, including Columbiformes (doves and pigeons), Pteroclidiformes (sandgrouse), Phoenicopteriformes (flamingos), Podicipediformes (grebes), Phaethontiformes (tropicbirds), Opisthocomiformes (hoatzin), Eurypigiformes (kagus and sunbitterns), and Mesitornithiformes (mesites) (Fain and Houde 2004; Ericson et al. 2006; Hackett et al. 2008; McCormack et al. 2013). Statistical support for Metaves was weak (Ericson et al. 2006; Hackett et al. 2008; G. Mayr 2011a) and was apparently driven by two nuclear genes, β-fibrinogen and rhodopsin (Fain and Houde 2004; Hackett et al. 2008). McCormack et al. (2013) suggested that Metaves may actually be due to long-branch attraction—the grouping of taxa together as sister taxa because of the accumulation of identical, independently evolved nucleotide substitutions (Bergsten 2005). Further evidence that Metaves may be an artifact of convergent evolution comes from phylogenetic analysis of complete mitochondrial genomes, which found no support for Metaves (Morgan-Richards et al. 2008). Recent whole-genome analysis including data from 48 species of birds representing all currently accepted orders confirmed the existence of two major divisions within Neoaves (Jarvis et al. 2014). The smaller clade, referred to by Jarvis et al.

(2014) as Columbea, included Columbiformes, Pteroclidiformes, Mesitornithiformes, Podicipediformes, and Phoenicopteriformes, with all other Neoaves encompassed by a larger clade named Passerea. The results of Jarvis et al. (2014) suggest that Phaethontiformes and Eurypygiformes are closely related to the waterbird assemblage and that together these formed a sister clade to the landbirds. Jarvis et al. (2014) recovered a lineage consisting of Charadriiformes, Gruiformes, and Opithocomiformes that formed a sister relationship with the larger landbird-waterbird clade. Caprimulgiformes, Otidiformes, Musophagiformes, and Cuculiformes occupied basal positions within Passerea (Jarvis et al. 2014).

Galliformes

Megapodidae is the most basal member of Galliformes and is a sister clade to the remaining families (Crowe et al. 2006; Kriegs et al. 2007). Cracidae is a sister clade to one composed of the remaining families of Phasianidae, Numididae, and Odontophoridae; however, the relationships among these three families are not entirely settled (Crowe et al. 2006; Cox, Kimball, and Braun 2007; Kriegs et al. 2007; Cohen et al. 2012; Meiklejohn et al. 2014). Cracidae, including guans, chachalacas, and curassows, consists of 51 forest-adapted species in nine genera that are mostly confined to the neotropics. Only one species, the Plain Chachalaca (*Ortalis vetula*), extends its range into the United States. The phylogenetic relationships among genera of Cracidae have been largely resolved (Birks and Edwards 2002; Pereira, Baker, and Wajntal 2002; Pereira and Baker 2004; Grau et al. 2005; Frank-Hoeflich et al. 2007). Guans (*Aburria, Pipile, Penelope, Chamaepetes*, and *Penelopina*) represent a sister clade to one composed of chachalacas (*Ortalis*), curassows (*Crax, Nothocrax, Pauxi*, and *Mitu*), and the Horned Guan (*Oreophasis derbianus*; Pereira, Baker, and Wajntal 2002). Within the chachalaca–curassow–horned guan clade, *Ortalis* is basal to the other genera and most closely related to the Horned Guan (Pereira, Baker, and Wajntal 2002). None of the cracids have been subjected to range-wide genetic assays.

Phasianidae is a large, diverse family of 47 genera and 150 species that occur naturally on all continents except South America, Australia, and Antarctica. The

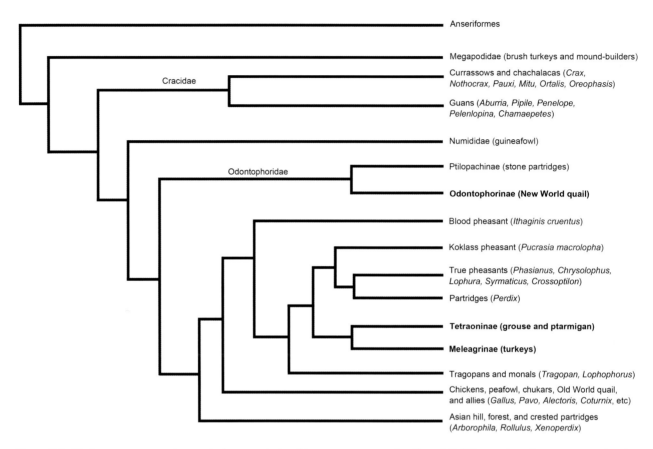

Figure 2.2. Cladogram representing evolutionary relationships among extant families of Galliformes based on recent molecular phylogenetic studies (Crowe et al. 2006; Cox, Kimball, and Braun 2007; Kriegs et al. 2007; Cohen et al. 2012).

taxonomy and phylogenetics of Phasianidae are far from fully resolved, but molecular data have helped answer some evolutionary questions. Although some ornithologists have classified grouse and turkeys as distinct families, Tetraonidae and Meleagridae, respectively, molecular phylogenetics has shown that these lineages are nested within Phasianidae and are best regarded as subfamilies (Tetraoninae and Meleagrinae; Gutiérrez, Barrowclough, and Groth 2000; Crowe et al. 2006; Kimball and Braun 2008; Wang et al. 2013).

The Ring-necked Pheasant (*Phasianus colchicus*), widespread in Eurasia, was introduced into North America during the 1800s and is now established in several states, including Texas. Thirty-one subspecies of the Ring-necked Pheasant have been described based on variations in morphology and plumage variation; however, studies based on mitochondrial DNA have found no support for any subspecies (Zhang et al. 2014). The lack of genetic differentiation among Ring-necked Pheasant subspecies may be due to the

different rates of evolution of phenotypic traits and neutral genetic variation, inadequate assessment of geographic variation and delineation of subspecies, and interbreeding with transplanted or escaped domestic stocks (Zhang et al. 2014). Although subspecies were not distinct, Ring-necked Pheasants in China did exhibit strong genetic structure closely associated with geography. No range-wide analysis of genetic variation has been conducted on North American Ring-necked Pheasants; however, nuclear marker data showed that populations in Iowa were highly structured, perhaps because of a combination of founder effects, inbreeding, and genetic drift (Giesel et al. 1997).

Genetic data indicate that Meleagrinae and Tetraoninae are sister taxa (Kimball et al. 1999; Crowe et al. 2006; Kriegs et al. 2007; Wang et al. 2013). Asian phasianids are the closest relatives of turkeys and grouse, which implies that their stem ancestor colonized North America from Asia (Kriegs et al. 2007). Turkeys diverged from grouse during the mid-Miocene (5–7 MYA; Drovetski 2003; Lucchini et al. 2011). Turkeys comprise two extant species, the Central American Ocellated Turkey (*Meleagris ocellata*) and the North American Wild Turkey (*M. gallopavo*). The Wild Turkey and prairie grouse (*Tympanuchus*) have been subjected to intense intraspecific phylogeographic research. Despite widespread reintroduction efforts, the Wild Turkey appears to have retained much of its historical phylogeographic structure. Mock et al. (2002) were able to recover historical biogeographic patterns of the Wild Turkey. Multiple genetic markers have generally supported the current subspecies taxonomy of the Wild Turkey except for the Eastern (*M. g. silvestris*) and Florida Wild Turkeys (*M. g. osceola*; Mock et al. 2002). Different demographic and historical factors have shaped the genetic structure of each of the Wild Turkey subspecies (Mock et al. 2002). Lack of differentiation among the Eastern and Florida subspecies is due to mostly continuous habitat that supports historical and ongoing gene flow between these two subspecies. Rio Grande Turkeys

(*M. g. intermedia*) are genetically distinct from the Eastern and Florida subspecies, but Mock et al. (2002) suggested that this might be due to the elimination of intermediate populations that formerly occupied areas within the subspecies range boundaries. Merriam's (*M. g. merriami*) and Gould's Turkeys (*M. g. mexicana*) were the most genetically distinct and also exhibited the lowest genetic diversity.

The diversification and speciation of grouse were influenced by climatic oscillations and glacial cycles in the Pliocene and Pleistocene (5.3–0.01 MYA) and possibly involved three separate invasions of Eurasia from North America across the Bering Land Bridge (Drovetski 2003; Lucchini et al. 2001). Grouse consist of 8 genera and 19 species (American Ornithologists' Union 1998; Sangster et al. 2012). Grouse genera comprise several distinct lineages, including a Palearctic/Holarctic clade of *Tetrao*, *Falcipennis*, and *Lagopus* that is sister to a clade composed of North American *Tympanuchus*, *Centrocercus*, and *Dendragapus*, with the Hazel and Chinese Grouse (*Tetrastes bonasia* and

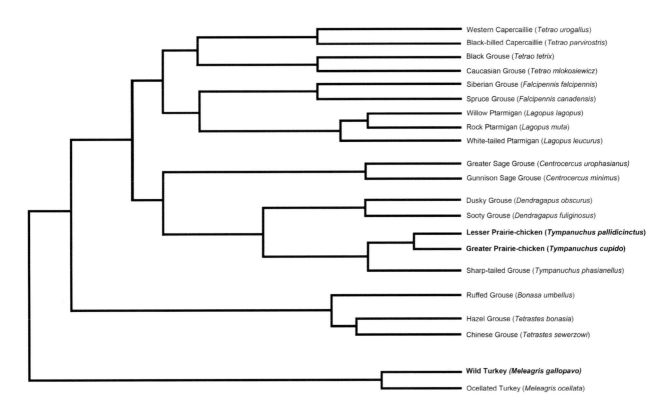

Figure 2.3. Cladogram representing evolutionary relationships among the grouse and turkeys based on recent phylogenetic studies (Lucchini et al. 2001; Gutiérrez, Barrowclough, and Groth 2000; Dimcheff, Drovetski, and Mindell 2002; Drovetski 2002, 2003).

T. sewerzowi) and the Ruffed Grouse (*Bonasa umbellus*) occupying successively basal positions (Drovetski 2002; Lucchini et al. 2001; DeYoung and Williford 2016).

Molecular clock data indicate that *Tympanuchus* arose and rapidly diversified during the mid- to late Pleistocene, beginning as early as 200,000 years ago (Drovetski 2003; Spaulding et al. 2006; J. Johnson 2008; Galla 2013). Studies based on mitochondrial DNA showed that the genetic structure of prairie grouse, in contrast to turkeys, was not concordant with the species and subspecies taxonomy despite the distinct morphological and behavioral differences among Sharp-tailed Grouse (*Tympanuchus phasianellus*) and Greater (*T. cupido*) and Lesser Prairie-Chickens (*T. pallidicinctus*; Ellsworth et al. 1994; Palkovacs et al. 2004; J. Johnson and Dunn 2006; Spaulding et al. 2006). Nuclear loci also failed to produce gene trees that were concordant with *Tympanuchus* species taxonomy, although sex-linked loci performed much better than autosomal nuclear or mitochondrial loci, with the Sharp-tailed Grouse being recovered as a distinct lineage (Galla 2013). Galla's (2013) phylogenetic reconstructions using combined mitochondrial and nuclear sequence data recovered each of the prairie grouse species as distinct lineages, demonstrating the power of multilocus data sets to resolve species limits among closely related taxa. Geographic patterns of genetic variation and ecological niche modeling indicate that the geographic ranges of all three species of prairie grouse were restricted during the latest glacial period (26.5–19 kya), suggesting that all three species underwent demographic and range expansions following the end of the last glacial period (Palkovacs et al. 2004; J. Johnson and Dunn 2006; Ross et al. 2006; Spaulding et al. 2006; J. Johnson 2008; Hagen et al. 2010; DeYoung and Williford 2016). Interspecific hybridization following secondary contact between expanding populations may account for some of the genetic indistinctness among prairie grouse, as do differences in the evolutionary rates of phenotypic traits and neutral genetic markers (Ellsworth et al. 1994; J. Johnson 2008).

New World quail have occasionally been treated as a subfamily of Phasianidae, but morphological and genetic data indicate that they represent a distinct clade closely related to Phasianidae and Numididae (Crowe et al. 2006; Cox, Kimball, and Braun 2007; Kriegs et al. 2007; Cohen et al. 2012; Meiklejohn et al. 2014). Odontophoridae is composed of nine extant genera and 24 extant species, including tree quail (*Dendrortyx* spp.), Banded Quail (*Philortyx fasciatus*), Mountain Quail (*Oreortyx pictus*), bobwhites (*Colinus* spp.), crested quail (*Callipepla* spp.), wood quail (*Odontophorus* spp.), harlequin quail (*Cyrtonyx* spp.), Singing Quail (*Dactylortyx thoracicus*), and the Tawny-faced Quail (*Rhynchortyx cinctus*). The most complete phylogenetic analysis of New Word quail is Holman's (1961) osteological study. Holman (1961) concluded that Odontophoridae was composed of two major lineages: one that included *Dendrortyx*, *Philortyx*, *Oreortyx*, *Colinus*, and *Callipepla* and another composed of *Odontophorus*, *Dactylortyx*, *Cyrtonyx*, and *Rhynchortyx*. Molecular phylogenetic studies of New World quail have been taxonomically limited (Gutiérrez, Zink, and Yang 1983; Zink and Blackwell 1998b; Eo, Bininda-Emonds, and Carroll 2009). Analysis of mitochondrial DNA sequences obtained from all odontophorid genera was largely congruent with Holman's (1961) conclusions, with the exception that *Rhynchortyx* appears to be the most basal (fig. 2.4). Multilocus data have shown that Odontophoridae also includes two African galliforms, the Stone Partridge (*Ptilopachus petrosus*) and Nahan's Francolin (*P. nahani*), which represent a sister lineage (Ptilopachinae) to New World taxa (Odontophorinae; Crowe et al. 2006; Cohen et al. 2012; Bowie, Cohen, and Crowe 2013; Meikeljohn et al. 2014). This unexpected finding suggests that Odontophoridae originated in Africa during the early Cenozoic and colonized the New World via the North Atlantic Land Bridge that connected Europe, Greenland, and North America or the Bering Land Bridge that connected eastern Asia and Alaska during the early Cenozoic (Cohen et al. 2012; Hosner, Braun, and Kimball 2015). The origin and diversification of extant genera and species of North American quail began during the Miocene and continued through the Pliocene and Pleistocene in response to climatic oscillations (Gutiérrez, Zink, and Yang 1983; Zink and Blackwell 1998b; Williford 2013; Hosner, Braun, and Kimball 2015).

Four genera and six species of New World quail inhabit the United States: Northern Bobwhite (*Colinus*

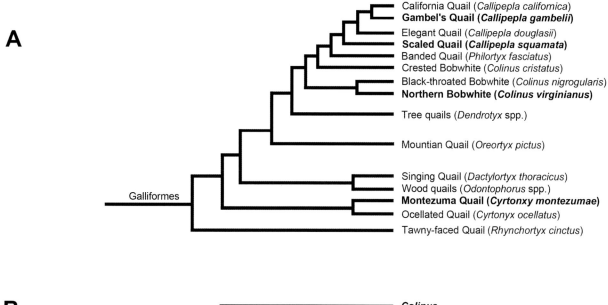

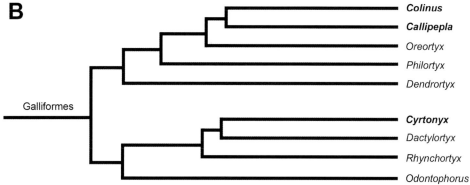

Figure 2.4. Cladograms representing the phylogenetic relationships among the New World quails based on *A*, mitochondrial ND2 sequences (Williford 2013), and *B*, skeletal anatomy and morphology (Holman 1964).

virginianus), Scaled Quail (*Callipepla squamata*), Gambel's Quail (*Callipepla gambelii*), California Quail (*Callipepla californica*), Mountain Quail (*Oreortyx pictus*), and Montezuma Quail (*Cyrtonyx montezumae*). Only the Mountain and California Quail are absent from Texas. *Colinus* includes two neotropical species in addition to the Northern Bobwhite, the Black-throated (*Colinus nigrogularis*) and Crested Bobwhites (*Colinus cristatus*). Holman (1961) noted that the skeletons of these three species were nearly indistinguishable from one another, and Hubbard (1973) hypothesized that the diversification of the bobwhites was driven by Pleistocene glacial cycles. However, mitochondrial DNA data indicate that the Crested Bobwhite diverged from the Northern and Black-throated Bobwhites during the Pliocene

(4–5 MYA), whereas the split between the Northern and Black-throated Bobwhites occurred much more recently (Williford 2013). The Northern Bobwhite exhibits greater geographic variation in plumage coloration than any other species of New World quail. Most of the variation, however, is due to geographic differences in male plumage, with females being very similar across the entire range (Brennan 1999). The dramatic differences in male plumage led many early ornithologists to describe morphologically distinct bobwhite populations as new species. During the early twentieth century, these "species" were relegated to subspecies status when they were lumped together as the "Northern Bobwhite." Approximately 16–22 subspecies of the Northern Bobwhite are considered valid today, although doubt and disagreement still exist about the status of many of these subspecies. Early studies based on a small sample size and limited taxonomic sampling suggested some degree of differentiation among some of the subspecies (Nedbal et al. 1997; White et al. 2000). Recent studies based on mitochondrial control region sequences that employed greater geographic sampling have shown that the Northern Bobwhite exhibits little phylogeographic structure across its range, and its geographic patterns of genetic diversity are not concordant with subspecies taxonomy (Eo, Wares, and Carroll 2010; Williford 2013; Williford et al. 2014c). The Northern Bobwhite does exhibit a strong signal of demographic expansion, which is most likely the result of late or post-Pleistocene population growth and range expansion (Eo, Wares, and Carroll 2010; Williford 2013; Williford et al. 2014c). The Northern Bobwhite exhibits greater genetic diversity in Mexico, which suggests that the expansion was largely northward (Williford 2013).

In addition to Scaled, Gambel's, and California Quail, *Callipepla* includes a fourth species, restricted to northwestern Mexico, the Elegant Quail (*C. douglasii*). Elegant, Gambel's, and California Quail were formerly placed in the genus *Lophortyx*, which was later merged with *Callipepla* based on molecular evidence (Gutiérrez, Zink, and Yang 1983; Zink and Blackwell 1998b). The Scaled Quail is assumed to be the most basal member of the group because of its more subdued coloration and less extravagant crest; however, previous studies based on mitochondrial DNA have not been able to fully resolve the phylogenetic positions of the four *Callipepla* species (Zink and Blackwell 1998b). Nuclear DNA may be necessary to accomplish this. The Scaled Quail exhibits little genetic structure throughout its geographic distribution, little differentiation among its four subspecies, and evidence of demographic expansion (Williford et al. 2014a). This suggests that much of the Scaled Quail's historical range was recently colonized, perhaps after passing through a severe bottleneck. The Gambel's Quail, in contrast, exhibits a strong phylogeographic structure that suggests former isolation in two separate populations in the Chihuahuan and Sonoran Deserts (Williford et al. 2014b). Like the Northern Bobwhite and the Scaled Quail, the Gambel's Quail also exhibits evidence of former demographic expansion and little

differentiation among its various subspecies (Williford et al. 2014b).

The Montezuma Quail (*Cyrtonyx montezumae*) is the only member of its genus that extends its range into the United States. Its congener, the Ocellated Quail (*C. ocellatus*), is restricted to parts of southern Mexico and northern Central America. Five subspecies have been described for the Montezuma Quail based on variations in male plumage, and the Ocellated Quail is sometimes considered to be a sixth subspecies (Johnsgard 1988). No phylogenetic or phylogeographic studies have been conducted on *Cyrtonyx*.

Columbiformes

The method by which doves and pigeons (Columbidae) feed their offspring makes this lineage unique among birds. Columbid adults feed their chicks a semiliquid diet of sloughed-off epithelial cells, known as "pigeon milk" or "crop milk." Pigeon milk contains high levels of fatty acids and amino acids that allow for rapid growth and development (Beams and Meyer 1931; Shetty et al. 1992). Molecular clock data suggest that Columbiformes originated in the Late Cretaceous (Pereira et al. 2007; Pacheco et al. 2011); however, the earliest fossils assigned to Columbiformes date from the Oligocene and Miocene (Olson 1985; Becker and Brodkorb 1992; Boles 2001). Morphological data suggest that doves and pigeons are closely related to sandgrouse (Pteroclidiformes; G. Mayr and Clarke 2003; Livezey and Zusi 2007), which is further supported by nuclear sequences (Ericson et al. 2006). Nuclear DNA also indicated that Columbiformes and Pteroclidiformes have affinities with the Madagascan mesites. In contrast, work based on complete mitochondrial genomes recovered a sister relationship between Columbiformes and Charadriiformes (Pacheco et al. 2011), although these taxa do not share derived morphological features to the exclusion of all other taxa (G. Mayr 2011a). To complicate matters further, recent phylogenetic studies based on nuclear clathrin heavy chain genes supported relationships between Columbiformes and the waterbird assemblage (Chojnowski, Kimball, and Braun 2008). Whole-genome analysis suggests that Columbiformes is a sister clade to the mesites and the sandgrouse, and together these form a sister lineage to flamingos and grebes (Jarvis et al. 2014).

The phylogenetic relationships within Columbiformes are well understood, and genetic data support the existence of three clades (K. Johnson and Clayton 2000b; Shapiro et al. 2002; Pereira et al. 2007; K. Johnson et al. 2010). One clade includes both New and Old World species divided into two subclades, in which the New World genera *Zentrygon*, *Leptotila*, *Leptotrygon*, *Zenaida*, and *Geotrygon* are a sister lineage to another that includes New World pigeons (*Patagioenas*, and the extinct Passenger Pigeon, *Ectopistes migratorius*) and Old World pigeons (*Columba*), turtledoves and collared doves (*Streptopelia*, *Spilopelia*, and *Nesoenas*), and cuckoo-doves (*Reinwardtoena*, *Macropygia*, and *Turacoena*). A second clade contains small New World ground-doves (*Columbina*, *Metriopelia*, *Uropelia*, and *Claravis*). The third clade includes genera from Africa, Asia, Australia, the East Indies, and New Zealand, including the extinct Dodo (*Raphus cucullatus*) and Rodrigues Solitaire (*Pezophaps solitaria*).

Eight native and three introduced species of doves and pigeons regularly breed in the United States, and of these nine species maintain breeding populations in Texas: the Band-tailed Pigeon (*Patagioenas fasciata*), Red-billed Pigeon (*P. flavirostris*), Mourning Dove (*Zenaida macroura*), White-winged Dove (*Z. asiatica*), Common Ground-Dove (*Columbina passerina*), Inca Dove (*C. inca*), and White-tipped Dove (*Leptotila verreauxi*), and the introduced Rock Pigeon (*Columba livia*) and Eurasian Collared-Dove (*Streptopelia decaocto*). Only the Mourning, White-winged, and White-tipped Doves are regularly targeted by hunters in Texas.

Phylogenetic relationships among *Zenaida* and *Leptotila* doves are well resolved. The closest relative of the White-winged Dove is the neotropical Pacific Dove (*Z. meloda*, formerly included in *Z. asiatica*), and this lineage is a sister clade to another composed of Mourning, Socorro (*Z. graysoni*), Eared

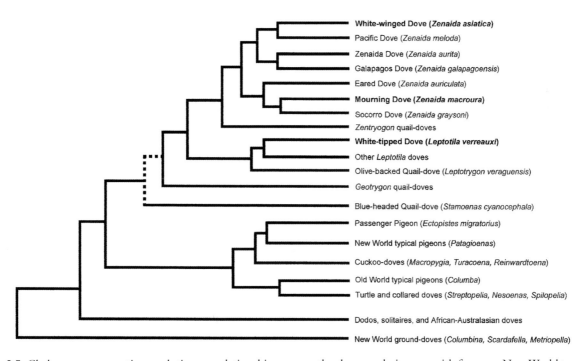

Figure 2.5. Cladogram representing evolutionary relationships among the doves and pigeons, with focus on New World taxa based on recent studies using molecular methods (K. Johnson and Clayton 2000a, 2000b; K. Johnson et al. 2001, 2010; Shapiro et al. 2002; Pereira et al. 2007; K. Johnson and Weckstein 2011; Banks et al. 2013). The dotted line represents the presumed phylogenetic relationship of the Blue-headed Quail-Dove (*Starnoenas cyanocephala*) to *Geotrygon*. The Blue-headed Quail-Dove has not yet been included in any molecular phylogenetic studies, but Goodwin (1958) hypothesized that its closest relatives were probably among *Geotrygon* quail-doves.

(*Z. auriculata*), Galapagos (*Z. galapagoensis*), and Zenaida Doves (*Z. aurita*; K. Johnson and Clayton 2000a). *Zenaida* is most closely related to *Leptotila* (K. Johnson and Clayton 2000a, 2000b; K. Johnson et al. 2010). The White-tipped Dove (*L. verreauxi*) appears to be the most basal member of its genus and is a sister lineage to the other *Leptotila* species (K. Johnson et al. 2010; R. C. Banks et al. 2013); however, no phylogenetic study as of yet has included all 11 species of *Leptotila*. Recent work by K. Johnson and Weckstein (2011) suggests that *Leptotila* originated in South America and speciated as it dispersed northward into North America beginning 3.4 MYA. The White-tipped Dove underwent rapid diversification beginning about 870,000 years ago and has reinvaded South America from Central America (K. Johnson and Weckstein 2011). Only the Mourning and White-winged Doves have been subjected to genetic assays, and these involved limited geographic sampling despite the ecological and economic importance of these two species. Ball and Avise (1992) found little population structure within the Mourning Dove and no genetic differentiation between two subspecies, Z. *m. carolinensis* and Z. *m. marginella*. Morphological and mitochondrial DNA sequence data indicate that White-winged Doves formerly existed as geographically distinct populations prior to the range expansion that began in the late twentieth century, conforming to the named subspecies of the Eastern (*Z. a. asiatica*) and Western White-winged Doves (*Z. a. mearnsi*; Pruett et al. 2000). Populations in range expansion areas sampled by Pruett et al. (2000) were intermediate in body size and genetically homogeneous, which suggests that the two subspecies now interbreed where their ranges overlap.

Gruiformes

Gruiformes, as traditionally delineated, is a collection of morphologically diverse families that includes the cranes (Gruidae), rails (Rallidae), Limpkin (*Aramus guarauna*, Aramidae), trumpeters (Psophiidae), seriemas (Cariamidae), sungrebes and finfoots (Heliornithidae), Sunbittern (*Eurypyga helias*, Eurypygidae), Kagu (*Rhynochetos jubatus*, Rhynochetidae), Plains Wanderer (*Pedionomus torquatus*, Pedionomidae), buttonquails (Turnicidae), Madagascan mesites

(Mesitornithidae), and bustards (Otididae). Morphological and molecular analyses, however, have failed to support this grouping. Buttonquails and the Plains Wanderer, despite superficial similarities to gruiforms, are actually part of Charadriiformes (Paton, Haddrath, and Baker 2002; Fain and Houde 2004; Paton and Baker 2006; Baker, Pereira, and Paton 2007; G. Mayr 2007, 2011b). Seriemas appear to be more closely related to falcons and caracaras (Falconidae; Ericson et al. 2006; Hackett et al. 2008; Jarvis et al. 2014). Molecular and morphological data support a sister relationship between the Kagu and Sunbittern (Eurypygiformes) that falls outside of Gruiformes, as do the bustards and mesites (Hacket et al. 2008; G. Mayr 2014; Jarvis et al. 2014). Molecular data strongly support the existence of two clades within Gruiformes, a Ralloidea (Rallidae and Heliornithidae) and Gruoidea (Gruidae, Aramidae, and Psophiidae; Fain and Houde 2004; Ericson et al. 2006; Fain, Krajewski, and Houde 2007; Hackett et al. 2008; G. Mayr 2007, 2011a). Multilocus genetic data suggest that Heliornithidae may actually be nested within Rallidae (Hackett et al. 2008), which is also supported by shared, derived features in the foot skeletal structure of the rail (*Sarothrura rufa*, the Red-chested Flufftail) and the Sungrebe (*Heliornis fulica*; G. Mayr 2011a).

Gruidae is composed of five genera and 15 species split into two subfamilies: the crowned cranes, Balearicinae (*Balearica*), and typical cranes, Gruinae (*Leucogeranus*, *Bugeranus*, *Anthropoides*, and *Grus*). The existence of these two subfamilies is supported by vocalizations (Archibald 1976), morphometrics (Wood 1979), and morphological and molecular phylogenetics (Ingold, Guttman, and Osborne 1987; Dressauer, Gee, and Rogers 1992; Krajewski and Fetzner 1994; Livezey 1998; Krajewski 1989; Krajewski et al. 1999; Krajewski, Sipiorski, and Anderson 2010; Fain 2001). *Grus* is composed of three subclades (Krajewski and Fetzner 1994; Krajewski and King 1996; Krajewski, Sipiorski, and Anderson 2010). The Antigone species group includes species that occur in Australia and southern Asia, the Sarus Crane (*G. antigone*), Brolga (*G. rubicunda*), and the White-naped Crane (*G. vipo*). The Common Crane (*G. grus*), Hooded Crane (*G. monachus*), Whooping Crane (*G. americana*), Black-necked Crane (*G. nigricollis*), and Red-crowned Crane (*G. japonensis*) make

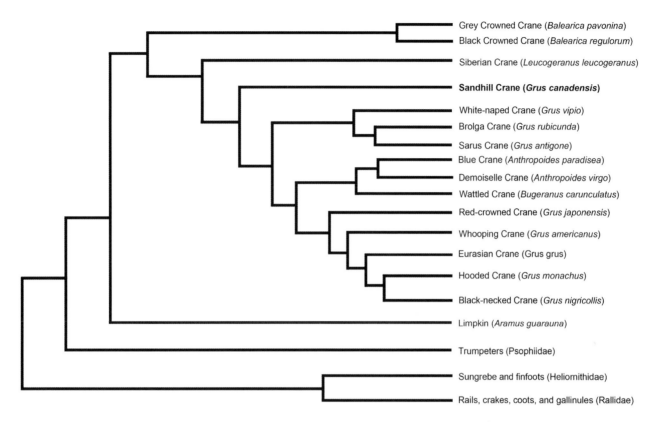

Figure 2.6. Cladogram representing evolutionary relationships among the cranes and their close relatives based on recent molecular phylogenetic studies (Krajewski and Fain 1994; Krajewski et al. 1999; Krajewski and King 1996; Krajewski, Sipiorski, and Anderson 2010).

up the Americana species group, which occurs in North America, Europe, and northern Asia. The Sandhill Crane (*G. canadensis*) represents the third subclade. Phylogenetic analyses based on the mitochondrial cytochrome *b* gene and whole mitochondrial genomes have not been able to resolve the evolutionary relationships among *Leucogeranus*, *Bugeranus*, *Anthropoides*, and the *Grus* species groups, with *Grus* appearing to be paraphyletic with respect to the other three genera (Krajewski and Fetzner 1994; Krajewski and King 1996; Krajewski, Sipiorski, and Anderson 2010). Nuclear DNA sequences are necessary to finally resolve the phylogenetic relationships and taxonomy within Gruidae (Krajewski, Sipiorski, and Anderson 2010).

Balearicinae and Gruinae may have diverged during the Oligocene about 31–37 MYA, but most crane diversification took place during the Miocene (20.4–7.2 MYA; Krajewski, Sipiorski, and Anderson 2010). The Sandhill Crane diverged from the Antigone species group 10–12 MYA after becoming isolated in either

North America or eastern Siberia, while the Antigone and Americana groups speciated during the Pliocene and Pleistocene (Krajewski, Sipiorski, and Anderson 2010).

Six subspecies have been described for the Sandhill Crane, three of which are migratory (Lesser, *G. c. canadensis*; Canadian, *G. c. rowani*; and Greater, *G. c. tabida*), and three of which are nonmigratory (Florida, *G. c. pratensis*; Mississippi, *G. c. pulla*; and Cuban, *G. c. nesiotes*). A deep phylogenetic split exists between the Arctic-nesting Lesser Sandhill Crane and the other mainland subspecies (the Cuban Sandhill Crane has yet to be included in a genetic study), which may have occurred during the Pleistocene 1.5 MYA (Rhymer et al. 2001). No other deep divergence exists within the Sandhill Crane; however, the frequency and geographic distribution of mitochondrial DNA haplotypes indicate a level of population structuring among migratory and nonmigratory subspecies (Rhymer et al. 2001). The lack of substantial genetic divergence among most

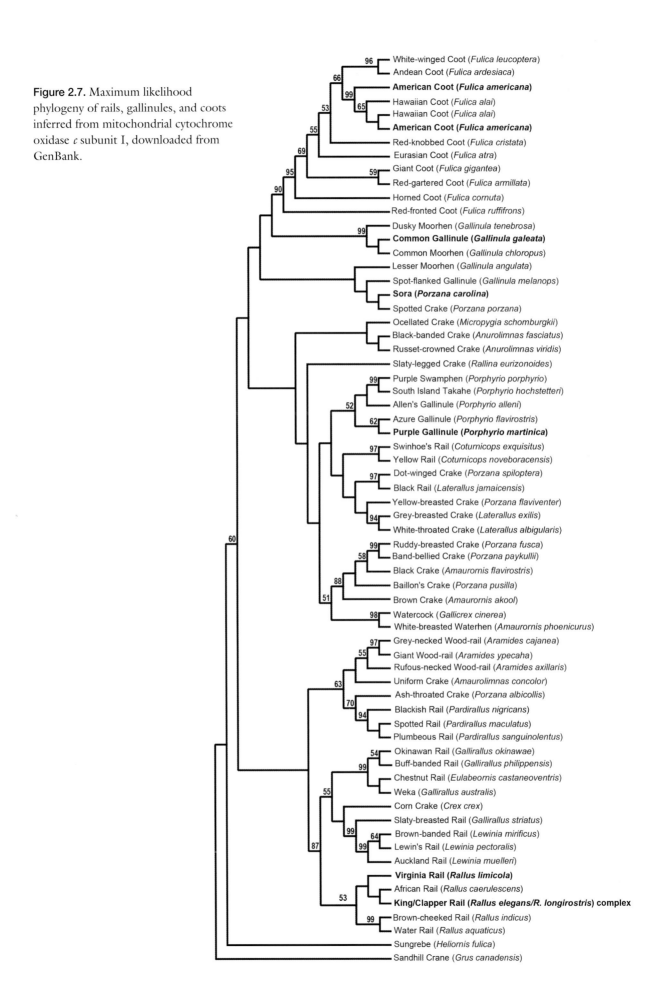

Figure 2.7. Maximum likelihood phylogeny of rails, gallinules, and coots inferred from mitochondrial cytochrome oxidase *c* subunit I, downloaded from GenBank.

Sandhill Crane subspecies is probably due to the recent divergence and gene flow stemming from postglacial secondary contact (Rhymer et al. 2001; Jones et al. 2005).

Rallidae is composed of 33 genera and 150 species (15 of which have become extinct since 1600), making it the largest family in the Gruidae. It includes rails, crakes, flufftails, coots, gallinules, and moorhens. Rails have traditionally been divided into the subfamilies Rallinae (typical rails), Gallinulinae (gallinules and moorhens), and Fulicinae (coots), although little justification for this exists (Olson 1973a). Despite several taxonomic revisions (Olson 1973a, 1973b; Sibley and Ahlquist 1985), there has not been a thorough phylogenetic study of the rails that included all extant genera and species. Although not all genera and species were included, Livezey's (1998) morphological analysis remains the most taxonomically complete study of rail phylogeny to date. The few phylogenetic studies employing molecular methods have focused on the evolution of flightlessness in rails on islands (Trewick 1997; Silkas, Olson, and Fleischer 2002; Kirchman 2012). Figure 2.7 is a maximum likelihood inferred phylogeny of Rallidae based on mitochondrial cytochrome *c* oxidase subunit I (COX1) gene sequences downloaded from GenBank. Similarities between the COX1-based tree and Livezey's (1998) results include lack of support for Gallinulinae and close relationships between *Rallus* and *Gallirallus* and between *Gallinula* and *Fulica*. *Porzana* and *Laterallus* appear to be artificial groupings, as others have suggested (Livezey 1998; Taylor 1998). Genetic data also suggest that the American (*Fulica americana*) and Hawaiian Coots (*F. atra*) do not represent phylogenetically distinct species. A comprehensive phylogenetic study of Rallidae that incorporates all genera and species and uses mitochondrial and nuclear DNA will be needed to resolve evolutionary relationships within this family.

Among North American rails, studies of intraspecific phylogenetics using molecular methods have been conducted only on the King–Clapper Rail complex (*Rallus elegans*–*R. longirostris*; Maley and Brumfield 2013) and the Yellow Rail (*Coturnicops noveboracensis*; Miller et al. 2012). Clapper and King Rails are highly similar to one another and can be differentiated by slight differences in body size and plumage coloration.

Both species are subdivided into several subspecies based on minor phenotypic variation, habitat, and geographic range. Early studies based on allozymic and mitochondrial DNA restriction-fragment data suggested that Clapper and King Rails were weakly differentiated at the genetic level (Avise and Zink 1988). Recent work using mitochondrial DNA sequences and multiple nuclear loci, however, has shown that the King Rail is paraphyletic with respect to the Clapper Rail and that genetic structure and species limits are concordant with geography rather than the current subspecies taxonomy (Maley and Brumfield 2013). Maley and Brumfield (2013) found five genetically distinct groups in the King–Clapper Rail complex and argued that these groups should be regarded as separate species. The American Ornithologists' Union (AOU) (Chesser et al. 2014) recently adopted the taxonomic changes proposed by Maley and Brumfield (2013). The name *Rallus longirostris* is now restricted to South American populations and given the common name "Mangrove Rail." The subspecies *R. e. tenuirostris* has been raised to species rank, Aztec Rail (*R. tenuirostris*). Ridgway's Rail (*R. obsoletus*) encompasses North American populations along the Pacific Coast. "King Rail" (*R. elegans*) is now restricted to subspecies in the eastern United States and Cuba (*R. e. elegans* and *R. e. ramsdeni*). Finally, "Clapper Rail" (*R. crepitans*) is restricted to populations along the Atlantic and Gulf Coasts, the Yucatán Peninsula, and Caribbean islands.

Charadriiformes

Charadriiformes is an ecologically and morphologically diverse clade that encompasses 3 suborders, 19 families, 96 genera, and more than 360 species of birds. The order includes familiar birds such as plovers (Charadriidae); oystercatchers (Haematopodidae); avocets and stilts (Recurvirostridae); auks, murres, and puffins (Alcidae); sandpipers, godwits, curlews, and snipes (Scolopacidae); gulls (Laridae); terns (Sternidae); and skimmers (Rhynchophidae). Charadriiformes also includes unusual and enigmatic taxa such as the galliform-like buttonquail (Turnicidae); raptorial skuas and jaegers (Stercorariidae); Antarctic sheathbills (Chionididae); swallow-like pratincoles and terrestrial coursers (Glareolidae); granivorous seed snipes (Thinocoridae); painted snipes (Rostratulidae); rail-like jacanas (Jacanidae); arid-adapted thick-knees (Burhinidae); Plains Wanderer (Pedionomidae); Crab Plover (*Dromas ardeola*, Dromadidae); Ibisbill (*Ibidorhyncha struthersii*, Ibidorhynchidae); Egyptian Plover (*Pluvianus aegyptius*, Pluvianidae); and Magellanic Plover (*Pluvianellus socialis*, Pluvianellidae).

Several studies utilizing nuclear gene sequences recovered Charadriiformes as a sister clade to the landbird assemblage (Fain and Houde 2004; Ericson et al. 2006; Hackett et al. 2008). However, this inferred relationship seems to be driven mostly by a single gene (β-fibrinogen), and the sister relationship between Charadriiformes and landbirds disappeared with the removal of β-fibrinogen (Ericson et al. 2006; G. Mayr 2011a). Other proposed sister clades include Gruiformes, the Hoatzin (*Opisthocomus hoazin*), Columbiformes, Cuculiformes, and Mirandornithes (flamingos and grebes) (Ericson et al. 2006; Brown et

al. 2008; Morgan-Richards et al. 2008; Pacheco et al. 2011; Kimball et al. 2013; McCormack et al. 2013; Yuri et al. 2013). Whole-genome analysis recovered a strongly supported sister-clade relationship between Gruiformes and Charadriiformes (Jarvis et al. 2014). Whole-genome data recovered the Hoatzin as the sister lineage to the gruiform-charadriiform clade, although this inferred relationship received less statistical support (Jarvis et al. 2014).

The evolutionary relationships among the various families and genera of Charadriiformes are better understood, with broad agreement between recent morphological and molecular studies (Paton et al. 2003; Baker, Pereira, and Paton 2007; G. Mayr 2011a, 2011b). Three distinct clades exist within Charadriiformes, including suborder Scolopaci (Jacanidae, Rostratulidae, Pedionomidae, Thinocoridae, and Scolopacidae), Lari (Laridae, Sternidae, Rhyncopidae, Stercorariidae, Alcidae, Glareolidae, Pluvianidae,

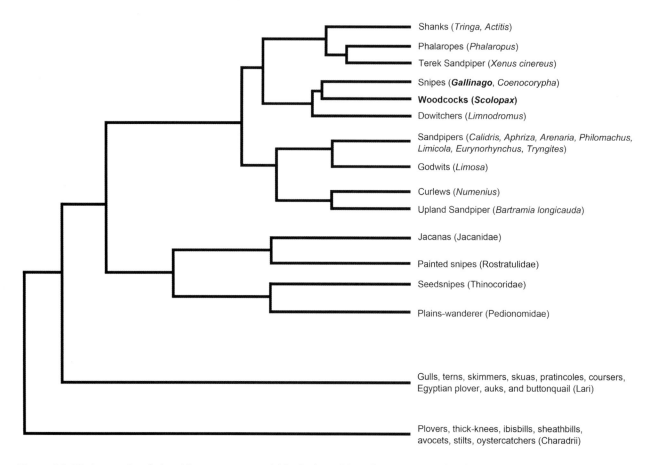

Figure 2.8. Phylogenetic relationships among taxa within Scolopaci based on recent molecular studies (Paton et al. 2003; Baker, Pereira, and Paton 2007; Gibson and Baker 2012).

Dromadidae, and Turnicidae), and Charadrii (Burhinidae, Chionidae, Pluvianellidae, Charadriidae, Ibidorhynchidae, Haematopodidae, and Recurvirostridae).

Genus- and species-level taxonomy of Scolopaci is currently in flux, as recent molecular studies have revealed that many genera are paraphyletic or polyphyletic (Pereira and Baker 2005; Gibson and Baker 2012), and the snipes are a good example. The austral or New Zealand snipes (*Coenocorypha* spp.) are classified in a separate genus, but Gibson and Baker (2012) found that this taxon was nested within typical snipes (*Gallinago* spp.). The *Gallinago-Coenocorypha* clade is sister to the woodcocks (*Scolopax* spp.), which in turn is sister to the dowitchers (*Limnodromus* spp.; fig. 2.8) (Baker, Pereira, and Paton 2007; Gibson and Baker 2012).

The Wilson's Snipe was formerly considered conspecific with the Common Snipe (*G. gallinago*) but is now regarded as a separate species by the AOU (R. J. Banks et al. 2002) and the British Ornithologists' Union (Knox et al. 2008) based on diagnostic differences in plumage and courtship display vocalizations as well as modest levels of genetic differentiation based on mitochondrial DNA restriction-fragment data (Zink et al. 1995). In contrast, recent DNA bar-coding studies were not able to distinguish the Wilson's Snipe from the Common Snipe, and phylogenetic analysis utilizing several mitochondrial genes resulted in the Wilson's Snipe being nested within the Common Snipe (Baker, Tavares, and Elbourne 2009). Several South American and African snipe species formerly treated as conspecific with the Common Snipe have recently been raised to species status (del Hoyo, Elliot, and Sargatal 1996). A detailed morphological and molecular phylogenetic study of the snipes that includes all currently recognized species is needed to determine species limits within *Gallinago* and *Coenocorypha*.

The species limits of *Scolopax* have not been determined either; however, the phylogeography of the American (*S. minor*) and European Woodcocks (*S. rusticola*) has been thoroughly studied (Burlando et al. 1996; Rhymer, McAuley, and Ziel 2005). The American Woodcock displays no phylogeographic structure across its geographic range despite high levels of genetic diversity. Rhymer, McAuley, and Ziel (2005) concluded that lack of population structure among the two migratory flyways used by American Woodcocks

was due to rapid postglacial expansion, recent or ongoing gene flow among populations, and movement of birds between flyways. In contrast, the closely related European Woodcock displays strong population structure that appears to be concordant with the species' migration routes (Burlando et al. 1996).

Conclusion

The evolutionary relationships within the Tree of Life are becoming better resolved thanks to increased computing power (to handle complex algorithms and evolutionary models) and technological advances in the sequencing of individual genes and, now, whole genomes. Molecular data have greatly enhanced our knowledge of evolutionary relationships within birds, confirming many relationships previously based only on phenotypic data. However, sequencing and genomic approaches have also revealed surprising relationships that were not apparent in morphological or behavioral traits (e.g., the grebe-flamingo clade and the parrot-passerine-falcon-seriema clade). But many questions regarding avian phylogenetics still remain. The following is a list of phylogenetic research priorities for species covered in this book.

1. A multilocus phylogenetic study of New World quail is needed to test Holman's (1961) hypotheses. In light of recent phylogeographic studies, revision of the Gambel's and Scaled Quail and Northern Bobwhite subspecies taxonomy is in order.

2. A phylogeographic study of the Plain Chachalaca is needed.

3. A phylogenetic study of New World columbid clades that includes all genera and species is needed. Thorough phylogeographic studies of Mourning, White-winged, and White-tipped Doves and other wide-ranging columbid species of the Western Hemisphere are also needed.

4. A phylogenetic study of cranes utilizing nuclear gene sequences is needed.

5. The phylogenetics and taxonomy of the rails are a mess. A multilocus phylogenetic study that includes data from all extant genera and from as many species as possible is desperately needed. Phylogeographic studies of the American Coot,

Common Gallinule, Purple Gallinule, Sora, and Virginia Rail are also needed.

6. The generic-, species-, and subspecies-level phylogenetics and taxonomy of *Gallinago* and *Coenocorypha* are unclear and will probably require a multilocus approach that thoroughly samples both genera. Phylogeographic study of the Wilson's Snipe is also needed.

Literature Cited

Allendorf, F. W., and J. J. Hard. 2009. Human-induced evolution caused by unnatural selection through harvest of wild animals. *Proceedings of the National Academy of Sciences of the United States of America* 106 (Suppl.): 9987–94.

American Ornithologists' Union. 1998. *Check-List of North American Birds*. 7th ed. Washington, DC: American Ornithologists' Union.

Archibald, G. W. 1976. Crane taxonomy as revealed by the unison call. In *Proceedings of the International Crane Workshop*, edited by J. C. Lewis, 225–51. Stillwater: Oklahoma State University Publishing and Printing Department.

Avise, J. C. 2000. *Phylogeography: The History and Formation of Species*. Cambridge, MA: Harvard University Press.

———. 2004. *Molecular Markers, Natural History, and Evolution*. 2nd ed. Sunderland, MA: Sinauer Associates.

Avise, J. C., and W. S. Nelson. 1989. Molecular genetic relationships of the extinct Dusky Seaside Sparrow. *Science* 243:646–48.

Avise, J. C., and D. Walker. 1998. Pleistocene phylogeographic effects on avian populations and the speciation process. *Proceedings of the Royal Society of London B* 265:457–63.

Avise, J. C., and R. M. Zink. 1988. Molecular genetic divergence between avian sibling species: King and Clapper Rails, Long-billed and Short-billed Dowitchers, Boat-tailed and Great-tailed Grackles, and Tufted and Black-crested Titmice. *Auk* 105:516–28.

Baker, A. J., S. L. Pereira, and T. A. Paton. 2007. Phylogenetic relationships and divergence times of Charadriiformes genera: Multigene evidence for the Cretaceous origin of at least 14 clades of shorebirds. *Biology Letters* 3:205–10.

Baker, A. J., E. S. Tavares, and R. F. Elbourne. 2009. Countering criticisms of single mitochondrial DNA gene barcoding in birds. *Molecular Ecology Resources* 9 (Suppl. 1): 257–68.

Ball, R. M., Jr., and J. C. Avise. 1992. Mitochondrial DNA phylogeographic differentiation among avian populations and the evolutionary significance of subspecies. *Auk* 109:626–36.

Banks, R. C., J. D. Weckstein, J. V. Remsen Jr., and K. P. Johnson. 2013. Classification of a clade of New World doves (Columbidae: Zenaidini). *Zootaxa* 3669:184–88.

Banks, R. J., C. Cicero, J. L. Dunn, A. W. Kratter, P. C. Rasmussen, J. V. Remsen Jr., J. D. Rising, and D. F. Stotz. 2002. Forty-third supplement to the American Ornithologists' Union *Check-List of North American Birds*. *Auk* 119:897–906.

Barrowclough, G. F., J. G. Groth, L. A. Mertz, and R. J. Gutiérrez. 2004. Phylogeographic structure, gene flow and species status in Blue Grouse (*Dendragapus obscurus*). *Molecular Ecology* 13:1911–22.

Battin, J. 2004. When good animals love bad habitats: Ecological traps and the conservation of animal populations. *Conservation Biology* 18:1482–91.

Beams, H. W., and R. K. Meyer. 1931. The formation of pigeon "milk." *Physiological Zoology* 4:486–500.

Becker, J. J., and P. Brodkorb. 1992. An early Miocene ground-dove (Aves: Columbidae) from Florida. *Natural History Museum of Los Angeles County Science Series* 36:189–93.

Beddard, F. E. 1898. *The Structure and Classification of Birds*. London: Longmans and Green.

Benton, M. J. 2004. *Vertebrate Paleontology*. 3rd ed. Malden, MA: Blackwell.

Bergsten, J. 2005. A review of long-branch attraction. *Cladistics* 21:163–93.

Birks, S. M., and S. V. Edwards. 2002. A phylogeny of the megapodes (Aves: Megapodiidae) based on nuclear and mitochondrial DNA sequences. *Molecular Phylogenetics and Evolution* 23:408–21.

Boles, W. E. 2001. A new emu (Dromaiinae) from the Late Oligocene Etadunna Formation. *Emu* 101:317–21.

Bowie, R. C. K., C. Cohen, and T. M. Crowe. 2013. Ptilopachinae: A new subfamily of the Odontophoridae (Aves: Galliformes). *Zootaxa* 3670:97–98.

Brennan, L. A. 1999. Northern Bobwhite (*Colinus virginianus*). In *The Birds of North America*, No. 397, edited by A. Poole and F. Gill. Philadelphia: Academy of Natural Sciences.

Brocklehurst, N., P. Upchurch, P. D. Mannion, and J. O'Connor. 2014. The completeness of the fossil record of Mesozoic birds: Implications for early avian evolution. *PLoS ONE* 7 (6): e39056.

Brown, J. W., J. S. Rest, J. García-Moreno, M. D. Sorenson, and D. P. Mindell. 2008. Strong mitochondrial DNA support for a Cretaceous origin of modern avian lineages. *BMC Biology* 6:6.

Burbridge, M. L., R. M. Colbourne, H. A. Robertson, and A. J. Baker. 2003. Molecular and other biological evidence supports the recognition of at least three species of Brown Kiwi. *Conservation Genetics* 4:167–77.

Burlando, B., A. Arilo, S. Spanò, and M. Machetti. 1996. A study of the genetic variability in populations of European Woodcock (*Scolopax rusticola*) by random amplification of polymorphic DNA. *Italian Journal of Zoology* 63:31–36.

Chesser, R. T., R. C. Banks, C. Cicero, J. L. Dunn, A. W. Krattler, I. J. Lovette, A. G. Navarro-Sigüenza, et al. 2014. Fifty-fifth supplement to the American Ornithologists' Union *Check-List of North American Birds*. *Auk* 131:CSi–CSxv.

Chiappe, L. M. 2009. Downsized dinosaurs: The evolutionary transition to modern birds. *Evolution Education and Outreach* 2:248–56.

Chojnowski, J. L., R. T. Kimball, and E. L. Braun. 2008. Introns outperform exons in analyses of basal avian phylogeny using clathrin heavy chain genes. *Gene* 410:89–96.

Clarke, J. A., C. P. Tambussi, J. L. Noriega, G. M. Erickson, and R. A. Ketcham. 2005. Definitive fossil evidence for the extant avian radiation in the Cretaceous. *Nature* 433:305–8.

Cohen, C., J. L. Wakeling, T. G. Mandiwana-Neudani, E. Sande, C. Dranzoa, T. M. Crowe, and R. C. K. Bowie. 2012. Phylogenetic affinities of evolutionary enigmatic African galliforms: The Stone Partridge *Ptilopachus petrosus* and Nahan's Francolin *Francolinus nahani*, and support for their sister relationship with New World quails. *Ibis* 154:768–80.

Cooper, A., C. Lalueza-Fox, S. Anderson, A. Rambaut, J. Austin, and R. Ward. 2001. Complete mitochondrial genome sequences of two extinct moas clarify ratite evolution. *Nature* 409:704–7.

Cooper, A., and D. Penny. 1997. Mass survival of birds across the Cretaceous-Tertiary boundary: Molecular evidence. *Science* 275:1109–13.

Corman, K. S. 2011. Conservation and landscape genetics of Texas Lesser Prairie-Chickens: Population structure and differentiation, genetic variability, and effective size. Master's thesis, Texas A&M University–Kingsville.

Cox, W. A., R. T. Kimball, and E. L. Braun. 2007. Phylogenetic position of the New World quail (Odontophoridae): Eight nuclear loci and three mitochondrial regions contradict morphology and the Sibley-Ahlquist tapestry. *Auk* 124:71–84.

Crandall, K. A., O. R. P. Bininda-Emonds, G. M. Mace, and R. K. Wayne. 2000. Considering evolutionary processes in conservation biology. *Trends in Ecology and Evolution* 15:290–95.

Crowe, T. M., R. C. K. Bowie, P. Bloomer, T. G. Mandiwana, T. A. J. Hedderson, E. Randi, S. L. Pereira, and J. Wakeling. 2006. Phylogenetics, biogeography and classification of, and character evolution in, gamebirds (Aves: Galliformes): Effects of character exclusion, data partitioning and missing data. *Cladistics* 22:495–532.

del Hoyo, J., A. Elliot, and J. Sargatal, eds. 1996. *Handbook of the Birds of the World*. Vol. 3, *Hoatzin to Auks*. Barcelona, Spain: Lynx Edicions.

DeYoung, R. W., and D. L. Williford. 2016. Genetic variation and population structure in the prairie grouse: Implications for conservation of the Lesser Prairie-Chicken. *Studies in Avian Biology* 48:77–97.

Dimcheff, D. E., S. V. Drovetski, and D. P. Mindell. 2002. Phylogeny of Tetraoninae and other galliform birds using mitochondrial 12S and ND2 genes. *Molecular Phylogenetics and Evolution* 24:203–15.

Dobzhansky, T. 1973. Nothing in biology makes sense except in the light of evolution. *American Biology Teacher* 35:125–29.

Dressauer, H. C., G. F. Gee, and J. S. Rogers. 1992. Allozyme evidence for crane systematics and polymorphisms within populations of Sandhill, Sarus, Siberian, and Whooping Cranes. *Molecular Phylogenetics and Evolution* 1:279–88.

Drovetski, S. V. 2002. Molecular phylogeny of grouse: Individual and combined performance of W-linked, autosomal, and mitochondrial loci. *Systematic Biology* 51:930–45.

———. 2003. Plio-Pleistocene climatic oscillations, Holarctic biogeography and speciation in an avian subfamily. *Journal of Biogeography* 30:1173–81.

Dyke, G. J., and M. van Tuinen. 2004. The evolutionary radiation of modern birds (Neornithes): Reconciling molecules, morphology and the fossil record. *Zoological Journal of the Linnean Society* 141:153–77.

Ellsworth, D. L, R. L. Honeycutt, N. J. Silvy, K. D. Rittenhouse, and M. H. Smith. 1994. Mitochondrial-DNA and nuclear-gene differentiation in North American prairie grouse (Genus *Tympanuchus*). *Auk* 111:661–71.

Eo, S. H., O. R. P. Bininda-Emonds, and J. P. Carroll. 2009. A phylogenetic supertree of the fowls (Galloanserae, Aves). *Zoological Scripta* 38:465–81.

Eo, S. H., J. P. Wares, and J. P. Carroll. 2010. Subspecies and units for conservation and management of the Northern Bobwhite in the eastern United States. *Conservation Genetics* 11:867–75.

Ericson, P. G. P. 2008. Current perspectives on the evolution of birds. *Contributions to Zoology* 77:109–16.

Ericson, P. G. P., C. L. Anderson, T. Britton, A. Elzanowksi, U. S. Johansson, M. Källersjö, J. I. Ohlson, T. J. Parsons, D. Zuccon, and G. Mayr. 2006. Diversification of Neoaves: Integration of molecular sequence data and fossils. *Biology Letters* 2:543–47.

Ericson, P. G. P., C. L. Anderson, and G. Mayr. 2007. Hangin' on to our rocks 'n clocks: A reply to Brown et al. *Biology Letters* 3:260–61.

Fain, M. G. 2001. Phylogeny and evolution of cranes (Aves: Gruidae) inferred from DNA sequences of multiple genes. PhD diss., Southern Illinois State University.

Fain, M. G., and P. Houde. 2004. Parallel radiations in the primary clades of birds. *Evolution* 58:2558–73.

Fain, M. G., C. Krajewski, and P. Houde. 2007. Phylogeny of "core Gruiformes" (Aves: Grues) and resolution of the Limpkin-Sungrebe problem. *Molecular Phylogenetics and Evolution* 43:515–29.

Frank-Hoeflich, K., L. F. Silveira, J. Estudillo-López, A. M. García-Koch, L. Ongay-Larios, and D. Piñero. 2007. Increased taxon and character sampling reveals novel intergeneric relationships in the Cracidae (Aves: Galliformes). *Journal of Zoological Systematics and Evolutionary Research* 45:242–54.

Freeman, S., and R. M. Zink. 1995. A phylogenetic study of the blackbirds based on variation in mitochondrial DNA restriction sites. *Systematic Biology* 44:409–20.

Friesen, V. L., D. J. Anderson, T. E. Steeves, H. Jones, and E. A. Schreiber. 2002. Molecular support for species status of the Nazca Booby (*Sula granti*). *Auk* 119:820–26.

Galla, S. J. 2013. Exploring the evolutionary history of North American prairie grouse (genus: *Tympanuchus*) using multi-locus coalescent analyses. Master's thesis, University of North Texas.

Gavin, T. A. 1989. What's wrong with the questions we ask in wildlife research? *Wildlife Society Bulletin* 17:345–50.

———. 1991. Why ask "why": The importance of evolutionary biology in wildlife science. *Journal of Wildlife Management* 55:760–66.

Gibb, G. C., and D. Penny. 2010. Two aspects along the continuum of pigeon evolution: A South-Pacific radiation and the relationships of pigeons within Neoaves. *Molecular Phylogenetics and Evolution* 56:698–706.

Gibson, R., and A. Baker. 2012. Multiple gene sequences resolve phylogenetic relationships in the shorebird suborder Scolopaci (Aves: Charadriiformes). *Molecular Phylogenetics and Evolution* 64:66–72.

Gienapp, P., C. Teplitsky, J. S. Alho, J. A. Mills, and J. Merilä. 2008. Climate change and evolution: Disentangling environmental and genetic responses. *Molecular Ecology* 17:167–78.

Giesel, J. T., D. Brazeau, R. Koopelman, and D. Shiver. 1997. Ring-necked Pheasant population genetic structure. *Journal of Wildlife Management* 61:1332–38.

Goodwin, D. 1958. Remarks on the taxonomy of some American Doves. *Auk* 75:330–34.

Grau, E. T., S. L. Pereira, L. F. Silveira, E. Höfling, and A. Wajntal. 2005. Molecular phylogenetics and biogeography of neotropical piping guans (Aves: Galliformes): *Pipile* Bonaparte, 1856 is synonym of *Aburria* Reichenbach, 1853. *Molecular Phylogenetics and Evolution* 35:637–45.

Graur, D., and W. Martin. 2004. Reading the entrails of chickens: Molecular timescales of evolution and the illusion of precision. *Trends in Ecology and Evolution* 20:80–86.

Gutiérrez, R. J. 1993. Taxonomy and biogeography of New World quail. *Proceedings of the National Quail Symposium* 3:8–15.

Gutiérrez, R. J., G. F. Barrowclough, and J. G. Groth. 2000. A classification of the grouse (Aves: Tetraoninae) based on mitochondrial DNA sequences. *Wildlife Biology* 6:205–11.

Gutiérrez, R. J., R. M. Zink, and S. Y. Yang. 1983. Genic variation, systematic, and biogeographic relationships of some galliform birds. *Auk* 100:33–47.

Hackett, S. J., R. T. Kimball, S. Reddy, R. C. K. Bowie, E. L. Braun, M. J. Braun, J. L. Chonjnowski, et al. 2008. A phylogenomic study of birds reveals their evolutionary history. *Science* 320:1763–68.

Haddrath, O., and A. J. Baker. 2012. Multiple nuclear genes and retroposons support vicariance and dispersal of the palaeognaths, and an Early Cretaceous origin of modern birds. *Proceedings of the Royal Society of London B* 279:4617–25.

Hagen, C. A., J. C. Pitman, B. K. Sandercock, D. H. Wolfe, R. J. Robel, R. D. Applegate, and S. J. Oyler-McCance. 2010. Regional variation in mtDNA of the Lesser Prairie-Chicken. *Condor* 112:29–37.

Hedges, S. B. 1994. Molecular evidence for the origin of birds. *Proceedings of the National Academy of Science of the United States of America* 91:2621–24.

Hewitt, G. M. 2000. The genetic legacy of the Quaternary ice ages. *Nature* 405:907–25.

———. 2004. The structure of biodiversity—insights from molecular phylogeography. *Frontiers in Zoology* 1:4.

Holman, J. A. 1961. Osteology of living and fossil New World quails (Aves, Galliformes). *Bulletin of the Florida State Museum* 6:131–233.

———. 1964. Osteology of gallinaceous birds. *Quarterly Journal of the Florida Academy of Science* 22:230–52.

Holtz, T. R., Jr. 2012. Theropods. In *The Complete Dinosaur*, edited by M. K. Brett-Surman, T. R. Holtz Jr., J. O. Farlow, and B. Walters, 347–78. Bloomington: Indiana University Press.

Hosner, P. A., E. L. Braun, and R. T. Kimball. 2015. Land connectivity changes and global cooling shaped the colonization history and diversification of New World quail (Aves: Galliformes: Odontophoridae). *Journal of Biogeography* 42:1883–95.

Hubbard, J. P. 1973. Avian evolution in the aridlands of North America. *Living Bird* 12:155–96.

Ingold, J. L., S. I. Guttman, and D. O. Osborne. 1987. Biochemical systematics and evolution of the cranes (Aves: Gruidae). In *Proceedings of the 1983 International Crane Workshop*, edited by G. W. Archibald and R. F. Pasquier, 575–84. Baraboo, WI: International Crane Foundation.

Jarvis, E. D., S. Mirarab, A. J. Aberer, B. Li, P. Houde, C. Li, S. Y. W. Ho, et al. 2014. Whole-genome analyses resolve early branches in the tree of life of modern birds. *Science* 346: 1321–31.

Jiang, F., Y. Miao, W. Liang, H. Ye, H. Liu, and B. Liu. 2010. The complete mitochondrial genomes of the whistling duck (*Dendrocygna javanica*) and Black Swan (*Cygnus atratus*): Dating evolutionary divergence in Galloanserae. *Molecular Biology Reports* 37:3001–15.

Johnsgard, P. A. 1988. *The Quails, Partridges, and Francolins of the World*. New York: Oxford University Press.

Johnson, J. A. 2008. Recent range expansion and divergence among North American prairie grouse. *Journal of Heredity* 99:165–73.

Johnson, J. A., and P. O. Dunn. 2006. Low genetic variation in the Heath Hen prior to extinction and implications for the conservation of prairie-chicken populations. *Conservation Genetics* 7:37–48.

Johnson, K. P., and D. H. Clayton. 2000a. A molecular phylogeny of the dove genus *Zenaida*: Mitochondrial and nuclear DNA sequences. *Condor* 102:864–70.

———. 2000b. Nuclear and mitochondrial genes contain similar phylogenetic signal for pigeons and doves (Aves: Columbiformes). *Molecular Phylogenetics and Evolution* 14:141–51.

Johnson, K. P., D. H. Clayton, J. P. Dumbacher, and R. C. Fleischer. 2010. The flight of the Passenger Pigeon: Phylogenetic and biogeographic history of an extinct species. *Molecular Phylogenetics and Evolution* 57:455–58.

Johnson, K. P., S. de Kort, K. Dinwoodey, A. C. Mateman, C. ten Cate, C. M. Lessells, and D. H. Clatyon. 2001. Molecular phylogeny of the dove genera *Streptopelia* and *Columba*. *Auk* 118:874–87.

Johnson, K. P., and J. D. Weckstein. 2011. The Central American land bridge as an engine of diversification in New World doves. *Journal of Biogeography* 38:1069–76.

Johnson, N. K., and C. Cicero. 2004. New mitochondrial DNA data affirm the importance of Pleistocene speciation in North American birds. *Evolution* 58:1122–30.

Jones, K. L., G. L. Krapu, D. A. Brandt, and M. V. Ashley. 2005. Population genetic structure in migratory Sandhill Cranes and the role of Pleistocene glaciations. *Molecular Ecology* 14:2645–57.

Kimball, R. T., and E. L. Braun. 2008. A multigene phylogeny of Galliformes supports a single origin of erectile ability in non-feathered facial traits. *Journal of Avian Biology* 39:438–45.

Kimball, R. T., E. L. Braun, P. W. Zwartjes, T. M. Crowe, and J. D. Ligon. 1999. A molecular phylogeny of pheasants and partridges suggests that these lineages are not monophyletic. *Molecular Phylogenetics and Evolution* 11:38–54.

Kirchman, J. J. 2012. Speciation of flightless rails on islands: A DNA-based phylogeny of the typical rails of the Pacific. *Auk* 129:56–69.

Klicka, J., and R. M. Zink. 1997. The importance of recent ice ages in speciation: A failed paradigm. *Science* 277:1666–69.

———. 1999. Pleistocene effects on North American songbird evolution. *Proceedings of the Royal Society of London B* 266:695–700.

Knox, A. G., J. M. Collinson, D. T. Parkin, G. Sangster, and L. Svensson. 2008. Taxonomic recommendations for British birds: Fifth report. *Ibis* 150:833–35.

Krajewski, C. 1989. Phylogenetic relationships among cranes (Gruiformes: Gruidae) based on DNA hybridization. *Auk* 106:603–18.

Krajewski, C., and M. G. Fain. 1994. Phylogeny of cranes (Gruiformes: Gruidae) based on cytochrome *b* DNA sequences. *Auk* 111:351–65.

Krajewski, C., M. G. Fain, L. Buckley, and D. G. King. 1999. Dynamically heterogenous partitions and phylogenetic inference: An evaluation of analytical strategies with cytochrome *b* and ND6 gene sequences in cranes. *Molecular Phylogenetics and Evolution* 13:302–13.

Krajewski, C., and J. W. Fetzner, Jr. 1994. Phylogeny of cranes (Gruiformes: Gruidae) based on cytochrome-B DNA sequences. *Auk* 111:351–65.

Krajewski, C., and D. G. King. 1996. Molecular divergence and phylogeny: Rates and patterns of cytochrome *b* evolution in cranes. *Molecular Biology and Evolution* 13:21–30.

Krajewski, C., J. T. Sipiorski, and F. E. Anderson. 2010. Complete mitochondrial genome sequences and the phylogeny of cranes (Gruiformes: Gruidae). *Auk* 127:440–52.

Kriegs, J. O., A. Matzke, G. Churakov, A. Kuritzin, G. Mayr, J. Brosius, and J. Schmitz. 2007. Waves of genomic hitchhikers shed light on the evolution of gamebirds (Aves: Galliformes). *BMC Evolutionary Biology* 7:190.

Ksepka, D. T. 2009. Broken gears in the avian molecular clock: New phylogenetic analyses support stem galliform status for *Gallinuloides wyomingensis* and rallid affinities for *Amitabha urbsinterdictensis*. *Cladistics* 25:173–97.

Ksepka, D. T., and C. A. Boyd. 2012. Quantifying historical trends in the completeness of the fossil record and the contributing factors: An example using Aves. *Paleobiology* 38:112–25.

Ksepka, D. T., J. L. Ware, and K. S. Lamm. 2014. Flying rocks and flying clocks: Disparity in fossil and molecular dates for birds. *Proceedings of the Royal Society of London B* 281: 2014.0677.

Lahammar, D., and R. J. Milner. 1989. Phylogenetic relationship of birds with crocodiles and mammals, as deduced from protein sequences. *Molecular Biology and Evolution* 6:693–96.

Law, R. 2000. Fishing, selection, and phenotypic evolution. *ICES Journal of Marine Science* 57:659–68.

Lee, C. E. 2002. Evolutionary genetics of invasive species. *Trends in Ecology and Evolution* 17:386–91.

Li, S.-H., J.-W. Li, L.-X. Han, C.-T. Yao, H. Shi, F.-M. Lei, and C. Yen. 2006. Species delimitation in the Hwamei *Garrulax canorus*. *Ibis* 148:698–706.

Livezey, B. C. 1998. A phylogenetic analysis of the Gruiformes (Aves) based on morphological characters, with an emphasis on the rails (Rallidae). *Philosophical Transactions of the Royal Society of London B* 353:2077–151.

Livezey, B. C., and R. L. Zusi. 2007. Higher-order phylogeny of modern birds (Theropoda, Aves: Neornithes) based on comparative anatomy. II. Analysis and discussion. *Zoological Journal of the Linnean Society* 149:1–95.

Longrich, N. R., T. Tokaryk, and D. J. Field. 2011. Mass extinction of birds at the Cretaceous-Paleogene (K-Pg) boundary. *Proceedings of the National Academy of Sciences of the United States of America* 108:15253–57.

Lovette, I. J. 2005. Glacial cycles and the tempo of avian speciation. *Trends in Ecology and Evolution* 20:57–59.

Lucchini, V., J. Höglund, S. Klaus, J. Swenson, and E. Randi. 2001. Historical biogeography and a mitochondrial DNA phylogeny of grouse and ptarmigan. *Molecular Phylogenetics and Evolution* 20:149–62.

Maley, J. M., and R. T. Brumfield. 2013. Mitochondrial and next-generation sequence data used to infer phylogenetic relationships and species limits in the Clapper/King Rail complex. *Condor* 115:316–29.

Martin, R. A., J. G. Honey, and P. Peláez-Campomanes. 2000. The Meade Basin rodent project: A progress report. *Paludicola* 3:1–32.

Mayr, E. 1961. Cause and effect in biology. *Science* 134:1501–6.

———. 1963. *Animal Species and Evolution*. Cambridge, MA: Belknap Press.

Mayr, G. 2005. The Paleogene fossil record of birds in Europe. *Biological Reviews* 80:515–42.

———. 2007. Avian higher-level phylogeny: Well-supported clades and what we can learn from a phylogenetic analysis of 2954 morphological characters. *Journal of Zoological Systematics and Evolutionary Research* 46:63–72.

———. 2008. The fossil record of galliform birds: Comments on Crowe et al. (2006). *Cladistics* 24:74–76.

———. 2009. *Paleogene Birds*. Berlin: Springer.

———. 2010. Phylogenetic relationships of the paraphyletic "caprimulgiform" birds (nightjars and allies). *Journal of Zoological Systematics and Evolutionary Research* 48:126–37.

———. 2011a. Metaves, Mirandornithes, Strisores and other novelties—A critical review of the higher-level phylogeny of neornithine birds. *Journal of Zoological Systematics and Evolutionary Research* 49:58–76.

———. 2011b. The phylogeny of charadriiform birds (shorebirds and allies)—Reassessing the conflict between morphology and molecules. *Zoological Journal of the Linnean Society* 161:916–34.

———. 2014. The origins of crown group birds: Molecules and fossils. *Palaeontology* 57:231–42.

Mayr, G., and J. Clarke. 2003. The deep divergences of neornithine birds: A phylogenetic analysis of morphological characters. *Cladistics* 19:527–53.

McCormack, J. E., M. G. Harvey, B. C. Faircloth, N. G.

Crawford, T. C. Glenn, and R. T. Blumfield. 2013. A phylogeny of birds based on over 1,500 loci collected by target enrichment and high-throughput sequencing. *PLoS ONE* 8 (1): e54848.

McDougall, P. T., D. Réale, D. Sol, and S. M. Reader. 2006. Wildlife conservation and animal temperament: Causes and consequences of evolutionary change for captive, reintroduced, and wildlife populations. *Animal Conservation* 9:39–48.

McKenna, M. C. 1983. Holarctic landmass rearrangement, cosmic events, and Cenozoic terrestrial organisms. *Annals of the Missouri Botanical Garden* 70:459–89.

Meiklejohn, K. A., M. J. Danielson, B. C. Faircloth, T. C. Glenn, E. L. Braun, and R. T. Kimball. 2014. Incongruence among different mitochondrial regions: A case study using complete mitogenomes. *Molecular Phylogenetics and Evolution* 78:314–23.

Miller, M. P., S. M. Haig, T. D. Mullins, K. J. Popper, and M. Green. 2012. Evidence for population bottlenecks and subtle genetic structure in the Yellow Rail. *Condor* 114:100–112.

Mitchell, J. S., and P. J. Makovicky. 2014. Low ecological disparity in Early Cretaceous birds. *Proceedings of the Royal Society B: Biological Sciences* 281:2014.0608.

Mitchell, K. J., B. Llamas, J. Soubrier, N. J. Rawlence, T. H. Worthy, J. Wood, M. S. Y. Lee, and A. Cooper. 2014. Ancient DNA reveals elephant birds and kiwi are sister taxa and clarifies ratite bird evolution. *Science* 344:898–900.

Mock, K. E., T. C. Theimer, O. E. Rhodes Jr., D. L. Greenberg, and P. Keim. 2002. Genetic variation across the historical range of the Wild Turkey (*Meleagris gallopavo*). *Molecular Ecology* 11:643–57.

Morgan-Richards, M., S. A. Trewick, A. Barosch-Härlid, O. Kardailsky, M. J. Phillips, P. A. McLenachan, and D. Penny. 2008. Bird evolution: Testing the Metaves clade with six new mitochondrial genomes. *BMC Evolutionary Biology* 8:20.

Naish, D. 2012. Birds. In *The Complete Dinosaur*, edited by M. K. Brett-Surman, T. R. Holtz Jr., J. O. Farlow, and B. Walters, 379–423. Bloomington: Indiana University Press.

Nedbal, M. A., R. L. Honeycutt, S. G. Evans, R. M. Whiting, and D. R. Dietz. 1997. Northern Bobwhite restocking in east Texas: A genetic assessment. *Journal of Wildlife Management* 61:854–63.

O'Connor, J., L. M. Chiappe, and A. Bell. 2011. Premodern birds: Avian divergences in the Mesozoic. In *Living Dinosaurs: The Evolutionary History of Modern Birds*, edited by G. Dyke and G. Kaiser, 39–114. London: John Wiley and Sons.

Olsen, E. M., M. Heino, G. R. Lilly, M. J. Morgan, J. Brattey, B. Ernade, and U. Dieckmann. 2004. Maturation trends indicative of rapid evolution preceded the collapse of northern cod. *Nature* 428:932–35.

Olson, S. L. 1973a. A classification of the Rallidae. *Wilson Bulletin* 85:380–416.

———. 1973b. Evolution of the rails in the South Atlantic islands (Aves: Rallidae). *Smithsonian Contributions in Zoology* 152:1–53.

———. 1985. Faunal turnover in South American fossil avifaunas: The insufficiencies of the fossil record. *Evolution* 39:1174–77.

Organ, C. L., M. H. Schweitzer, W. Zheng, L. M. Freimark, L. C. Cantley, and J. M. Asara. 2008. Molecular phylogenetics of mastodon and *Tyrannosaurus rex*. *Science* 320:5875.

Pacheco, M. A., F. U. Battistuzzi, M. Lentino, R. F. Aguilar, S. Kumar, and A. A. Escalante. 2011. Evolution of modern birds revealed by mitogenomics: Timing the radiation and origin of major orders. *Molecular Biology and Evolution* 28:1927–42.

Palkovacs, E. P., A. J. Oppenheimer, E. Gladyshev, J. E. Toepfer, G. Amato, T. Chase, and A. Caccone. 2004. Genetic evaluation of a proposed introduction: The case of the Greater Prairie Chicken and the extinct Heath Hen. *Molecular Ecology* 13:1759–69.

Parmesan, C. 2006. Ecological and evolutionary responses to recent climate change. *Annual Reviews in Ecology, Evolution, and Systematics* 37:637–69.

Paton, T. A., and A. J. Baker. 2006. Sequences from 14 mitochondrial genes provide a well-supported phylogeny of the charadriiform birds congruent with the nuclear RAG-1 tree. *Molecular Phylogenetics and Evolution* 39:657–67.

Paton, T. A., A. J. Baker, J. G. Groth, and G. F. Barrowclough. 2003. RAG-1 sequences resolve phylogenetic relationships within charadriiform birds. *Molecular Phylogenetics and Evolution* 29:268–78.

Paton, T., O. Haddrath, and A. J. Baker. 2002. Complete mitochondrial DNA genome sequences show that modern birds are not descended from transitional shorebirds. *Proceedings of the Royal Society of London B* 269:839–46.

Pavlova, A., R. M. Zink, S. V. Drovetski, Y. Red'kin, and S. Rohwer. 2003. Phylogeographic patterns in *Motacilla flava* and *Motacilla citreola*: Species limits and population history. *Auk* 120:744–58.

Pereira, S. L., and A. J. Baker. 2004. Vicariant speciation of curassows (Aves, Cracidae): A hypothesis based on mitochondrial DNA phylogeny. *Auk* 121:882–94.

———. 2005. Multiple gene evidence for parallel evolution and retention of ancestral morphological states in the shanks (Charadriiformes: Scolopacidae). *Condor* 107:514–26.

———. 2006. A molecular timescale for galliform birds accounting for uncertainty in time estimates and heterogeneity of rates of DNA substitutions across lineages and sites. *Molecular Phylogenetics and Evolution* 38:499–509.

Pereira, S. L., A. J. Baker, and A. Wajntal. 2002. Combined nuclear and mitochondrial DNA sequences resolve generic relationships within the Cracidae (Galliformes, Aves). *Systematic Biology* 51:946–58.

Pereira, S. L., K. P. Johnson, D. H. Clayton, and A. J. Baker. 2007. Mitochondrial and nuclear DNA sequences support a Cretaceous origin of Columbiformes and a dispersal-driven radiation in the Paleogene. *Systematic Biology* 56:656–72.

Phillips, M. J., G. C. Gibb, E. A. Crimp, and D. Penny. 2010. Tinamous and moa flock together: Mitochondrial genome sequence analysis reveals independent losses of flight among ratites. *Systematic Biology* 59:90–107.

Pruett, C. L., S. E. Henke, S. M. Tanksley, M. F. Small, K. M. Hogan, and J. Roberson. 2000. Mitochondrial DNA and morphological variation of White-winged Doves in Texas. *Condor* 102:871–80.

Prum, R. O. 2002. Why ornithologists should care about the theropod origin of birds. *Auk* 119:1–17.

Pulquério, M. J. F., and R. A. Nichols. 2007. Dates from the molecular clock: How wrong can we be? *Trends in Ecology and Evolution* 22:180–84.

Rhymer, J. M., M. G. Fain, J. E. Austin, D. H. Johnson, and C. Krajewski. 2001. Mitochondrial phylogeography, subspecies taxonomy, and conservation genetics of Sandhill Cranes (*Grus canadensis*, Aves: Gruidae). *Conservation Genetics* 2:203–18.

Rhymer, J. M., D. G. McAuley, and H. L. Ziel. 2005. Phylogeography of the American Woodcock (*Scolopax minor*): Are management units based on band recovery data reflected in genetically based management units? *Auk* 122:1149–60.

Rising, J. D. 2007. Named subspecies and their significance in contemporary ornithology. *Ornithological Monographs* 63:45–54.

Rosene, W. 1969. *The Bobwhite Quail: Its Life and Management*. New Brunswick, NJ: Rutgers University Press.

Ross, J. D., A. D. Arndt, R. F. C. Smith, J. A. Johnson, and J. L. Bouzat. 2006. Re-examination of the historical range of the Greater Prairie Chicken using provenance data and DNA analysis of museum collections. *Conservation Genetics* 7:735–51.

Sangster, G., J. M. Collinson, P.-A. Crochet, A. G. Knox, D. T. Parkin, and S. C. Voiter. 2012. Taxonomic recommendations for British birds: Eighth report. *Ibis* 154:874–83.

Sax, D. F., J. J. Stachowicz, J. H. Brown, J. F. Bruno, M. N. Dawson, S. D. Gaines, R. K. Grosberg, et al. 2007. Ecological and evolutionary insights from species invasions. *Trends in Ecology and Evolution* 22:465–71.

Schlaepfer, M. A., M. C. Runge, and P. W. Sherman. 1998. Ecological and evolutionary traps. *Trends in Ecology and Evolution* 17:474–80.

Schweitzer, M. H., W. Zheng, C. L. Organ, R. Avci, Z. Suo, L. M. Freimark, V. S. Lebleu, et al. 2008. Biomolecular characterization and protein sequences of the Campanian hadrosaur *B. canadensis*. *Science* 324:626–31.

Semel, B., and P. W. Sherman. 1986. Dynamics of nest parasitism in Wood Ducks. *Auk* 103:813–16.

Semel, B., P. W. Sherman, and S. M. Byers. 1988. Effects of brood parasitism and nest-box placement on Wood Duck breeding ecology. *Condor* 90:920–30.

Shapiro, B., D. Sibthorpe, A. Rambaut, J. Austin, G. M. Wragg, O. R. P. Bininda-Emonds, P. L. M. Lee, and A. Cooper. 2002. Flight of the Dodo. *Science* 295:1683.

Shetty, S., L. Bharathi, K. B. Shenoy, and S. N. Hegde. 1992. Biochemical properties of pigeon milk and its effects on growth. *Journal of Comparative Physiology B* 162:632–36.

Sibley, C. G., and J. E. Ahlquist. 1985. The relationships of some groups of African birds, based on comparisons of the genetic material, DNA. In *Proceedings of the International Symposium on African Vertebrates: Systematics, Phylogeny, and Evolutionary Ecology*, edited by K.-L. Schuchmann, 115–62. Bonn, Germany: Zoologisches Forschungsinstitut und Museum Alexander Koenig.

Silkas, B., S. L. Olson, and R. C. Fleischer. 2002. Rapid, independent evolution of flightlessness in four species of Pacific Island rails (Rallidae): An analysis based on mitochondrial sequence data. *Journal of Avian Biology* 33:5–14.

Simonetta, A. M. 1963. Cinesi e morfologia del cranio negli uccelli non-passeriformi: Studio su varie tendenze evolutive, parte I. *Archivo Zoologico Italiano* 48:53–135.

Soulé, M. E. 1985. What is conservation biology? *BioScience* 35:727–34.

Spaulding, A. W., K. E. Mock, M. A. Schroeder, and K. I. Warheit. 2006. Recency, range expansion, and unsorted lineages: Implications for interpreting neutral genetic variation in the Sharp-tailed Grouse (*Tympanuchus phasianellus*). *Molecular Ecology* 15:2317–32.

Stockwell, C. A., A. P. Hendry, and M. T. Kinnison. 2003. Contemporary evolution meets conservation biology. *Trends in Ecology and Evolution* 18:94–101.

Strauss, S. Y., J. A. Lau, S. P. Carroll. 2006. Evolutionary responses of natives to introduced species: What do introductions tell us about natural communities? *Ecology Letters* 9:357–74.

Taylor, B. 1998. *Rails: A Guide to the Rails, Crakes, Gallinules and Coots of the World*. New Haven, CT: Yale University Press.

Tordoff, H. B. 1951. Osteology of *Colinus hibbardi*, a Pliocene quail. *Condor* 53:23–30.

Trewick, S. A. 1997. Flightlessness and phylogeny amongst endemic rails (Aves: Rallidae) of the New Zealand region. *Philosophical Transactions of the Royal Society of London B* 352:429–46.

van Tuinen, M., and G. J. Dyke. 2004. Calibration of galliform molecular clocks using multiple fossils and genetic partitions. *Molecular Phylogenetics and Evolution* 30:74–86.

Vargas, A. O., and J. F. Fallon. 2005. Birds have dinosaur wings: The molecular evidence. *Journal of Experimental Zoology B: Molecular and Developmental Evolution* 304B:86–90.

Voelker, G. 2002. Systematics and historical biogeography of wagtails: Dispersal versus vicariance revisited. *Condor* 104:725–39.

Wang, N., R. T. Kimball, E. L. Braun, B. Liang, and Z. Zhang. 2013. Assessing phylogenetic relationships among Galliformes: A multigene phylogeny with expanded taxon sampling in Phasianidae. *PLoS ONE* 8 (5): e64312.

Weir, J. T. 2006. Divergent timing and patterns of species accumulation in lowland and highland neotropical birds. *Evolution* 60:842–55.

Weir, J. T., and D. Schluter. 2004. Ice sheets promote speciation in boreal birds. *Proceedings of the Royal Society of London B* 271:1881–87.

Wetmore, A. 1944. Remains of birds from the Rexroad fauna of the Upper Pliocene of Kansas. *University of Kansas Science Bulletin* 30:89–105.

White, S. L., K. R. Nolte, W. P. Kuvlesky Jr., and F. S. Guthery. 2000. Comparative morphology and phylogenetic relatedness among bobwhites in the southern U.S. and Mexico. *Proceedings of the National Quail Symposium* 4:111–14.

Williford, D. L. 2013. Molecular genetics of the Northern Bobwhite, Scaled Quail, and Gambel's Quail. PhD diss., Texas A&M University–Kingsville.

Williford, D., R. W. DeYoung, R. L. Honeycutt, L. A. Brennan, and F. Hernández. 2014a. Phylogeography of the Scaled Quail in the American Southwest. *Western North American Naturalist* 74:18–32.

Williford, D., R. W. DeYoung, R. L. Honeycutt, L. A. Brennan, F. Hernández, J. R. Heffelfinger, and L. A. Harveson. 2014b. Phylogeography of the Gambel's Quail (*Callipepla gambelii*) of western North America. *Wilson Journal of Ornithology* 126:218–35.

Williford, D., R. W. DeYoung, R. L. Honeycutt, L. A. Brennan, F. Hernández, E. M. Wehland, J. P. Sands, S. J. DeMaso, K. S. Miller, and R. M. Perez. 2014c. Contemporary genetic structure of the Northern Bobwhite west of the Mississippi River. *Journal of Wildlife Management* 78:914–29.

Winker, K. 2010. Subspecies represent geographically partitioned variation, a gold mine of evolutionary biology, and a challenge for conservation. *Ornithological Monographs* 67:6–23.

Witmer, L. M., and L. M. Chiappe. 2002. *Mesozoic Birds: Above the Heads of Dinosaurs*. Berkeley: University of California Press.

Wood, D. S. 1979. Phenetic relationships within the family Gruidae. *Wilson Bulletin* 91:384–99.

Wright, T. F., E. E. Schirtzinger, T. Matsumoto, J. R. Eberhard, G. R. Graves, J. J. Sanchez, S. Capelli, et al.

2008. A multilocus molecular phylogeny of the parrots (Psittaciformes): Support for a Gondwanan origin during the Cretaceous. *Molecular Biology and Evolution* 25:2141–56.

Yuri, T., R. T. Kimball, J. Harshman, R. C. K. Bowie, M. J. Braun, J. L. Chojnowski, K.-L. Han, et al. 2013. Parsimony and model-based analyses of indels in avian nuclear genes reveal congruent and incongruent phylogenetic signals. *Biology* 2:419–44.

Zhang, L., B. An, N. Backström, and N. Liu. 2014. Phylogeography-based delimitation of subspecies boundaries in the common pheasant (*Phasianus colchicus*). *Biochemical Genetics* 52:38–51.

Zheng, X., J. K. O'Connor, F. Huchzermeyer, X. Wang, Y. Wang, X. Zhang, and Z. Zhou. 2014. New specimens of *Yanornis* indicate a piscivorous diet and modern alimentary canal. *PLoS ONE* 9 (4): e95036.

Zhonge, Z. 2006. Evolutionary radiation of the Jehol Biota: Chronological and ecological perspectives. *Geological Journal* 41:377–93.

Zhou, Z. 2004. The origin and early evolution of birds: Discoveries, disputes, and perspectives from fossil evidence. *Naturwissenschaften* 91:455–71.

Zhou, Z., P. M. Barrett, and J. Hilton. 2003. An exceptionally preserved Lower Cretaceous ecosystem. *Nature* 421:807–14.

Zink, R. M. 1996. Comparative phylogeography and North American birds. *Evolution* 50:308–17.

———. 2004. The role of subspecies in obscuring avian biological diversity and misleading conservation policy. *Proceedings of the Royal Society of London Series B* 271:561–64.

Zink, R. M., and R. C. Blackwell. 1998a. Molecular systematics and biogeography of aridland gnatcatchers (genus *Polioptila*), and evidence supporting species status of the California Gnatcatcher (*P. californica*). *Molecular Phylogenetics and Evolution* 9:26–32.

———. 1998b. Molecular systematics of the Scaled Quail complex (genus *Callipepla*). *Auk* 115:394–403.

Zink, R. M., S. Rohwer, A. V. Andreev, and D. L. Dittmann. 1995. Trans-Beringian comparisons of mitochondrial DNA differentiation in birds. *Condor* 97:639–49.

Zink, R. M., S. Rohwer, S. Drovetski, R. C. Blackwell-Rago, and S. L. Farrell. 2002. Holarctic phylogeography and species limits of Three-toed Woodpeckers. *Condor* 104:167–70.

3

Sandhill Crane

More abundant and easier to kill than whooping cranes, they [sandhill cranes] were "very good eating" and a favorite of the local markets throughout the 1800s.—SAWYER (2013, 21)

Introduction

The Sandhill Crane (*Grus canadensis*) is a large, long-necked, long-legged bird well known for its resonating calls. It stands up to 1.2 m (4 ft) tall, with a wingspan reaching over 1.8 m (6 ft), and weighs 3.4 to 5 kg (7.5 to 11 lb). Sexes have similar uniform gray plumage, which can appear mottled with brownish staining that occurs primarily on wing and upper breast feathers, apparently caused by soil (Nesbitt 1975). In adults, the cheeks are whitish, and the forehead, lores, and crown are unfeathered, with reddish papillose skin. Young of the year can be distinguished from adults by a fully feathered head as well as brown nape feathers. Males are typically larger (~ 10%) than females, but much variation occurs in structural measurements, even within subspecies (Tacha, Nesbitt, and Vohs 1992).

The vocal repertoire of the Sandhill Crane is quite diverse, but its most recognizable vocalizations include loud, rattling bugles that can be heard for well over a mile. Cranes often make these calls when they are flying or on the ground, and pairs often make them in unison. Because of the cranes' social and gregarious nature, vocalizations are common and are most frequent during migration and winter.

Up to six subspecies of Sandhill Crane have been recognized (Tacha, Nesbitt, and Vohs 1992), with three of these occurring in Texas during winter. The subspecies with winter distributions in Texas include the large, aptly named Greater subspecies (*G. c. tabida*), the more diminutive Lesser subspecies (*G. c. canadensis*), and the intermediate Canadian subspecies (*G. c. rowani*). Subspecies designations were previously based on geographical distribution, and subtle differences in plumage and morphology (Walkinshaw 1973). However, more recent genetic analyses from cranes sampled in Texas during winter suggest that two of these presumed subspecies, the Greater and Canadian, are genetically indistinguishable (Glenn et al. 2002). Since then, other studies have corroborated the finding that there are two, not three, genetically distinct subspecies in the midcontinent population (Peterson et al. 2003; Jones et al. 2005).

Distribution in Texas

The winter distribution of midcontinent Sandhill Cranes ranges from the Gulf Coast of Texas west into southern New Mexico and southeastern Arizona and south into north-central Mexico. However, 80%–90% of the midcontinent population winters in western Texas, particularly in the southern High Plains region, where there are clusters of alkaline pluvial lakes within an agricultural landscape. This region contains

Figure 3.1. *(Top)*, Sandhill Crane flying. Photo credit: Larry Ditto. *(Right)*, note mud on bill of Sandhill Crane from foraging in moist soil. Photo credit: Greg Lasley.

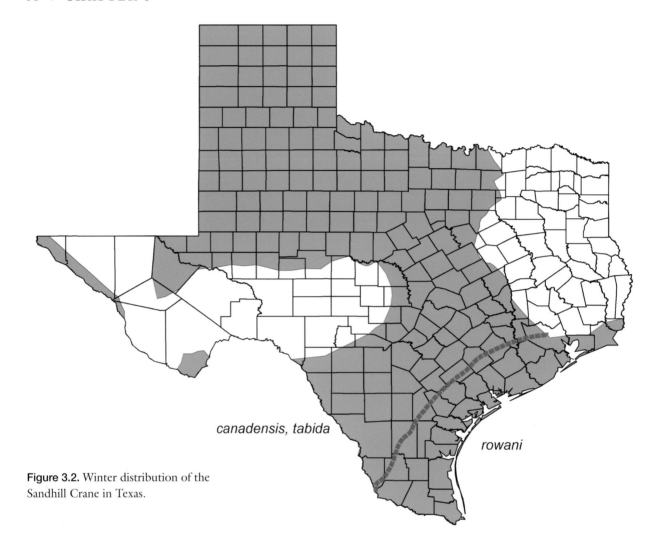

canadensis, tabida

rowani

Figure 3.2. Winter distribution of the Sandhill Crane in Texas.

the largest concentration of Sandhill Cranes during winter in North America, with more than 300,000 Sandhill Cranes estimated to use the area (Iverson, Vohs, and Tacha 1985a). Cranes in western Texas are primarily the Lesser subspecies, with breeding affiliations mainly in western Alaska, eastern Siberia, and northern Canada, and to a lesser extent from western Canada and interior Alaska to east-central Canada and Minnesota.

The Gulf Coast region of Texas between Houston and the Mexican border contains the second-highest abundance of cranes in the state, with around 120,000 spending the winter (Ballard et al. 1999; Krapu et al. 2011). Cranes wintering in this region are primarily larger Sandhill Cranes (Greaters and Canadians), with a few individuals of the Lesser subspecies. Breeding affiliation of cranes is primarily from east-central Canada

and Minnesota along northern portions of the coast, in western Canada and interior Alaska, and along the lower Texas coast (Krapu et al. 2011).

In Texas, the winter distribution of the Sandhill Crane has likely expanded into areas where land-use practices have changed to row crop agriculture (e.g., corn, sorghum, rice), allowing cranes to successfully inhabit new areas. Historically, the winter range of the Sandhill Crane extended well into eastern Arizona and southward into northwestern and central Mexico.

Biology

The Sandhill Crane has a broad breeding range across much of North America and into eastern Siberia. In North America, the breeding range of the midcontinent population extends from western Alaska through northern Canada to Hudson Bay, and south to the southern end of the prairie provinces of Alberta, Saskatchewan, and Manitoba. Nests are usually over water, either attached to vegetation or floating, and often occur in marshes dominated by grasses and sedges. However, cranes nesting in the Arctic will regularly nest on land (Walskinshaw 1973).

Migratory routes and timing

Midcontinent cranes migrate through the central part of the continent to wintering areas in Texas, southern New Mexico, southeastern Arizona, and north-central Mexico. They begin to depart breeding areas in late August, with the latest departures occurring in early October. The large nonbreeding cohort typically initiates fall migration before family units (pairs and pairs with young); however, nonbreeding groups tend to remain on staging areas longer and, as a result, arrive on wintering areas later than family units (Carlisle and Tacha 1983). Sandhill Cranes arrive on Texas wintering areas from October to January, with peak numbers in western Texas occurring in early February (Iverson, Vohs, and Tacha 1985a, 1985b). Most cranes depart Texas wintering areas in late February and early March to initiate their northward migration. Approximately 90% of the midcontinent population stages along the Platte River in Nebraska during mid- to late March. Many wildlife viewers, photographers, and tourist groups travel to the Platte River Valley each year to experience the large number of cranes staging there. Because nearly the entire midcontinent population of Sandhill Cranes concentrates along the Platte River during spring migration, surveys to estimate population size occur at this time. Cranes depart the Platte River staging area in early to mid-April and arrive at nesting areas from late April to mid-May (Melvin and Temple 1980).

Timing of breeding

Sandhill Cranes initiate pair bonds during spring migration with their elaborate, well-known courtship dance, which plays an important role in mate selection. Sandhill Cranes are perennially monogamous and delay breeding for 2 to 7 years after hatching. In the midcontinent population, pairs form as early as 3 years of age (~ 20% of birds), but most are not paired until

7 years (and most are not successful reproductively until > 8 years of age). Interestingly, in the Florida subspecies, most are paired at 2 years. Pair bonds may form and dissolve before successful reproduction, but following reproduction, mate changes are rare unless a mate dies (Littlefield 1981; Nesbitt and Wenner 1987). Average nest initiation date ranges from early April to mid-May in migratory populations (Walkinshaw 1973).

Behavior

Sandhill Cranes are known for their elaborate courtship dances, comprising 8 primary displays, 3 of which are used only by paired adults, and 5 of which are used by all social classes. Pair formation is accomplished through courtship dancing, and all 8 courtship displays play a role. The diverse array of courtship, agonistic, and other social behaviors are explained in detail by Tacha (1988).

Clutch size and incubation

Sandhill Cranes typically lay a clutch of 2 eggs, but fledging more than 1 young per year is rare. Eggs are light brown to light olive and are irregularly blotched with darker brown. Incubation starts when the first egg is laid and lasts for 30 days on average (Drewien 1973). Males and females share equally in incubation duties during the day, but only females incubate at night (Littlefield and Ryder 1968; Drewien 1973).

Phenology

Sandhill Cranes raise a single brood per year, but pairs will renest if a clutch is lost early in the incubation period. Chicks typically leave the nest within 24 hours of hatching, and fledging occurs around 70 days following hatching (Drewien 1973). Family units (parents and young) typically remain together for 9–10 months, at which time the young join groups of other nonbreeding individuals (Tacha 1988).

Diet and foraging

Sandhill Cranes are omnivorous but capitalize on agricultural grains whenever they are available (Tacha, Nesbitt, and Vohs 1992; Ballard and Thompson 2000). During winter in Texas, Ballard and Thompson (2000) found that the dominant cereal grain grown in the region was the dominant food in the diet of Sandhill Cranes. For instance, cranes fed primarily on sorghum in southern Texas, on corn and rice along the central coast, and on wheat and sorghum in the Rolling Plains. Nutgrass (*Cyperus* spp.) tubers extracted from natural wetlands are also common foods consumed by Sandhill Cranes. Animal material is important but rarely makes up more than 10% of the diet. Beetles, crickets, grasshoppers, and snails are the major animal foods found in the diet of Sandhill Cranes during winter.

Demography and vital rates

Sandhill Cranes are long-lived. The maximum age documented in the wild is 21 years (Tacha, Nesbitt, and Vohs 1992). Survival from hatching to fledging averages 65%, increases to 82% between fledging and independence, and is more than 85% for adults. Once independent, Sandhill Cranes are rarely preyed on, and nonhunting mortality is estimated to be about 5%. Most natural mortality appears to be due to disease (avian botulism and avian cholera; Windingstad 1988), lead poisoning, and collision with power lines. Windingstad et al. (1989) reported that an estimated 9,500 Sandhill Cranes died in Gaines County, Texas, and Roosevelt County, New Mexico, between 1982 and 1987 from a previously unknown mycotoxin produced by *Fusarium* fungi in waste peanuts under cold, wet weather conditions. Convincing peanut growers to till under waste peanuts eliminated this source of mortality.

Age at first reproduction

Delayed maturation occurs, with most individuals paired by their seventh year, but about 20% pair by their fourth year. Many first-time pairs are unsuccessful at producing young that survive to independence, and consequently, most successful reproduction occurs in birds 8 years of age and older (Tacha, Haley, and Vohs 1989).

Age and sex ratios

The more k-selected life-history characteristics (i.e., long life span, delayed sexual maturation, small clutch size) of Sandhill Cranes result in fall age ratios that are lower than those of other harvested game birds. The percentage of first-year individuals ranges from 6% to 18% during fall in most populations, averaging around 11% (Tacha, Nesbitt, and Vohs 1992). Winter sex ratios of Sandhill Cranes in Texas are slightly skewed toward males (55%–58% males) (Tacha and Vohs 1984; Ballard et al. 1999).

Population Status and Trends

The midcontinent population of Sandhill Cranes is by far the largest of nine recognized populations of Sandhill Cranes, making up about 87% of all Sandhill Cranes in North America. The midcontinent population has fluctuated between 282,702 and 893,160 individuals since 1982 (mean = 464,206; SE = 22,215), according to the coordinated US Fish and Wildlife Service annual survey conducted across all survey areas during spring migration, when most cranes are concentrated along the Platte River in Nebraska (Kruse, Dubovsky, and Cooper 2012). Four of the highest counts have occurred in the last six years, suggesting that the population has increased in recent years. Overall, the survey shows a highly fluctuating but increasing trend from 1982 to 2013. Another source of information to calculate population trends is the Christmas Bird Count, which is an annual citizen-based survey across North America. Based on results only from Texas, the number of cranes wintering in Texas appeared to decline in the mid-1980s, remained relatively stable through 2005, and became relatively high from 2006 to 2014. Thus, based on these two surveys, it appears that Sandhill Cranes in the midcontinent population and wintering in Texas have increased in abundance in recent years.

Specific Habitat Requirements

Nesting habitat typically consists of freshwater marsh dominated by sedges, often adjacent to wooded areas (Carlisle 1982; Tacha, Nesbitt, and Vohs 1992). During migration and winter, Sandhill Cranes feed primarily in agricultural fields of cereal grains (e.g., corn, sorghum, wheat, and rice), hay fields, pastures, and freshwater wetlands. Also critical for Sandhill Cranes is adequate roost habitat, which is characterized by relatively large, freshwater wetlands with open, shallow water.

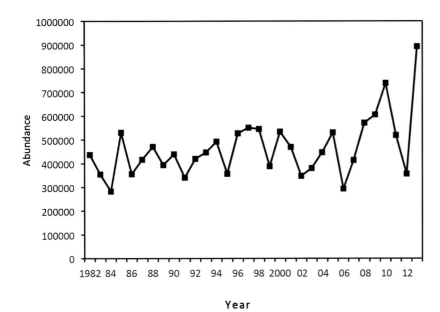

Figure 3.3. Estimated size of midcontinent Sandhill Crane population during the annual US Fish and Wildlife Service spring survey, 1982–2013.

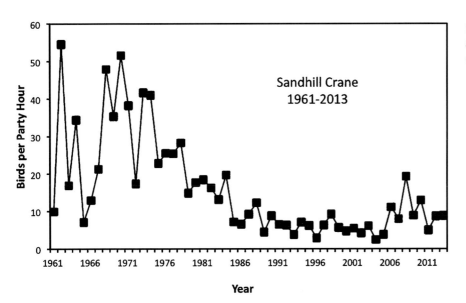

Figure 3.4. Population trend of the Sandhill Crane in Texas, based on Christmas Bird Count data.

Winter habitat use

During winter, Sandhill Cranes require three primary resources: food that comes primarily from agricultural fields and shallow wetlands, sources of fresh water to drink, and relatively large, shallow bodies of water in which to roost (Iverson, Vohs, and Tacha 1985b). Cranes typically roost in shallow water with a maximum depth of 16 inches but will also roost on mudflats surrounding water if such areas are expansive enough to provide an adequate distance barrier from cover that may hide predators. In western Texas, roost sites are typically saline pluvial lakes with freshwater springs. In fact, numbers of cranes roosting on these lakes are directly related to the number of freshwater springs and the amount of milo stubble around the lake. Sandhill Cranes that winter along the Gulf Coast of Texas typically use shallow water in estuaries as well as shallow wetlands farther inland for roost sites. During winter, Sandhill Cranes depart from their nighttime roost sites about 30 minutes after sunrise and travel up to eight miles to foraging sites. Cranes return to the roost about one hour prior to sunset, except on cold days (mean daily temperature below 10°C, or 50°F), when foraging time increases and arrival on roost sites approximates sunset (Iverson, Vohs, and Tacha 1985a, 1985b).

Diet varies seasonally and regionally based on food availability. In particular, Sandhill Cranes appear to capitalize on available waste grain from agricultural fields at wintering sites. Sandhill Cranes wintering in western Texas consume primarily milo, and 75% of their time away from the roost site is spent in milo fields (Iverson, Tacha, and Vohs 1982; Iverson, Vohs, and Tacha 1985b). Along the Gulf Coast of Texas, sorghum fields, coastal prairie, and freshwater marshes are commonly used habitats (Guthery 1975; Ballard and Thompson 2000). Thus, winter distribution is highly tied to agricultural areas.

Conservation and management

There are nine populations of Sandhill Cranes identified that have distinct breeding and/or winter ranges (see below). The midcontinent population is by far the largest, comprising over 500,000 cranes, most of which winter in Texas.

In Texas, the midcontinent population is dispersed between two subpopulations, the western and the Gulf Coast. The western subpopulation winters in western Texas, westward into southern New Mexico and southeastern Arizona, and south into north-central Mexico (Tacha, Nesbitt, and Vohs 1992). The Gulf Coast subpopulation winters along the Texas Gulf Coast. During winter in Texas, the Lesser subspecies is more prevalent in the western subpopulation that winters primarily in the Panhandle region of Texas, whereas the Greater is more prevalent in the Gulf Coast subpopulation (Tacha, Nesbitt, and Vohs 1992; Ballard et al. 1999).

Because of their omnivorous diet and great reliance on agricultural fields, foraging habitat is rarely limited for Sandhill Cranes in the midcontinent. The availability and distribution of roost sites, however, can limit the use of foraging areas, particularly in western Texas. In this arid part of the state, fewer than 20 lakes support the majority of midcontinent Sandhill Cranes during winter, resulting in greater concentrations of cranes on roost sites and greater competition for food near roost sites. Management activities that promote water availability or water conservation in roost lakes is

beneficial to Sandhill Cranes in western Texas. Tacha, Nesbitt, and Vohs (1992, 92) specifically recommended that the US Fish and Wildlife Service and the Texas Parks and Wildlife Department prioritize and fund protection of key saline pluvial lakes used in winter by Sandhill Cranes in Texas.

Hunting and Conservation

The Sandhill Crane was traditionally harvested for food and recreation in the United States and Canada prior to the Migratory Bird Treaty Act of 1918. Because of unregulated harvest and changes to habitat, its abundance declined considerably and the hunting season on Sandhill Cranes in the United States and Canada was closed, remaining so for 45 years. Because farmers complained of severe crop depredation in wintering areas from Sandhill Crane foraging, the season was reopened in portions of New Mexico in 1960 and the following year in western Texas. By 1975, Sandhill Crane hunting seasons had been opened in seven other states within the Central Flyway. Currently, all or portions of all states in the Central Flyway, except Nebraska, have a regulated Sandhill Crane hunting season.

From 1975 to 2012 the estimated annual harvest of midcontinent Sandhill Cranes ranged from 8,030 to 24,704 per year. Texas harvests more cranes than any other state and annually accounts for 42%–70% of the total annual harvest on midcontinent Sandhill Cranes. The number of active Sandhill Crane hunters in Texas has ranged from a low of 1,553 in 1982 to a high of 6,338 in 2008. Since 2012, an average of 4,362 active Sandhill Crane hunters per year in Texas have killed an average of 10,463 cranes per year (Kruse, Dubovsky, and Cooper 2012).

Texas hunting season dates

Texas is divided into three Sandhill Crane hunting zones based on the migration chronology of Sandhill Cranes through the zone, composition of subspecies within the zone, and the chronology of Whooping Crane (*Grus americana*) migration through the zone to minimize accidental harvest (fig. 3.5). Zone A is the westernmost zone and was the first (in 1961) to allow a Sandhill Crane hunting season in Texas.

Dates for the Sandhill Crane hunting season in Zone A have generally run from early to mid-November to early February over the last 25 years. Zone B lies east of Zone A, north of Austin, and has had an active Sandhill Crane hunting season since 1968. The hunting season in Zone B opens about three weeks later than in Zone A (late November) and runs through early February. Zone C covers the southeastern part of Texas and first allowed a Sandhill Crane hunting season in 1983. The season in Zone C opens in mid- to late December to allow for Whooping Cranes to pass through and settle on their wintering area at Aransas National Wildlife Refuge near Austwell. The season in Zone C originally closed in early February, but since the conservation order on light geese was put into effect in 2001, the season has closed in late January to allow for liberal hunting methods to increase harvest on light geese.

Texas bag limits

In recent years, the bag limit in Zones A and B has been three cranes per day, and in Zone C it has been two cranes per day, with a possession limit of twice the daily bag.

Research Needs and Priorities

The Sandhill Crane is a relatively well-studied game bird. Tacha, Nesbitt, and Vohs (1994) provided several recommendations for Sandhill Crane research. Below are six recommendations for the midcontinent population that remain relevant today.

1. Develop an annual wintering ground survey to better understand numbers and trends of Sandhill Cranes wintering in western Texas and along the Gulf Coast.

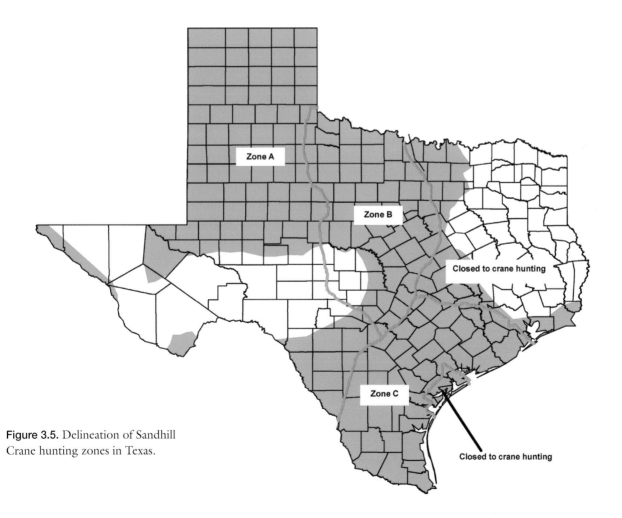

Figure 3.5. Delineation of Sandhill Crane hunting zones in Texas.

2. Gain a better understanding of harvest, including subsistence harvest, recreational harvest in Mexico and Siberia, and unretrieved harvest in major harvest areas.

3. Investigate how changes in regulations (e.g., bag limits, season lengths, and season dates) influence the number of birds harvested in regions that harvest significant numbers of Sandhill Cranes.

4. Develop operational surveys to understand annual variation in recruitment of Sandhill Cranes from the different subpopulations.

5. Evaluate techniques to reduce crop depredations by Sandhill Cranes.

6. Develop and test models that can be used to understand the population dynamics of subpopulations within the midcontinent population of Sandhill Cranes.

Literature Cited

Ballard, B. M., and J. E. Thompson. 2000. Winter diets of Sandhill Cranes from central and coastal Texas. *Wilson Bulletin* 112:263–68.

Ballard, B. M., J. E. Thompson, M. T. Merendino, J. D. Ray, J. A. Roberson, and T. C. Tacha. 1999. Demographics of the Gulf Coast subpopulation of mid-continent Sandhill Cranes. *Proceedings of the Annual Conference of the Southeastern Association of Fish and Wildlife Agencies* 53:449–63.

Carlisle, M. 1982. Nesting habits of Sandhill Cranes in central Alberta. In *Proceedings of the 1981 International Crane Workshop*, edited by J. C. Lewis, 44–55. Tavernier, FL: National Audubon Society.

Carlisle, M. J., and T. C. Tacha. 1983. Fall migration of Sandhill Cranes in west central North Dakota. *Journal of Wildlife Management* 47:818–21.

Drewien, R. C. 1973. *Ecology of Rocky Mountain Greater Sandhill Cranes*. PhD diss., University of Idaho.

Glenn, T. C., J. E. Thompson, B. M. Ballard, J. A. Roberson, and J. O. French. 2002. Mitochondrial DNA variation among wintering mid-continent Gulf Coast Sandhill Cranes. *Journal of Wildlife Management* 66:339–48.

Guthery, F. S. 1975. Food habits of Sandhill Cranes in southern Texas. *Journal of Wildlife Management* 39:221–23.

Iverson, G. C., T. C. Tacha, and P. A. Vohs. 1982. Food contents of Sandhill Cranes during winter and spring. In *Proceedings of the 1981 International Crane Workshop*, edited by J. C. Lewis, 95–98. Tavernier, FL: National Audubon Society.

Iverson, G. C., P. A. Vohs, and T. C. Tacha. 1985a. Distribution and abundance of Sandhill Cranes wintering in western Texas. *Journal of Wildlife Management* 49:250–55.

———. 1985b. Habitat use by Sandhill Cranes wintering in western Texas. *Journal of Wildlife Management* 49:1074–83.

Jones, K. L., G. L. Krapu, D. A. Brandt, and M. V. Ashley. 2005. Population genetic structure in migratory Sandhill Cranes and the role of Pleistocene glaciation. *Molecular Ecology* 14:2645–57.

Krapu, G. L., D. A. Brandt, K. L. Jones, and D. H. Johnson. 2011. Geographic distribution of the mid-continent population of Sandhill Cranes and related management implications. *Wildlife Monographs* 175:1–38.

Kruse, K. L., J. A. Dubovsky, and T. R. Cooper. 2012. *Status and Harvest of Sandhill Cranes: Mid-continent, Rocky Mountain, Lower Colorado River Valley and Eastern Populations*. Lakewood, CO: US Fish and Wildlife Service.

Littlefield, C. D. 1981. Mate swapping of Sandhill Cranes. *Journal of Field Ornithology* 52:244–45.

Littlefield, C. D., and R. A. Ryder. 1968. Breeding biology of the greater Sandhill Crane on Malheur National Wildlife Refuge, Oregon. *Transactions of the North American Wildlife and Natural Resources Conference* 33:444–54.

Melvin, S. M., and S. A. Temple. 1980. *Migration Ecology and Wintering Grounds of Sandhill Cranes from the Interlake Region of Manitoba*. Washington, DC: US Fish and Wildlife Service.

Nesbitt, S. A. 1975. Feather staining in Florida Sandhill Cranes. *Florida Field Naturalist* 3:28–30.

Nesbitt, S. A., and A. S. Wenner. 1987. Pair formation and mate fidelity in Sandhill Cranes. In *Proceedings of the 1985 International Crane Workshop*, edited by J. C. Lewis, 117–22. Grand Island, NE: US Fish and Wildlife Service.

Peterson, J. L., R. Bischof, G. L. Krapu, and A. L. Szalanski. 2003. Genetic variation in the mid-continent population of Sandhill Cranes, *Grus canadensis*. *Biochemical Genetics* 41:1–12.

Sauer, J. R., J. E. Hines, J. E. Fallon, K. L. Pardieck, D. J. Ziolkowski Jr., and W. A. Link. 2014. *The North American Breeding Bird Survey, Results and Analysis 1966–2013*. Version 01.30.2015. Laurel, MD: USGS Patuxent Wildlife Research Center.

Sawyer, R. K. 2013. *Texas Market Hunting: Stories of Waterfowl, Game Laws and Outlaws*. College Station: Texas A&M University Press.

Tacha, T. C. 1988. Social organization of Sandhill Cranes from mid-continent North America. *Wildlife Monographs* 99.

Tacha, T. C., D. E. Haley, and P. A. Vohs. 1989. Age of sexual maturity in Sandhill Cranes from mid-continent

North America. *Journal of Wildlife Management* 53:43–46.

Tacha, T. C., S. A. Nesbitt, and P. A. Vohs. 1992. Sandhill Crane. In *The Birds of North America*, No. 31, edited by A. Poole, P. Stettenheim, and F. Gill. Philadelphia: Academy of Natural Sciences.

———. 1994. Sandhill Crane. In *Migratory Shore and Upland Game Bird Management in North America*, edited by T. C. Tacha and C. E. Braun, 77–96. Washington, DC: International Association of Fish and Wildlife Agencies.

Tacha, T. C., and P. A. Vohs. 1984. Some population parameters of Sandhill Cranes from mid-continental North America. *Journal of Wildlife Management* 48:89–98.

Walkinshaw, L. H. 1973. *Cranes of the World*. New York: Winchester Press.

Windingstad, R. M. 1988. Nonhunting mortality in Sandhill Cranes. *Journal of Wildlife Management* 52:260–63.

Windingstad, R. M., R. J. Cole, P. E. Nelson, T. J. Roffe, R. R. George, and J. W. Dorner. 1989. *Fusarium* mycotoxins from peanuts suspected as a cause of Sandhill Crane mortality. *Journal of Wildlife Diseases* 25:38–46.

4

Clapper Rail

Hunting is done from a boat, poled through the marsh at high tide when the birds can be put to flight.—LEOPOLD, GUTIÉRREZ, AND BRONSON (1981, 18)

Introduction

The Clapper Rail (*Rallus longirostris*) is a large rail of salt marsh habitat. It has grayish to tannish plumage streaked with brown above, a somewhat buffy color on its breast and belly, and gray and white barring on its flanks. It has a relatively long, slightly decurved bill used for capturing crustaceans and other aquatic insects. Its body is laterally compressed like that of most true rails, to aid in its ability to travel through thick stands of marsh vegetation. The Clapper Rail is more often heard than observed; its repetitious "kek-kek-kek" call can be heard resonating from coastal salt marsh habitat throughout spring.

Several subspecies of Clapper Rail are recognized based primarily on differences in plumage coloration and structural size. The King Rail (*Rallus elegans*) resembles the Clapper Rail but is larger and typically less drab in coloration. The Clapper Rail and King Rail are known to hybridize where their geographic ranges overlap.

Distribution in Texas

This common year-round resident is found in salt marshes along the immediate Texas coast. The Clapper Rail has a fairly wide distribution in coastal areas of the United States and throughout the Americas, south to Brazil and Peru.

Biology

The Clapper Rail is presumed to be annually monogamous and males are territorial throughout the breeding season. The male uses the typical "kek-kek-kek" call to advertise its territory and to attract females. Both males and females take equal roles during incubation and brood rearing. They will often renest and produce a second brood. Clapper Rails are solitary outside the breeding season.

Migratory routes and timing

Individuals from northern portions of the range tend to be migratory, but most populations throughout the range remain resident. Timing of fall migration is variable but depends largely on cold fronts to push birds south. Arrival on wintering grounds begins in mid-September and extends through early November. Timing of spring migration and migratory routes taken are relatively unknown. The Clapper Rail is thought to migrate mainly at night.

Behavior

The Clapper Rail is a secretive marsh bird that stays in or near emergent vegetation. Most often it is observed walking or running on the ground, as it flies infrequently except during migration. It typically holds its tail in an upright position when walking, often flicking it up and

Figure 4.1. Clapper Rail and wetland habitat. Note dense grass in background. Photo credit: Larry Ditto.

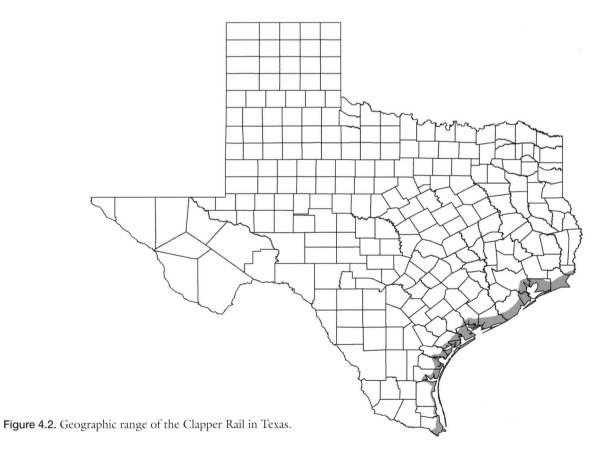

Figure 4.2. Geographic range of the Clapper Rail in Texas.

down. Flight appears quite laborious, with legs hanging down during takeoff, and shorter flights. The Clapper Rail can swim effectively and uses this form of locomotion to cross short segments of deep water.

Phenology

Courtship calls are initiated in early March in Texas, with birds starting to pair by mid-March. First nests occur in mid- to late March, with peak nest initiation in late April to mid-May. First broods are typically observed in early May, but peak brood rearing occurs in June and July. Chicks become independent of adults at around 6 weeks after hatching and are able to fly at around 10 weeks after hatching.

Clutch size and incubation

Clutch size varies among subspecies but averages 8 eggs for Clapper Rails breeding along the western Gulf Coast. Both males and females contribute to incubation, which lasts around 21 days.

Diet and foraging

Clapper Rails are omnivorous and feed opportunistically on available foods. The majority of their diet comprises animal material, primarily crustaceans (e.g., crabs and shrimp) but also snails, clams, benthic worms, and insects. Plant material makes up a much smaller component of the diet; up to 11% in winter, less than 5% in fall and spring, and none in summer. Plant foods consumed by Clapper Rails are primarily emergent plant seeds.

Demography and vital rates

The Clapper Rail is a relatively short-lived bird. Adults have an estimated annual survival rate of 49%–67%, with most mortality occurring during fall migration and winter. The oldest known individual Clapper Rail from the wild, banded as an adult, was at least 7.5 years old.

Nest success ranges from 42% to 94%, with most nest failures the result of high tides or predation. Brood mortality is thought to be high during the first few weeks after hatching, when chicks are most vulnerable.

Age at first reproduction

Age at first reproduction is thought to be 1 year, but no information is available.

Age and sex ratios

Age ratios of the Clapper Rail appear to be quite variable during fall, ranging from 2 to 5.8 juveniles per adult. Sex ratios have been shown to be skewed toward males, but hunter-harvested samples often show an equal sex ratio.

Population Status and Trends

There is no integrated survey of Clapper Rails across their range. The California, Light-footed, and Yuma subspecies of Clapper Rail, all occurring in California, are classified as federally endangered. However, populations along the Atlantic and Gulf Coasts appear to be stable, and no state currently lists them as a species of concern in the eastern part of North America.

According to the Christmas Bird Count, Clapper Rail abundance has remained relatively stable since 1961.

Specific Habitat Requirements

Clapper Rails show an affinity for cordgrass-dominated salt marsh habitats that are flooded by high tides at least daily. Nest sites are often associated with dense stands of cordgrass in the higher extent of the salt marsh, thus reducing the chance of tides flooding the nest. Clapper Rails forage on mudflats and along tidal creeks where prey densities are high, but they are rarely far from dense plant cover.

Winter habitat use

Clapper rails remain in salt marsh habitats year round but appear to move to denser cordgrass cover during winter.

Habitat management

The largest factor affecting Clapper Rail habitat is development within and around the coastal marsh that

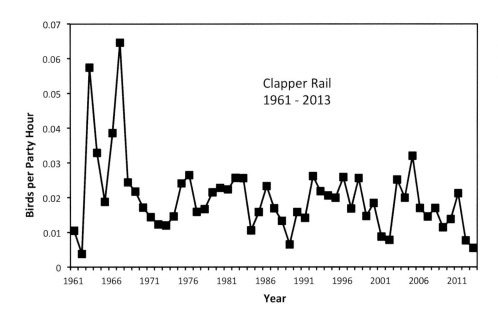

Figure 4.3. Population trend of the Clapper Rail in Texas, based on Christmas Bird Count data.

influences habitat structure or modifies tidal flows. Management practices that prevent alteration to tidal flows or restore tidal flow activity within the salt marsh are most common for Clapper Rails.

Texas Hunting Regulations

The bag limit is 15 (in aggregation with King Rail), and the possession limit is 45. There is currently a 40-day season, from mid- to late September and from early November to late December. There is no geographic restriction on hunting in Texas; the season is open in all 254 counties.

Research Needs and Priorities

The most important research needs were summarized by Eddleman and Conway (1994), and these are still relevant today. Because most populations of the Clapper Rail appear to be doing quite well, particularly in eastern portions of its range, little emphasis has been placed on researching much of this information.

1. Improve monitoring techniques to acquire estimates of distribution, abundance, and population trends.

2. Increase banding throughout the range to better understand survival rates.

3. Develop standardized methods to assess harvest of the Clapper Rail throughout its range.

4. Gain a better understanding of habitat use by Clapper Rails, particularly how habitat management practices influence populations.

5. Fill gaps in our knowledge of the basic life history of the Clapper Rail.

Literature Cited

Eddleman, W. R., and C. J. Conway. 1994. Clapper Rail. In *Migratory Shore and Upland Game Bird Management in North America*, edited by T. C. Tacha and C. E. Braun, 167–79. Washington, DC: International Association of Fish and Wildlife Agencies.

———. 1998. Clapper Rail (*Rallus longirostris*). In *The Birds of North America*, No. 340, edited by A. Poole and F. Gill. Philadelphia: Birds of North America.

Leopold, A. S., R. J. Gutiérrez, and M. S. Bronson. 1981. *North American Game Birds and Mammals.* New York: Charles Scribner's Sons.

Sauer, J. R., J. E. Hines, and J. Fallon. 2005. *The North American Breeding Bird Survey, Results and Analysis 1966–2005.* Version 6.2.2006. Laurel, MD: USGS Patuxent Wildlife Research Center. http://www.mbr-pwrc.usgs.gov/bbs/BBS_Results_and_Analysis_2005.html.

5

King Rail

They are weak flyers, but nonetheless they make long seasonal migrations, flying exclusively at night as is true of other rails.—LEOPOLD, GUTIÉRREZ, AND BRONSON (1981, 18)

Introduction

The King Rail (*Rallus elegans*) is our largest true rail, found in fresh to brackish marshes throughout the eastern half of North America. It is a secretive marshbird, more often heard than seen. It has a laterally compressed body like that of most true rails, a moderately long, slender bill that is slightly decurved, relatively long legs and toes, and a short tail. Coloration is streaked brown to rusty on its upper parts, rusty orange on the breast, and black-and-white barring on the flanks. Sexes are quite similar, but females tend to be somewhat smaller and have duller-colored plumage. There are two recognized subspecies, one with its distribution in North America (*R. e. elegans*), and the second restricted to Cuba (*R. e. remsdeni*). The King Rail closely resembles the Clapper Rail (*Rallus longirostris*), but the King Rail tends to be larger and more colorful than the drabber, grayish Clapper Rail.

A game bird along the Atlantic and Gulf Coasts, the King Rail has a relatively small harvest with a traditional following. The King Rail is a focal species of the US Fish and Wildlife Service.

Distribution in Texas

The King Rail is relatively common throughout the coastal zone of Texas, and rare to casual across the eastern third of the state. Less common during summer, it becomes more common as migrants from more northerly areas pass through or winter along the Texas coast. The King Rail winters along the Gulf Coast as far south as southern Mexico. Because of its secretive nature, it may be more common than records indicate.

Biology

Several aspects of the King Rail's biology have not been thoroughly studied. The mating system is thought to be monogamous, as both members of the pair contribute to incubation and brooding. Nests are constructed in thickets of emergent vegetation and elevated above the water. Chicks are mobile soon after hatching but are fed by adults until 4–6 weeks of age. By 7–9 weeks of age, young feed themselves, and they become independent by late summer.

Figure 5.1. King Rail and habitat. Photo credit: Greg Lasley.

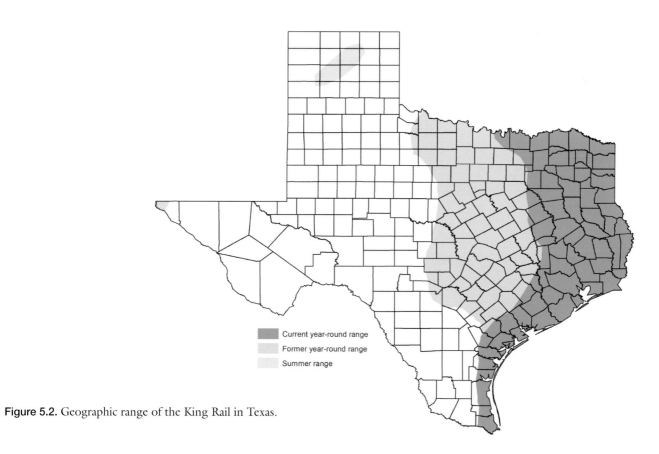

Current year-round range
Former year-round range
Summer range

Figure 5.2. Geographic range of the King Rail in Texas.

Migratory routes and timing

Little is known about the migration of the King Rail. It is believed that northern and inland populations are migratory and southern and coastal populations remain resident year round. Thus, the Texas coast is believed to support resident populations as well as migratory individuals during winter. Anecdotal information suggests that King Rails migrate solitarily and nocturnally. Fall migration occurs primarily in September and October, and spring migration occurs primarily in April and May. Information on migratory routes is lacking.

Phenology

Pairing in the King Rail is thought to occur in January and early February in southern portions of the range, such as Texas. Nesting occurs in late February to early August (Poole et al. 2005). First broods occur in late March to early April. It is unknown whether double brooding occurs, but it does in the closely related Clapper Rail. Young fledge 9–10 weeks after hatching.

Clutch size and incubation

Clutch size appears to vary little across the geographic distribution, averaging 10.5 to 11.2 eggs. Both males and females take part in incubation, which lasts from 21 to 23 days and is initiated when the clutch is complete.

Diet and foraging

Although King Rails are omnivorous, their diet is dominated by animal foods, particularly crustaceans and aquatic insects. In freshwater marshes, crayfish (Cambaridae) are one of the most important foods consumed by King Rails, whereas fiddler crabs (*Uca* spp.) tend to be the food of choice in tidal marsh habitats. Animal material makes up 90%–95% of their diet in spring and summer, 74% in fall, and 58% in winter. Other foods commonly consumed include frogs, fish, grasshoppers, crickets, and wetland plant seeds (Poole et al. 2005).

Demography and vital rates

Currently, there is no information on life span and survivorship of King Rails. Raccoon (*Procyon lotor*),
mink (*Neovison vison*), striped skunk (*Mephitis mephitis*), Northern Harrier (*Circus cyaneus*), and American alligator (*Alligator mississippiensis*) are likely culprits for nest depredation and mortality of adults and young (Poole et al. 2005). It is believed that low brood survival may be a limiting factor in King Rail population dynamics.

Age at first reproduction

No information is available.

Age and sex ratios

No information is available.

Behavior

The King Rail is typically observed walking or running through emergent vegetation more than flying. Courtship display by males includes walking with tail upright to expose white undertail coverts. Often the male will flick its tail up and down to flash the white coverts. Mating calls are frequently given during the courtship display to attract a female.

Population Status and Trends

The King Rail appears to be relatively stable throughout most of the southern portions of its range, but it appears to be declining in the northern parts of its range, particularly throughout the Midwest and along the Atlantic Coast (e.g., Maryland and Delaware). The King Rail is listed as a Species of Management Concern by the US Fish and Wildlife Service and is classified as endangered by nine states and as threatened by three others. Thirty states list the King Rail as a Species of Greatest Conservation Need (Cooper 2008). Declines in abundance are believed to be related primarily to loss of wetland habitats (Poole et al. 2005)

Analysis of count data from 13 Breeding Bird Survey routes for the King Rail in Texas from 1966 to 2012 suggests a declining trend of 6.26% per year. According to the Breeding Bird Survey, the King Rail has shown some of the largest declines among species in the United States. However, the small number of routes and low detection of King Rails suggest that these results should be interpreted with caution (Sauer, Hines, and Fallon 2005).

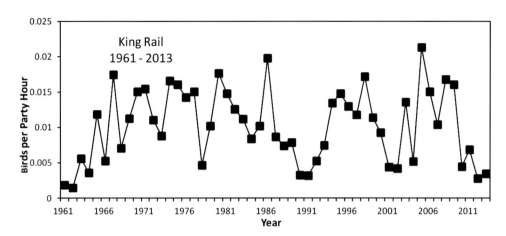

Figure 5.3. King Rail population trend in Texas, based on Christmas Bird Count data.

In contrast to the Breeding Bird Survey data, Christmas Bird Count data from 1961 to 2013 indicate a fluctuating population, but no discernible increasing or decreasing trend in Texas.

Specific Habitat Requirements

The King Rail uses shallow-water marshes (fresh to brackish), rice fields, and shrub swamps. Nesting habitat is characterized by water depths of less than 1 and up to 20 cm, and a vegetation community dominated by emergent perennials such as cattails, grasses, sedges, and rushes (Poole et al. 2005). Foraging habitat tends to be associated with water depths of up to 25 cm with tall, dense, emergent vegetation, except during the brood-rearing period when open mudflats with shallow water are typically used.

Winter habitat use

King Rails tend to use wetlands associated with river floodplains during winter. Areas of robust emergent vegetation with damp soils or shallow water are characteristic of King Rail habitat.

Habitat management

Loss of habitat is a primary concern across the range of the King Rail. Natural topography of floodplain wetlands is an important habitat attribute; thus, land-use practices that promote land leveling should be discouraged. Protection and management of shallow, seasonally flooded wetlands with perennial emergent vegetation should be promoted. Nest success is most influenced by the extent of shallow, flooded, emergent marshes. Most habitat loss and degradation are related to agricultural impacts, development, habitat fragmentation, and invasion of nonnative plant species.

Texas Hunting Regulations

The bag limit is 15 (in aggregation with Clapper Rail), and the possession limit is 45. There is currently a 40-day season, from mid- to late September and from early November to late December. There is no geographic restriction on hunting in Texas; the season is open in all 254 counties.

Research Needs and Priorities

Several key aspects of the King Rail's ecology are relatively unknown; thus, research and monitoring will be critical to informing managers of best management practices to positively impact populations. Reid, Meanley, and Fredrickson (1994) and the King Rail Conservation Plan (Cooper 2008) provided recommendations for management and research activities that would most benefit King Rails across their range.

1. Increase our understanding of habitat use during all aspects of the annual cycle.

2. Investigate how attributes of habitat patches and landscape characteristics influence King Rail abundance, in particular their nest success and brood survival.

3. Increase our understanding of the foraging ecology, nutrition, and energetics of King Rails.

4. Evaluate techniques to effectively assess current status and distribution.

5. Gain an understanding of active wetland management techniques that are best suited for providing optimal King Rail habitat.

6. Assess the relationship between harvest regulations and annual survival.

Literature Cited

Cooper, T. R. 2008. *King Rail Conservation Plan.* Version 1. Fort Snelling, MN: US Fish and Wildlife Service.

Leopold, A. S., R. J. Gutiérrez, and M. T. Bronson. 1981. *North American Game Birds and Mammals.*

New York: Charles Scribner's Sons.

Poole, A. F., L. R. Bevier, C. A. Marantz, and B. Meanley. 2005. King Rail (*Rallus elegans*). In *The Birds of North America Online*, edited by A. Poole. Ithaca, NY: Cornell Laboratory of Ornithology. http://bna.birds.cornell.edu/BNA/account/King_Rail/.

Reid, F. A., B. Meanley, and L. H. Fredrickson. 1994. King Rail. In *Migratory Shore and Upland Game Bird Management in North America*, edited by C. Tacha and C. E. Braun, 181–91. Washington, DC: International Association of Fish and Wildlife Agencies.

Sauer, J. R., J. E. Hines, and J. Fallon. 2005. *The North American Breeding Bird Survey, Results and Analysis 1966–2005.* Version 6.2.2006. Laurel, MD: USGS Patuxent Wildlife Research Center. http://www.mbr-pwrc.usgs.gov/bbs/BBS_Results_and_Analysis_2005.html.

Virginia Rail

In their southern migrations in the autumn with ranks recruited by the summer's broods, the Virginia rails are more easily seen than in the spring and their course is a more leisurely one. At this time of the year I have occasionally found them in the salt marshes of the coast.—SAUNDERS (1918)

Introduction

The Virginia Rail (*Rallus limicola*) is a secretive marshbird that is often heard but rarely seen (Conway 1995). Adults have an orange-buff throat, neck, and breast contrasting with black-and-white stripes on the rear flanks, gray cheeks, and a dark brown crown. The bill is long, decurved, and reddish, and the legs are reddish pink (Peterson 1980; Conway and Eddleman 1994; Sterry and Small 2009). Adults are small, 23–27 cm (9.1–10.6 in) in length, and weigh 55–124 g (1.9–4.4 oz). Chicks are covered in black natal down (Gillette 1897; Billard 1948). Juveniles are similar to adults, except the plumage that is orange in adults is gray or dark brown, and the bill color is dark (Conway and Eddleman 1994; Sterry and Small 2009).

Currently, North America has only one recognized subspecies (*Rallus limicola limicola*; Conway 1995). Because of poor information about seasonal distributions, the species should be managed as one continental race (Conway and Eddleman 1994). Texas is primarily wintering range for the species, providing wintering habitat in freshwater and intermediate (i.e., brackish) marshes along the Gulf of Mexico.

Distribution in Texas

Texas is not included in the Virginia Rail breeding range (Conway 1995). Although distributed broadly across Texas, it is typically found during fall, winter, and early spring (September–April) along the Texas coast and in major river drainages and their associated wetlands. This results in a somewhat scattered, clumpy distribution of wintering Virginia Rails because of the ephemeral nature of these wetlands.

Biology

Currently, the most comprehensive publication on the Virginia Rail is its species account in the *Birds of North America* series (Conway 1995), which covers its annual life cycle, habitats, and demography. Most of the information on Virginia Rail biology and life history in this chapter is summarized from Conway (1995), unless otherwise cited.

Migratory routes and timing

Virginia Rails exhibit irregular migration irruptions, which may be adaptive for a species that inhabits

Figure 6.1. Virginia Rail in marshland habitat. Photo credit: Greg Lasley.

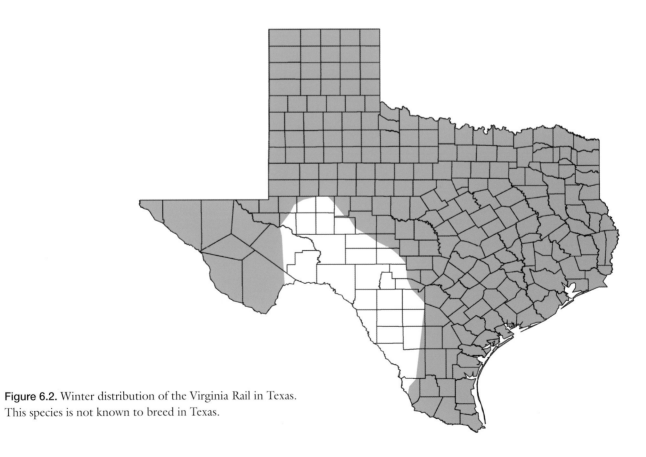

Figure 6.2. Winter distribution of the Virginia Rail in Texas.
This species is not known to breed in Texas.

ephemeral habitats. Fall departure dates vary with latitude and elevation, but departure from northern breeding areas occurs in late September to mid-October, and the birds begin to arrive on wintering grounds in September (Cooke 1914). In the central United States, birds concentrate in larger marshes prior to the fall migration (Pospichal and Marshall 1954). In Kansas, birds are present through October, but vocalizations end by late September (Baird 1974). In Colorado, fall migration peaks between mid-August and mid-September (Griese, Ryder, and Braun 1980). Birds may leave southern portions of the breeding range as late as November.

Birds usually depart wintering grounds by early April. Virginia Rails can arrive at southern breeding grounds in mid-March and northern breeding grounds from late April to mid-May (Cooke 1914; Crandall 1920; Bent 1926; Baird 1974; Glahn 1974; Tacha 1975; Griese, Ryder, and Braun 1980; Conway and Eddleman 1994). Males usually arrive on breeding grounds 7–10 days before females (Audubon 1842). Virginia Rail migration routes and important staging areas are unknown.

Timing of breeding

The timing of breeding is variable depending on geographic location; it can range from mid-March to mid-July. Kaufmann (1989) described pair formation.

Behavior

Long toes allow the birds to walk on floating marsh vegetation, and laterally compressed bodies allow them to walk through dense understory marsh vegetation. The tail is normally fanned and erect while walking, exposing black-and-white banded undertail coverts.

They rarely fly except during migration. Flight muscles are poorly developed. Flight involves rapid wing beats with short, rounded wings. They often drop to the ground abruptly and ungracefully after a short flight.

Virginia Rails can dive and swim, using their wings for propulsion underwater, most likely to avoid potential predators (Forbush 1925). After a dive, they often extend their head, or sometimes only their bill and eyes (Forbush 1925; Pospichal and Marshall 1954), slightly above the water surface, keeping their body

underwater. They forage actively at dawn and dusk and remain active throughout the day.

Breeding pairs are monogamous and territorial (Conway 1995). As pair bonds are formed, pairs engage in precopulatory chases, exchanges of calls, and vigorous defense of their territory (Audubon 1842; Nice 1962; Kaufmann 1988, 1989). Males perform the majority of territorial defense (Kaufmann 1989). Parents protect young aggressively, approaching intruders with regular rasping calls, head and neck bowed and outstretched (Allen 1934; Pospichal and Marshall 1954). Both sexes engage in nest defense and defend their young after they leave the nest; the female is usually more aggressive (Burtch 1917; Mousley 1940; Pospichal and Marshall 1954; Weins 1966; Ripley 1977).

Kaufmann (1983) identified 4 Virginia Rail displays associated with hostile interactions: (1) birds may engage in fights by jumping into the air, pecking and clawing at their opponent's breast; (2) incubating adults may leap at, peck, or strike intruders severely and utter low grunts (Burtch 1917; Walkinshaw 1937); (3) a captive male may often "attack an opponent's back, raking it with his claws, striking with the edges of his wings, and repeatedly pecking the head," forcing his subordinate underwater; (4) when fleeing, birds may jump or turn abruptly and stand motionless to avoid detection (Walkinshaw 1937).

Virginia Rail territory defense is vigorous during territory establishment and pair formation. With the onset of nesting, pairs defend the area around their nest vigorously but do not aggressively defend their territory boundaries. Distances between adjacent Virginia Rail nests range between 1.5 m (Billard 1948; Pospichal and Marshall 1954) and 46 m (Pospichal and Marshall 1954).

Sexual behavior

Virginia Rails are considered socially monogamous, but the extent of extrapair fertilizations is unknown. Mated pairs perform allopreening, precopulatory chases, courtship displays, copulations, and exchanges of calls (Audubon 1842; Kaufmann 1988). The male performs courtship displays to the female, running around the female with wings raised above his body and flitting his tail, bowing in front of her at each pass (Audubon

1842). Mated pairs perform courtship feeding (Kaufmann 1983). The actual courtship period is brief and can be identified by the short duration of "tick-it" calls in the spring (Bent 1926; Glahn 1974). Copulations have been observed 20 days or more prior to laying the first egg. The pair bond breaks down before dispersal, shortly after the young fledge (Johnson and Dinsmore 1985), but the adults may return to a nest site the following year if habitat conditions are stable (Mousley 1931; Pospichal and Marshall 1954).

Virginia Rails are typically found in pairs during the breeding season. Aggregations observed during migration may be a response to drying of suitable habitat and concurrent concentration of aquatic invertebrates, rather than social gatherings. They are known to co-occur with Sora Rails (Pospichal and Marshall 1954).

They avoid predators by performing distraction displays and submerging their body underwater. Adults perform distraction displays around nest sites by lowering their wings, tilting their body forward, and running in tight circles (Burtch 1917; Walkinshaw 1937).

Clutch size and incubation

Virginia Rail mean clutch size is 8.5 eggs (n = 115 clutches from across the North American range; minimum = 4.0 eggs; maximum = 13.0 eggs) (Walkinshaw 1937; Ripley 1977; Kaufmann 1989). Clutch size may be larger in northern areas, but data are limited (Walkinshaw 1937).

The incubation period is normally 19 days, ranging from 18 to 20 days (Walkinshaw 1937; Wood 1937; Mousley 1940; Billard 1948; Pospichal and Marshall 1954; Ripley 1977). The peak of incubation is late May through mid-June.

Nest losses

Information about Virginia Rail nest losses is very limited. Estimates of annual nesting success (when ≥ 1 chick leaves the nest successfully) average about 53% across North America using Mayfield estimates from nest card programs (Conway, Eddleman, and Anderson 1994). Many nests do not successfully hatch all eggs. No data exist on Virginia Rail brood or juvenile survival, or on the proportion of females successfully nesting each year.

Phenology

One parent broods hatchlings while the other incubates the remaining eggs (Pospichal and Marshall 1954; Kaufmann 1989). After all eggs hatch, the brooding mate brings food to the incubating mate at the nest, and they pass it to a chick, but as chicks grow older, they rush from the nest to accept food from the approaching adult (Kaufmann 1989). Females brood chicks about 67% of the time (range = 50%–90%) (Kaufmann 1989). The proportion of food brought to the nest by each sex of the brooding pair varies (Kaufmann 1989).

Both parents brood the chicks immediately after departure from the nest (Kaufmann 1987, 1989). Chicks are brooded constantly by parents for the first 4–7 days, then less during the following 2 weeks (Kaufmann 1989). Parents brood chicks as a family group within the breeding territory for 3–4 weeks (Kaufmann 1987, 1989), and then parents expand their movements beyond their territory as young become independent (Johnson and Dinsmore 1985). Brooding parents frequently preen chicks.

Virginia Rail parents have been observed carrying young nestlings in their bill (Burtch 1917; Bent 1926; Walkinshaw 1937; Kaufmann 1987, 1989). However, the frequency of this occurrence is unknown. Parents occasionally carry eggs in their bill, moving clutches to alternative nest sites (Kaufmann 1989).

Diet and foraging

Diet varies by season. During the breeding season it consists of small aquatic invertebrates, mainly beetles, snails, spiders, true bugs, and dipteran larvae. The winter diet consists of invertebrates, aquatic plants, and seeds of emergent plants.

Summer diet includes slugs, snails, small fish, insect larvae, aquatic invertebrates, caterpillars, beetles, flies, earthworms, amphipods (*Gammarus* spp.), crayfish, frogs, and small snakes (Audubon 1842; Cahn 1915; Forbush 1925; Richter 1948; Pospichal and Marshall 1954). They also eat a variety of aquatic plants and seeds of emergent plants (Fassett 1940; Pospichal and Marshall 1954; Irish 1974). Seeds of marsh plants, including wild rice (*Ziziana* spp.), sedge (*Carex* spp.), buttonbush (*Cephalanthus* spp.), *Cyperus*, cow lily (*Nuphar* spp.), smartweed (*Polygonum* spp.), and cordgrass (*Spartina* spp.) are consumed more commonly in the fall than in other seasons (Martin, Zim, and Nelson 1951).

Virginia Rails forage mainly in shallow water or on mudflats. They prefer unstable, moist, silty substrates. They occasionally forage in adjacent upland habitats (Walkinshaw 1937; Pospichal and Marshall 1954; Horak 1970). Virginia Rails feed standing up, probing mud and shallow water with their long bill. They feed primarily at dawn and dusk (Gillette 1897). They also probe under mats of vegetation and floating vegetation (Kaufmann 1989). They will climb vegetation in pursuit of food.

Demography and vital rates

Chick mortality is thought to be high prior to fledging. Brood sizes are relatively small compared to estimates of clutch size (Hunt 1908; Allen 1934; Lowther 1961; Weins 1966; Irish 1974), assuming all brood members were counted. The estimated daily survival rate of 36 radio-marked Virginia Rails in Arizona was 0.998 ± 0.001 (SE), with an annual survival rate of 0.526 ± 0.195 (SE) in Arizona pooled over all age and sex classes (Conway, Eddleman, and Anderson

1994). Although seasonal survival rates did not differ, mortality was highest in winter (Conway, Eddleman, and Anderson 1994). The annual survival rate of 88 banded Virginia Rails in Arizona was 0.532 ± 0.128 pooled over age and sex classes (Conway, Eddleman, and Anderson 1994).

Age at first reproduction

Both sexes can breed in their first year (Pospichal and Marshall 1954).

Age and sex ratios

Age and sex ratios are unknown.

Population Status and Trends

According to the Texas Parks and Wildlife Department (2010), the US Fish and Wildlife Service estimate of annual harvest of all rails combined in Texas is approximately 500 birds.

Breeding Bird Survey results for Virginia Rail population trends in the United States, based on data from 301 routes from 1966 to 2013, indicate that populations are increasing at a rate of 0.81% per year (Sauer et al. 2014). However, the 95% confidence interval of the estimate overlaps 0.0; therefore, there

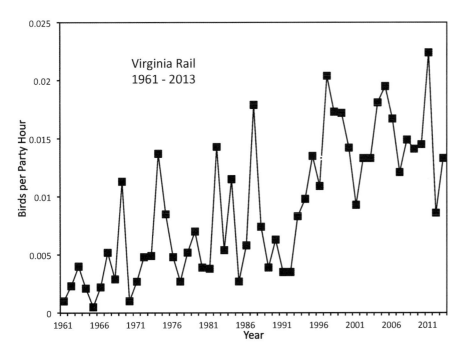

Figure 6.3. Trend in Virginia Rail wintering population in Texas, based on Christmas Bird Count data. Note that while numbers are highly variable from year to year, wintering populations of this species in Texas appear to be increasing.

Figure 6.4. *(Top)*, Virginia Rail habitat in coastal marsh; *(bottom)*, Virginia Rail habitat in rice field. Photo credit: Gulf Coast Joint Venture.

is no evidence of an increase in the breeding population of Virginia Rails in the United States (Sauer et al. 2014).

Data from the Christmas Bird Count from 1961 to 2013 indicate that the winter population of Virginia Rails in Texas is highly variable from year to year but shows an increasing trend for that period.

Specific Habitat Requirements

Winter habitat use

Virginia Rails prefer drier areas of marsh than Sora Rails (Conway 1995). Winter Virginia Rail habitat consists of robust emergent vegetation within freshwater and brackish marshes and wetlands, though they are occasionally found in coastal salt marshes (Horak 1964; Post and Enders 1970; Johnson and Dinsmore 1985; Sayre and Rundle 1984; Eddleman et al. 1988). They will also use Gulf Coast rice fields that have adequate cover (Eadie et al. 2008).

Important features of Virgina Rail habitat include shallow water, emergent cover, and substrates with abundant invertebrates (Berger 1951; Andrews 1973; Baird 1974; Glahn 1974; Tacha 1975; Griese, Ryder, and Braun 1980; Rundle and Fredrickson 1981; Sayre and Rundle 1984; Fredrickson and Reid 1986). They need standing water, moist soil, or mudflats for foraging and avoid dry emergent vegetation (Fredrickson and Reid 1986; Manci and Rusch 1988; Gibbs et al. 1991). They sometimes use deep-water habitats but prefer depths of 15 cm or less with muddy, unstable substrates for foraging (Billard 1948; Pospichal and Marshall 1954; Irish 1974; Tacha 1975; Griese, Ryder, and Braun 1980; Rundle and Fredrickson 1981; Sayre and Rundle 1984; Johnson and Dinsmore 1985). They can also occupy deeper-water habitats where there is collapsed or floating vegetation on which they can walk and forage (Sayre and Rundle 1984; Johnson and Dinsmore 1985).

Virginia Rails avoid wetlands that lack adequate shallow-water pools or mudflats (Conway 1995). They are most common in wetlands with 40%–70% upright emergent vegetation interspersed with open water, mudflats, and/or matted vegetation (Krapu and Green 1978; Fredrickson and Reid 1986).

Habitat management

Few management activities have been implemented specifically for Virginia Rails, but they may respond positively to some waterfowl management programs (Rundle and Fredrickson 1981). Activities that increase wetland cover of emergent perennial vegetation, while retaining 30%–60% of the wetland in open water or mudflat, will provide foraging habitat for Virginia Rails.

Fall flooding stimulates growth and productivity of many invertebrate species. However, if flooding is too deep, it reduces the habitat quality for Virginia Rails (Fredrickson and Reid 1986; Eddleman et al. 1988). Fall or winter drawdowns that are maintained through August can provide good habitat for migrating rails (Johnson 1984).

Virginia Rail management should encourage a diversity of emergent vegetation and seed-producing annuals that are well interspersed with aquatic bed vegetation (Cowardin et al. 1979) and open water. Management activities that eliminate elevation diversity in wetlands (e.g., land leveling) and reduce vegetation-to-water interfaces should be avoided (Sayre and Rundle 1984; Eddleman et al. 1988).

Hunting and Conservation

Sora and Virginia Rails are combined for Texas regulatory purposes. The total number of days and the daily bag limit in the Texas rail season are constant; however, the annual dates for legal rail hunting in Texas vary slightly (table 6.1). The estimated numbers of Texas rail hunters (all rail species combined) as well as harvest numbers vary annually, and large 95% confidence intervals can be attributed to small sample sizes for rails in the Texas Parks and Wildlife annual Small Game Harvest Survey (table 6.2).

Table 6.1. Texas Sora and Virginia Rail (combined) hunting season dates, total number of days, and daily bag limit, 1990 to 2014 (S. Oldenburger, Small Game Program, Texas Parks and Wildlife, personal communication).

Year	Season dates	No. of days	Daily bag limit
1990	1 Sep–9 Nov	70	25
1991	1 Sep–9 Nov	70	25
1992	1 Sep–9 Nov	70	25
1993	1 Sep–9 Nov	70	25
1994	1 Sep–9 Nov	70	25
1995	16 Sep–24 Sep; 18 Nov–17 Jan	70	25
1996	14 Sep–22 Sep; 9 Nov–8 Jan	70	25
1997	13 Sep–21 Sep; 8 Nov–7 Jan	70	25
1998	12 Sep–27 Sep; 24 Oct–16 Dec	70	25
1999	11 Sep–26 Sep; 23 Oct–15 Dec	70	25
2000	15 Sep–30 Sep; 28 Oct–20 Dec	70	25
2001	15 Sep–30 Sep; 27 Oct–19 Dec	70	25
2002	14 Sep–29 Sep; 26 Oct–18 Dec	70	25
2003	20 Sep–28 Sep; 25 Oct–24 Dec	70	25
2004	11 Sep–26 Sep; 30 Oct–22 Dec	70	25
2005	10 Sep–25 Sep; 29 Oct–21 Dec	70	25
2006	16 Sep–24 Sep; 4 Nov–3 Jan	70	25
2007	15 Sep–30 Sep; 3 Nov–26 Dec	70	25
2008	13 Sep–28 Sep; 1 Nov–24 Dec	70	25
2009	12 Sep–27 Sep; 31 Oct–23 Dec	70	25
2010	11 Sep–26 Sep; 30 Oct–22 Dec	70	25
2011	10 Sep–25 Sep; 5 Nov–28 Dec	70	25
2012	15 Sep–30 Sep; 3 Nov–26 Dec	70	25
2013	14 Sep–29 Sep; 2 Nov–25 Dec	70	25
2014	13 Sep–28 Sep; 1 Nov–24 Dec	70	25

Table 6.2. Estimated number of Texas rail hunters (all legal rail species combined) and total rail harvest in Texas, 1994–2013 (Texas Parks and Wildlife Department, Small Game Harvest Survey).

Year	Hunters (95% CI)	Harvest (95% CI)
1994–95	892 (76–1,708)	3,261 (40–10,652)
1995–96	614 (61–1,168)	1,069 (4–2,348)
1996–97	146 (2–544)	0
1997–98	731 (204–1,259)	1,027 (97–1,958)
1998–99	506 (7–1,104)	1,733 (29–6,537)
1999–00	628 (6–1,325)	1,562 (22–5,119)
2000–01	731 (7–1,624)	1,286 (9–2,834)
2001–02	545 (4–1,285)	1,288 (17–6,589)
2002–03	404 (2–905)	312 (4–1,730)
2003–04	141 (2–622)	0
2004–05	377 (2–877)	1,220 (13–5,474)
2005–06	49 (1–278)	98 (2–557)
2006–07	210 (1–444)	0
2007–08	238 (3–933)	79 (1–481)
2008–09	33 (1–187)	267 (8–1,493)
2009–10	241 (2–503)	1,073 (25–5,699)
2010–11	83 (2–348)	166 (4–916)
2011–12	47 (1–271)	512 (11–2,979)
2012–13	49 (1–289)	146 (3–868)
2013–14	760 (148–1,373)	453 (4–1,124)

Research Needs and Priorities

Most research has been conducted in the Virginia Rail breeding range. Priority research needs related to the wintering range include the following:

1. Implement a national monitoring program.

   A monitoring program conducted on a national scale is critical to inform harvest management of Virginia Rails. Virginia Rails are difficult to monitor because of their secretive habits, cryptic coloration, infrequent vocalizations, and use of difficult-to-access dense wetland habitats. Annual harvest management decisions are made with considerable uncertainty because of limited abundance information and/or relative population trends. Uncertainty also exists concerning population response to habitat management because of the lack of basic trend information (Case and McCool 2009).

2. Continue to improve the Harvest Information Program (HIP) sampling frame.

   Screening questions asked during the HIP certification process are used to identify hunters by type (e.g., duck, goose, woodcock) in order to increase the efficiency of the sampling procedure. This allows the sampling effort to be concentrated on the hunters who hunt specific species. However, estimates of hunter numbers suggest that screening data are not accurately identifying rail hunters (Case and McCool 2009). Better sampling will decrease the variance associated with estimates of rail hunters and harvest.

3. Improve the rail and snipe Parts Collection Survey (PCS).

   The PCS for rails enables the estimation of the species composition of the rail harvest. Rail wings received from hunters are identified to species. Species-specific harvest estimates for rails are then derived by adjusting HIP harvest estimates by the five-year running average of species composition from the wings collected. Age ratios provide an index to recruitment from the breeding season prior to the hunting season. Wings collected as part of the PCS could be used for additional purposes to better inform management for rails (Case and McCool 2009).

4. Estimate vital rates to support population modeling.

   By predicting future population size or trends under alternative harvest management, habitat management, or climate change scenarios, population models support science-based adaptive management decisions. Very few studies have estimated vital rates for rails, and there are significant knowledge gaps. For rails, small-scale, regionally replicated studies offer the best opportunity to provide initial estimates of vital rates. In particular, limited water availability on the landscape, a result of climate and of management decisions, likely has a strong negative influence on vital rates, as appropriate water levels are thought to reduce predation and ensure high-quality forage during some life stages (Case and McCool 2009).

Literature Cited

Allen, A. A. 1934. The Virginia Rail and the Sora. *Bird Lore* 36:196–204.

Andrews, D. A. 1973. Habitat utilization by Soras, Virginia Rails, and King Rails near southwestern Lake Erie. Master's thesis, Ohio State University.

Audubon, J. J. 1842. *The Birds of America*. Vol. 5. New York: J. J. Audubon.

Baird, K. E. 1974. Field study of the King, Sora, and Virginia Rails at Cheyenne Bottoms in west-central Kansas. Master's thesis, Fort Hays Kansas State College.

Bent, A. C. 1926. *Life Histories of North American Marsh Birds*. US National Museum Bulletin 135. Washington, DC: Smithsonian Institution.

Berger, A. J. 1951. Nesting density of Virginia and Sora Rails in Michigan. *Condor* 53:202.

Billard, R. S. 1948. An ecological study of the Virginia Rail and the Sora in Connecticut Swamps, 1947. Master's thesis, Iowa State University.

Burtch, V. 1917. The summer life of the Virginia Rail. *Bird Lore* 19:243–48.

Cahn, A. R. 1915. Notes on a captive Virginia Rail. *Auk* 32:91–95.

Case, D. J., and D. D. McCool. 2009. *Priority Information Needs for Rails and Snipe: A Funding Strategy*. Mishawaka, IN: D. J. Case and Associates.

Conway, C. J. 1995. Virginia Rail (*Rallus limicola*). In *The Birds of North America Online*, edited by A. Poole. Ithaca, NY: Cornell Laboratory of Ornithology. http://bna.birds.cornell.edu/bna/species/173.

Conway, C. J., and W. R. Eddleman. 1994. Virginia Rail. In *Migratory Shore and Upland Game Bird Management in North America*, edited by T. C. Tacha and C. E. Braun, 193–206. Washington, DC: International Association of Fish and Wildlife Agencies.

Conway, C. J., E. W. Eddleman, and S. H. Anderson. 1994. Nesting success and survival of Virginia Rails and Soras. *Wilson Bulletin* 106:466–73.

Cooke, W. W. 1914. *Distribution and Migration of North American Rails and Their Allies.* Bulletin 128. Washington, DC: US Department of Agriculture.

Cowardin, L. M., V. Carter, F. C. Golet, and E. T. LaRoe. 1979. *Classification of Wetlands and Deepwater Habitats of the United States.* FWS/OBS-79/31. Washington, DC: US Fish and Wildife Service, Office of Biological Service.

Crandall, L. S. 1920. Early Virginia Rail in New York. *Auk* 37:452.

Eadie, J. M., C. S. Elphick, K. J. Reinecke, and M. R. Miller. 2008. Wildlife values of North American ricelands. In *Conservation of Ricelands in North America*, edited by S. W. Manley, 7–90. Stuttgart, AR: Rice Foundation.

Eddleman, W. R., F. L. Knopf, B. Meanley, F. A. Reid, and R. Zernbal. 1988. Conservation of North American rallids. *Wilson Bulletin* 100:458–75.

Fasset, N. C. 1940. *A Manual of Aquatic Plants.* New York: McGraw-Hill.

Forbush, E. H. 1925. *Birds of Massachusetts and Other New England States. Part 1: Water Birds, Marsh Birds and Shore Birds.* Boston: Massachusetts Department of Agriculture.

Fredrickson, L. H., and F. A. Reid. 1986. Wetland and riparian habitats: A nongame management overview. In *Management of Nongame Wildlife in the Midwest: A Developing Art*, edited by J. B. Hale, L. B. Best, and R. L. Clawson, 59–96. Chelsea, MI: North Central Section of the Wildlife Society.

Gibbs, J. P., J. R. Longcore, D. G. McAuley, and J. K. Ringleman. 1991. *Use of Wetland Habitats by Selected Nongame Water Birds in Maine.* Fish and Wildlife Research Report 9. Washington, DC: US Fish and Wildlife Service.

Gillette, D. C. 1897. Notes on the Virginia and Sora Rails. *Oologist* 14:21–23.

Glahn, J. F. 1974. Study of breeding rails with recorded calls in north-central Colorado. *Wilson Bulletin* 86:206–14.

Griese, H. J., R. A. Ryder, and C. E. Braun. 1980. Spatial and temporal distribution of rails in Colorado. *Wilson Bulletin* 92:96–102.

Horak, G. J. 1964. A comparative study of Virginia and Sora Rails with emphasis on foods. Master's thesis, Iowa State University.

———. 1970. A comparative study of the foods of the Sora and Virginia Rail. *Wilson Bulletin* 82:207–13.

Hunt, C. J. 1908. *Rallus virginianus* a Delaware Valley breeder. *Auk* 25:81.

Irish, J. 1974. Postbreeding territorial behavior of Soras and Virginia Rails in several Michigan marshes. *Jack-Pine Warbler* 52:115–24.

Johnson, R. R. 1984. Breeding habitat use and post-breeding movements by Soras and Virginia Rails. Master's thesis, Iowa State University.

Johnson, R. R., and J. J. Dinsmore. 1985. Brood-rearing and postbreeding habitat use by Virginia Rails and Soras. *Wildlife Society Bulletin* 97:551–54.

Kaufmann, G. W. 1983. Displays and vocalizations of the Sora and the Virginia Rail. *Wilson Bulletin* 95:42–59.

———. 1987. Growth and development of Sora and Virginia Rail chicks. *Wilson Bulletin* 99:432–40.

———. 1988. Social preening in Soras and Virginia Rails. *Loon* 60:59–63.

———. 1989. Breeding ecology of the Sora, *Porzana carolina*, and the Virginia Rail, *Rallus limicola*. *Canadian Field-Naturalist* 103:270–82.

Krapu, G. L., and G. L. Green. 1978. Breeding bird populations of selected semipermanent wetlands in south-central North Dakota. *American Birds* 32:110–12.

Lowther, J. K. 1961. Virginia Rail (*Rallus limicola limicola* Vieillot) breeding at Vermillion, Alberta. *Auk* 78:271.

Manci, K. M., and D. H. Rusch. 1988. Indices to distribution and abundance of some inconspicuous waterbirds on Horicon Marsh. *Journal of Field Ornithology* 59:67–75.

Martin, A. C., H. S. Zim, and A. L. Nelson. 1951. *American Wildlife and Plants.* New York: McGraw-Hill.

Mousley, H. 1931. Notes on the home life of the Virginia Rail. *Canadian Field-Naturalist* 45:65–66.

———. 1940. Further notes on the nesting habits of the Virginia Rail. *Wilson Bulletin* 52:87–90.

Nice, M. M. 1962. Development of behavior of precocial birds. *Transactions of the Linnean Society* 8:1–211.

Peterson, R. T. 1980. *A Field Guide to the Birds.* Boston: Houghton-Mifflin.

Pospichal, L. B., and W. H. Marshall. 1954. A field study of Sora Rail and Virginia Rail in central Minnesota. *Flicker* 2:2–32.

Post, W., and F. Enders. 1970. Notes on a saltmarsh Virginia Rail population. *Kingbird* 20:61–67.

Richter, C. 1948. Virginia Rail catches frog. *Passenger Pigeon* 10:32.

Ripley, S. D. 1977. *Rails of the World: A Monograph of the Family Rallidae.* Toronto: M. F. Freheley.

Rundle, W. D., and L. H. Fredrickson. 1981. Managing seasonally flooded impoundments for migrant rails and shorebirds. *Wildlife Society Bulletin* 9:80–87.

Sauer, J. R., J. E. Hines, J. E. Fallon, K. L. Pardieck, D. J. Ziolkowski Jr., and W. A. Link. 2014. *The North*

American Breeding Bird Survey, Results and Analysis 1966–2013. Version 01.30.2015. Laurel, MD: USGS Patuxent Wildlife Research Center.

Saunders, W. E. 1918. An episode with the Virginia Rail. *Ottawa Naturalist* 32:1–77.

Sayre, M. W., and W. D. Rundle. 1984. Comparison of habitat use by migrant Soras and Virginia Rails. *Journal of Wildlife Management* 48:599–605.

Sterry, P., and B. E. Small. 2009. *Birds of Eastern North America: A Photographic Guide.* Princeton, NJ: Princeton University Press.

Tacha, R. W. 1975. A survey of rail populations in Kansas, with emphasis on Cheyenne Bottoms. Master's thesis, Fort Hays Kansas State College.

Texas Parks and Wildlife Department. 2010. *Webless Migratory Gamebird Strategic Plan: 2011–2015.* Austin: Texas Parks and Wildlife Department.

Walkinshaw, L. H. 1937. The Virginia Rail in Michigan. *Auk* 54:464–75.

Weins, J. A. 1966. Notes on the distraction display of the Virginia Rail. *Wilson Bulletin* 78:229–31.

Wood, H. B. 1937. Incubation period of Virginia Rail. *Auk* 102:179–80.

7

Sora Rail

The flight of the sora is slow and labored but some individuals travel more miles between the summer and winter homes than almost any other rails in the Western Hemisphere.—COOKE (1914)

Introduction

The Sora Rail (*Porzana carolina*) may be more popular with nonconsumptive users than with hunters (Odom 1977). Many of the wetlands most important to Sora Rails rank among the most threatened in the United States, including coastal marshes in California, Florida, Louisiana, New Jersey, and Texas (Melvin and Gibbs 2012).

The adult male has a blue-gray face, neck, and breast, with a black wedge between the eye and the bill that continues as a line down the center of the chest (Sterry and Small 2009). The belly is pale, with flanks that are barred brown, black, and white. The undertail is a cream white. Upper parts are brown, with white streaks. The bill is yellow and legs are yellowish green (Sterry and Small 2009). Nonbreeding plumage is similar, with duller bill and leg colors, and less black on the face. Adult females are similar to nonbreeding males (Sterry and Small 2009). Adults are small, 20.3–22.9 cm (8.0–9.0 in) in length (Sterry and Small 2009), and weigh 60–110 g (2.1–3.9 oz) (Ridgway and Friedmann 1941). On average males are larger and heavier than females (Melvin and Gibbs 2012). Juveniles are similar to adult females but parts of the plumage that are blue gray in adults are buff,

and the bill is darker (Sterry and Small 2009). There are no subspecies for the Sora Rail (Ripley 1977).

Distribution in Texas

Texas is not included in the Sora Rail's breeding range (Melvin and Gibbs 2012). Although widely distributed across a broad area of Texas, during fall and winter the Sora Rail is found largely on the Coastal Prairies (Lockwood and Freeman 2004). The Sora Rail is rare to uncommon in inland Texas during the winter (Lockwood and Freeman 2004).

Biology

Most Sora Rail breeding biology, ecology, and behavior studies have occurred in the midwestern United States (Walkinshaw 1940; Pospichal and Marshall 1954; Tanner and Hendrickson 1956; Kaufmann 1983, 1987, 1989). The most comprehensive volume on the Sora Rail is its species account in the *Birds of North America* series (Melvin and Gibbs 2012), which covers its annual life cycle, habitats, and demography. Unless citations indicate otherwise, much of the biology and life history summarized here is based on Melvin and Gibbs (2012).

Figure 7.1. Sora Rail. Photo credit: Larry Ditto.

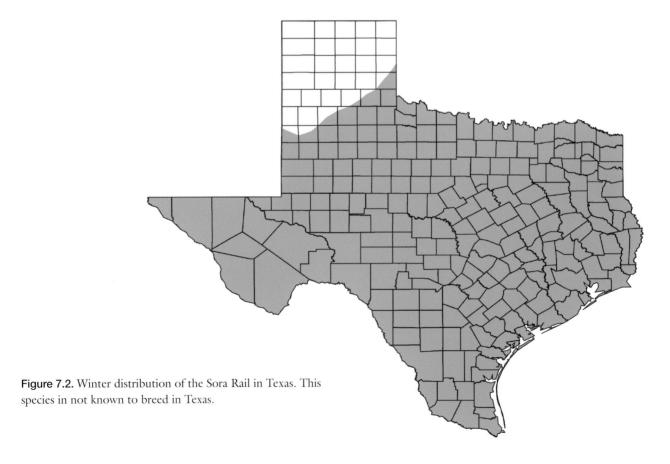

Figure 7.2. Winter distribution of the Sora Rail in Texas. This species in not known to breed in Texas.

Migratory routes and timing

Sora Rails are reclusive and hard to observe, and migrant Soras are difficult to detect. Timing of fall migration may be determined in part by timing of frosts (Bent 1926; Walkinshaw 1940; Tanner and Hendrickson 1956). In some areas, shifts may occur from smaller breeding wetlands and the birds may congregate in larger wetlands with abundant food in August and early September (Pospichal and Marshall 1954).

Peak arrival on breeding grounds is from the third week in April to the second week in May in Arkansas (Meanley 1960; James and Neal 1986), Missouri (Robbins and Easterla 1992), Michigan (Walkinshaw 1940), Iowa (Tanner and Hendrickson 1956), Wisconsin (Robbins 1991), Minnesota (Pospichal and Marshall 1954), Ohio (Peterjohn 1989), and Colorado (Griese, Ryder, and Braun 1980).

Peak fall migration is from September to early October in northern latitudes (Walkinshaw 1940; Tanner and Hendrickson 1956; Peterjohn 1989; Robbins 1991). In Missouri, migrants begin appearing in late August and peak in early to mid-September (Robbins and Easterla 1992). In Arkansas, fall migrants are seen primarily in September and October, and the majority have moved south by early November (Meanley 1960; James and Neal 1986).

Timing of breeding

The timing of breeding is variable depending on geographic location; it can range from early May to the end of August. Kaufmann (1989) described pair formation.

Behavior

Sora Rails move mostly by walking or running through and over wetland vegetation and debris. They are reluctant to fly and difficult to flush (Walkinshaw 1940). They appear to be strong fliers during migration, more so than when flushed from wetlands (Bent 1926).

Soras can swim and dive (Ripley 1977). At times, they will submerge with only their bill and eyes above the water (Pospichal and Marshall 1954).

Soras often preen themselves and their chicks; breeding adults preen their mates, apparently as part of courtship and pair-bond maintenance (Kaufmann 1983, 1987, 1989). Preening between pair members lasts 1–5 minutes and appears more ritualized than in Virginia Rails (Kaufmann 1983). Chicks more than 1 day old can preen themselves, and siblings frequently preen each other in the nest. Chicks of this age also perform other behaviors including yawning, stretching their wings and legs, shaking their bill and body, and scratching their bill. Sora chicks bathe at 1 week of age, and oiling of feathers can occur at 18 days or older (Kaufmann 1987).

Sora Rails vigorously defend territories against conspecifics. Threat displays include assuming an extended upright posture, stretching the head toward the opponent, pecking the substrate, and swanning (Kaufmann 1983). Swanning displays are given by opposing males at territorial boundaries and usually involve variations of bending down and forward while lifting wing feathers and spreading undertail coverts. The black facial mask and bright yellow bill appear to augment frontal threat displays. The facial coloration is intense during the breeding season (Kaufmann 1983).

Chasing appears to be the most important method of establishing and maintaining territories (Kaufmann 1989). Sparring consists of jumping up and down while facing each other, but not actually fighting. Fighting includes jumping up and simultaneously pecking and clawing the opponent, or clawing the opponent while lying backward supported on wings. Sora fighting is most frequent between males but does occur between females (Kaufmann 1983). Chasing by males is a primary means of interspecific territory defense (mostly against Virginia Rails), while combinations of swanning displays and chasing are a primary means of intraspecific defense. Territory defense appears to play a greater role in the breeding biology of Soras compared to that of Virginia Rails (Kaufmann 1983).

Depending on the location, the minimum distance between Sora nests ranges from 12 m (39.4 ft; Glahn 1974) to 25 m (82.0 ft; Berger 1951). The minimum distance between Sora and Virginia Rail nests ranges from 4.3 m (14.1 ft; Berger 1951) to 25 m (82.0 ft; Glahn 1974), depending on location. Active nests of Sora and King Rails (*Rallus elegans*) were 31.1 m (102.0 ft) or more apart in Iowa (Tanner and Hendrickson 1956). It is unknown whether Soras maintain winter territories.

Sora Rails are thought to be monogamous. There is no evidence of polygamy or a significant nonbreeding component of the population. In the early stages of pair formation, male and female Soras stand immobile within sight of each other for up to 30 minutes (Kaufmann 1983). Pairs bathe, feed, and preen near each other, and mated pairs preen each other while bowing and facing toward or away from their mate (Kaufmann 1983).

Sora pairs usually preen before copulation (Kaufmann 1983). The male will approach the female in a precopulatory chase with his head held rigid and elevated, while softly cooing. Receptivity of the female increases as egg laying nears. The male mounts the female from behind and lowers her head to the substrate or water (Kaufmann 1983). Copulation lasts only a few seconds, and then the male dismounts or the female runs out from underneath the male. During copulation, the male flaps his wings to maintain balance. Postcopulatory displays include the male bowing his head and elevating his wing and tail feathers, and the female giving a "body shake" (Kaufmann 1983). Pair bond duration is unknown. The degree of sociality with conspecifics after the breeding season is also unknown. Soras vigorously defend their territory against Virginia Rails during the breeding season (Kaufmann 1983, 1989).

Clutch size and incubation

Sora Rail mean clutch size ranges from 9.4 to 11.7 eggs per clutch (minimum = 5.0 eggs, maximum = 16 eggs) (Walkinshaw 1940; Billard 1948; Pospichal and Marshall 1954; Tanner and Hendrickson 1956; Kaufmann 1989).

The incubation period ranges from 16 to 22 days depending on location (Walkinshaw 1940; Pospichal and Marshall 1954; Tanner and Hendrickson 1956). The peak of incubation is mid-May through mid-July.

Nest losses

Predation is thought to be the primary cause of egg loss (Pospichal and Marshall 1954). Top egg predators include the Marsh Wren (*Cistothorus palustris*); Common Grackle (*Quiscalus quiscula*); American Crow (*Corvus brachyrhynchos*); striped skunk (*Mephitis mephitis*); coyote (*Canis latrans*); and raccoon (*Procyon lotor*)

(Allen 1934; Lowther 1977; Tanner and Hendrickson 1956). Pospichal and Marshall (1954) reported 2 clutches crushed by muskrats (*Ondatra zibethicus*) that used nests as feeding platforms. Lowther (1977) reported 2 nests trampled by cattle after water was no longer present under the nests.

Phenology

Sora hatchlings may be brooded by 1 parent near the nest, even in shallow (≤ 15 cm; ≤ 5.9 in) water, while the other parent incubates the remaining eggs (Allen 1934; Walkinshaw 1940). Chicks are brooded by 1 parent for 4–7 days after hatching. Diurnal brooding decreases over the next 2 weeks, but nocturnal brooding continues longer. Chicks are brooded until about 1 month old, and diurnal brooding decreases over the next 2 weeks. Parents often build a brood nest on which young chicks are brooded and where chicks are frequently preened and oiled by adults (Kaufmann 1987, 1989). Food items brought by adults are presumably important in influencing chicks' ability to recognize food.

Diet and foraging

Soras feed on both plant and animal material in freshwater marshes. Seeds are the predominant food, especially in late summer, fall, and winter (Martin, Zim, and Nelson 1951; Meanley 1960, 1965; Webster 1964; Horak 1970; Rundle and Sayre 1983). The percentage of invertebrates in the diet increases in spring (Martin, Zim, and Nelson 1951; Rundle and Sayre 1983). Common plant foods include seeds of wild or cultivated rice, smartweeds, sedges, bulrushes, and grasses (Martin, Zim, and Nelson 1951; Pospichal and Marshall 1954; Horak 1970; Rundle and Sayre 1983), and some vegetative plant material, including leaves or stems (Pospichal and Marshall 1954). Principal animal foods include adults, larvae, and pupae of a variety of aquatic invertebrates including beetles, flies, bugs, dragonflies, and snails (Pospichal and Marshall 1954; Horak 1970; Gochfeld 1972). Soras consume more plant material, primarily seeds, and less animal material than Virginia Rails (Martin, Zim, and Nelson 1951; Horak 1970).

Sora Rails search for food by raking floating vegetation with their feet or pulling aside vegetation with

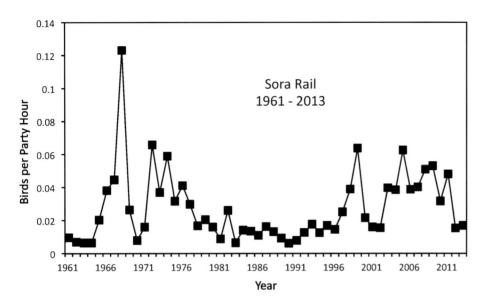

Figure 7.3. Trend in Sora Rail wintering population in Texas, based on Christmas Bird Count data. Note that while numbers are highly variable from year to year, wintering populations of this species in Texas appear to be increasing.

their bill and visually searching for food (Kaufmann 1989). They feed while standing and will stand on plant stems or debris. In autumn, they will strip seed heads of maturing smartweeds and annual grasses (Meanley 1965; Rundle and Sayre 1983).

Demography and vital rates

There is no information on Sora Rail life span or annual survival (Melvin and Gibbs 2012). The non-breeding (August–April) Sora survival rate in southwest Arizona was estimated to be 0.31 ± 0.26 SE pooled over age and sex classes (Conway, Eddleman, and Anderson 1994). Survival may have been lowered by effects of radio transmitters or underestimated because of emigration.

Age at first reproduction

Age at first reproduction is unknown.

Age and sex ratios

Sora Rail age ratios are unknown. Pospichal and Marshall (1954) reported male-to-female ratios of 1.9:1.0 and 1.8:1.0 in Minnesota.

Population Status and Trends

According to the Texas Parks and Wildlife Department (2010), the US Fish and Wildlife Service estimate of the annual harvest of all rails combined in Texas is about 500 birds.

Breeding Bird Survey results for Sora Rail population trends in the United States, based on data from 553 routes from 1966 to 2013, indicate that populations are increasing at a rate of 1.60% per year (Sauer et al. 2014). However, the 95% confidence interval of the estimate overlaps 0.0; therefore, there is no evidence of an increase in the breeding population of Sora Rails in the United States (Sauer et al. 2014).

Christmas Bird Count data from 1961 to 2013 indicate that the winter population of Sora Rails in Texas is highly variable from year to year but shows a statistically stable trend for that period.

Specific Habitat Requirements

Winter habitat use

Very little is known about Sora Rail winter habitat use, other than that they use freshwater, brackish, and salt marshes (Eddleman et al. 1988; Small 1994). During winter, they are probably most abundant in marshes with good interspersion of shallow water and emergent vegetation (Gochfeld 1972; Conway 1990), but Soras also use vegetated canals and ditches, rice fields, impoundments, mangroves, wet pastures, overgrown and cultivated fields, and emergent vegetation along edges of small ponds and rivers (Gochfeld 1972; Raffaele 1989; Stiles and Skutch 1989; Rosenberg et al. 1991; Howell and Webb 1995).

Soras wintering in emergent wetlands along the Colorado River in southwest Arizona occur primarily

Figure 7.4. *(Top)*, Sora Rail habitat in coastal marsh; *(bottom)*, Sora Rail habitat in rice field. Photo credit: Gulf Coast Joint Venture.

in shallow-water cattail and bulrush habitats and occasionally in mixed shrubs near wetland-upland edges (Conway 1990). Sora and Virginia Rails use similar habitat types, although Soras seem to select areas with shallower water in winter and deeper water in spring (Melvin and Gibbs 2012).

Habitat management

The top priority is the preservation of emergent wetlands that provide breeding, migration, and wintering habitat for Soras (Melvin and Gibbs 2012). Soras will benefit from policies and management that eliminate or minimize the effects of wetland draining and filling. Other threats to emergent wetland Sora habitat include siltation, eutrophication, contaminants, and invasive exotic plants (Melvin and Gibbs 2012).

Habitat management to benefit Soras should encourage diverse stands of both fine-leaved and robust emergent vegetation, including sedges, bulrushes, and cattails, as well as moist-soil annuals around wetland edges (Rundle and Sayre 1983; Johnson and Dinsmore 1986). Management activities should maximize interspersion of emergent vegetation and open-water areas (Weller and Spatcher 1965), because Soras seem most abundant near the edges of vegetation and open water (Walkinshaw 1940; Pospichal and Marshall 1954; Johnson and Dinsmore 1986; Crowley 1994). Wetland impoundments constructed with irregular or sloping bottoms provide a greater diversity of water levels and topography that will increase vegetation-water edges (Eddleman et al. 1988). Impoundments drawn down during early summer can be followed by late summer–fall reflooding to provide habitat for postbreeding and migrant Soras (Rundle and Fredrickson 1981). Soras may respond positively to some waterfowl management programs (Rundle and Fredrickson 1981).

Hunting and Conservation

Sora and Virginia Rails are combined for Texas regulatory purposes. The total number of days and the daily bag limit in the Texas rail season are constant; however, the annual dates for legal rail hunting in Texas vary slightly (table 6.1). The estimated numbers of Texas rail hunters (all rail species combined) as well as harvest numbers vary annually, and large 95% confidence intervals can be attributed to small sample sizes for rails in the Texas Parks and Wildlife annual Small Game Harvest Survey (table 6.2)

Research Needs and Priorities

Most research has been conducted in the Sora Rail breeding range. Research priorities for Soras are summarized by Melvin and Gibbs (1994, 2012).

Priority research needs related to Sora wintering range include the following:

1. Implement a national monitoring program.

   A monitoring program conducted on a national scale is critical to inform harvest management of Sora Rails. Sora Rails are difficult to monitor because of their secretive habits, cryptic coloration, infrequent vocalizations, and use of difficult-to-access dense wetland habitats. Annual harvest management decisions are made with considerable uncertainty because of limited abundance information and/or relative population trends. Uncertainty also exists concerning population response to habitat management because of the lack of basic trend information (Case and McCool 2009).

2. Continue to improve the Harvest Information Program (HIP) sampling frame.

   Screening questions asked during the HIP certification process are used to identify hunters by type (e.g., duck, goose, woodcock) in order to increase the efficiency of the sampling procedure. This allows the sampling effort to be concentrated on the hunters who hunt specific species. However, estimates of hunter numbers suggest that screening data are not accurately identifying rail hunters (Case and McCool 2009). Better sampling will decrease the variance associated with estimates of rail hunters and harvest.

3. Improve the rail and snipe Parts Collection Survey (PCS).

   The PCS for rails enables the estimation of the species composition of the rail harvest. Rail wings received from hunters are identified to species. Species-specific harvest estimates for rails are then derived by adjusting HIP harvest estimates by the five-year running average of species composition from the wings collected. Age ratios provide an index to recruitment from the breeding season prior to the hunting season. Wings collected as part of the PCS could be used for additional purposes to better inform management for rails (Case and McCool 2009).

4. Estimate vital rates to support population modeling.

By predicting future population size or trends under alternative harvest management, habitat management, or climate change scenarios, population models support science-based adaptive management decisions. Very few studies have estimated vital rates for rails, and there are significant knowledge gaps. For rails, small-scale, regionally replicated studies offer the best opportunity to provide initial estimates of vital rates. In particular, limited water availability on the landscape, a result of climate and of management decisions, likely has a strong negative influence on vital rates, as appropriate water levels are thought to reduce predation and ensure high-quality forage during some life stages (Case and McCool 2009).

Literature Cited

Allen, A. A. 1934. The Virginia Rail and the Sora. *Bird Lore* 36:196–204.

Bent, A. C. 1926. *Life Histories of North American Marsh Birds.* US National Museum Bulletin 135. Washington, DC: Smithsonian Institution.

Berger, A. J. 1951. Nesting density of Virginia and Sora Rails in Michigan. *Condor* 53:202.

Billard, R. S. 1948. An ecological study of the Virginia Rail and the Sora in Connecticut Swamps, 1947. Master's thesis, Iowa State University.

Case, D. J., and D. D. McCool. 2009. *Priority Information Needs for Rails and Snipe: A Funding Strategy.* Mishawaka, IN: D. J. Case and Associates.

Conway, C. J. 1990. Seasonal changes in movements and habitat use by three sympatric species of rails. Master's thesis, University of Wyoming.

Conway, C. J., E. W. Eddleman, and S. H. Anderson. 1994. Nesting success and survival of Virginia Rails and Soras. *Wilson Bulletin* 106:466–73.

Cooke, W. W. 1914. *Distribution and Migration of North American Rails and Their Allies.* Bulletin 128. Washington, DC: US Department of Agriculture.

Crowley, S. K. 1994. Habitat use and population monitoring of secretive waterbirds in Massachusetts. Master's thesis, University of Massachusetts.

Eddleman, W. R., F. L. Knopf, B. Meanley, F. A. Reid, and R. Zernbal. 1988. Conservation of North American rallids. *Wilson Bulletin* 100:458–75.

Glahn, J. F. 1974. Study of breeding rails with recorded calls in north-central Colorado. *Wilson Bulletin* 86:206–14.

Gochfeld, M. 1972. Observations on the status, ecology, and behavior of Soras wintering in Trinidad, West Indies. *Wilson Bulletin* 84:200–201.

Griese, H. J., R. A. Ryder, and C. E. Braun. 1980. Spatial and temporal distribution of rails in Colorado. *Wilson Bulletin* 92:96–102.

Horak, G. J. 1970. A comparative study of the foods of the Sora and Virginia Rail. *Wilson Bulletin* 82:207–13.

Howell, S. N. G., and S. Webb. 1995. *A Guide to the Birds of Mexico and Northern Central America.* New York: Oxford University Press.

James, D. A., and J. C. Neal. 1986. *Arkansas Birds: Their Distribution and Abundance.* Fayetteville: University of Arkansas Press.

Johnson, R. R., and J. J. Dinsmore. 1986. Habitat use by breeding Virginia Rails and Soras. *Journal of Wildlife Management* 50:387–92.

Kaufmann, G. W. 1983. Displays and vocalizations of the Sora and the Virginia Rail. *Wilson Bulletin* 95:42–59.

———. 1987. Growth and development of Sora and Virginia Rail chicks. *Wilson Bulletin* 99:432–40.

———. 1989. Breeding ecology of the Sora, *Porzana carolina*, and the Virginia Rail, *Rallus limicola. Canadian Field-Naturalist* 103:270–82.

Lockwood, M. W., and B. Freeman. 2004. *Handbook of Texas Birds.* College Station: Texas A&M University Press.

Lowther, J. K. 1977. Nesting biology of the Sora at Vermillion, Alberta. *Canadian Field-Naturalist* 91:63–67.

Martin, A. C., H. S. Zim, and A. L. Nelson. 1951. *American Wildlife and Plants.* New York: McGraw-Hill.

Meanley, B. 1960. Fall food of the Sora Rail in the Arkansas rice fields. *Journal of Wildlife Management* 24:339.

———. 1965. Early fall food and habitat of the Sora in Patuxent River marshes, Maryland. *Chesapeake Science* 6:235–37.

Melvin, S. M., and J. P. Gibbs. 1994. Sora Rail. In *Migratory Shore and Upland Game Bird Management in North America*, edited by T. C. Tacha and C. E. Braun, 209–17. Washington, DC: International Association of Fish and Wildlife Agencies.

———. 2012. Sora (*Porzana carolina*). In *The Birds of*

North America Online, edited by A. Poole. Ithaca, NY: Cornell Laboratory of Ornithology. http://bna.birds.cornell.edu/bna/species/250.

Odom, R. R. 1977. Sora. In *Management of Migratory Shore and Upland Game Birds in North America*, edited by G. C. Sanderson, 57–65. Washington, DC: International Association of Fish and Wildlife Agencies.

Peterjohn, B. G. 1989. *The Birds of Ohio*. Bloomington: Indiana University Press.

Pospichal, L. B., and W. H. Marshall. 1954. A field study of Sora Rail and Virginia Rail in central Minnesota. *Flicker* 2:2–32.

Raffaele, H. A. 1989. A guide to the birds of Puerto Rico and the Virgin Islands. Princeton, NJ: Princeton University Press.

Ridgway, R., and H. Friedmann. 1941. *The Birds of North and Middle America, Part 9*. US National Museum Bulletin 50. Washington, DC: Smithsonian Institution.

Ripley, S. D. 1977. *Rails of the World*. Boston: David R. Godine.

Robbins, M. B., and D. A. Easterla. 1992. *Birds of Missouri: Their Distribution and Abundance*. Columbia: University of Missouri Press.

Robbins, S. D., Jr. 1991. *Wisconsin Birdlife: Population and Distribution Past and Present*. Madison: University of Wisconsin Press.

Rosenberg, K. V., R. D. Ohmart, W. C. Hunter, and B. W. Anderson. 1991. *Birds of the Lower Colorado River Valley*. Tucson: University of Arizona Press.

Rundle, W. D., and L. H. Fredrickson. 1981. Managing seasonally flooded impoundments for migrant rails and shorebirds. *Wildlife Society Bulletin* 9:80–87.

Rundle, W. D., and M. W. Sayre. 1983. Feeding ecology of migrant Soras in southwestern Missouri. *Journal of Wildlife Management* 47:1153–59.

Sauer, J. R., J. E. Hines, J. E. Fallon, K. L. Pardieck, D. J. Ziolkowski Jr., and W. A. Link. 2014. *The North American Breeding Bird Survey, Results and Analysis 1966–2013*. Version 01.30.2015. Laurel, MD: USGS Patuxent Wildlife Research Center.

Small, A. 1994. *California Birds: Their Status and Distribution*. Vista, CA: Ibis.

Sterry, P., and B. E. Small. 2009. *Birds of Eastern North America: A Photographic Guide*. Princeton, NJ: Princeton University Press.

Stiles, F. G., and A. F. Skutch. 1989. *A Guide to the Birds of Costa Rica*. Ithaca, NY: Cornell University Press.

Tanner, W. D., and G. O. Hendrickson. 1956. Ecology of the Sora in Clay County Iowa. *Iowa Bird Life* 26:78–81.

Texas Parks and Wildlife Department. 2010. *Webless Migratory Gamebird Strategic Plan: 2011–2015*. Austin: Texas Parks and Wildlife Department.

Walkinshaw, L. H. 1940. Summer life of the Sora Rail. *Auk* 57:153–68.

Webster, C. G. 1964. Fall foods of Soras from two habitats in Connecticut. *Journal of Wildlife Management* 28:163–65.

Weller, M. W., and C. E. Spatcher. 1965. *Role of Habitat in the Distribution and Abundance of Marsh Birds*. Iowa Agricultural Home Economic Experiment Station Special Report No. 43.

American Coot

American Coots migrate at night, singly or in loose flocks.—ALISAUSKAS AND ARNOLD (1994, 128)

Introduction

The American Coot (*Fulica americana*) is one of the most abundant and widely distributed marshbirds in North America. It is quite distinctive, with slate-gray plumage, a white bill, and a red spot on top of an otherwise white frontal shield. Juveniles can be distinguished from adults into October by their gray bill as opposed to the white bill in adults. The age of breeding American Coots, up to four years of age, can also be determined by the color of their tarsus (Crawford 1978).

The American Coot is a very noticeable member of the avifauna in most types of wetland habitats, from vegetated marshes to open-water lakes. It is often heard announcing its presence with its loud grunting and croaking calls. It is most often seen swimming and appears superficially duck-like compared to other rails.

Distribution in Texas

The American Coot is a locally common to rare summer resident throughout Texas, depending on the availability of marshy habitats. It is common through-out the state during winter.

Biology

Older females are known to lay eggs in nests of other coots (conspecific brood parasitism), apparently to increase their reproductive success (Lyon 2003). Conspecific brood parasitism has been found to be a strategy in about 25% of nesting coots in some populations.

Migratory routes and timing

American Coots migrate at night. Southern popula-tions are thought to remain resident, whereas more northerly populations are migratory. Fall migration initiates in late August from northern breeding areas, and migratory movements continue into November. The largest movements are often observed follow-ing cold fronts in fall. Most migrants from northern populations usually arrive in Texas during October and November. Adult and juvenile males and juvenile females tend to migrate simultaneously in fall, followed by adult females (Eddleman, Knopf, and Patterson 1985). Most migratory individuals depart Texas during February and March to initiate their spring migration. Adult Coots typically migrate before juveniles in spring. Migration routes of the American Coot are not fixed, as individuals regularly cross flyways.

Figure 8.1. *(Top)*, American Coot standing on a branch in marshland habitat. Photo credit: Larry Ditto. *(Bottom)*, American Coot initiating flight. Coots often appear to get started by "running" across the surface of the water for a few steps before taking to the air. Photo credit: Greg Lasley.

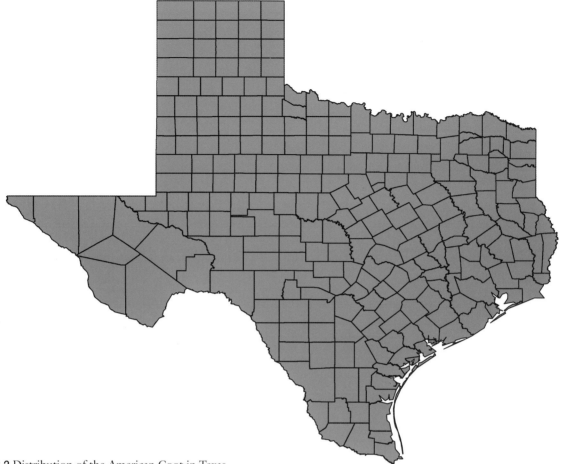

Figure 8.2 Distribution of the American Coot in Texas.

Phenology

Pair formation occurs during spring migration and as late as during nest building (Brisbin, Lehr, and Mowbray 2002). Nest initiation starts as early as March in Texas but peaks in April and May. Coots that are 3 years old and older begin nesting at about the same time, relatively early in the breeding season. Younger American Coots tend to nest later in the breeding season. Parents feed chicks for the first 2 weeks following hatching. American Coots fledge 60–70 days following hatching, and fledgling success is about 50%. In southern portions of their range where the breeding season is relatively long, as in Texas, American Coots may raise 2 broods.

Clutch size and incubation

Clutch size of the American Coot ranges from 6 to 12 eggs, but a typical clutch has 7 to 9 eggs. Clutch size

tends to increase with the age of the nesting female (Crawford 1980). Both males and females take part in incubation, which lasts for 23 to 25 days, with the male usually incubating at night. Incubation is initiated at variable times during laying, often resulting in large variation in hatching times of eggs. Coots are known to be prolific renesters if the initial nest fails. Renesting efforts typically result in clutches with 1 to 2 fewer eggs than in the initial clutch (Arnold 1993). Coots are also known to overlap clutches, laying a second clutch in the same nest at around the time the first clutch hatches (Hill 1986). This typically occurs in pairs that initiate their first nest early in the breeding season. When a pair overlaps their clutches, or when hatching is highly asynchronous, 1 adult will depart with older chicks, while the other remains at the nest to incubate the remainder of the clutch and to brood recently hatched chicks. Young leave the nest within the first 2 days following hatching (Brisbin, Lehr, and Mowbray

2002). Coots are known to be persistent renesters; some individuals have been documented renesting as many as 4 times in a season, following losses of clutches or broods (Alisauskas and Arnold 1994).

Diet and foraging

The American Coot eats predominantly plant material, although animal foods become important during the breeding season, especially for young coots that are growing. Plant foods found to be important include pondweeds (*Potamogeton* spp.), wigeongrass (*Ruppia maritima*), hydrilla (*Hydrilla* spp.), spike rush (*Eleocharis* spp.), and algae, to name a few. Depending on the plant species, coots may consume leaves, stems, roots, or seeds. Animal foods that become important during the breeding season include aquatic insects, mollusks, and crustaceans.

Foraging behavior is dominated by either diving in shallow water or pecking at food near the surface. However, foraging tactics are often diverse and can include fly catching, scavenging, tipping up, and terrestrial grazing (Frederickson et al. 1977). Chicks obtain food from parents for the first 2 weeks after hatching and then become more independent of parents after 3–10 weeks.

Demography and vital rates

Annual survival is estimated at 49% per year for adults and 44% per year for juveniles (Ryder 1963). Severe weather during late winter and spring can be an important mortality factor. Chick survival tends to be related to hatch date, with chicks from later-hatching nests exhibiting lower survival than those from early-hatching nests. This is thought to be the result of poorer-quality habitats used by later-nesting pairs (Brinkhof, Cavé, and Perdeck 1997). The longest known life span of an adult American Coot is 22 years, based on a band recovery. Severe spring weather can result in widespread mortality (Frederickson 1969). Alligators (*Alligator mississippiensis*) often prey on adults and juveniles.

Age at first reproduction

In a study from Iowa, 58% of American Coots nested in their first year, as opposed to 96% of coots 2 years old and older that nested (Crawford 1980).

Age and sex ratios

The sex ratios of American Coots appear to be skewed toward males. Alisauskas (1987) found that males outnumbered females 1.44:1 on Delta Marsh in Manitoba. Because American Coots exhibit differential migration, wherein females migrate to wintering areas farther south than males, sex ratios during migration and winter can be highly variable depending on time and location.

In a study on breeding American Coots, 58% of those breeding in the population were 1 year, 25% were 2 years, 14% were 3 years, and 4% were 4 years old and older (Crawford 1980).

Behavior

The American Coot appears more duck-like in behavior than other rails. It is less secretive than other rails and commonly uses open-water habitats, often far from vegetation cover. Swimming is the most common mode of locomotion, and they pump their heads forward while swimming. Flight is initiated by running across the surface of the water during takeoff and appears somewhat labored during initial stages. American Coots are often observed squabbling over food with other coots or ducks and are quite vocal in the process.

American Coots are quite territorial during the breeding season, often chasing conspecifics as well as other waterbirds out of their territory. Both sexes contribute to territory establishment, and interspecific aggression tends to peak soon after the young hatch (Ryan and Dinsmore 1979). American Coots are also known to defend territories during winter. Resident individuals typically defend core areas around the nest site they occupied during the previous breeding season. Migrant individuals tend to set up territories later in winter.

Population Status and Trends

American Coots breed across most of North America. Their abundance fluctuates annually based on average wetland habitat conditions across their range, declining in drought years and rebounding when wetland conditions are optimal. Christmas Bird Count data indicate a stable population trend in Texas between

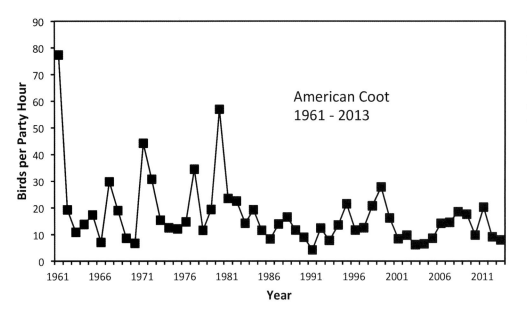

Figure 8.3. Population trend of the American Coot in Texas, 1961–2013, based on Christmas Bird Count data.

1961 and 2013. After 1961, abundance appeared to be highest from 1971 to 1980.

Specific Habitat Requirements

Coots prefer to nest in freshwater wetlands with a relatively even interspersion of open water and thick stands of emergent vegetation (Alisauskas and Arnold 1994). Maximum densities are related to well-flooded wetlands with interspersion of open water and emergent vegetation (Weller and Fredrickson 1973). Emergent vegetation typically comprises robust macrophytes like cattail (*Typha* spp.) and bulrush (*Scirpus* spp.) that provide nesting cover. Open-water areas often have submerged aquatic vegetation that harbors aquatic invertebrates, which are important at this time of year as a food source for growing chicks. Several species of submerged aquatic vegetation are also important food sources for adults. During the nonbreeding period, American Coots are less particular regarding the wetland habitat they inhabit and frequently use many different wetland types. Villamagna, Murphy, and Trauger (2010) found that the occurrence of wintering coots was positively related to the presence of water hyacinth (*Eichhornia crassipes*), and that coots tended to use their typical shallow-water foraging habitat less, choosing to forage in deeper water in association with water hyacinth.

Winter habitat use

During winter, American Coots can be readily found on a variety of wetland types. They have adjusted well to human settings and can often be found in park and golf course ponds in urban areas, in agricultural wetlands (including rice fields and catfish and crayfish ponds), and warm-water outflows from factories. Studies from Texas and Florida found that the distribution of coots was positively related to the presence of wetlands with hydrilla (a submerged aquatic plant) (Montalbano, Hardin, and Hetrick 1979; Esler 1990). There is little published information on winter habitat use and ecology of American Coots (Alisauskas and Arnold 1994). They have been documented using human-constructed wetlands such as catfish ponds, brackish impoundments, and coal mine sediment ponds.

Habitat management

For breeding habitat, managing drawdowns, mowing, and burning to promote high dispersion of patches of emergent vegetation and open marsh produce ideal breeding conditions. Beneficial management of wetlands on migration and wintering areas includes maintaining diverse plant species (emergent and submergent) that provide both food and cover. The growth of preferred foods such as pondweeds, wigeongrass, muskgrass (*Chara* spp.), water milfoils (*Myriophyllum* spp.), and bulrushes should be promoted (Alisauskas and Arnold 1994). American Coots are known for their ability to pioneer new habitats and they respond positively to wetland restoration efforts (Weller and Frederickson 1973). How saltwater intrusion influences American Coots in freshwater habitats in important overwintering states such as Texas is unknown.

Texas hunting regulations

The bag limit is 15, and the possession limit is 45. There is currently a 74- to 89-day season, depending on the zone. The season runs concurrently with the duck season. There is no geographic restriction on hunting in Texas; the season is open in all 254 counties.

Research Needs and Priorities

Although the American Coot has been studied more than most other rails in North America, there are still many information needs relative to its biology and management. In their review of the American Coot, Alisauskas and Arnold (1994) laid out several research priorities that included population dynamics, habitat requirements, general ecology, and improved harvest estimation.

1. Gain a better understanding of the accuracy of breeding population estimates for the American Coot during the Breeding Ground Survey and Breeding Bird Survey.

2. Investigate aspects of movement ecology, including natal and breeding site philopatry, migration routes, and winter site fidelity.

3. Initiate research to improve our understanding of vital rates, including estimates of annual survival, and identify sources of variation in recruitment such as brood and postfledging survival.

4. Conduct genetic analyses to investigate population structuring of American Coots across North America.

5. Increase our understanding of how diseases may limit populations.

6. Examine habitat requirements during post-breeding, migration, and winter.

7. Investigate potential sources of bias in the harvest survey, such as band reporting rates, crippling loss, and illegal kill.

8. Experiment with harvest regulations to increase hunter interest in coots.

Literature Cited

Alisauskas, R. T. 1987. Morphological correlates of age and breeding status in American coots. *Auk* 104:640–46.

Alisauskas, R. T., and T. W. Arnold. 1994. American coot. In *Migratory Shore and Upland Game Bird Management in North America*, edited by T. C. Tacha and C. E. Braun, 127–43. Washington, DC: International Association of Fish and Wildlife Agencies.

Arnold, T. W. 1993. Factors affecting renesting in American Coots. *Condor* 95:273–81.

Brinkhof, M. W. G., A. J. Cavé, and A. C. Perdeck. 1997. The seasonal decline in the first-year survival of juvenile coots: An experimental approach. *Journal of Animal Ecology* 66:73–82.

Brisbin, I. Lehr, Jr., and T. B. Mowbray. 2002. American Coot (*Fulica americana*). In *The Birds of North America Online*, edited by A. Poole. Ithaca, NY: Cornell Laboratory of Ornithology. http://bna.birds.cornell.edu/bna/search?SearchableText=Fulica%20americana.

Crawford, R. D. 1978. Tarsal color of American Coots in relation to age. *Wilson Bulletin* 90:536–43.

———. 1980. Effects of age on reproduction in American Coots. *Journal of Wildlife Management* 44:183–89.

Eddleman, E. R., F. L. Knopf, and C. T. Patterson. 1985. Chronology of migration by American Coots in Oklahoma. *Journal of Wildlife Management* 49:241–46.

Esler, D. 1990. Avian community responses to hydrilla invasion. *Wilson Bulletin* 102:427–40.

Frederickson, L. H. 1969. Mortality of coots during severe spring weather. *Wilson Bulletin* 81:450–53.

Frederickson, L. H., J. M. Anderson, F. M. Kozlik, and R. A. Ryder. 1977. American coot (*Fulica americana*). In *Management of Migratory Shore and Upland Game Birds in North America*, edited by G. C. Sanderson, 123–47. Washington, DC: International Association of Fish and Wildlife Agencies.

Hill, W. L. 1986. Clutch overlap in the American coot. *Condor* 88:96–97.

Lyon, B. E. 2003. Ecological and social constraints on conspecific brood parasitism by nesting female American coots (*Fulica americana*). *Journal of Animal Ecology* 72:47–60.

Montalbano, F., III, S. Hardin, and W. M. Hetrick. 1979. Utilization of hydrilla by ducks and coots in central Florida. *Proceedings of the Southeastern Association of Fish and Wildlife Agencies* 33:36–42.

Ryan, M. R., and J. J. Dinsmore. 1979. A quantitative study of the behavior of breeding in American Coots. *Auk* 96:704–13.

Ryder, R. A. 1963. Migration and population dynamics of American coots in western North America. *Proceedings of the International Ornithological Congress* 13:441–53.

Villamagna, A. M., B. R. Murphy, and D. L. Trauger. 2010. Behavioral response of the American Coot (*Fulica americana*) to water hyacinth (*Eichhornia crassipes*) in Lake Chapala, Mexico. *Waterbirds* 33:550–55.

Weller, M. W., and L. H. Frederickson. 1973. Avian ecology in a managed glacial marsh. *Living Bird* 12:269–91.

Common Gallinule and Common Moorhen

In Texas we found it breeding on some of the deep ponds near Brownsville, while we were hunting for nests of the Mexican grebe, on May 23, 1923, wading in water waist deep or more. These ponds are more or less overgrown, especially around the borders, with water huisache bushes and scattered clumps of cat-tail flags. Some of the nests were in the flags and similar in construction to those described above.—BENT (1926)

Introduction

The Common Gallinule (*Gallinula galeata*) and the Common Moorhen (*Gallinula chloropus*) were formerly considered the same species, or conspecifics. In this chapter they will be treated as conspecifics (Common Gallinule), despite the fact that contemporary ornithologists consider them separate species based on minor differences in vocalizations, bill and shield morphology, and mitochondrial DNA; see the 52nd Supplement to the AOU *Check-List of North American Birds* for details (Bannor and Kiviat 2002). At least 37 other common or local names have been recorded in the United States and Canada for the Common Gallinule and/or Common Moorhen (McAtee 1923). Most Common Gallinule harvest appears to be incidental to waterfowl hunting and is thought to be light (Strohmeyer 1977). From 1977 to 1992, Texas hunters brought in 4.1% of the total US gallinule harvest (Greij 1994).

Both sexes have similar plumage. Adults look all dark, with a dark blue-gray head, neck, and underparts, and a brownish back, wings, and tail (Sterry and Small 2009). The Common Gallinule has a yellow-tipped red bill, a red frontal shield on the forehead, and yellowish legs and toes. The sides of the undertail are white and there are white lines on the flanks (Sterry and Small 2009). Juveniles are grayish brown with white on the throat, sides of the undertail coverts, and flanks (Sterry and Small 2009). Adults are 33.0–35.6 cm (13.0–14.0 in) in length (Sterry and Small 2009) and weigh 192–493 g (6.2–15.9 oz) (Bannor and Kiviat 2002). Males are larger than females in all body measurements (Greij 1994).

Twelve subspecies are recognized following B. Taylor (1998); four of these occur in North America and the West Indies and one in the Hawaiian Islands. See Bannor and Kiviat (2002) for subspecies descriptions and locales.

Distribution in Texas

Common Gallinules are found year round in Texas. *The Texas Breeding Bird Atlas* (TBBA; http://txtbba.tamu.edu/species-accounts/common-moorhen/) has evidence of breeding by the Common Gallinule

Figure 9.1. *(Top)*, Common Gallinule. Photo credit: Larry Ditto. *(Bottom)*, Common Moorhen. Photo credit: Larry Ditto.

COMMON GALLINULE AND COMMON MOORHEN | 81

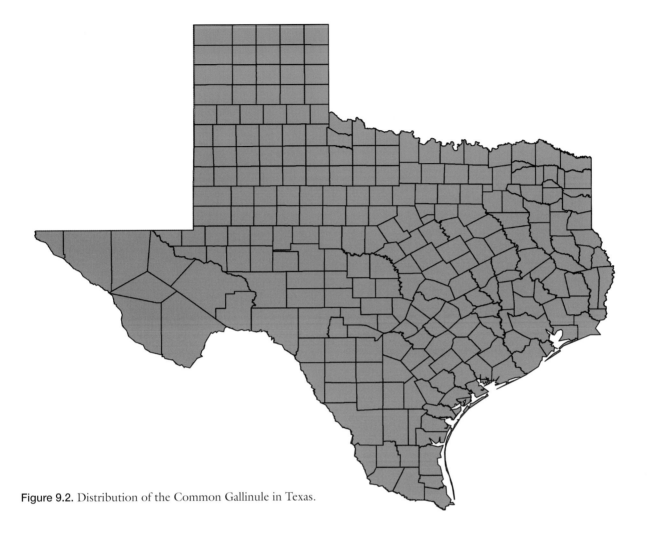

Figure 9.2. Distribution of the Common Gallinule in Texas.

in parts of Texas where breeding was not previously reported. The TBBA map shows that Common Gallinules breed throughout much of Texas, in sharp contrast to previously published maps of the species distribution. Oberholser (1974) showed breeding by Common Gallinules only in the eastern half of Texas and in the El Paso area. Greij (1994) illustrated a broader distribution in west Texas, including nearly all the Trans-Pecos. Neither the map by Oberholser (1974) nor that by Greij (1994) includes the Panhandle or southern plains within the Common Gallinule's breeding range. Nesting in the Panhandle was not reported until 1976 (Seyffert 2001). Reported Common Gallinule occurrences appear to be lowest in the Texas Hill Country. During winter the species is most common from the central coast southward (Lockwood and Freeman 2004).

Biology

Most American research on this species has been conducted in the southern United States, especially Louisiana and Florida, where gallinules are more common and conspicuous than they are elsewhere. Gallinule diet has been well studied in Florida (Mulholland and Percival 1982; O'Meara et al. 1982; Haag et al. 1987), and breeding biology has been investigated in Louisiana (Bell and Cordes 1977; Matthews 1983; Helm, Pashley, and Zwank 1987). Currently, the most comprehensive publication on the Common Gallinule is its species account in the *Birds of North America* series (Bannor and Kiviat 2002). Unless citations indicate otherwise, much of the information on Common Gallinule biology and life history in this chapter is based on Bannor and Kiviat (2002).

Migratory routes and timing

Common Gallinules are nocturnal migrants (Bullis and Lincoln 1952; W. Taylor and Anderson 1973). In North America, they arrive on the breeding grounds from March to early May and depart for wintering areas from mid-September to mid-November.

Timing of breeding

The timing of breeding is variable depending on geographic location; it can range from early April to mid-August.

Behavior

Large feet and long toes allow Common Gallinules to walk on floating plants and soft soils (Bent 1926). When foraging while walking, they carry their body low "in a crouching attitude," lifting and putting their feet down slowly and gently, continually jerking their tail up to reveal undertail coverts (Brewster 1891). They can run across the water surface with flapping wings when repelling an intruder in their territory (Krauth 1972). They can also climb on plants, logs, and rocks.

Common Gallinules are rarely seen flying. If startled or pursued, they are likely to take cover in vegetation rather than fly. When they are flushed on their breeding grounds, flights are short, with legs hanging down, appearing to be "feeble and labored" and ending with an abrupt drop into vegetation (Brewster 1891). In migration or when flying from pond to pond, they fly directly and fairly swiftly with their head and feet extended (Bent 1926).

Their swimming appears as if they are attempting to stride through the water (Abbott 1907). Feet may be lifted out of the water in front of the body alternately in swimming, probably to pass over aquatic plants (Abbott 1907; Saunders 1926). Common Gallinules dive to forage or escape; they may hide underwater with their head or bill concealed in vegetation (Bent 1926). They bathe while standing still and plunging their head into the water, then throwing water up over their back and vibrating their opened wings (Brewster 1891). After bathing, they run individual feathers through their bill. Common Gallinule preening lasts for up to 15 minutes (Brewster 1891).

Both males and females defend territories and nests (Bannor and Kiviat 2002). Aggressive and sexual displays are similar to those of the American Coot (*Fulica americana*); postures are illustrated for the coot by Gullion (1952) but have direct counterparts in Common Gallinule behavior. Gallinules aggressively defend territories, repelling conspecifics and other animals. Intraspecific aggression may begin with patrolling, escalate with a charging and splattering attack, and finally end with a retreat by the intruder or with a hunched display and mutual retreat at the territory boundary, sometimes followed by foot slapping. Aggression can include challenging and violent fighting.

In Louisiana, Matthews (1983) found that radio-marked nesting Common Gallinules occupied an average home range of 1.22 ha (3.0 ac; range: 0.21–3.20 ha [0.5–7.9 ac]). It should be noted that these estimates "may or may not be consistent with territories" (Matthews 1983).

In North America, the mating system, pair bonding, and copulation have not been described (Bannor and Kiviat 2002). European information is available on the mating system (Siegfried and Frost 1975; Petrie 1983, 1986), pair bonding (Morley 1936; Cramp and Simmons 1980; Petrie 1983), and copulation (Selous 1902; Cramp and Simmons 1980). Common Gallinules appear territorial on breeding grounds. However, they are apparently more social on their wintering grounds: mean flock size in coastal Texas was 12.6 birds (Anderson et al. 1996).

Clutch size and incubation

Clutch sizes based on 5 North American and Hawaiian studies range from 5.6 to 9.1 eggs (Cottam and Glazener 1959; Byrd and Zeillemaker 1981; Brackney and Bookhout 1982; Helm, Pashley, and Zwank 1987; Greij 1994). In Louisiana, the mean clutch size was significantly larger in rice fields (8.8 eggs) than in marshes (6.7 eggs) (Helm, Pashley, and Zwank 1987). The incubation period ranges from 19 to 22 days (Ripley 1977; Greij 1994).

Nest losses

Common Gallinule adult, chick, and egg predators include raccoons (*Procyon lotor*), crows (*Corvus* spp.), coyotes (*Canis latrans*), weasels (*Mustela* spp.), mink

(*Mustela vison*), muskrats (*Ondatra zibethicus*), marsh rice rats (*Oryzomys palustris*), Norway rats (*Rattus norvegicus*), opossums (*Didelphis marsupialis*), grackles (*Quiscalus* spp.), snapping turtles (*Chelydra serpentina*), snakes, bowfins (*Amia calva*), gars (Lepisosteidae), and American alligators (*Alligator mississippiensis*) (Bent 1926; Miller 1946; Cottam and Glazener 1959; Krauth 1972; Bell and Cordes 1977; Brackney 1979; Helm 1982; Post and Seals 1991).

Phenology

Both sexes brood chicks. Daytime brooding decreases after 7 days, and at 14 days chicks are brooded only in cold weather events (Wood 1974). Fredrickson (1971) found that only 1 adult (sex unspecified) broods overnight. Wood (1974) found that chicks hatching synchronously generally stay in the nest for only the first 12–24 hours before venturing out with adults. When hatching takes place over several days, chicks often leave the nest and are cared for by 1 adult while the other incubates the remaining eggs (Wood 1974).

Adults may bring food to chicks on the nest within 1 hour after hatching and for 2–4 days after chicks hatch (Fredrickson 1971; Bell and Cordes 1977). Chicks first feed themselves at about 7 days but continue to rely on adults and related juveniles to provide food until about 21–25 days old (Wood 1974; Siegfried and Frost 1975; Byrd and Zeillemaker 1981). After they are 25 days old, chicks rely less on adults for food, until adults completely discontinue feeding at about 45 days old (Wood 1974).

Young Common Gallinules learn to follow adults soon after leaving the nest (Hinde, Thorpe, and Vince 1956). When accompanying a foraging adult, chicks typically cluster behind the adult as it traverses a linear route (Bell and Cordes 1977). Upon finding food, the adult snatches items in its bill and presents them to the chicks. At the approach of an adult, a chick on land or in water begs by extending its head and body upward and forward. The chick typically spreads and quivers its wings while gently swaying its head. At about 14 days old, the chick modifies its begging display by squatting with its hindquarters elevated and its neck held low, its head pointed slightly upward, and its wings outstretched and quivering (Wood 1974).

Parental aggression toward chicks is common, possibly related to feeding demands. Parental aggression may reduce sibling competition and encourage chick independence (Leonard, Horn, and Eden 1988).

Diet and foraging

Common Gallinule chicks feed on both animal and plant matter. Significant foods in diets of chicks are nymphs of dragonflies and mayflies (Ephemeroptera), leeches, duckweed (*Lemna*), and bladderwort (*Utricularia vulgaris*; Miller 1946; Fredrickson 1971; Wood 1974; Greij 1994). Chicks seldom reject a food item presented to them by adults (Bell and Cordes 1977).

The adult diet consists mainly of small, hard items (Bannor and Kiviat 2002). Sedge (Cyperaceae) seeds and snails are most important (Wetmore 1916; Mulholland and Percival 1982; O'Meara et al. 1982; Haag et al. 1987). The animals most frequently eaten are snails, beetles (Coleoptera), true bugs (Hemiptera), ants and wasps (Hymenoptera), true flies (Diptera), spiders (Araneida), crustaceans (Crustacea), dragonflies and damselflies (Odonata), leeches, and moss animals (Bryozoa) (Wetmore 1916; Forbush 1925; Saunders 1926; Simpson 1939; Bell 1976; Mulholland and Percival 1982; O'Meara et al. 1982; Haag et al. 1987; Greij 1994). Exotic invasive plants eaten in the United States include Eurasian watermilfoil (*Myriophyllum spicatum*), hydrilla, water hyacinth, and climbing nightshade (*Solanum dulcamara*; Saunders 1926; Mulholland and Percival 1982; O'Meara et al. 1982; Haag et al. 1987).

Common Gallinules obtain food from the water surface and leaves of floating plants while swimming or walking on these plants or along the shore. They also forage beneath the water surface by dipping their head, tipping up, or occasionally diving in submerged vegetation among emergent plants (Bent 1926; Cogswell 1977). They often flip floating leaves to capture animals attached to the lower surfaces (Bell 1976). They commonly forage on lawns, fields, and golf courses adjoining water (Bent 1926; Bull et al. 1985).

Demography and vital rates

One Common Gallinule banded in Louisiana was recaptured 9 years and 10 months later at an estimated age of about 10 years and 6 months (Clapp,

Klimkiewicz, and Kennard 1982). There is no information on annual survival.

Common Gallinule nest-success rates (nests with ≥ 1 egg hatching) range from 55% to 80% (Cottam and Glazener 1959; Byrd and Zeillemaker 1981; Brackney and Bookhout 1982; Helm 1987). Both of the extremes were from Louisiana, where Helm, Pashley, and Zwank (1987) found a success rate of 55% in coastal marshes and 80% in rice fields. In Louisiana, up to 40% of chicks may perish within 10 days after hatching, primarily because of predation and adverse weather. Thirty percent more may be lost between 10 and 25 days (Bell 1976; Bell and Cordes 1977). Foraging on water away from emergent vegetation is believed to make chicks particularly vulnerable to predation (Bell 1976).

Age at first reproduction

Common Gallinules breed the first year after hatching (Greij 1994).

Age and sex ratios

Common Gallinule age and sex ratios are unknown.

Population Status and Trends

According to the Texas Parks and Wildlife Department (2010), the US Fish and Wildlife Service estimate of annual harvest of all gallinules combined in Texas is about 500 birds.

Breeding Bird Survey results for Common Gallinule population trends in the United States, based on data from 244 routes from 1966 to 2012, indicate that populations are decreasing at a rate of 1.30% per year (Sauer et al. 2014). However, the 95% confidence interval of the estimate overlaps zero; therefore, there is evidence of a stable breeding population of Common Gallinules in the United States (Sauer et al. 2014).

Christmas Bird Count data from 1961 to 2013 indicate high annual variance in the winter population of Common Gallinules in Texas but show a statistically increasing trend for that period.

Specific Habitat Requirements

Breeding habitat

Common Gallinule habitat is mainly freshwater marshes (Greij 1994). They also use shallow edges of lakes and impoundments (primarily coastal, but also inland) with stable water levels and dense stands of floating vegetation that provide excellent habitat for nesting (Greij 1994). In Texas, Common Gallinules will nest in panicum (*Panicum* spp.) and paspalum (*Paspalum* spp.) (Reagan 1977), as well as flooded rice fields (Helm 1982).

Habitat requirements are places to walk and feed over water, plentiful vegetable food, tall cover for nesting, open water, and a healthy system containing invertebrate foods (Greij 1994). Wetlands used contain predominantly lily pads and floating vegetation, emergent cattails, sedges, and grasses. Rice fields are a preferred habitat as soon as rice is tall enough to provide cover or to begin ripening (Helm 1982).

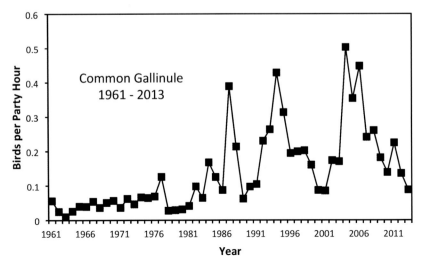

Figure 9.3. Trend in Common Gallinule wintering population in Texas, based on Christmas Bird Count data. Note that while numbers are highly variable from year to year, wintering populations of this species in Texas appear to be increasing.

Figure 9.4. Common Gallinule habitat in coastal marsh. Photo credit: Gulf Coast Joint Venture.

Winter range

In southern and southwestern states, Common Gallinules winter in a variety of marshes, swamps, canals, ponds, and lakes. In coastal Texas, they used 23 of 83 wetland types, with a preference for aquatic-bed rooted vascular and emergent persistent types of the palustrine subclass (Anderson et al. 1996). Cordgrass (*Spartina spartinae*) dominates some wintering habitats in Louisiana (Meanley 1969).

Habitat management

Extensive wetland losses in Louisiana, Florida, Texas, Arkansas, and Mississippi (Eddleman et al. 1988) correspond with the breeding range of the Common Gallinule. These wetland losses might be mitigated by rice fields, national and state wildlife refuges, and water-conservation impoundments. However, a trend toward faster-maturing rice varieties may not allow sufficient time for completion of the nesting cycle (Helm 1982).

Hunting and Conservation

The total number of days and the daily bag limit in the Texas gallinule season are constant; however, the annual dates for legal gallinule hunting in Texas vary slightly based on federal regulation frameworks (table 9.1). The estimated numbers of Texas gallinule hunters (all gallinule species combined) as well as harvest numbers vary annually; large 95% confidence intervals can be attributed to small sample sizes for gallinules in the Texas Parks and Wildlife annual Small Game Harvest Survey (table 9.2)

Table 9.1. Texas Common Gallinule (formerly Common Moorhen) and Purple Gallinule (combined) hunting season dates, total number of days, and daily bag limit, 1990–2014.

Year	Season dates	No. of days	Daily bag limit
1990	1 Sep–9 Nov	0	15
1991	1 Sep–9 Nov	70	15
1992	1 Sep–9 Nov	70	15
1993	1 Sep–9 Nov	70	15
1994	1 Sep–9 Nov	70	15
1995	16 Sep–24 Sep; 18 Nov–17 Jan	70	25
1996	14 Sep–22 Sep; 9 Nov–8 Jan	70	15
1997	13 Sep–21 Sep; 8 Nov–7 Jan	70	15
1998	12 Sep–27 Sep; 24 Oct–16 Dec	70	15
1999	11 Sep–26 Sep; 23 Oct–15 Dec	70	15
2000	15 Sep–30 Sep; 28 Oct–20 Dec	70	15
2001	15 Sep–30 Sep; 27 Oct–19 Dec	70	15
2002	14 Sep–29 Sep; 26 Oct–18 Dec	70	15
2003	20 Sep–28 Sep; 25 Oct–24 Dec	70	15
2004	11 Sep–26 Sep; 30 Oct–22 Dec	70	15
2005	10 Sep–25 Sep; 29 Oct–21 Dec	70	15
2006	16 Sep–24 Sep; 4 Nov–3 Jan	70	15
2007	15 Sep–30 Sep; 3 Nov–26 Dec	70	15
2008	13 Sep–28 Sep; 1 Nov–24 Dec	70	15
2009	12 Sep–27 Sep; 31 Oct–23 Dec	70	15
2010	11 Sep–26 Sep; 30 Oct–22 Dec	70	15
2011	10 Sep–25 Sep; 5 Nov–28 Dec	70	15
2012	15 Sep–30 Sep; 3 Nov–26 Dec	70	15
2013	14 Sep–29 Sep; 2 Nov–25 Dec	70	15
2014	13 Sep–28 Sep; 1 Nov–24 Dec	70	15

Table 9.2. Estimated number of Texas gallinule hunters (all legal gallinule species combined) and total gallinule harvest in Texas, 1994–2013.

Year	Hunters (95% CI)	Harvest (95% CI)
1994–95	811 (55–1,566)	1,549 (19–5,966)
1995–96	80 (1–399)	0
1996–97	146 (2–544)	512 (7–2,028)
1997–98	766 (239–1,293)	504 (5–1,138)
1998–99	506 (54–959)	1,171 (21–5,701)
1999–00	617 (124–1,110)	3,820 (14–7,806)
2000–01	151 (2–629)	0
2001–02	781 (140–1,422)	1,740 (7–3,734)
2002–03	638 (5–1,421)	857 (11–3,288)
2003–04	437 (3–1,026)	1,998 (22–8,843)
2004–05	469 (2–968)	852 (7–3,001)
2005–06	49 (1–278)	0
2006–07	100 (2–431)	199 (4–1,136)
2007–08	158 (2–726)	0
2008–09	197 (3–462)	267 (8–1,493)
2009–10	129 (3–449)	472 (11–2,053)
2010–11	83 (2–348)	166 (4–758)
2011–12	47 (1–271)	279 (6–1,625)
2012–13	97 (2–438)	1,994 (41–11,628)
2013–14	49 (1–323)	0

Research Needs and Priorities

Research priorities for Common Gallinules were summarized by Greij (1994) and Bannor and Kiviat (2002). Priority research needs related to the Common Gallinule include the following:

1. Implement a National Marshbird Monitoring Program.

   An operational marshbird monitoring program conducted on a national scale is critical to assist with harvest management decisions for gallinules (Case and Sanders 2010). Gallinules are difficult to monitor because of their elusive habits, cryptic coloration, and use of difficult-to-access dense wetland habitats (Case and Sanders 2010). Lack of basic population trend and habitat information also causes uncertainty concerning population response to habitat management. Existing field protocols have the potential to provide a national monitoring framework for coots, moorhens, gallinules, rails, snipes, and similar nongame species (Conway 2009; Johnson et al. 2009).

2. Update the National Wetland Inventory.

   The National Wetland Inventory program was established by the US Fish and Wildlife Service in 1974. Its initial purpose was to conduct a nationwide inventory of wetlands on a relatively coarse scale (1:250,000) that could be used for wildlife management (Case and Sanders 2010). The National Wetland Inventory could fulfill a fundamental need for the management of wetland-dependent birds by providing data on the status and trends of their habitat (Case and Sanders 2010). Updated National Wetland Inventory data are critically needed to manage all wetland-associated birds and other wildlife. Uncertainty about the status and trends of wetlands could make all other management actions inefficient and/or ineffective (Case and Sanders 2010).

3. Continue to improve the Harvest Information Program (HIP) sampling frame.

   The HIP provides the sampling frame for annual nationwide surveys of migratory bird hunters in the United States (Case and Sanders 2010). However, HIP certification is required only of legally licensed hunters. In some states, certain hunters (e.g., juniors, landowners, seniors) who are exempted from state licensing requirements are not required to become HIP certified and thus are not included in the sampling frame. The resulting incomplete sampling frame is a source of bias that should be reduced or, preferably, eliminated from the annual HIP estimates (Case and Sanders 2010).

   Individuals who report hunting various migratory bird species the previous year are sampled at much higher rates than those who did not, thereby concentrating sampling effort on the few hunters who hunt these species (Case and Sanders 2010). However, estimates of hunter numbers suggest that screening data are not accurately identifying snipe, coot, rail, or gallinule hunters. It appears that many hunters are responding inaccurately to screening questions, and/or some license vendors are not recording hunters' responses accurately (Case and Sanders 2010). As a result, stratification based on the current screening questions has not been as efficient as expected, and annual HIP estimates of hunter activity and harvest have been imprecise, especially at state levels (Case and Sanders 2010).

Literature Cited

Abbott, C. G. 1907. Summer bird-life of the Newark, New Jersey marshes. *Auk* 24:1–11.

Anderson, J. T., T. C. Tacha, G. T. Muehl, and D. Lobpries. 1996. *Wetland Use by Waterbirds That Winter in Coastal Texas.* Information and Technical Report No. 8. Washington, DC: US Department of the Interior.

Bannor, B. K., and E. Kiviat. 2002. Common Gallinule (*Gallinula galeata*). In *The Birds of North America Online*, edited by A. Poole. Ithaca, NY: Cornell Laboratory of Ornithology. http://bna.birds.cornell.edu/bna/species/685.

Bell, G. 1976. Ecological observations of Common and Purple Gallinules on Lacassine National Wildlife Refuge. Master's thesis, University of Louisiana at Lafayette.

Bell, G. R., and C. L. Cordes. 1977. Ecological investigation of Common and Purple Gallinules on Lacassine National Wildlife Refuge, Louisiana. *Proceedings of the Annual Conference of the Southeastern Association of Fish and Wildlife Agencies* 31:295–99.

Bent, A. C. 1926. *Life Histories of North American Marsh Birds*. US National Museum Bulletin 135. Washington, DC: Smithsonian Institution.

Brackney, A. W. 1979. Population ecology of Common Gallinules in southwestern Lake Erie marshes. Master's thesis, Ohio State University.

Brackney, A. W., and T. A. Bookhout. 1982. Population ecology of Common Gallinules in southwestern Lake Erie marshes. *Ohio Journal of Science* 82:229–37.

Brewster, W. 1891. A study of Florida Gallinules, with some notes on a nest found at Cambridge, Massachusetts. *Auk* 8:1–7.

Bull, J., E. Bull, G. Gold, and P. D. Prall. 1985. *Birds of North America: Eastern Region*. New York: Macmillan.

Bullis, H. R., Jr., and F. C. Lincoln. 1952. A trans-Gulf migration. *Auk* 69:34–39.

Byrd, G. V., and C. F. Zeillemaker. 1981. Ecology of nesting Hawaiian Common Gallinules at Hanalei, Hawaii. *Western Birds* 12:105–16.

Case, D. J., and S. J. Sanders. 2010. *Information Needs for American Coots, Purple Gallinules and Common Moorhens: A Funding Strategy*. Mishawaka, IN: D. J. Case and Associates.

Clapp, R. B., M. K. Klimkiewicz, and J. H. Kennard. 1982. Longevity records of North American birds: Gaviidae through Alcidae. *Journal of Field Ornithology* 53:81–124.

Cogswell, H. L. 1977. *Water Birds of California*. Berkeley: University of California Press.

Conway, C. J. 2009. *Standardized North American Marsh Bird Monitoring Protocols*. Wildlife Research Report #2009–01. Tucson: USGS Arizona Cooperative Fish and Wildlife Research Unit.

Cottam, C., and W. C. Glazener. 1959. Late nesting of water birds in south Texas. *Transactions of the North American Wildlife and Natural Resources Conference* 24:382–95.

Cramp, S., and K. E. L. Simmons. 1980. *The Birds of the Western Palearctic*. Vol. 2, *Hawks to Bustards*. Oxford: Oxford University Press.

Eddleman, W. R., F. L. Knopf, B. Meanley, F. A. Reid, and R. Zernbal. 1988. Conservation of North American rallids. *Wilson Bulletin* 100:458–75.

Forbush, E. H. 1925. *Birds of Massachusetts and Other New England States*. Vol. 1. Massachusetts Department of Agriculture. Norwood, MA: Norwood Press.

Fredrickson, L. H. 1971. Common Gallinule breeding biology and development. *Auk* 88:914–19.

Greij, E. D. 1994. Common Moorhen. In *Migratory Shore and Upland Game Bird Management in North America*, edited by T. C. Tacha and C. E. Braun, 145–57. Washington, DC: International Association of Fish and Wildlife Agencies.

Gullion, G. W. 1952. The displays and calls of the American Coot. *Wilson Bulletin* 64:83–97.

Haag, K. H., J. C. Joyce, W. M. Hetrick, and J. C. Jordan.

1987. Predation on water hyacinth weevils and other aquatic insects by three wetland birds in Florida. *Florida Entomology* 70:457–71.

Helm, R. N. 1982. Chronological nesting study of Common and Purple Gallinules in marshlands and rice fields of southwestern Louisiana. Master's thesis, Louisiana State University.

Helm, R. N., D. N. Pashley, and P. J. Zwank. 1987. Notes on the nesting of the Common Moorhen and Purple Gallinule in southwestern Louisiana. *Journal of Field Ornithology* 58:55–61.

Hinde, R. A., W. H. Thorpe, and M. A. Vince. 1956. The following response of young coots and moorhens. *Behaviour* 9:214–243.

Johnson, D. H., J. P. Gibbs, M. Herzog, S. Lor, N. Neimuth, C. A. Ribic, M. E. Seamans, et al. 2009. A sampling design framework for monitoring secretive marshbirds. *Waterbirds* 32 (2): 203–15.

Krauth, S. 1972. The breeding biology of the Common Gallinule. Master's thesis, University of Wisconsin.

Leonard, M. L., A. G. Horn, and S. F. Eden. 1988. Parent-offspring aggression in moorhens. *Behavioral Ecology and Sociobiology* 23:265–70.

Lockwood, M. W., and B. Freeman. 2004. *Handbook of Texas Birds*. College Station: Texas A&M University Press.

Matthews, W. C. 1983. Home range and movements and habitat selection of nesting gallinules in a Louisiana freshwater marsh. Master's thesis, Louisiana State University.

McAtee, W. L. 1923. *Local Names of Migratory Game Birds*. Miscellaneous Circular 13. Washington, DC: US Department of Agriculture.

Meanley, B. 1969. *Natural History of the King Rail*. North American Fauna, no. 67.

Miller, R. F. 1946. The Florida Gallinule: Breeding birds of the Philadelphia region, Part III. *Cassinia* 36:1–16.

Morley, A. 1936. The winter behaviour of moor-hens. *British Birds* 6:120–24.

Mulholland, R., and H. F. Percival. 1982. Food habits of Common Moorhens and Purple Gallinules in north-central Florida. *Proceedings of the Annual Conference of the Southeastern Association of Fish and Wildlife Agencies* 36:527–36.

Oberholser, H. C. 1974. *The Bird Life of Texas*. Vols. 1 and 2. Austin: University of Texas Press.

O'Meara, T. E., W. R. Marion, O. B. Myers, and W. M. Hetrick. 1982. Food habits of three bird species in phosphorus-mine settling ponds and natural wetlands. *Proceedings of the Annual Conference of the Southeastern Association of Fish and Wildlife Agencies* 36:515–26.

Petrie, M. 1983. Female moorhens compete for small fat males. *Science* 220:413–15.

———. 1986. Reproductive strategies of male and female moorhens (*Gallinula chloropus*). In *Ecological Aspects of*

Social Evolution: Birds and Mammals, edited by D. L. Rubenstein and R. W. Wrangham, 43–63. Princeton, NJ: Princeton University Press.

Post, W., and C. A. Seals. 1991. Bird density and productivity in an impounded cattail marsh. *Journal of Field Ornithology* 62:195–99.

Reagan, W. W. 1977. Resource partitioning in the North American gallinules in southern Texas. Master's thesis, Utah State University.

Ripley, S. D. 1977. *Rails of the World*. Washington, DC: Smithsonian Institution Press.

Sauer, J. R., J. E. Hines, J. E. Fallon, K. L. Pardieck, D. J. Ziolkowski Jr., and W. A. Link. 2014. *The North American Breeding Bird Survey, Results and Analysis 1966–2013*. Version 01.30.2015. Laurel, MD: USGS Patuxent Wildlife Research Center.

Saunders, A. 1926. The summer birds of central New York marshes. *Roosevelt Wildlife Bulletin* 3:334–476.

Selous, E. 1902. Note on the pairing of moor-hens. *Zoologist* 6:196–97.

Seyffert, K. D. 2001. *Birds of the Texas Panhandle*. College Station: Texas A&M University Press.

Siegfried, W. R., and P. G. H. Frost. 1975. Continuous breeding and associated behavior in the moorhen *Gallinula chloropus. Ibis* 117:102–9.

Simpson, T. W. 1939. The feeding habits of the Coot, Florida Gallinule, and Least Bittern on Reelfoot Lake. *Journal of the Tennessee Academy of Science* 14:110–15.

Sterry, P., and B. E. Small. 2009. *Birds of Eastern North America: A Photographic Guide*. Princeton, NJ: Princeton University Press.

Strohmeyer, D. L. 1977. Common Gallinule. In *Management of Migratory Shore and Upland Game Birds in North America*, edited by G. C. Sanderson, 110–17. Washington, DC: International Association of Fish and Wildlife Agencies.

Taylor, B. 1998. *Rails: A Guide to Rails, Crakes, Gallinules, and Coots of the World*. New Haven, CT: Yale University Press.

Taylor, W. K., and B. H. Anderson. 1973. Nocturnal migrants killed at a central Florida TV tower, autumn 1969–1971. *Wilson Bulletin* 85:42–51.

Wetmore, A. 1916. *Birds of Puerto Rico*. Bulletin No. 326. Washington, DC: US Department of Agriculture.

Wood, N. A. 1974. Breeding behavior and biology of the moorhen. *British Birds* 67:104–15, 137–58.

Purple Gallinule

A nest described in his notes as: a shallow platform located among the cat-tails and rushes near the shore in shallow water and in an isolated clump. The cat-tails were bent down and woven together in the manner of our least bittern and the nest would easily be taken for one. The nest was about 30 inches above the water and a shallow but well made platform of live flat leaves.
—HERBERT W. BRANDT, BEXAR COUNTY, TEXAS, JUNE 8, 1919

Introduction

The Purple Gallinule (*Porphyrula martinica*) is probably the least frequently harvested game bird in North America because hunting season starts after the fall migration has begun. Purple Gallinules have a reputation of being unpalatable, but those harvested in rice fields of Louisiana and South America are considered excellent table fare when served over rice (West and Hess 2002).

Both sexes have similar plumage. Adults have a mostly bluish-purple head, neck, and underparts, with a green back and wing coverts (Sterry and Small 2009). Undertail coverts are mostly white. The legs are yellow, the eye is red, and the bill is red with a yellow tip (Sterry and Small 2009). Adults are 30.5–35.6 cm (12.0–14.0 in) in length (Sterry and Small 2009) and weigh 190.3–230.1 g (6.1–7.4 oz) (Gross and Van Tyne 1929). Males are larger than females (West and Hess 2002). Juveniles have an orange-buff head, neck, and flanks, with grayish-green back and wing coverts. Underparts and undertail coverts are white. Bill and legs are a dull brown (Sterry and Small 2009). There are no subspecies recognized despite the broad range of Purple Gallinules.

Distribution in Texas

Texas is not included in the Purple Gallinule wintering range (West and Hess 2002). Distribution during spring and summer is tied largely to the upper and middle coast during summer (Lockwood and Freeman 2004). The Purple Gallinule is rare in Texas during winter.

Biology

Currently, the most comprehensive volume on the Purple Gallinule is its species account in the *Birds of North America* series (West and Hess 2002), which covers its annual life cycle, habitats, and demography. Little is known about this seldom-hunted game species, and much of what is known is in unpublished theses (Bell 1976; Reagan 1977; Helm 1982; Matthews 1983; Mulholland 1983).

Migratory routes and timing

Purple Gallinules arrive in Texas from mid-April to late May and depart from early August to late October (extremes in arrival are March 5–June 24, and for

Figure 10.1. Purple Gallinule in wetland habitat. Photo credit: Greg Lasley.

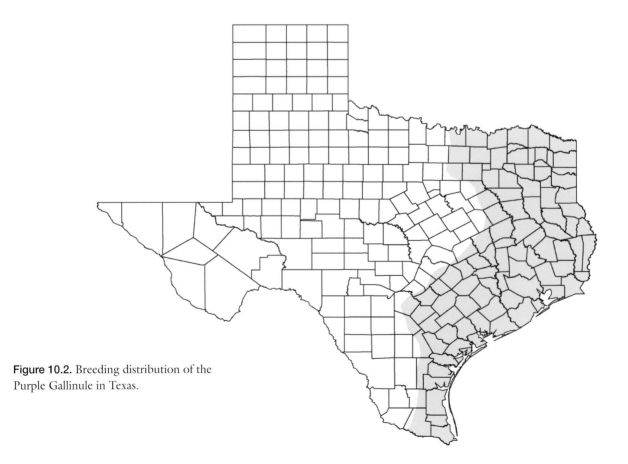

Figure 10.2. Breeding distribution of the
Purple Gallinule in Texas.

departure, July–December 1; Oberholser 1974). In Louisiana, the earliest Purple Gallinule arrival was the last week in March (Lowery 1960). The average arrival in the breeding range of Georgia, Texas, and Louisiana is mid-April, and the third week of April in Arkansas (Meanley 1963; Reagan 1977; Helm 1982; James and Neal 1986). Fall departure is mainly in late August, but some adults with young remain into September and early October (West and Hess 2002).

Purple Gallinules frequently land on ships in the Gulf of Mexico (Audubon 1838). Purple Gallinules arriving earlier on the northern Gulf Coast than on the Texas coast provide circumstantial evidence of trans-Gulf migration (Stevenson 1957).

Timing of breeding

The timing of breeding is variable depending on geographic location; in the United States it can range from mid-April to May.

Behavior

Purple Gallinules are able to walk on water lilies and other floating vegetation, on uneven surfaces of tangled masses of grass stems, and along muddy margins of wetlands (West and Hess 2002). They can climb through bushes and trees up to 20 m (65.6 ft) aboveground (Gross and Van Tyne 1929; Mulholland 1983). When they walk, their neck is alternately bridled up or thrown forward, and their short black-and-white tail alternates between semi-erect and perpendicular (Gosse 1847). Jerking motions of the tail are quick and repetitive (Audubon 1838).

Typical flight over breeding marshes is weak and slow, with legs hanging down, and is not long and protracted; the birds hover feebly along, just clearing the tops of vegetation, and then suddenly drop down out of sight (Bent 1926). When taking flight, they are capable of rising directly, but not far, out of the water. They land with legs held far forward and can come to a sudden stop on lily pads or reed stems (Slud 1964; Sick 1993).

Purple Gallinules swim and dive readily (West and Hess 2002). When swimming in secure situations, they throw their head forward with every propelling motion of their feet (Audubon 1838). They use diving as an escape mechanism and can remain underwater with only their bill pointing up out of the water (Wayne 1910).

Little is known about Purple Gallinule daily activities. However, in a South Texas study where a breeding area was scanned at intervals from a tower, feeding was noted in 54 of 99 observations, territorial encounters in 10, swimming in 9, preening in 8, resting in 5, calling in 3, flying in 2, incubating in 2, and unknown in 6 (Reagan 1977). Since the individuals observed remained concealed most of the time, data are biased toward more obvious behaviors.

Purple Gallinule territorial interactions involve adults of both sexes and often juveniles. When neighbors of either sex meet at ill-defined borders, confrontations sometimes escalate into physical combat in which one flies up and strikes the other with its feet and also pecks its opponent. Sometimes a fight begins when an adult attacks a neighboring juvenile. The juvenile runs to the center of its territory and older birds chase away the intruder (Krekorian 1978; Hunter 1986). Purple Gallinule territories are established after pair formation, prior to nesting, and are maintained throughout brood rearing (Hunter 1986; Helm 1994). Pairs are highly territorial during the breeding season, but territories begin to break down in mid-winter in central Florida, when residential birds from several territories will share the same feeding station (West and Hess 2002). Estimated Purple Gallinule home range was 1.03 ha (2.5 ac) for 4 radio-marked birds in a Louisiana impoundment (range 0.63–1.68 ha [1.6–4.2 ac]; Matthews 1983).

Territorial defense among Purple Gallinules rarely includes fighting (West and Hess 2002). Charging and chasing are more common behaviors. Resident birds often bow following a confrontation on the edge of a territory (Helm 1982). When nonterritorial birds intrude on a territory, the resident runs or flies at the intruder and chases it off the territory. Intruders quickly leave, and confrontations rarely escalate beyond the staring and chasing stages (Krekorian 1978; Hunter 1986).

Purple Gallinules arrive in the Gulf states in mid-April, coinciding with the establishment of territories by early-nesting Common Gallinules (*Gallinula chloropus*). The 2 species often compete for nesting habitat (Reagan 1977). Common Gallinules appear to be competitively superior; a short charge or chase is usually sufficient to send an intruding Purple Gallinule into flight (Helm 1982). Purple Gallinules appear to be present in consistently smaller numbers than Common Gallinules when nesting sympatrically in natural wetlands.

In south Louisiana, where Boat-tailed Grackles (*Quiscalus major*) nest in emergent vegetation bordering waterways, Purple Gallinules are immediately attacked if they land in a shrub occupied by nesting grackles. Purple Gallinules are often forced to the ground by grackles as they fly over grackle nesting areas (Helm 1982).

Purple Gallinules are monogamous (Helm 1994). Some large clutches found in Louisiana rice fields (Helm 1982) suggest that 1 or more females are responsible. There is no information about Purple Gallinule sex ratios (West and Hess 2002).

Social structure of Purple Gallinules in North America is usually limited to a breeding pair and their hatch-year young (West and Hess 2002). These family units are maintained through the breeding season (Helm 1994). Under ideal conditions, more than 1 brood may be attempted per year (Helm 1982; West and Hess 2002).

Clutch size and incubation

Purple Gallinule clutch size varies greatly (range 2–14 eggs). North American clutches average more than 6 eggs, and in the tropics about 4 eggs (West and Hess 2002). In Louisiana, clutches in rice fields averaged 3 eggs more than those found in either an impounded marsh or a disturbed natural marsh in 1977 and 1978 (Helm 1982). Higher food availability in rice fields may have increased egg production or egg dumping, resulting in larger clutch sizes (Helm, Pashley, and Zwank 1987).

The incubation period in Louisiana ranges from 18 to 20 days (Matthews 1983).

Nest losses

Purple Gallinule nest and egg predators include Boat-tailed Grackles (Cottam and Glazener 1959; Helm 1982), Common Gallinules (Nicholson 1929), American alligators (*Alligator mississippiensis*; Helm 1982), and raccoons (*Procyon lotor*; Helm 1982).

Phenology

Purple Gallinule adults share brooding and incubating duties. The brooding period is primarily at night after the first week; chicks are also brooded during the day for short periods, and during rain showers (Helm 1982). The brooding adults sometimes rise to examine the chicks, but more often they put their head under their breast feathers without rising (Gross and Van Tyne 1929).

For 1–4 days after hatching, the precocial young become excited when an adult peers over the edge of the nest, peeping and waving their heads before jumping up and grasping the adult's bill (West and Hess 2002). The adult offers small insects and spiders, reaching into the nest with its neck outstretched and presenting the food to the eldest chick, which grabs at it (West and Hess 2002). Food items delivered to Louisiana nests included mollusks, crayfish (*Procambarus clarkii*), dragonflies, grasshoppers, garter snakes (*Thamnophis* spp.), water beetles, spiders, and insect larvae (Helm 1982). Animal food is the primary diet for the first 2 weeks. Chicks begin to feed themselves at 7–10 days and are primarily self-feeding by 21 days. Coontail, duckweed, pondweed, and flowers of water hyacinth are foods consumed directly by downy young (Gross and Van Tyne 1929; Bell 1976; Helm 1982).

Diet and foraging

Diet varies greatly with season and local availability, but plant material predominates over animal items (Howell 1932; McKay 1981; Mulholland and Percival 1982). Flowers and fruits of the water-lily family are major food items (McKay 1981; Mulholland and Percival 1982; Hunter 1986). Portions of 2 invasive exotic plants (water hyacinth flowers and hydrilla leaves and tubers) in the southern United States can be major food items for Purple Gallinules (Mulholland and Percival 1982; Esler 1990; Helm 1994). American lotus is a staple food in Florida and South Carolina (Olsen 1963).

Individuals of all ages spend much time walking or running on lily pads, frequently rolling back the edges of the pads with their bills and then stepping on them and holding them in that position so they can pick off aquatic insects from the underside (Stoddard 1978).

Birds bend down or climb stalks of rice and other grains to feed on seed heads. They also obtain food in bushes and trees (Bent 1926; Oberholser 1974).

Demography and vital rates

No information on Purple Gallinule life span or annual survival is available (West and Hess 2002). A 2-year Texas study showed that nest-success rates (percentage of nests hatching ≥ 1 egg) varied greatly, between 91% and 49% (Cottam and Glazener 1959). In Louisiana rice fields, 85.2% of eggs hatched from nests observed throughout the incubation period (Causey, Bonner, and Graves 1968). Analysis of failed nests, pooled over species (Purple Gallinule, $n = 38$; Common Moorhen, $n = 71$) in Louisiana, suggested that 39% were depredated, 24% were lost to unknown causes, 23% were abandoned, 9% were lost in severe weather, 3% floated away, and 2% were lost when black ants (Formicidae) entered pipping eggs (Helm 1982).

In Louisiana studies, average brood size was 1.8 chicks for 9 broods 4–6 weeks of age (Bell 1976), and the average brood size at fledging varied from 1.5 (Matthews 1983) to 3.1 (Helm 1982). Brood sizes observed through roadside counts in Louisiana show a decreasing trend as the young grow from less than 2 weeks to more than 6 weeks of age (Helm 1982).

Age at first reproduction

Age at first reproduction is unknown, but Purple Gallinules probably breed when 1 year old, like small rallids (West and Hess 2002).

Age and sex ratios

Purple Gallinule sex ratios are unknown (West and Hess 2002). Surveys conducted from air boats each August during 1979–1992 on Lacassine National Wildlife Refuge in southwestern Louisiana indicated an average production rate of 1.6 (range 0.6–2.8) young per adult (Lacassine National Wildlife Refuge, unpublished data).

Population Status and Trends

According to the Texas Parks and Wildlife Department (2010), the US Fish and Wildlife Service estimate of annual harvest of all gallinules combined in Texas is about 500 birds.

Breeding Bird Survey results for Purple Gallinule population trends in the United States, based on data from 57 routes from 1966 to 2012, indicate that populations are declining at a rate of 2.80% per year (Sauer et al. 2014). However, the 95% confidence interval of the estimate does not overlap 0.0; therefore,

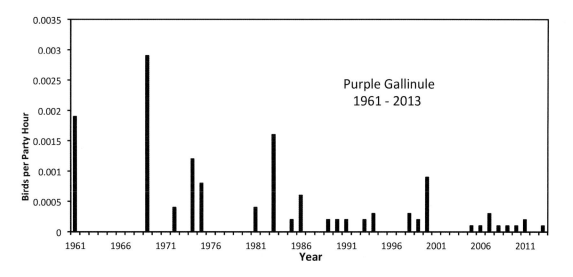

Figure 10.3. Trend in Purple Gallinule wintering population in Texas, based on Christmas Bird Count data. Note that while numbers are highly variable from year to year, wintering populations of this species in Texas appear to be declining.

there is evidence of a decline in the breeding population of Purple Gallinules in the United States (Sauer et al. 2014).

Christmas Bird Count data from 1961 to 2012 indicate that the winter population of Purple Gallinules in Texas is highly variable from year to year, but there is a declining trend for that period.

Specific Habitat Requirements

Breeding habitat

Purple Gallinule habitat is mainly fresh to intermediate marshes (≤ 5 ppt salt content; Helm 1994). They also use deep-water marshes (0.25–1 m; 0.8–3.3 ft depth), shallow edges of lakes, and impoundments (primarily coastal, but also inland) with stable water levels and dense stands of floating vegetation that provide excellent habitat for nesting (Helm 1994). Preferred breeding habitats also include a large amount of edge created by interspersion of open-water areas and robust emergent vegetation such as water lilies, sedges, grasses, rushes, juncus, floating and submerged vegetation, and hydrilla (Trautman and Glines 1964; Sprunt and Chamberlain 1970; Oberholser 1974; Helm 1982).

Habitat requirements are places to walk and feed over water, plentiful vegetable foods, tall cover for nesting, open water, and a wetland system containing invertebrate food (West and Hess 2002). Some wetlands used are predominantly lily pads and floating vegetation; others are primarily emergent cattails, sedges, and grasses. Rice fields are a preferred habitat as soon as rice is tall enough to provide cover or to begin ripening (McKay 1981; Helm 1982).

Figure 10.4. Purple Gallinule habitat. Photo credit: Gulf Coast Joint Venture.

Spring and fall migration

Purple Gallinule vagrants appear in urban habitats, such as lawns and industrial sites. Trans-Gulf spring migrants frequent the first marshes they encounter on barrier islands until they regain their strength (West and Hess 2002).

Winter habitat

Winter habitat is generally similar to breeding habitat, except that movement to warmer and wetter locations is necessary because of seasonal changes, drying of wet areas, and harvesting of rice fields. Purple Gallinules appear to be more tolerant of open situations (50%–75% open water compared to 25% water) during winter (Mulholland 1983).

Habitat management

Extensive wetland losses in Louisiana, Florida, Texas, Arkansas, and Mississippi (Eddleman et al. 1988) correspond with the breeding range of the Purple Gallinule. These wetland losses might be mitigated by rice fields, national and state wildlife refuges, and water-conservation impoundments. However, a trend toward quicker-maturing rice varieties may not allow sufficient time for completion of the nesting cycle (Helm 1982). Also, there have been declines in rice farming on the Texas coast, which may account for the declines in Purple Gallinule populations seen there.

Purple Gallinules may have benefited from the introduction of exotic aquatic plants. Water hyacinth and hydrilla provide food and habitat for Purple Gallinules and may provide needed isolation for breeding. Removing emergent vegetation from ponds to improve fishing and hunting may harm Purple Gallinule reproduction, but only anecdotal data exist on this practice (West and Hess 2002).

Hunting and Conservation

Purple and Common Gallinules are combined for Texas regulatory purposes. The total number of days and the daily bag limit in the Texas gallinule season are constant; however, the annual dates for legal gallinule hunting in Texas vary slightly (table 9.1). The estimated numbers of Texas gallinule hunters (all gallinule species combined) as well as harvest numbers vary annually, and large 95% confidence intervals can be attributed to small sample sizes for gallinules in the Texas Parks and Wildlife annual Small Game Harvest Survey (table 9.2).

Research Needs and Priorities

Most research has been conducted in the Purple Gallinule breeding range. Research priorities for Purple Gallinules are summarized by Helm (1994) and West and Hess (2002). Priority research needs related to the Purple Gallinule include the following:

1. Implement a National Marshbird Monitoring Program.

   An operational marshbird monitoring program conducted on a national scale is critical to assist with harvest management decisions for gallinules (Case and Sanders 2010). Gallinules are difficult to monitor because of their elusive habits, cryptic coloration, and use of difficult-to-access dense wetland habitats (Case and Sanders 2010). Lack of basic population trend and habitat information also causes uncertainty concerning population response to habitat management. Existing field protocols have the potential to provide a national monitoring framework for coots, moorhens, gallinules, rails, snipes, and similar nongame species (Conway 2009; Johnson et al. 2009).

2. Update the National Wetland Inventory.

   The National Wetland Inventory program was established by the US Fish and Wildlife Service in 1974. Its initial purpose was to conduct a nationwide inventory of wetlands on a relatively coarse scale (1:250,000) that could be used for wildlife management (Case and Sanders 2010). The National Wetland Inventory could fulfill a fundamental need for the management of wetland-dependent birds by providing data on the status and trends of their habitat (Case and Sanders 2010). Updated National Wetland Inventory data are critically needed to manage all wetland-associated birds and other wildlife. Uncertainty about the status and trends of wetlands could make all other management actions inefficient and/or ineffective (Case and Sanders 2010).

3. Continue to improve the Harvest Information Program (HIP) sampling frame.

The HIP provides the sampling frame for annual nationwide surveys of migratory bird hunters in the United States (Case and Sanders 2010). However, HIP certification is required only of legally licensed hunters. In some states, certain hunters (e.g., juniors, landowners, seniors) who are exempted from state licensing requirements are not required to become HIP certified and thus are not included in the sampling frame. The resulting incomplete sampling frame is a source of bias that should be reduced or, preferably, eliminated from the annual HIP estimates (Case and Sanders 2010).

Hunters who report hunting various migratory bird species the previous year are sampled at much higher rates than those who did not, thereby concentrating sampling effort on the few hunters who hunt these species (Case and Sanders 2010). However, estimates of hunter numbers suggest that screening data are not accurately identifying snipe, coot, rail, or gallinule hunters. It appears that many hunters are responding inaccurately to screening questions, or else some license vendors are not recording hunters' responses accurately (Case and Sanders 2010). Because of these problems, stratification based on the current screening questions has not been as efficient as expected. As a result, annual HIP estimates of hunter activity and harvest have been imprecise, especially at state levels (Case and Sanders 2010).

Literature Cited

Audubon, J. J. 1838. *Ornithological Biography.* Vol. 4. Edinburgh: Adam and Charles Black.

Bell, G. 1976. Ecological observations of Common and Purple Gallinules on Lacassine National Wildlife Refuge. Master's thesis, University of Louisiana at Lafayette.

Bent, A. C. 1926. *Life Histories of North American Marsh Birds.* US National Museum Bulletin 135. Washington, DC: Smithsonian Institution.

Case, D. J., and S. J. Sanders. 2010. *Information Needs for American Coots, Purple Gallinules and Common Moorhens: A Funding Strategy.* Mishawaka, IN: D. J. Case and Associates.

Causey, M. K., F. L. Bonner, and J. B. Graves. 1968. Dieldrin residues in the gallinules *Porphyrula martinica* L. and *Gallinula chloropus* L. and its effect on clutch size and hatchability. *Bulletin of Environmental Contamination and Toxicology* 3:274–83.

Conway, C. J. 2009. *Standardized North American Marsh Bird Monitoring Protocols.* Wildlife Research Report #2009–01. Tucson: USGS Arizona Cooperative Fish and Wildlife Research Unit.

Cottam, C., and W. C. Glazener. 1959. Late nesting of water birds in south Texas. *Transactions of the North American Wildlife and Natural Resources Conference* 24:382–95.

Eddleman, W. R., F. L. Knopf, B. Meanley, F. A. Reid, and R. Zernbal. 1988. Conservation of North American rallids. *Wilson Bulletin* 100:458–75.

Esler, D. 1990. Avian community responses to hydrilla invasion. *Wilson Bulletin* 102:427–40.

Gosse, P. H. 1847. *The Birds of Jamaica.* London: John Van Voorst.

Gross, A. O., and J. Van Tyne. 1929. The Purple Gallinule (*Ionornis martinicus*) of Barro Colorado Island, canal zone. *Auk* 46:431–46.

Helm, R. N. 1982. Chronological nesting study of Common and Purple Gallinules in marshlands and rice fields of southwestern Louisiana. Master's thesis, Louisiana State University.

———. 1994. Purple Gallinule. In *Migratory Shore and Upland Game Bird Management in North America*, edited by T. C. Tacha and C. E. Braun, 158–65. Washington, DC: International Association of Fish and Wildlife Agencies.

Helm, R. N., D. N. Pashley, and P. J. Zwank. 1987. Notes on the nesting of the Common Moorhen and Purple Gallinule in southwestern Louisiana. *Journal of Field Ornithology* 58:55–61.

Howell, A. H. 1932. *Florida Bird Life.* New York: Coward-McCann.

Hunter, L. A. 1986. Cooperative breeding behavior of Purple Gallinules. PhD diss., University of Montana.

James, D. A., and J. C. Neal. 1986. *Arkansas Birds: Their Distribution and Abundance.* Fayetteville: University of Arkansas Press.

Johnson, D. H., J. P. Gibbs, M. Herzog, S. Lor, N. Neimuth, C. A. Ribic, M. E. Seamans, et al. 2009. A sampling design framework for monitoring secretive marshbirds. *Waterbird* 32 (2): 203–15.

Krekorian, C. O. 1978. Alloparental care in the Purple Gallinule. *Condor* 80:382–90.

Lockwood, M. W., and B. Freeman. 2004. *Handbook of Texas Birds.* College Station: Texas A&M University Press.

Lowery, G. H., Jr. 1960. *Louisiana Birds*. Baton Rouge: Louisiana State University Press.

Matthews, W. C. 1983. Home range and movements and habitat selection of nesting gallinules in a Louisiana freshwater marsh. Master's thesis, Louisiana State University.

McKay, W. D. 1981. Notes on Purple Gallinules in Colombian rice fields. *Wilson Bulletin* 93:267–71.

Meanley, B. 1963. Pre-nesting activity of the Purple Gallinule near Savannah, Georgia. *Auk* 80:545–47.

Mulholland, R. 1983. Feeding ecology of the Common Moorhen and Purple Gallinule on Orange Lake, Florida. Master's thesis, University of Florida, Gainesville.

Mulholland, R., and H. F. Percival. 1982. Food habits of Common Moorhens and Purple Gallinules in north-central Florida. *Proceedings of the Annual Conference of the Southeastern Association of Fish and Wildlife Agencies* 36:527–36.

Nicholson, D. J. 1929. Egg-eating habits of the Florida Gallinule. *Auk* 46:380–81.

Oberholser, H. C. 1974. *The Bird Life of Texas*. Vol. 1. Austin: University of Texas Press.

Olsen, S. L. 1963. The Purple Gallinule feeding on the yellow lotus. *Florida Naturalist* 36:63.

Reagan, W. 1977. Resource partitioning of North American gallinules in southern Texas. Master's thesis, Utah State University.

Sauer, J. R., J. E. Hines, J. E. Fallon, K. L. Pardieck, D. J. Ziolkowski Jr., and W. A. Link. 2014. *The North American Breeding Bird Survey, Results and Analysis 1966–2013*. Version 01.30.2015. Laurel, MD: USGS Patuxent Wildlife Research Center.

Sick, H. 1993. *Birds in Brazil: A Natural History*. Princeton, NJ: Princeton University Press.

Slud, P. 1964. *The Birds of Costa Rica*. American Museum of Natural History, Bulletin 128.

Sprunt, A., Jr., and E. B. Chamberlain. 1970. *South Carolina Bird Life*. Rev. ed. Columbia: University of South Carolina Press

Sterry, P., and B. E. Small. 2009. *Birds of Eastern North America: A Photographic Guide*. Princeton, NJ: Princeton University Press.

Stevenson, H. M. 1957. Relative magnitude of the trans-Gulf and circum-Gulf spring migration. *Wilson Bulletin* 69:39–77.

Stoddard, H. 1978. *Birds of Grady County, Georgia*. Bulletin Number 21. Tallahassee, FL: Tall Timbers Research Station.

Texas Parks and Wildlife Department. 2010. *Webless Migratory Gamebird Strategic Plan: 2011–2015*. Austin: Texas Parks and Wildlife Department.

Trautman, M. B., and S. J. Glines. 1964. A nesting of Purple Gallinule (*Porphyrio martinicus*) in Ohio. *Auk* 81:224–26.

Wayne, A. T. 1910. *Birds of South Carolina*. Charleston, SC: Daggett Printing.

West, R. L., and G. K. Hess. 2002. Purple Gallinule (*Porphyrio martinicus*). In *The Birds of North America Online*, edited by A. Poole. Ithaca, NY: Cornell Laboratory of Ornithology. http://bna.birds.cornell.edu/bna/species/626.

Wilson's Snipe

The sportsman who brings in a limit of Snipe can be proud of his shooting and happy with the thought of a fine meal to come.—LEOPOLD, GUTIÉRREZ, AND BRONSON (1981, 24)

Introduction

Wilson's Snipe (*Gallinago delicata*) is a midsized shorebird that is widely hunted across the United States. Adults are 23–28 cm (9.1–11.0 in) long, with a wingspan of 39–45 cm (15–18 in). The species exhibits what ornithologists call "reverse sexual dimorphism" in that adult females are slightly larger than males (Mueller 1999). This is typical of most species in the Scolopacidae. The size differences between males and females may play a role in their habitat use during winter (McClosky and Thompson 2000), or perhaps in the mating behaviors of males (Mueller 1999).

Originally considered a subspecies of the Common Snipe (*Gallinago gallinago*), Wilson's Snipe was designated a separate species by the American Ornithologists' Union (Banks et al. 2002). Wilson's Snipe was named in honor of Alexander Wilson, who many consider to be the first ornithologist in North America to conduct scientific study of wild birds. The literature citations in this chapter that contain "Common Snipe" in the title actually refer to the same bird as the Wilson's Snipe.

Distribution in Texas

Wilson's Snipe is distributed across Texas during fall, winter, and early spring (September–April). Winter distribution of Wilson's Snipe in Texas is highly scattered because the birds are tied to shallow wetlands that are often ephemeral. Meaningful density estimates for this species have not been reported from Texas. The huge variation in annual precipitation across most of Texas is a major driver in expanding or reducing the amount of usable space available for the birds during winter.

Biology

The landmark monograph on the snipes by Tuck (1972) is the standard reference for the biology and life history of this species. Much of the information on the annual life cycle of Wilson's Snipe presented here is summarized from Tuck (1972). Dr. Leslie Tuck studied this species in Canada, Louisiana, Florida, and Venezuela for more than 15 years. In contrast to other species of snipe in Europe, the Wilson's Snipe in the United States has received very little research attention since Tuck's monograph was published.

Migratory routes and timing

Migration flights occur at night, typically during full or near-full moon. The initiation of northward movements from wintering to breeding grounds typically occurs in March, with migration lasting through April and well into May, depending on the location.

Figure 11.1. Wilson's Snipe. Males and females have similar plumage, and females are slightly larger than males. Photo credit: Larry Ditto.

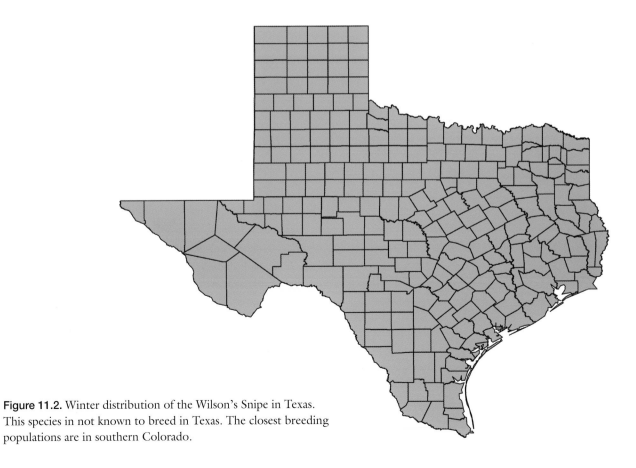

Figure 11.2. Winter distribution of the Wilson's Snipe in Texas. This species in not known to breed in Texas. The closest breeding populations are in southern Colorado.

Typically, arrivals are much later on the northern breeding grounds than on the southern ones. In Newfoundland, Canada, males arrive on the breeding grounds an average of 10–14 days earlier than females. This is also typical of more southerly breeding locations in the United States. Presumably, males arrive earlier than females in order to establish breeding territories. The timing of migration can also vary greatly with weather. Cold fronts can delay migration or even cause it to cease, while warm fronts accelerate migration.

The initiation of southward movements begins in late August. Wilson's Snipes typically migrate southward as single birds or in small flocks called "wisps" (Leopold, Gutiérrez, and Bronson 1981).

Timing of breeding

The timing of breeding is highly variable depending on geographic location; it can range from late May to well into August.

Behavior

Wilson's Snipe exhibits spectacular territorial displays called "winnowing." Birds will fly up 50–100 or more ft (approximately 30 m or more) in altitude and then make a steep, downward, *j*-shaped flight at a 45° angle that causes the retrices (outer tail feathers) to vibrate and make a tremolo-type sound. Females also will winnow, but to a much lesser extent than males.

Tuck (1972) described 5 other basic display behaviors:

1. Arched wing. In flight, males arch their wings above their body while holding their body and bill 45° below horizontal. Typically used for pair formation and to entice a female into the male's territory.

2. Sparring. The body and bill are held horizontally and the tail is fanned so it is aligned with the body. An agnostic display restricted to males.

3. Displacement feeding. The bill is pointed perpendicular to the ground and the tail is fanned vertically. Sometimes displayed by both sexes after copulation, by males after sparring or intense aerial displays, and by females after returning to the nest from being disturbed.

4. Distraction display. Carried out by both sexes to distract potential threats to the nest or chicks. Typically the bill is held at 90° to the ground while 1 wing is flapped and the tail is pointed toward the ground.

5. Flutter leap. Sometimes precedes copulation, but not always. Consists of short-duration bouts of leaping and fluttering in the air before returning to feeding. May also be agonistic when migrants are crowded on small patches of foraging habitat.

Typical breeding-season ground vocalizations, a monotonous "cut-a-cut-a-cut," are used by both sexes to maintain contact and call lost chicks. Other common vocalizations are called yakking and vary greatly: "gick-jack," "keet-koot," and "tjick-tjuck" are a few examples.

Clutch size and incubation

Clutch size averages 4 eggs. Incubation period is 19 days by the female. After the chicks hatch males typically care for 2 chicks, and females for the other 2 chicks.

Nest losses

Wilson's Snipe nest losses are poorly documented. Tuck (1972) seems to dismiss or perhaps overlook losses to predators but mentions that nests are often lost to trampling by cattle. The spotted camouflage patterns on the eggs make an unattended nest extremely difficult to locate.

Phenology

Adults brood and care for chicks for the first 3 weeks of life. After this time, the young birds are able to make sustained flight and start to become independent of the adults. Birds are nearly fully grown at 14 weeks after hatching.

Diet and foraging

Like many other shorebirds, Wilson's Snipes have a prehensile bill that allows them to probe soft, muddy substrates and soils to extract food. Remarkably, these birds can procure food and swallow it without removing their bills from the ground. Under close observation, it is easy to watch them swallow their food while simultaneously probing moist soils without removing their bills.

Isopods, along with aquatic or wetland insect larvae and gastropods, are among the most common foods eaten. Plant fibers, seeds, and grit are also ingested but are not typically considered food (Tuck 1972). Wilson's Snipes cast pellets of indigestible materials such as chitin, mollusk shell fragments, grit, plant parts, and seeds.

Demography and vital rates

This is a relatively short-lived species with considerable population turnover. Overwintering mortality, based on banding returns, averages slightly greater than 50%. Twenty-five percent of band recoveries were alive after year 3, and 4% in year 6 (Tuck 1972, 357). Life expectancy for juveniles is about 1.3 years, and for adults older than 1 year, 1.5 years. The oldest band recovery was of a 12-year-old bird, which is truly exceptional.

Age at first reproduction

Wilson's Snipes breed as yearlings.

Age and sex ratios

Differential distributions of adult and juvenile birds on the wintering grounds (see comments below on wintering habitat use) make it difficult to obtain reliable age ratios. Adults typically linger on the breeding grounds while they complete their postnuptial molt, while juveniles are gregarious and often migrate southward earlier. Based on sample sizes ranging from 159 to 260 in Louisiana, Tuck (1972, 354) documented a male-to-female ratio of 63:37, and an adult-to-juvenile ratio of 58:42. While there is a preponderance of males in most wintering populations, the relatively low proportion of juveniles may indicate that the year these data were collected was a relatively unproductive breeding season. Alternatively, juveniles may have been wintering in other locations. The differential winter habitat use by males and females, as well as by juveniles and adults, makes estimation of population ratios for this species challenging.

Population Status and Trends

According to the Texas Parks and Wildlife Department (2010), the US Fish and Wildlife Service estimate of annual harvest of Wilson's Snipe in Texas is approximately 5,000 birds. Most snipes are hunted in association with waterfowl, and many hunters will bag snipes opportunistically while walking to and from duck blinds and other haunts. Quail and dove hunters in regions such as South Texas can often avail themselves

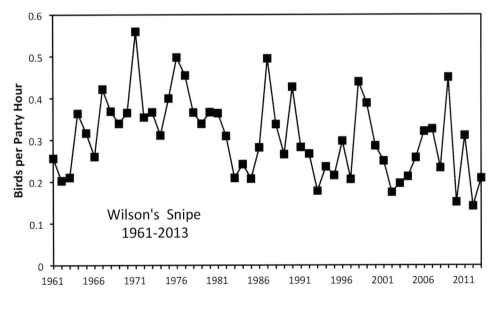

Figure 11.3. Trend in Wilson's Snipe wintering populations in Texas, based on Christmas Bird Count data. Note that while numbers are highly variable from year to year, wintering populations of this species in Texas appear to be stable.

of opportunistically bagging a snipe or two on their way back home after a hunt.

Breeding Bird Survey results for Wilson's Snipe population trends in the United States, based on data from 711 routes from 1966 to 2006, indicate that populations are declining at a rate of 0.25% per year. The probability value associated with this trend estimate indicates that this apparent decline is not statistically different from zero, and thus there is no evidence for a decline in breeding populations of Wilson's Snipe in the United States.

Christmas Bird Count data from 1961 to 2013 also indicate that wintering populations of Wilson's Snipe in Texas are highly variable from year to year but are stable and not declining.

Specific Habitat Requirements

Shallow and often ephemeral wetlands are the most common type of habitat used by Wilson's Snipe year round. Wilson's Snipe typically breeds in peat lands and organic soils in the boreal forest region of North America (Tuck 1972). In the south-central part of their breeding range in Colorado, wetlands containing large amounts of sedges in the genus *Carex* were present in 60% of sampling locations (Johnson and Ryder 1977). In California, at the southwestern extreme of their breeding distribution in North America, bogs and shallow wetlands that contain the sedges *Carex simulata* and *C. rostrata* are particularly important as breeding habitat (McKibben and Hofmann 1985).

Figure 11.4. Wilson's Snipe habitat. Photo credit: Eric Grahmann.

Winter habitat use

McClosky and Thompson (2000) found females more frequently than males in "heavily vegetated" habitats such as coastal marshes and rice fields. Males were more common than females in "open" habitats such as mudflats.

During winter months at locations in Texas, Wilson's Snipe is closely associated with shallow, boggy wetlands that are often ephemeral. In nearby Louisiana, Tuck (1972) documented winter densities ranging from 2.7 birds per acre (about 7 birds per hectare) in rice fields up to nearly 5 birds per acre (about 12 birds per hectare) in coastal marshes. These numbers are the highest densities recorded for this species and may potentially be similar in Texas in such habitats. However, at inland locales, densities of wintering snipes across Texas are certainly much, much lower than in coastal marshes and areas with rice production.

Habitat management

Habitat management is rarely, if ever, directed at influencing Wilson's Snipe abundance. Human activities that actively regulate water flow such as rice cultivation, moist-soil management for waterfowl, and creation of other impoundments are generally considered favorable for this species. Wilson's Snipe has also been known to take up temporary winter residence in flooded grassy yards and on golf courses where areas of shallow standing water are present.

Hunting and Conservation

Annual harvest of Wilson's Snipe in Texas has ranged from a high of nearly 50,000 birds in 2002 to a low of about 3,500 birds in 2008. While there seems to be evidence for a declining trend in annual harvest, there are years such as 1994, 2001, 2002, and 2007 when more than 40,000 birds were bagged. Conversely, there have been several years such as 2003, 2006, 2008, and 2012 when fewer than 10,000 birds were bagged (Purvis 2014).

Texas hunting season length, 2013–2014

The Texas hunting season started on November 2, 2013, and ended on February 16, 2014.

Texas bag limits

The daily bag limit is 8 birds, and the possession bag limit is 24 birds. Hunting is permitted one-half hour before sunrise until sunset.

Geographic restrictions on hunting in Texas

There are no geographic restrictions on snipe hunting in Texas. All 254 counties in Texas are open for hunting Wilson's Snipe. Hunters must be HIP (Harvest Information Program) certified by answering a set of questions when they renew their hunting license, and they must purchase a Texas Migratory Game Bird Hunting Stamp. Wilson's Snipe is hunted in 49 of 50 states and Puerto Rico.

Note that the regulations listed above may change from year to year and are intended to indicate hunting opportunities at the time this book was published.

Research Needs and Priorities

Mueller (1999) noted, "Marshy habitat, cryptic coloration, and crepuscular habits make for remarkably poor knowledge of this common species." Arnold (1994, 117) pointed out that "snipe remain one of the least studied of North American game birds. During 1971–93, only 4 papers were published on the North American subspecies." Note here that the subspecies Arnold is referring to is now considered its own species, the Wilson's Snipe, as mentioned earlier. Nevertheless, Arnold's point is well taken, as it seems that very little research attention has been paid to this species. The relatively recent study by McClosky and Thompson (2000) is a notable exception. Arnold (1994, 123) made four recommendations for management research topics that remain relevant today. Recommendations 2 through 4 are particularly germane to Texas.

1. Implement breeding-ground censuses.

   Conduct hunter surveys in the United States, Canada, and Latin America to assess harvest pressure on migratory and wintering populations.

2. Inventory wintering habitat to identify trends in loss and condition.

Develop techniques to classify age and sex of hunter-harvested birds.

Case and McCool (2009) updated these priorities as follows for the United States, as well as for Canada and Mexico:

1. Implement a national monitoring program.

2. Continue to improve the Harvest Information Program sampling frame.

3. Improve the snipe parts collection survey.

4. Estimate vital rates to support population modeling.

Along with the priorities mentioned above, a reliable estimate of the number of Wilson's Snipes that winter in Texas would be extremely useful for conservation and management of this species.

Literature Cited

Arnold, K. A. 1994. Common Snipe. In *Migratory Shore and Upland Game Birds in North America*, edited by T. C. Tacha and C. E. Braun, 116–25. Washington, DC: International Association of Fish and Wildlife Agencies.

Banks, R. C., C. Cicero, J. L. Dunn, A. W. Kratter, P. Rasmussen, J. V. Remsen Jr., J. D. Rising, and D. F. Stotz. 2002. Forty-third supplement to the America Ornithologists' Union *Check-List of North American Birds. Auk* 119 (3): 897–906.

Case, D. J., and D. C. McCool. 2009. *Priority Information Needs for Rails and Snipe*. Washington, DC: Association of Fish and Wildlife Agencies.

Johnson, B. R., and R. A. Ryder. 1977. Breeding densities and migration periods of the Common Snipe in Colorado. *Wilson Bulletin* 89:116–21.

Leopold, A. S., R. J. Gutiérrez, and M. T. Bronson. 1981. *North American Game Birds and Mammals*. New York: Charles Scribner's Sons

McClosky, J. T., and J. E. Thompson. 2000. Sex-related differences in migration chronology and winter habitat use of the Common Snipe. *Wilson Bulletin* 112:143–48.

McKibben, L. A., and P. Hofmann. 1985. Breeding range and population studies of Common Snipe in California. *California Fish and Game* 71:68–75.

Mueller, H. 1999. Wilson's Snipe (*Gallinago delicata*). In *The Birds of North America Online*, edited by A. Poole. Ithaca, NY: Cornell Laboratory of Ornithology. http://bna.birds.cornell.edu.bnaproxy.birds.cornell.edu/bna/species/417. doi:10.2173/bna.417

Purvis, J. 2014. *Small Game Harvest Survey Results 1994–95 thru 2013–14*. Austin: Texas Parks and Wildlife Department.

Texas Parks and Wildlife Department. 2010. *Webless Migratory Gamebird Strategic Plan: 2011–2015*. Austin: Texas Parks and Wildlife Department.

Tuck. L. M. 1972. *The Snipes: A Study of the Genus* Capella. Canadian Wildlife Service Monograph Series, Number 5. Ottawa: Environment Canada.

American Woodcock

Woodcock prefer thick brushy woods that make for difficult hunting.—LEOPOLD, GUTIÉRREZ, AND BRONSON (1981, 24)

Introduction

The American Woodcock (*Scolopax minor*) is a medium-sized shorebird that breeds and winters in East Texas. Like the Wilson's Snipe, the American Woodcock exhibits reverse sexual dimorphism. Females weigh about 170 g (6.0 oz) and are slightly larger than males, which average 140 g (4.9 oz). Plumage is similar for both males and females. Bill length can be used to determine the sex of a woodcock: birds with a bill longer than 77 mm (about 3 in) are female, and birds with a bill less than 64 mm (about 2.5 in) are male (Mendall and Aldous 1943). The width of the outermost primary wing feather (Greeley 1953) or a combination of primary feather width and bill length (Blankenship 1957) can be used to determine sex in the range where bill lengths (64 to 77 mm, or 2.5 to 3 in) overlap. Whiting and Richardson (2007) claim that sex can be determined by inserting a dollar bill into a woodcock's beak: if the beak is longer than the dollar bill is wide, the bird is a female; otherwise it is a male.

The American Woodcock is one of the most challenging game birds to hunt in the United States. A combination of dense, brushy, forested habitats and explosive zigzag flight behavior make them almost impossible to bag with a shotgun. Nevertheless—or perhaps because of these factors—there is a relatively small but hugely fanatical group of hunters who pursue woodcock in East Texas during the hunting season.

Distribution in Texas

The American Woodcock is distributed across the eastern third of Texas. Winter distribution extends in a wide arc west and south of the breeding distribution. Meaningful density estimates have not been reported for this species in Texas. Straw et al. (1994) reported that the density and extent of American Woodcock abundance in East Texas ranges from "scattered to common" to "common to abundant." Although the green area on the map in figure 12.2 indicates that American Woodcock is a year-round resident in Texas, Whiting and Richardson (2007) assert that hardly any woodcocks are present during July and August in Texas.

Before nesting was documented in Florida (McAuley, Keppie, and Whiting 2013), Texas was thought to be the southernmost nesting location of the American Woodcock (Cain, Whyte, and Micks 1977). East Texas is still the western limit of breeding (McAuley, Keppie, and Whiting 2013). During 1992, there were 5 documented instances of American Woodcock breeding in East Texas. By 2007, there were more than 35

Figure 12.1. American Woodcock. Photo credit: S. J. Lang/VIREO.

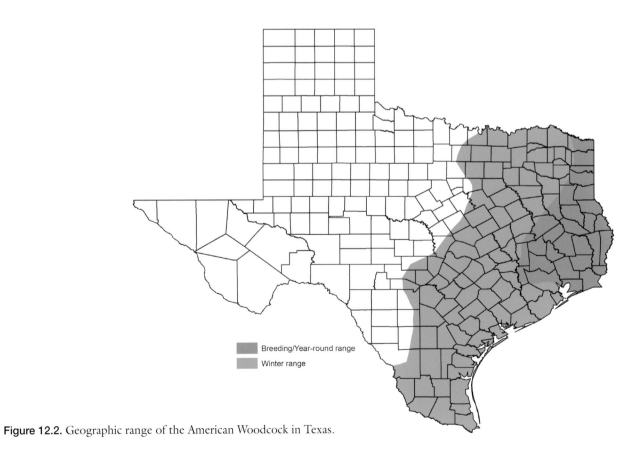

Breeding/Year-round range
Winter range

Figure 12.2. Geographic range of the American Woodcock in Texas.

(Whiting and Richardson 2007), and today American Woodcock breeding in East Texas is almost taken for granted. Whether this represents an expansion of the breeding population or is simply the result of increased survey effort is unknown.

Biology

The landmark monograph by Sheldon (1967) remains the standard reference for the American Woodcock even after nearly 50 years. The *Birds of North America* species account by McAuley, Keppie, and Whiting (2013) and the account in the *Texas Breeding Bird Atlas* by Whiting and Richardson (2007) contain recent updated information on the American Woodcock that is summarized in this section and referenced throughout this chapter.

Migratory routes and timing

The American Woodcock typically arrives in Texas during late October; southward migration is complete by mid-December. West of the Appalachian Mountains, the Mississippi River and associated tributaries are thought to orient migration routes. During warm winters, northward migration may start as early as January, but most birds have moved north by late February. Males may initiate spring migration earlier than females, but both sexes have been documented arriving in Maine at the same time (McAuley, Keppie, and Whiting 2013).

Migration occurs at night, typically in small loose flocks or as single birds. Migration from breeding to wintering grounds takes about 2 to 3 weeks. One bird was recorded flying from Wisconsin to northeast Texas (1406 km, or about 874 miles) in just less than 16 days.

Timing of breeding

American Woodcocks are polygamous; males attempt to attract multiple females as breeding partners. The timing of American Woodcock breeding varies greatly because the birds are distributed across a large north-south latitudinal gradient. In the southern United States, the American Woodcock is one of the earliest-nesting species. Males initiate courtship in December and have established territories by mid-January.

Courtship peaks in mid-February. Egg laying begins as early as mid-January; most nests are initiated in February.

Behavior

Males exhibit spectacular courtship displays, typically at twilight. After making a repeated series of "peent" vocalizations while walking back and forth on the ground, a male will fly in circles or ellipses to an altitude of more than 85 m (275 ft), hover while making a series of chirps, and then fly quickly to the ground in a mostly zigzag pattern, landing in nearly the same spot from which he launched. This display will be repeated every 2 to 3 minutes until darkness falls. Displays resume at dawn for a period of an hour or more.

"Peent" is the most common male vocalization. Others include "tuko," chirping, and cackles during dawn and dusk displays. Females are known to make a catlike sound when trying to distract predators. There is no evidence that females make the "peent" vocalization.

Clutch size and incubation

Clutch size averages 4 eggs. Incubation takes 20–22 days. Precocial chicks can fly 14 days after hatching. Males do not incubate eggs or brood chicks (Sheldon 1967).

Nest losses

Nest losses are poorly documented. Sheldon (1967) listed fire as a major hazard to nests and commented that a reduction in prescribed fires on Martha's Vineyard and Cape Cod probably resulted in a population increase during the first half of the twentieth century. Otherwise, typical predators of ground-nesting birds such as mesomammals, snakes, and house cats are primary factors responsible for nest losses (McAuley, Keppie, and Whiting 2013). Nest success typically ranges from 43% to 50%.

Phenology

Hens brood and care for chicks. Chicks have been documented to gain 5.3 g (0.18 oz) during the first 3 days, then 32.2 g (1.2 oz) in 7 days, and 55 g (2.0 oz) by the end of 14 days (Sheldon 1967). Within a month after hatching, juveniles are almost fully grown and nearly indistinguishable from adults. Most broods disperse within 6 to 8 weeks after hatching.

Diet and foraging

Earthworms (Oligochaeta) of various genera are the primary food of adult American Woodcocks. In the various diet studies summarized by Sheldon (1967), earthworms (Sheldon called them "angleworms") made up from 17% to 86% of the diet by volume, based on stomach analyses. McAuley, Keppie, and Whiting (2013) summarized the contents of 1,446 digestive tracts from 11 different studies and found that 77% of the animal food eaten by American Woodcocks was earthworms. Of plant material ingested, 22% was seeds of grasses and sedges.

Like the Wilson's Snipe, the American Woodcock has a prehensile bill that allows it to apparently "feel" in the soil for the worms that it extracts and consumes. The close relationship between woodcocks and earthworms has important implications for their habitat use and management.

Demography and vital rates

One completed nest is attempted per year, with a clutch that typically contains 4 eggs. Nesting success ranges from 43% to 50%. There is no information about lifetime reproductive success. McAuley, Keppie, and Whiting (2013) estimated approximately 1.5 chicks per female alive at breeding time. Maximum life span is 11 years and 4 months, for a banded female woodcock

in Wisconsin. Survival during winter in southern states (December 15 to February 15) is estimated to be 65% for all age and sex classes combined.

Age at first reproduction

Yearling females breed, and yearling males display on singing grounds the first spring after hatching (McAuley, Keppie, and Whiting 2013).

Age and sex ratios

Age ratios (juvenile to adult) can vary widely. In a summary of more than 30,000 birds from the northern tier of states where American Woodcocks breed, age ratios ranged from 1.1:1 to more than 5:1 juveniles per adult (Sheldon 1967). The average age ratio was slightly more than 2:1, which is the critical threshold for population persistence.

Based on a summary of more than 2,000 birds from 4 studies, sex ratios in American Woodcock populations range from 70 to 86 adult females to males, whereas sex ratios of juvenile females to males are nearly even. Sheldon (1967) attributed this discrepancy to the vulnerability of males to predation during their mating displays.

Population Status and Trends

In Texas, American Woodcock numbers appear to be stable, based on Christmas Bird Count data from 1961 to 2013. In contrast, Straw et al. (1994) showed a shallow but significant declining trend in woodcock

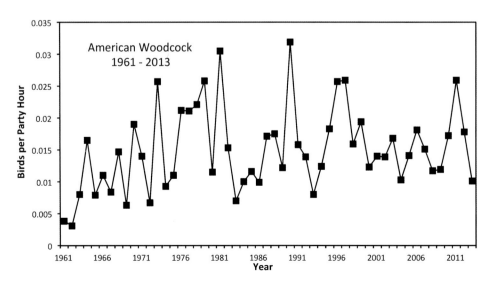

Figure 12.3. Trend in American Woodcock population abundance in Texas, based on Audubon Society Christmas Bird Count data. American Woodcock populations in Texas appear to be stable.

numbers in the eastern and central management zones, based on singing-ground surveys from 1968 to 1993; these declines have continued since that time (McAuley, Keppie, and Whiting 2013).

Specific Habitat Requirements

Young forests with openings and relatively rich organic soils that support abundant earthworm populations typically provide woodcock habitat. Heavy clay soils in the south and acidic boreal forest soils in the north are typically avoided by woodcocks because they lack earthworms. Ground-cover vegetation structure is an extremely important factor that influences whether an area can or cannot support woodcocks. This is because the structure of the ground cover must be sufficiently open to allow the birds to forage for earthworms. Open areas for chick foraging are also essential.

In East Texas, young pine woodlands with openings are essential for male displays. Whiting and Richardson

(2007) noted that during drought, woodcocks will move south and west out of pine woodlands into marshes along the coast of Texas. During periods of drought, woodcocks have also been observed on lawns and in flower beds in suburbs.

Habitat management

Sheldon (1967, 127) called the woodcock the "neglected stepchild of wildlife management." This is because few wildlife agencies undertake direct management of habitat for the woodcock. Additionally, there is a strong belief that the main tactic for woodcock management is harvest regulation.

Typical habitat management actions that seem to enhance woodcock habitat are those that either arrest or set back vegetation succession such as fire, grazing, herbicides, and cutting. The most intensive efforts to manage American Woodcock habitat have been at the Moosehorn National Wildlife Refuge in Maine (USFWS 2015), where this refuge was organized

Figure 12.4. American Woodcock habitat in East Texas. Photo credit: Eric Grahmann.

specifically for this objective. Over the years, managers at Moosehorn have learned that they can manipulate three major habitat components to benefit woodcock: (1) forest clearings for male displays during breeding, (2) dense thickets with rich, moist soil to provide earthworms, and (3) young hardwood (or in Texas, pine) forests that provide nesting and brood cover. Although Maine is a long way from Texas, these three management tactics can be employed to enhance woodcock habitat virtually anywhere within the geographic range of the species.

Hunting and Conservation

Annual American Woodcock harvest estimates in Texas are highly variable, ranging from a high of more than 11,000 birds in 1995 to only about 220 birds in 2000. During most hunting seasons, somewhere between 2,000 and 8,000 birds are bagged in Texas (Purvis 2014).

Texas hunting season length, 2014–2015

The gun season began on December 18, 2014, and ended on January 31, 2015. The falconry season began on January 26 and ended on February 9, 2015.

Texas bag limits

The daily bag limit is three birds, and the possession limit is nine birds.

Geographic restrictions on hunting in Texas

There are no geographic restrictions on hunting in Texas. American Woodcocks can be hunted wherever they are found in all 254 counties of Texas. Hunters must purchase a Migratory Game Bird Hunting Stamp and be HIP (Harvest Information Program) certified.

Research Needs and Priorities

Whiting and Richardson (2007) noted that the extent and distribution of woodcock nesting in Texas is unclear. Thus, a survey to better assess woodcock nesting distribution in East Texas is certainly warranted. Woodcock nesting in Texas was once considered rare (Oberholser 1974), yet a little more than a decade later 35% of the adult hens present in East Texas were

documented nesting (Whiting et al. 1985). The factors that influence American Woodcock nesting in the southern portions of its geographic range are most likely influenced by climate and thus deserve study.

A better understanding of how hunter harvest might or might not influence woodcock populations is also needed. This is especially true for Texas, where wings submitted to the wing-collection survey are often insufficient to estimate harvest (Kelly and Rau 2006).

Literature Cited

Blankenship, L. H. 1957. *Investigations of the American Woodcock in Michigan.* Michigan Department of Conservation Report Number 2123. Lansing, MI.

Cain, B. W., R. J. Whyte, and P. Micks. 1977. Southern nesting record of the American Woodcock. *Bulletin of the Texas Ornithological Society* 10:46.

Greeley, F. 1953. Sex and age studies in fall-shot woodcock (*Philohela minor*). *Journal of Wildlife Management* 17:29–32.

Kelly, J. R., Jr., and R. D. Rau. 2006. *American Woodcock Population Status, 2006.* Laurel, MD: US Fish and Wildlife Service.

Leopold, A. S, R. J. Gutiérrez, and M. T. Bronson. 1981. *North American Game Birds and Mammals.* New York: Charles Scribner's Sons.

McAuley, D., D. M. Keppie, and R. M. Whiting Jr. 2013. American Woodcock (*Scolopax minor*). In *The Birds of North America Online*, edited by A. Poole. Ithaca, NY: Cornell Laboratory of Ornithology. http://bna .birds.cornell.edu.bnaproxy.birds.cornell.edu/bna /species/100/.

Mendall, H. L., and C. M. Aldous. 1943. *The Ecology and Management of the American Woodcock.* Orono: Maine Cooperative Wildlife Research Unit, University of Maine.

Oberholser, H. C. 1974. *The Bird Life of Texas.* Austin: University of Texas Press.

Purvis, J. 2014. *Small Game Harvest Survey Results 1994–95 thru 2013–14.* Austin: Texas Parks and Wildlife Department.

Sheldon, W. G. 1967. *The Book of the American Woodcock.* Amherst: University of Massachusetts Press.

Straw, J. A., Jr., D. G. Kremnitz, M. W. Olinde, and G. F. Speik. 1994. American Woodcock. In *Migratory Shore and Upland Game Bird Management in North America*, edited by T. C. Tacha and C. E. Braun, 97–116. Washington, DC: International Association of Fish and Wildlife Agencies.

USFWS (US Fish and Wildlife Service). 2015. Moosehorn National Wildlife Refuge. Accessed June 15, 2015.

http://www.fws.gov/refuge/Moosehorn/wildlife_and
_habitat/woodcock.html.

Whiting, R. M., Jr., R. R. George, M. K. Causey, and T. H. Roberts. 1985. February hunting of breeding American Woodcock: Breeding implications. *Game Harvest Management*, edited by S. L. Beasom and S. F. Roberson,
309–17. Kingsville, TX: Caesar Kleberg Wildlife Research Institute.

Whiting, R. M., Jr., and S. E. Richardson. 2007. American Woodcock. *Texas Breeding Bird Atlas.* Accessed June 16, 2015. http://txtbba.tamu.edu/species-accounts /american-woodcock/.

13

White-tipped Dove

White-tipped doves are the only species of the genus Leptotila *that occurs in the United States.*
—WAGGERMAN ET AL. (1995, 53)

Introduction

The White-tipped Dove (*Leptotila verreauxi*) is a medium-sized dove that is a popular game bird throughout its extensive geographic range. Adults are 25–31 cm (9.8–12.2 in) long and weigh 145–229.7 g (5.1–8.1 oz). Males and females vary only slightly in body size and in plumage coloration and intensity (Wetmore 1968). The former common name for this species was "White-fronted Dove," which referred to the light-colored forehead (Waggerman et al. 1995). The White-tipped Dove has special attenuated outer primaries on its wings that are similar to those found on the American Woodcock (*Scolopax minor*), another bird that inhabits densely wooded habitats (Leopold 1959). This adaptation allows *Leptotila* doves and woodcocks to maneuver quickly around objects during flight (Leopold 1959; Goodwin 1983) or to attain rapid liftoff from the ground when fleeing predators (Mahler and Tubaro 2001). The characteristic call of this species most often alerts one to their presence. The call, when heard from a distance, is similar to the sound produced by a person blowing across the mouth of an empty glass soft-drink bottle (Waggerman et al. 1995).

Distribution in Texas

The White-tipped Dove occurs from southern Texas through Mexico and Central America to southern South America. Within Texas, White-tipped Doves are common to uncommon residents throughout the South Texas Brush Country to Dimmit, McMullen, and Refugio Counties (Lockwood and Freeman 2004). White-tipped Doves were restricted to counties in the extreme southern tip of Texas during much of the twentieth century (Oberholser 1974), but they expanded their range rapidly during the 1980s and 1990s and are continuing to slowly expand northward (Lockwood and Freeman 2004; Tweit 2007). Recent climate warming may have contributed to this range expansion (Rappole, Blacklock, and Norwine 2007). They have been recorded several times from Calhoun County since 1999, and there have been additional reports from the Edwards Plateau (Val Verde, Real, and Comal Counties) and from Big Bend National Park (Lockwood and Freeman 2004; Brush 2005).

Biology

Despite the White-tipped Dove's extensive geographic distribution and abundance, and its importance as a game bird, little is known about its ecology and

Figure 13.1. White-tipped Dove. Males and females have similar plumage. Photo credit: Larry Ditto.

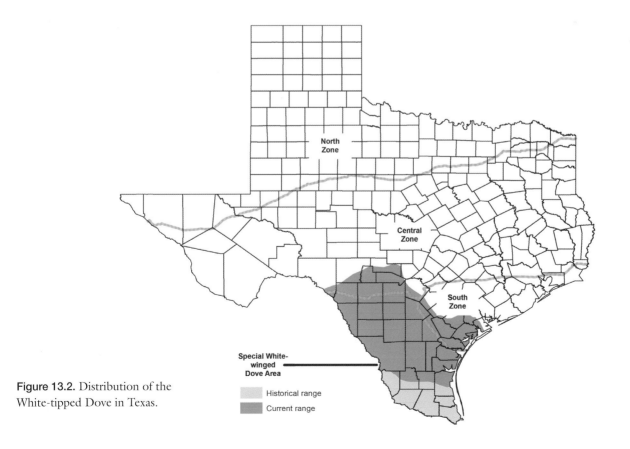

Figure 13.2. Distribution of the White-tipped Dove in Texas.

behavior. In fact, the most intensive field studies of this species have been conducted in southern Texas—the northernmost portion of its range.

Migratory routes and timing

The White-tipped Dove is a permanent resident; no evidence of migration or seasonal movements has been found (Hogan 1999 and references therein).

Timing of breeding

The timing of breeding varies throughout the range, but it can occur throughout the year. Texas populations begin pair formation and courtship in February and March. Nest building begins in February, reaches its peak between April and August, and ends by September (Boydstun 1982).

Behavior

White-tipped Doves are seasonally monogamous. Courtship behaviors observed in White-tipped Doves include allopreening, charging, bow cooing, and flap gliding (Hogan 1999).

> Allopreening. Consists of males and females touching bills and preening each other's neck feathers (Skutch 1964).

> Charging. The male lowers his body and tail horizontally and then walks rapidly toward the female.

> Bow cooing. Often follows charging displays. The male repeatedly raises and lowers his head while cooing (Kaufman 1996). Bow cooing and charging displays often end with the male driving the female toward the nest, which is a common behavior of many species of doves and pigeons (Goodwin 1983).

> Flap gliding. Observed in Mexico and Central America; consists of the male flying upward with 2 to 3 wing flaps and then gliding downward.

Clutch size and incubation

Clutch size is 1–3 eggs, with an average of 2 eggs, which are incubated for about 14 days by both parents (Skutch 1964; Boydstun and DeYoung 1987;

Waggerman et al. 1995). White-tipped Doves occasionally double brood, at least in Texas (Boydstun 1982; Boydstun and DeYoung 1987), but this requires further study. However, this species will attempt to renest after a nest failure (Skutch 1964).

Phenology

Observations of White-tipped Doves in Costa Rica suggest that parents continue to care for their offspring until the young are fully feathered and capable of flight (Skutch 1964). Fledglings leave the nest 12–15 days after hatching and become independent after 4 weeks (Skutch 1964).

Diet and foraging

The diet and foraging behavior of this species are poorly known, but as with most doves and pigeons, its diet consists mostly of seeds and fruit. White-tipped Doves in southern Texas and northeastern Mexico are known to eat seeds of Texas ebony (*Ebenopsis ebano*), cedar elm (*Ulmus crassifolia*), honey mesquite (*Prosopis glandulosa*), various native grasses, and domestic crops such as sunflower, corn, and sorghum. Fruits consumed include those of Texas prickly pear (*Opuntia lindheimeri*), anacua (*Ehretia anacua*), coma (*Bumelia celastrina*), brasil (*Condalia hookeri*), pigeonberry (*Rivina humilis*), spiny hackberry (*Celtis ehrenbergiana*), Texas sugarberry (*C. laevigata*), Texas nightshade (*Solanum triquetrum*), and citrus fruits (Smith 1910; Bent 1932; Oberholser 1974; Boydstun 1982; Waggerman et al. 1995). White-tipped Doves regularly visit bird feeders in the Lower Rio Grande Valley to feed on sunflower, cracked corn, and milo (Keener and Tewes 1994; Brush 2005).

Demography and vital rates

No information is available on survivorship. One banded dove lived 8 years after being banded (Clapp, Klimkiewicz, and Futcher 1983).

Age at first reproduction

Age at first reproduction is unknown.

Age and sex ratios

No information is available on age and sex ratios.

Population Status and Trends

White-tipped Doves are harvested in smaller numbers than either Mourning or White-winged Doves, since becoming a legal game bird in 1984 (Waggerman et al. 1995). The White-tipped Dove harvest has been relatively stable, with approximately 5,000 birds harvested annually in Texas (Texas Parks and Wildlife Department 2010). Limited information is available on abundance or population trends. Coo-count surveys conducted by the TPWD indicate that the White-tipped Dove population was relatively stable between 1983 and 1993 (Waggerman et al. 1995). Christmas Bird Count data from 1961 to 2013 indicate that White-tipped Dove populations in southern Texas are relatively stable and have increased slightly since 1999 (fig. 13.3).

Specific Habitat Requirements

White-tipped Doves utilize the same type of habitat throughout the year. Plant composition of habitats used by White-tipped Doves varies throughout their range, but habitat structure is generally the same—dense, tangled thickets of woody vegetation. White-tipped Doves were formerly restricted to native riparian habitat composed of Texas ebony, honey mesquite, retama (*Parkinsonia aculeata*), huisache (*Acacia farnesiana*), cedar elm, Texas sugarberry, and spiny hackberry that grew along the Rio Grande

and associated resacas (Bent 1932; Oberholser 1974; Boydstun 1982; Boydstun and DeYoung 1988). Texas ebony and spiny hackberry are heavily used as nest sites (Hayslette, Tacha, and Waggerman 2000). About 95% of the native vegetation of the Lower Rio Grande Valley was cleared during the twentieth century (Jahrsdoerfer and Leslie 1988). However, this does not seem to have adversely affected White-tipped Doves, as they have now become common nesting species in citrus groves and suburban areas, provided that dense patches of woody vegetation are available (Boydstun and DeYoung 1985; Waggerman et al. 1995; Brush 2005). Native grasslands have declined and dense woody brush has become more common in coastal southern Texas during the twentieth century as a result of overgrazing and fire suppression (Johnston 1963), which may have played a role in the range expansion of the White-tipped Dove. White-tipped Doves in Central and South America inhabit open and disturbed woodlands, brushy clearings, orchards, coffee and banana plantations, and gardens (Hogan 1999 and references therein).

Habitat management

No specific habitat management for White-tipped Doves is undertaken in Texas. The greatest threat to maintaining sustainable populations of White-tipped Doves is the decreasing availability of native brush and woodland habitat. Much of the surviving native brush habitat in the Lower Rio Grande Valley is now

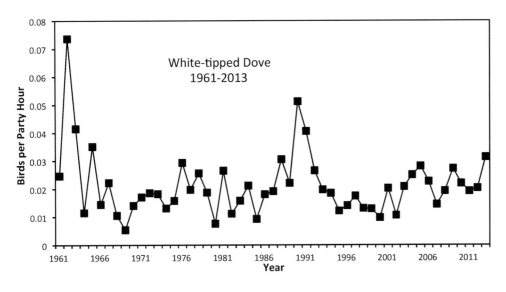

Figure 13.3. Trends in White-tipped Dove populations in Texas, based on Christmas Bird Count data. Although numbers vary from year to year, populations appear to be stable.

Figure 13.4. White-tipped Dove habitat in South Texas. Photo credit: Damon Williford.

protected as a series of state parks, wildlife management areas, and wildlife refuges (US Fish and Wildlife Service 1983; Waggerman et al. 1995). Hayslette, Tacha, and Waggerman (2000) recommended that wooded areas dominated by Texas ebony and Texas sugarberry should be given high priority for preservation and restoration, as White-tipped, White-winged, and Mourning Doves favor these two tree species as nest sites. Nesting habitat plantings for White-tipped Doves must reach over 3 m (10 ft) in height and should strive to provide more than 70% canopy cover (Hayslette, Tacha, and Waggerman 2000).

Hunting and Conservation

Texas hunting season length

White-tipped Doves occur mostly in the South Zone. The first hunting season lasts from about September 19 to October 20, and the second season from about December 19 to January 25. White-tipped Doves can also be taken during the Special White-winged Dove Season, which occurs during the first two weekends of September. The highest White-tipped Dove harvest estimate was about 270,000 birds (2009), and the lowest was about 144,000 birds (2006; Purvis 2014).

Texas bag limits

The daily bag limit is two birds per bag.

Geographic restrictions on hunting in Texas

There are no geographic restrictions on hunting in Texas. Dove hunters must complete the Harvest Information Program (HIP) questionnaire when they renew their hunting licenses. Dove hunters must also purchase the Texas Migratory Game Bird Hunting Stamp.

Research Needs and Priorities

White-tipped Doves are one of the least studied columbids in North America. Research priorities have been outlined by Waggerman et al. (1995) and Hogan (1999), but little research is currently underway. Basic research needs for White-tipped Doves include the following:

1. Research is needed on basic life history questions such as annual productivity, nesting success, molt, food habits, bioenergetics, water requirements, specific habitat use, ecological interactions with other species of doves and pigeons, predation, and parasites and disease.

2. Studies on the systematic relationships among the White-tipped Dove subspecies and other *Leptotila* species are needed. The White-tipped Dove exhibits geographic variation in eye-ring coloration and habitat use throughout its range (Hogan 1999). Although the *Leptotila* species and subspecies closely resemble one another, Hogan (1999) suggested that these taxa may be similar to deer mice (*Peromyscus* spp.) in that highly similar species, subspecies, and populations may have very different evolutionary histories. A range-wide genetic analysis using nuclear and mitochondrial DNA sequences of the White-tipped Dove that incorporates all subspecies and representatives of congeners is needed to resolve *Leptotila* systematics and provide insight into the ecological factors leading to speciation. Greater understanding of how genetic diversity and variation is distributed among populations of White-tipped Doves would help managers develop specific management strategies to protect genetically distinct populations.

Management research needs at the state level include the following:

1. An active banding program for White-tipped Doves is needed to provide information on survival and harvest rates.

2. Call-count surveys conducted in the Lower Rio Grande Valley for White-tipped Doves need to be expanded to the rest of southern Texas.

Waggerman et al. (1995) suggested that this could be accomplished with slight modifications to the Mourning Dove call-count routes.

Literature Cited

Bent, A. C. 1932. *Life Histories of North American Gallinaceous Birds.* US National Museum Bulletin 162. Washington, DC: Smithsonian Institution.

Boydstun, C. P. 1982. Evaluations of the current status of White-fronted Doves in South Texas. Master's thesis, Texas A&I University–Kingsville.

Boydstun, C. P., and C. A. DeYoung. 1985. Distribution and relative abundance of White-tipped Doves in South Texas. *Southwestern Naturalist* 30:565–71.

———. 1987. Nesting success of White-tipped Doves in South Texas. *Journal of Wildlife Management* 33:365–67.

———. 1988. Movements of White-tipped Doves in southern Texas. *Southwestern Naturalist* 33:365–67.

Brush, T. 2005. *Nesting Birds of a Tropical Frontier: The Lower Rio Grande Valley of Texas.* College Station: Texas A&M University Press.

Burger, J. 1992. Drinking, vigilance, and group size in White-tipped Doves and Common Ground-Doves in Costa Rica. *Wilson Bulletin* 104:357–59.

Clapp, R. B., M. K. Klimkiewicz, and A. G. Futcher. 1983. Longevity records of North American birds: Columbidae through Paridae. *Journal of Field Ornithology* 54:123–37.

Goodwin, D. 1983. *Pigeons and Doves of the World.* Ithaca, NY: Cornell University Press.

Hayslette, S. E., T. C. Tacha, and G. L. Waggerman. 2000. Factors affecting White-winged, White-tipped, and Mourning Dove reproduction in Lower Rio Grande Valley. *Journal of Wildlife Management* 64:286–95.

Hogan, K. M. 1999. White-tipped Dove (*Leptotila verreauxi*). In *The Birds of North America Online,* edited by A. Poole. Ithaca, NY: Cornell Laboratory of Ornithology. http://bna.birds.cornell.edu.bnaproxy.birds.cornell.edu/bna/search?SearchableText=White-tipped+dove.

Jahrsdoerfer, S. E., and D. M. Leslie Jr. 1988. *Tamaulipan Brushland of the Lower Rio Grande Valley of Texas: Description, Human Impacts, and Management Options.* Biological Report 88. Washington, DC: US Fish and Wildlife Service.

Johnston, M. C. 1963. Past and present grasslands of southern Texas and northeastern Mexico. *Ecology* 44:456–66.

Kaufman, K. 1996. *Lives of North American Birds.* Boston: Houghton Mifflin.

Keener, J. M., and M. E. Tewes. 1994. Seed preferences of nongame birds in the Rio Grande Valley. *Proceedings of the Annual Conference of the Southeastern Association of Fish and Wildlife Agencies* 48:302–9.

Leopold, A. S. 1959. *Wildlife of Mexico*. Berkeley: University of California Press.

Lockwood, M. W., and B. Freeman. 2004. *The TOS Handbook of Texas Birds*. College Station: Texas A&M University Press.

Mahler, B., and P. L. Tubaro. 2001. Attenuated outer primaries in pigeons and doves: A comparative test fails to support the flight performance hypothesis. *Condor* 103:449–54.

Oberholser, H. C. 1974. *The Bird Life of Texas*. Austin: University of Texas Press.

Purvis, J. 2014. *Small Game Harvest Survey Results 1994–95 thru 2013–14*. Austin: Texas Parks and Wildlife Department.

Rappole, J. H., G. W. Blacklock, and J. Norwine. 2007. Apparent rapid range change in South Texas birds: Response to climate change? In *The Changing Climate of South Texas 1900–2100: Problems and Prospects, Impacts and Implications*, edited by J. Norwine and K. John, 133–45. Kingsville: CREST-RESSACA, Texas A&M University–Kingsville.

Skutch, A. F. 1964. Life histories of Central American pigeons. *Wilson Bulletin* 76:211–47.

Smith, A. P. 1910. Miscellaneous bird notes from the Lower Rio Grande Valley. *Condor* 12:93–103.

Texas Parks and Wildlife Department. 2010. *Webless Migratory Game Bird Strategic Plan 2011–2015*. Austin: Texas Parks and Wildlife Department.

Tweit, R. C. 2007. White-tipped Dove. *The Texas Breeding Bird Atlas*. College Station: Texas A&M University System. http://txtbba.tamu.edu/species-accounts/white-tipped-dove.

US Fish and Wildlife Service. 1983. *Department of the Interior Land Protection Plan: Lower Rio Grande Valley National Wildlife Refuge in Cameron, Hidalgo, Starr, and Willacy Counties, Texas*. Albuquerque, NM: US Fish and Wildlife Service Region 2.

Waggerman, G. L., G. E. Homestad, R. R. George, and W. A. Shifflett. 1995. In *Migratory Shore and Upland Game Bird Management in North America*, edited by T. C. Tacha and C. E. Braun, 53–59. Washington, DC: International Association of Fish and Wildlife Agencies.

Wetmore, A. 1968. The birds of the Republic of Panama, Part 2, Columbidae (Pigeons) to Picidae (Woodpeckers). *Smithsonian Miscellaneous Collections* 150:37–40.

14

Mourning Dove

The mourning dove is an important game species in the southern half of the United States. It withstands heavy shooting, yet it continues to be abundant and widespread.—LEOPOLD, GUTIÉRREZ, AND BRONSON (1981, 26)

Introduction

The Mourning Dove (*Zenaida macroura*) is a medium-sized dove that is hunted throughout most (36 states) of the United States. Adults are approximately 30.48 cm (12 in) long, with a wingspan of 127–145 cm (50–57 in), and weigh 108–130 g (3.8–4.6 oz). Body measurements and weights vary by sex, with males being larger and heavier, and geographically, with *Z. m. carolinensis* of the eastern United States being the largest of the five subspecies (Otis et al. 2008). The name "Mourning Dove" originates from its mournful-sounding song, which is heard frequently during the spring and summer.

Distribution in Texas

The Mourning Dove is a common to abundant breeding and winter resident throughout Texas (Lockwood and Freeman 2004). The breeding range of the Mourning Dove includes all of the 48 contiguous states in the United States, southern Canada (British Columbia, Saskatchewan, Alberta, Manitoba, Ontario, and Quebec), and most of Mexico. Populations north of the 39th parallel are migratory. For management purposes, the US Fish and Wildlife Service (USFWS)

divided the US breeding range into three management units. The Eastern Management Unit (EMU) includes populations east of the Mississippi River, the Central Management Unit (CMU) includes populations west of the Mississippi River and east of the Rocky Mountains, and the Western Management Unit (WMU) includes all populations west of the Rocky Mountains.

Biology

The standard reference for the biology and management of the Mourning Dove is Baskett et al. (1993). Other comprehensive references for the Mourning Dove include Keeler et al. (1977), Tomlinson et al. (1995), and Otis et al. (2008). Much of the information presented in this chapter is summarized from these 4 references.

Migratory routes and timing

Baskett et al. (1993) provide an excellent overview of Mourning Dove migration. Upon becoming independent of their parents, immature Mourning Doves band together in flocks and, beginning in June, may wander over large areas in search of food and water, sometimes north of their natal areas. During late summer these flocks swell from the addition of adults that have

Figure 14.1. Mourning Dove. Photo credit: Greg Lasley.

Figure 14.2. Year-round distribution of the Mourning Dove in Texas. Most of the Mourning Doves that breed in Texas winter here as well. Texas is also a major wintering area for Mourning Doves from the eastern and central United States and provides important stopover habitats for spring and fall migrants.

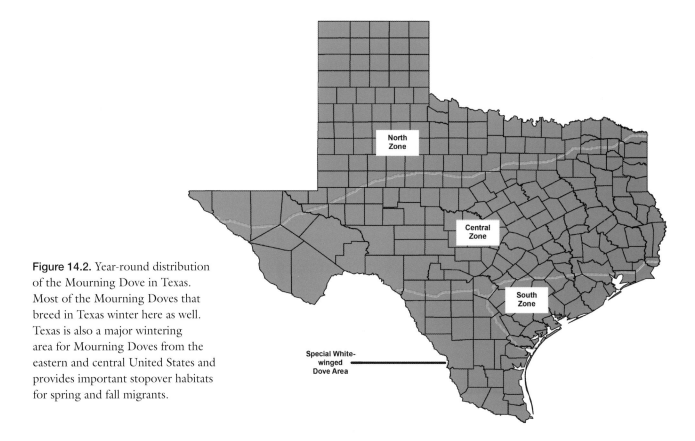

finished nesting. These apparently random movements continue until mid-August, when migration begins. Mourning Doves migrate during both the day and night, usually at low altitudes, and average about 30–55 km (19–34 mi) per day. Autumn-migrating Mourning Doves from the northern states begin to arrive in Texas in September and October (Dunks et al. 1982). Band recovery studies indicate that the majority of Mourning Doves that breed in Texas also winter here, but Texas also serves as an important wintering area for northern Mourning Doves and as a resting and staging area for doves headed farther south into Mexico (Dunks et al. 1982; Baskett et al. 1993). Forty-one percent of the harvest in Texas consists of immigrant doves from the EMU and the CMU. Most immigrant Mourning Doves in Texas derive from the CMU, with a smaller contribution from the EMU, whereas few doves from the WMU spend the winter in Texas. Spring migration is not as well studied as fall migration, but it apparently begins in March and ends by mid- or late May, terminating in southern areas sooner than in northern areas.

Timing of breeding

The breeding season of the Mourning Dove is one of the longest of any North American bird (Baskett et al. 1993). It has been recorded breeding during all months in Texas, although most breeding takes place from March to September (Tweit 2007).

Behavior

Mourning Doves are seasonally monogamous and may re-pair for subsequent breeding seasons. Mourning Doves exhibit several distinct courtship behaviors including "perch cooing," "flap gliding," and "bow cooing," as well as charging and allopreening (Baskett et al. 1993; Otis et al. 2008).

Perch cooing. Main advertisement behavior of male Mourning Doves. Consists of a double-syllable coo followed by 2–3 louder coos (*coo-oo, OO, OO, OO*), during which the male arches his neck, puffs out his throat, stiffens his body, and bobs his tail at each note. Females occasionally utter a fainter version, but the significance is unknown (Frankel and Baskett 1961).

Flap gliding. An advertising behavior in which the male leaves his perch while vigorously flapping his wings and clapping them loudly. The tips of the wings touch underneath the body during the exaggerated wingbeats. The male may fly to a height of over 30 m (98 ft). The male then extends his wings and keeps them motionless during the subsequent long, spiraling glide that terminates when he lands on the same or a different perch.

Bow cooing. The male bows his head and body until his head nearly touches the ground (up to 10 times). He then rises to an erect position, holds his head forward, and gives a loud coo. The female may react by flying away (usually the male follows), ignoring the male and continuing to feed or preen, pecking at the male, or permitting copulation.

Charging. The male approaches the female with his body raised, head held horizontally forward, and tail held horizontally back.

Allopreening. Consists of gentle nibbling of head and neck feathers with the beak, and usually occurs during pair formation, nest-site selection, nest construction, nest exchanges, and prior to copulation.

Clutch size and incubation

Both parents care for the eggs and young. Clutch size is usually 2 eggs. Reports of 3–4 eggs may be the result of dump nesting by other females, a behavior that occurs with some regularity in Mourning Doves (Weeks and Weeks 1980). Incubation lasts for 14–15 days. Male and female parents share incubation responsibilities.

Phenology

Brooding and feeding is shared by both the male and female. Brooding of chicks is constant for 4–5 days, but by the sixth or seventh day nestlings will be left unattended for long periods. Night brooding stops at 9–10 days, and brooding decreases rapidly at 12–15 days.

Nestlings are fed with regurgitated pigeon milk for the first 3–4 days. Beginning on the fifth or sixth day, the parents will also feed the young regurgitated seeds.

Seeds gradually replace pigeon milk. The female is responsible for most of the feeding of chicks for 4–15 days after hatching, while the male takes on most of the feeding duties beginning 12 days after hatching. Fledging normally occurs 13–15 days after hatching but may occur as early as 9 days after hatching. Fledglings are independent by 30 days after hatching.

Diet and foraging

Mourning Doves are primarily granivorous ground foragers that consume seeds of agricultural crops as well as wild grasses, forbs, shrubs, and trees. Most food habit studies are based on the examination of crops of harvested Mourning Doves. The most abundant items found in dove crops are often assumed to be the preferred foods; however, these studies often do not include data on food availability. Without this information, it is not possible to determine whether a food item was consumed in large quantities because it was preferred or simply because it was the appropriate size and readily available (Baskett et al. 1993). Food selection studies have shown that Mourning Doves are highly selective feeders (Browning 1959; Davison and Sullivan 1963; Stickney 1967; Hayslette and Mirarchi 2001). There are only a few food habit studies of Mourning Doves in Texas, and food selection studies in wild Mourning Doves have been restricted largely to the southeastern United States (Baskett et al. 1993). Agricultural crops documented in the diets of Mourning Doves include sunflowers, corn, wheat, grain sorghum, millet, buckwheat, barley, and peanuts. Mourning Doves also readily consume the seeds of signal grasses (*Brachiaria* spp.), bristlegrasses (*Setaria* spp.), bluegrasses (*Poa* spp.), paspalum grasses (*Paspalum* spp.), spurges (*Croton* spp.), lambsquarters (*Chenopodium album*), saltbushes (*Atriplex* spp.), common sunflower (*Helianthus annuus*) and other composites, ragweeds (*Ambrosia* spp.), pokeweed (*Phytolacca americana*), prickly poppies (*Argemone* spp.), pigweeds (*Amaranthus* spp.), smartweeds (*Polygonum* spp.), hemp (*Cannabis sativa*), mustards (*Brassica* spp.), and pines (*Pinus* spp.). In addition to the food items listed above, Mourning Doves in Texas are also known to consume Johnson grass (*Sorghum halepense*), panic grasses (*Panicum* spp.), verbena (*Verbena* spp.), caltrops (*Kallstroemia* spp.), noseburn (*Tragia* spp.), stillingia (*Stillingia* spp.), spurges (*Euphorbia* spp.), prickly ash (*Xanthoxylum* spp.), rye (*Secale cereale*), and chestnutleaf false croton (*Caperonia castaneifolia*) (Dillon 1961).

Demography and vital rates

The Mourning Dove is a relatively short-lived species, with high population turnover. Long-term banding studies have shown that annual mortality and survival rates vary geographically and with age (Otis et al. 2008). Adult annual mortality rates range from 56% to 66% in the EMU, 45% to 57% in the CMU, and 54% to 63% in the WMU, while mortality rates for immature doves range from 66% to 74% in the EMU, 56% to 68% in the CMU, and 67% to 70% in the WMU. Overall, survival probabilities are greater for northern-latitude breeding populations than for those in southern latitudes, and they are greater for adults than for immatures. There is currently no evidence of significantly different mortality rates among males and females. Average life span for adults is about 1.5 years, and about 1 year for immatures (Tomlinson and Dolton 1987), but individual Mourning Doves have been recorded living 10 years or more, with the longevity record being 19.3 years (Clapp, Klimkiewicz, and Futcher 1983).

Age at first reproduction

Most Mourning Doves first breed at 1 year old. Males are sexually mature at 80 days and females at 90 days (White, Mirarchi, and Lisano 1987). Because of rapid sexual maturity, it is possible for a Mourning Dove to begin breeding during its hatch year. Whether hatch-year birds attempt to breed depends on the time of year they reach sexual maturity, as there must be sufficient day length (about 31–32 hours) to stimulate reproductive responses (White, Mirarchi, and Lisano 1987), and it is further influenced by food resources and weather (Brown 1967; Armbuster 1983). The number of hatch-year birds contributing to recruitment is probably negligible (Otis et al. 2008).

Age and sex ratios

The age of an individual bird can be determined by examination of the wings (Ruos and Tomlinson 1968). Buff or cream-colored tips on primary wing coverts indicate a juvenile bird that was produced during the spring prior to the current hunting season. Wings of harvested Mourning Doves can be classified as hatch-year (juveniles) or after-hatch-year (adults). Some states collected wings from 2005 to 2007 to determine the fall age structure of their Mourning Dove populations (Miller and Otis 2010; Seamans and Sanders 2014). The USFWS in 2007 initiated a national effort to collect Mourning Dove wings to determine age ratios in each management unit and state (Seamans and Sanders 2014). Based on birds harvested from 2007 to 2013, Mourning Dove age ratios in the 3 management units were 1.51 (EMU), 1.05 (CMU), and 1.21 (WMU) (Seamans and Sanders 2014).

Sex ratios (males per 100 females) vary geographically within each management unit, from equal numbers of males and females (100:100) in Illinois to male-biased ratios as high as 433:100 in Arkansas (Baskett et al. 1993). Sex ratios vary monthly and seasonally as well as geographically, but most ratios tend to be skewed toward males (Baskett et al. 1993).

Population Status and Trends

The Mourning Dove is one of the most common bird species in North America. Among 251 avian species, the Mourning Dove ranked eleventh in relative abundance throughout its distribution (Droege and Sauer 1990). In terms of numbers of birds harvested and person-days of recreation provided, the Mourning Dove is the most important game bird in the United States and in Texas (Baskett et al. 1993; Texas Parks and Wildlife Department 2010). Prior to the hunting season, the US population estimate for Mourning Doves was 274 million (Seamans and Sanders 2014). Over 14 million Mourning Doves were harvested in the United States during the 2013–2014 hunting season, with more than 6 million harvested in the EMU, more than 5.9 million in the CMU, and more than 1.8 million in the WMU (Seamans and Sanders 2014). In Texas, more than 3.5 million Mourning Doves were harvested in the 2013–2014 hunting season.

The Mourning Dove population is monitored by the US Fish and Wildlife Service using Breeding Bird Surveys (BBS), and formerly by Call Count Surveys (CCS). The CCS was developed to provide an annual index of abundance (i.e., relative abundance; Baskett et al. 1993). The CCS was conducted from 1966 to 2013 but was abandoned because the harvest strategy adopted for Mourning Doves in 2013 relied on absolute abundance estimates. BBS and CCS often produced conflicting results because of differences in sample sizes and methodology (Sauer, Dolton, and Droege 1994; Sauer et al. 2010). BBS data suggest that the population declined in the United States and Canada by 0.52% per year from 1966 to 2012 (Sauer et al. 2014). The overall negative population trend is probably a result of population declines in the CMU and WMU, although BBS indicated that the EMU population increased (Seamans and Sanders 2014).

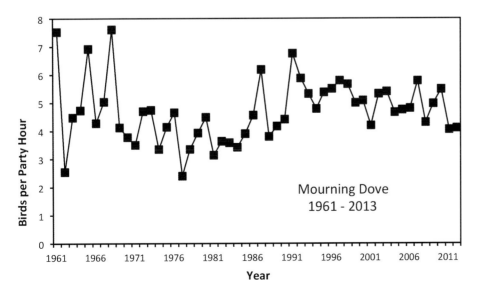

Figure 14.3. Trend in Mourning Dove wintering populations in Texas, based on Christmas Bird Count data. Note that while numbers are highly variable from year to year, wintering Mourning Dove populations in Texas have been fairly stable since 1992 and are higher than they were in the 1970s and 1980s.

Figure 14.4. *(Top)*, Mourning Dove habitat in grassy pasture. Photo credit: Damon Williford. *(Bottom)*, Mourning Dove habitat in field of croton. Photo credit: Eric Grahmann.

In Texas, the Mourning Dove population declined by 1.36% per year from 1966 to 2012. BBS does not usually include urban areas, which may contain important populations of Mourning Doves (Otis et al. 2008). In contrast, Christmas Bird Count data indicate that the Mourning Dove population in Texas has been relatively stable since 1992.

Specific Habitat Requirements

The Mourning Dove benefited greatly from the alteration of original North American vegetation by European settlers. Specifically, these doves benefited from the thinning of woodlands and the creation of open areas in forests, the conversion of prairies to farmland for cereal grain production, the creation of stock ponds, and the planting of shelterbelts (Basket et al. 1993; Tomlinson et al. 1995; Otis et al. 2008). Mourning Doves utilize a wide range of habitats for nesting but generally avoid extensive forests and use open woodlands and forest-prairie edges as well as agricultural, urban, and surburban areas (Basket et al. 1993; Hayslette, Tacha, and Waggerman 2000; Otis et al. 2008). Hayslette, Tacha, and Waggerman (2000) found that Mourning Doves in the Lower Rio Grande Valley of Texas nested in a broader range of habitats than did White-tipped and White-winged Doves. Mourning Doves in the Lower Rio Grande Valley nested in woodlots, parks, and citrus orchards with nearly equal frequency, with smaller numbers nesting in brushlands or shrublands (Hayslette, Tacha, and Waggerman 2000). Habitats used in winter and migration are similar to breeding habitat (Otis et al. 2008).

Habitat management

Landowners and wildlife scientists have not usually managed land for Mourning Doves because of their migratory nature and historical abundance; however, this has changed as a result of the decline of Mourning Dove populations in some areas and the increasing economic value of dove hunting (Taylor et al. 2006). The guidelines below are based on George (1988) and Taylor et al. (2006), who provide general recommendations for improving and managing land for Mourning Doves in Texas. The Texas Parks and Wildlife Department (TPWD) offers specific recommendations on its website for managing Mourning Dove habitat in the Panhandle, Post Oak Savannah, and Blackland Prairie. Baskett et al. (1993) include a detailed chapter on the management of fields for Mourning Dove shooting.

Mourning Doves require open areas for feeding that support seed-producing plants such as sunflowers, croton, and native grasses, brushy or wooded areas for nesting and loafing, and water for drinking; however, little research has been done to determine the best habitat management strategies for Mourning Doves. Although food plots can be planted for Mourning Doves, waste grain left over from harvesting and native and naturalized plants are the least expensive and most easily implemented method of providing food (George 1988). Soil disturbance from disking and plowing stimulates the growth of grasses and forbs that doves consume as food, but such action must be undertaken before the spring plant growth begins. Clean farming techniques, which involve the plowing under of field stubble and weedy vegetation after the completion of harvesting, rob Mourning Doves of important foraging areas, and these methods should be abandoned if farmland is to be managed for doves. Mourning Doves drink twice a day, in midmorning and late evening, and prefer to visit sources of water that are open and free of vegetation that might conceal predators. Any permanent or temporary water source can be improved for Mourning Doves by removing rank vegetation so as to produce a bare landing area 9–15 m (30–50 feet) from the water's edge (George 1988).

Hunting and Conservation

Texas hunting seasons

Dove hunting season varies in timing and length throughout Texas. The TPWD divides Texas into three dove hunting zones: North, Central, and South (fig. 14.2). The North Zone is that portion of Texas north of a line from Fort Hancock to Texarkana. The South Zone is that portion of Texas south of a line from Del Rio to Orange. The Central Zone is that portion of Texas between the North and South Zones. Hunters should consult the current Texas Parks and Wildlife Outdoor Annual for an exact description of these zones. Each zone has two separate hunting seasons for doves. The first hunting season in the North and Central Zones lasts from early September to late October, and the second starts in late December and ends in early January. The first South Zone hunting season lasts from late September to late October and the second from late December to late January. Hunting can begin one-half hour before sunrise and can continue until sunset.

A special season for the White-winged Doves takes place in the western portion of the South Zone, during which Mourning Doves may also be taken. The Special White-winged Dove Area is that portion of the South Zone west of a line from San Antonio to Corpus Christi. Hunters should consult the current Texas Parks and Wildlife Outdoor Annual for an exact description of this area. The Special White-winged Dove Season takes place on the first two weekends of September. Hunting begins at noon and continues until sunset.

Texas bag limits

For normal hunting seasons, the daily bag limit is 15 Mourning, White-winged, and White-tipped Doves in aggregate, to include not more than two White-tipped Doves. The possession limit is three times the daily bag limit. The daily bag limit for the Special White-winged Dove Season is 15 White-winged, Mourning, and White-tipped Doves in aggregate, to include not more than two Mourning Doves and two White-tipped Doves.

Geographic restrictions on hunting in Texas

Although the timing of the hunting seasons varies in Texas, Mourning Doves are currently hunted throughout the state. Dove hunters must complete the Harvest Information Program (HIP) questionnaire when they renew their hunting licenses. Dove hunters must also purchase the Texas Migratory Game Bird Hunting Stamp.

Research Needs and Priorities

The Mourning Dove is a relatively well-studied species, but several unanswered questions still present challenges for its management, especially in light of

the ongoing declines in the CMU and WMU. The exact cause or causes of the ongoing declines in the CMU and WMU are still unknown. Potential causes that have been suggested include changes in farming practices and crops grown, urbanization, increased hunting pressure, pesticides, parasites and diseases, and competition with other avian species (Baskett et al. 1993). Investigation of all aspects of Mourning Dove biology will be necessary in order to stop and reverse ongoing population declines. Baskett et al. (1993) and Otis et al. (2008) provide an extensive list of research needs, which is summarized below.

1. Statistical and predictive models that incorporate annual survival rates, harvest rates, hunting regulations, and annual recruitment as a function of physiographic region, land use, and climate are needed to improve harvest management. To do this, improved survey methods for the estimation of abundance and age and sex ratios are needed as well as additional studies of regional differences in recruitment and standardization of the collection of harvest data.

2. Study of urban and suburban Mourning Dove populations is needed to estimate the relative contributions of both to regional population densities and harvest.

3. Additional hunting occurs in Mexico and Central America, but Mourning Doves are poorly studied in these regions. Studies of the population dynamics of winter populations in Mexico and Central America are needed to better understand the impact of hunting on total and regional populations. Abundance estimates for Mourning Doves from Mexico and Central America are also lacking.

4. Evaluation of long-term sustainability of breeding populations under differing levels of hunting pressure is needed.

5. Although fall migration of Mourning Doves is well understood, spring migration is poorly studied. Aspects of spring migration that need study include the exact timing of its start, end, and duration; habitat use; and whether the routes used in spring are identical to those taken in fall migration.

6. Life history attributes of migratory and nonmigratory populations are lacking.

7. The Eurasian Collared-Dove (*Streptopelia decaocto*) was initially viewed as a potential threat to Mourning Doves as an aggressive competitor for the same food resources. However, Poling and Hayslette (2006) concluded that despite a high degree of dietary overlap, negative impacts on Mourning Doves by Eurasian Collared-Doves may be less than previously hypothesized. This may be because both species are generalist granivores and food resources may be abundant throughout the year, collared-doves may use alternative foods when in the presence of other dove species, and home-range sizes and habitat preferences may limit overlap in food resources (Poling and Hayslette 2006). Although Eurasian Collared-Doves can be aggressive toward native bird species, Mourning Doves have also been recorded chasing Eurasian Collared-Doves away from food resources (Poling and Hayslette 2006). Fronimos (2011) suggests that in urban settings access to feeding stations by Mourning Doves may be limited because of aggression from larger White-winged Doves and Great-tailed Grackles (*Quiscalus mexicanus*). Competition for food resources between Mourning Doves and White-winged Doves requires additional study. Eurasian Collared-Doves and Mourning and White-winged Doves may also compete for nesting and roosting sites, but studies are currently lacking.

8. Assessment of the relative importance of specific causes of nest failure and fledgling mortality is also needed, as well as estimates of temporal and spatial variation in the number of nesting attempts per season and the contribution of this to recruitment.

9. Impacts of pesticides on Mourning Dove mortality and reproductive success should be studied.

10. Little is known about the impact of parasites and pathogens on Mourning Dove populations. The protozoan *Trichomonas gallinae* heavily parasitizes White-winged Doves. The expansion of White-winged Doves may represent a threat to Mourning Doves, as increased contact between the two species may lead to higher rates of trichomoniasis in Mourning Doves (Conti and Forrester 1981). However, studies of Mourning Doves in Fillmore, Utah, indicated that trichomoniasis was not a factor in population declines in the area (Ostrand, Bissonette, and Conover 1995). Pathogens and parasites can have a significant impact on isolated or stressed populations, and additional data are required to determine the impact of infectious diseases in each of the three management units.

11. Detailed studies of how changes in land use during the last 100 years have affected Mourning Dove abundance and distribution are needed to formulate plans to improve habitat in management units. It is generally agreed that the conversion of grasslands to farmland and the thinning and opening of forests in the late nineteenth and early twentieth centuries benefited Mourning Doves (Baskett et al. 1993). Little research has focused on how new clean farming techniques, changes in crops grown, and urbanization have impacted Mourning Doves.

12. Finally, it is necessary to assess how habitat management strategies affect local populations. The wide distribution of the Mourning Dove suggests that optimal habitat management strategies will vary regionally, as they do in other widespread species such as the Northern Bobwhite (*Colinus virginianus*; Guthery 2000; Brennan 2007).

Literature Cited

Armbuster, M. J. 1983. Analysis of behavior in various components of breeding Mourning Dove populations. PhD diss., University of Missouri.

Baskett, T. S., M. W. Sayre, R. E. Tomlinson, and R. E. Mirarchi, eds. 1993. *Ecology and Management of the Mourning Dove*. Harrisburg, PA: Stackpole Books.

Brennan, L. A., ed. 2007. *Texas Quails: Ecology and Management*. College Station: Texas A&M University Press.

Brown, J. L. 1967. The extent of breeding by immature Mourning Doves (*Zenaida macroura marginella*) in southern Arizona. Master's thesis, University of Arizona.

Browning, B. M. 1959. An ecological study of the food habits of the Mourning Dove in California. *California Fish and Game* 48:91–115.

Clapp, R. B., M. K. Klimkiewicz, and A. G. Futcher. 1983. Longevity records of North American birds: Columbidae through Paridae. *Journal of Field Ornithology* 54:123–37.

Conti, J. A., and D. J. Forrester. 1981. Interrelationships of parasites of White-winged and Mourning Doves in Florida. *Journal of Wildlife Diseases* 17:529–36.

Davison, V. E., and E. G. Sullivan. 1963. Mourning Doves' selection of foods. *Journal of Wildlife Management* 27:373–83.

Dillon, O. W., Jr. 1961. Mourning Dove foods in Texas during September and October. *Journal of Wildlife Management* 25:334–36.

Droege, S., and J. R. Sauer. 1990. *North American Breeding Bird Survey Annual Summary 1989.* Federal Government Biological Report 90(8). Washington, DC: US Fish and Wildlife Service.

Dunks, J. H., R. E. Tomlinson, H. M. Reeves, D. D. Dolton, C. E. Braun, and T. P. Zapatka. 1982. *Migration, Harvest, and Population Dynamics of Mourning Doves Banded in the Central Management Unit, 1967–1977.* Special Science Report—Wildlife 249. Washington, DC: US Fish and Wildlife Service.

Frankel, A. I., and T. S. Baskett. 1961. The effect of pairing on cooing of penned Mourning Doves. *Journal of Wildlife Management* 25:352–84.

Fronimos, A. B. 2011. Use of food resources by White-winged Doves and Great-tailed Grackles at urban bird feeders in central Texas with observations on columbid wing raising behavior. Master's thesis, Texas State University–San Marcos.

George, R. R. 1988. *Mourning Doves in Texas: Life History, Habitat Needs, and Management Suggestions.* Austin: Texas Parks and Wildlife Department.

Guthery, F. S. 2000. *On Bobwhites.* College Station: Texas A&M University Press.

Hayslette, S. E., and R. E. Mirarchi. 2001. Patterns of food preferences in Mourning Doves. *Journal of Wildlife Management* 65:816–27.

Hayslette, S. E., T. C. Tacha, and G. L. Waggerman. 2000. Factors affecting White-winged, White-tipped, and Mourning Dove reproduction in Lower Rio Grande Valley. *Journal of Wildlife Management* 64:286–95.

Keeler, J. E., C. C. Allin, J. M. Anderson, S. Gallizioli, K. E. Gamble, D. W. Hayne, W. H. Kiel Jr., et al. 1977. Mourning Dove (*Zenaida macroura*). In *Management of Migratory Shore and Upland Game Birds in North America*, edited by G. C. Sanderson, 275–98. Washington, DC: International Association of Fish and Wildlife Agencies.

Leopold, A. S., R. J. Gutiérrez, and M. T. Bronson. 1981. *North American Game Birds and Mammals.* New York: Charles Scribner's Sons.

Lockwood, M. W., and B. Freeman. 2004. *The TOS Handbook of Texas Birds.* College Station: Texas A&M University Press.

Miller, D. A., and D. L. Otis. 2010. Calibrating recruitment estimates for Mourning Doves from harvest age ratios. *Journal of Wildlife Management* 74:1070–79.

Oberholser, H. C. 1974. *The Bird Life of Texas.* Austin: University of Texas Press.

Ostrand, W. D., J. A. Bissonette, and M. R. Conover. 1995. Trichomoniasis as a factor in Mourning Dove population decline in Fillmore, Utah. *Journal of Wildlife Diseases* 31:87–89.

Otis, D. L., J. H. Schulz, D. Miller, R. E. Mirarchi, and T. S. Baskett. 2008. Mourning Dove (*Zenaida macroura*). In *The Birds of North America Online*, edited by A. Poole. Ithaca, NY: Cornell Laboratory of Ornithology.

Poling, T. D., and S. E. Hayslette. 2006. Dietary overlap and foraging competition between Mourning Doves and Eurasian Collared-Doves. *Journal of Wildlife Management* 70:998–1004.

Ruos, J. L., and R. E. Tomlinson. 1968. *Mourning Dove Status Report, 1966.* US Fish and Wildlife Service Special Scientific Report, Wildlife No. 115.

Sauer, J. R., D. D. Dolton, and S. Droege. 1994. Mourning Dove population trend estimates from call-count and North American Breeding Bird Surveys. *Journal of Wildlife Management* 58:506–15.

Sauer, J. R., J. E. Hines, J. E. Fallon, K. L. Pardieck, D. J. Ziolkowski Jr., and W. A. Link. 2014. *The North American Breeding Bird Survey, Results and Analysis 1966–2012.* Version 02.19.2014. Laurel, MD: USGS Patuxent Wildlife Research Center. http://www.mbr-pwrc.usgs.gov/bbs/bbs.html.

Sauer, J. R., W. A. Link, W. L. Kendall, and D. D. Dolton. 2010. Comparative analysis of Mourning Dove population change in North America. *Journal of Wildlife Management* 74:1059–69.

Seamans, M. E., R. D. Rau, and T. A. Sanders. 2012. *Mourning Dove Population Status, 2012.* Washington, DC: US Fish and Wildlife Service.

Seamans, M. E., and T. A. Sanders. 2014. *Mourning Dove Population Status, 2014.* Washington, DC: US Fish and Wildlife Service.

Stickney, H. W. 1967. Preferences exhibited by the Mourning Dove and blackbirds for 19 kinds of seeds. Master's thesis, Auburn University.

Taylor, B., D. Rollins, J. Johnson, J. Roberson, T. W. Schwertner, and N. J. Silvy. 2006. *Dove Management in Texas.* College Station, TX: Cooperative Extension Service.

Texas Parks and Wildlife Department. 2010. *Webless Migratory Game Bird Strategic Plan 2011–2015.* Austin: Texas Parks and Wildlife Department.

Tomlinson, R. E., and D. D. Dolton. 1987. Current status of Mourning Dove in the Western Management Unit. *Proceedings of the Annual Conference of the Western Association of Fish and Wildlife Agencies* 67:119–33.

Tomlinson, R. E., D. D. Dolton, R. R. George, and R. E. Mirarchi. 1995. Mourning Dove. In *Migratory Shore and Upland Game Bird Management in North America*, edited by T. C. Tacha and C. E. Braun, 5–26. Washington, DC: International Association of Fish and Wildlife Agencies.

Tweit, R. C. 2007. Mourning Dove. *The Texas Breeding Bird Atlas.* College Station: Texas A&M University System. http://txtbba.tamu.edu/species-accounts/mourning-dove.

Weeks, H. P., and H. P. Weeks Jr. 1980. Unusual egg deposition in Mourning Doves. *Wilson Bulletin* 92:258–60.

White, L. M., R. E. Mirarchi, and M. E. Lisano. 1987. Reproductive capability of wild hatching-year Mourning Doves in Alabama. *Journal of Wildlife Management* 51:204–11.

15

White-winged Dove

Nesting white-winged doves seem to prefer the older more established residential neighborhoods with large live oak, pecan, and ashe [sic] trees. This may be due to better protection from predators and . . . consistent food and water sources due to watering of lawns and bird feeders.—TEXAS PARKS AND WILDLIFE DEPARTMENT (2015)

Introduction

The White-winged Dove (*Zenaida asiatica*) is a large dove that is easily recognized by the bold white crescent on the upper wing. Adults measure about 29 cm (11.4 in) in length and weigh approximately 150 g (5.3 oz), with females being slightly smaller than males (Schwertner et al. 2002). The White-winged Dove has undergone a dramatic range expansion and population increase during the past 40 years by taking advantage of urban nest sites and water and food resources (Schwertner et al. 2002; Small, Baccus, and Schwertner 2006; Veech, Small, and Baccus 2011), although increasingly warm climate may also have played a role (Rappole, Blacklock, and Norwine 2007). Urban areas support some of the largest White-winged Dove populations; for example, San Antonio is now home to nearly 500,000 resident White-winged Doves (Lockwood and Freeman 2004).

The Pacific Dove (*Z. meloda*), which occurs along the Pacific coast of South America, was formerly considered conspecific with and a subspecies of the White-winged Dove. Vocal and morphological differences and genetic distinctiveness between Pacific and White-winged Doves led to the recognition of these

disjunct taxa as separate species (Goodwin 1983; K. Johnson and Clayton 2000; American Ornithologists' Union 2002).

Distribution in Texas

The current breeding range of the White-winged Dove stretches from the southwestern United States throughout much of Mexico and Central America to northwestern Costa Rica, as well as many Caribbean islands and southern Florida. The historical breeding range of the White-winged Dove in Texas was restricted to riparian forests of the Lower Rio Grande Valley; however, the conversion of forest to farmland and the severe freezes of the 1950s pushed the species northward into mesquite brushland (Cottam and Trefethen 1968; Oberholser 1974; Tweit 2007). The White-winged Dove has since expanded its range in Texas, and breeding has been confirmed by the Texas Parks and Wildlife Department (TPWD) in most Texas counties (Tweit 2007). Counties in which breeding has not been confirmed are mostly within the High Plains and Piney Woods ecoregions (Lockwood and Freeman 2004; Tweit 2007). Range expansion by the White-winged Dove involves both of the subspecies historically found in Texas, with the

Figure 15.1. White-winged Dove. Males and females have similar plumage. Adults and juveniles are similar, but juveniles have paler faces. Photo credit: Greg Lasley.

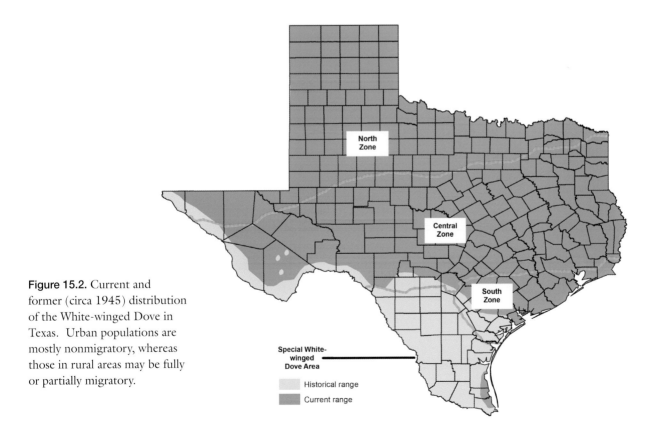

Figure 15.2. Current and former (circa 1945) distribution of the White-winged Dove in Texas. Urban populations are mostly nonmigratory, whereas those in rural areas may be fully or partially migratory.

Eastern White-winged Dove (*Z. a. asiatica*) contributing mostly to expansion into the eastern part of the state, and the Western White-winged Dove (*Z. a. mearnsi*) expanding statewide (Pruett et al. 2000). The genetic diversity of White-winged Doves in recently colonized areas is relatively high because of ongoing gene flow and immigration from multiple population sources (Pruett et al. 2011).

Biology

Most of what is known about the White-winged Dove is based on studies of US populations. Cottam and Trefethen (1968), Brown et al. (1977), George et al. (1995), and Schwertner et al. (2002) provide excellent reviews on the ecology and management of the White-winged Dove. Much of the information presented here is summarized from these 4 sources, supplemented with data from more recent studies.

Migratory routes and timing

The White-winged Dove is largely nonmigratory throughout most of its tropical range, but migratory tendencies vary widely among populations and individuals. White-winged Doves largely withdraw from California, Nevada, Utah, Arizona, and northern Texas during winter; however, small but increasing numbers winter in urban areas as far north as the Texas Panhandle (Schwertner et al. 2002; Lockwood and Freeman 2004). White-winged Doves are also found in parts of the southern United States, southeastern Mexico, and Belize, though they are absent from the latter during the breeding season (Schwertner et al. 2002). Fall migration in Texas begins in early September and continues until early October. Some Eastern White-winged Doves migrate to Central America as far south as Costa Rica (George et al. 2000). Some doves from western Texas may spend the winter in the highlands of Morelos and Guerrero, Mexico (Cottam and Trefethen 1968). Migratory White-winged Doves begin returning to Texas breeding grounds during late March and early April, with the number of returning birds peaking in mid-May and continuing until early June (George et al. 2000; Tweit 2007). Migrating White-winged Doves may make direct flights to winter destinations, or they may stop to feed if food

is available (Schwertner et al. 2002). Food availability and weather conditions may serve as stimuli to begin fall migration (Schwertner et al. 2002). It is unknown what stimulates northward movements in spring.

Timing of breeding

The timing of breeding is not well known. Pair formation may take place before arrival on breeding grounds (Cottam and Trefethen 1968). The breeding season of urban White-winged Doves begins earlier and lasts longer than in populations inhabiting native brush in the Lower Rio Grande Valley (West et al. 1993; Hayslette and Hayslette 1999; Small et al. 2005).

Behavior

Males defend nest sites and cooing perches. A perch-owning male will attack an invading male by flying toward the intruder and will often land on the spot formerly occupied by the intruder. Defending males may use wing slaps to drive away an intruder. Mated males defend smaller territories than unmated males. Territorial defense is greatest during courtship, nest-site selection, and nest building, in which mating, nesting, and feeding areas are defended; however, territorial defense declines once incubation begins and is limited to defending the mating and nesting area. Males use cooing and visual displays, such as preening, bowing, and spreading their wings and tail, to attract a potential mate. Once a female has been attracted, the male will perform a courtship flight. The male flies upward in a spiraling manner, circling 1–2 times, and then glides back to the perch. Prior to copulation, the male lowers his body forward, raises his wings straight up, lifts and fans his tail, and rocks backward to normal perching position. This may be repeated 8–9 times. White-winged Doves usually breed in large colonies (more than 25 pairs/ha, or 10 pairs/ac); however, smaller colonies or solitary pairs occur in parts of the range, depending on the availability of nest sites, food, and water (Cottam and Trefethen 1968; Schwertner et al. 2002).

Clutch size and incubation

Usually 2 eggs are laid, although rare clutches of 1 or 3 eggs do occur. Length of incubation varies geographically, from 13–15 days in southern Texas to

15–20 days in Arizona. Nest building among returning migrants begins in late April and continues until mid-May, whereas resident urban birds in Texas begin nest building as early as March. Egg laying begins in April and continues until August in Texas. Two broods per season are normal, but brood number depends on environmental conditions, with desert populations usually producing a single brood per season. Pairs will attempt to renest immediately following destruction of the current clutch. The maximum number of renesting attempts by White-winged Doves in Waco, Texas, was 4 (Small et al. 2005). New nesting attempts begin 4–15 days following the previous brood.

Phenology

Male and female parents incubate the eggs and brood and care for the chicks. Young fledge after 14 days but continue to be fed by the parents for more than a month despite being able to feed themselves around the third week of life. Young join feeding flights 14 days after fledging. Approximately 90% of hatch-year White-winged Doves in Alice, Texas, enter the local population by the beginning of August (Collier et al. 2013).

Diet and foraging

The diet varies geographically, but seeds, mast, and fruit are the primary foods. Fruits of spiny hackberry (*Celtis pallida*), anacua (*Ehretia anacua*), chittamwood (*Bumelia lanuginosa*), brasil (*Condalia hookeri*), and pigeonberry (*Rivina humilis*), and seeds of common sunflower, doveweed (*Croton texensis*), native grasses, corn, and grain sorghum are the most heavily consumed foods in southern Texas (Cottam and Trefethen 1968; Schacht, Tacha, and Waggerman 1995). White-winged Doves in central Texas consume seeds of Chinese tallow (*Sapium sebiferum*) during the winter, and leatherweed (*Jatropha dioica*) is heavily consumed in West Texas and New Mexico (Engel-Wilson and Ohmart 1978; Scudday, Gallucci, and West 1980). Arizona populations feed heavily on the nectar and fruit of saguaro cactus (*Carnegiea gigantea*), limebrush (*Jatropha cuneata*), Mexican jumping bean (*Sapium biloculare*), and ocotillo (*Fouquieria splendens*) (Haughey 1986; Wolf and Martinez del Rio 2000).

Demography and vital rates

Juveniles exhibit lower survival rates than adults (George et al. 2000; Collier et al. 2012). Based on band recoveries from Texas and Mexico, survival rates for hatch-year birds is 21%–36%, and 47%–54% for birds older than 1 year (Collier et al. 2012). The longevity record among wild White-winged Doves is a little over 22 years (Clapp, Klimkiewicz, and Futcher 1983).

Age at first reproduction

Sexual maturity is achieved in the first year of life. Early-hatched White-winged Doves may be able to breed during the hatch year (Cottam and Trefethen 1968; Schwertner et al. 2002).

Age and sex ratios

No data are available.

Population Status and Trends

The Lower Rio Grande Valley of Texas may have supported as many as 4–12 million White-winged Doves in 1923 (Jones 1945). Tamaulipan populations of White-winged Doves varied from 5.3 to 6.2 million birds in the late 1960s, to 1.7–8.9 million in the 1970s, to 16 million in the 1980s (Y. Johnson et al. 2009 and references therein). The highest density of nesting White-winged Doves ever recorded was in June 1973, with 141 active nests in a 0.1 ha (0.04 ac) belt transect of native brush 30 km east of San Fernando, Tamaulipas, Mexico (Waggerman 1973; Schwertner et al. 2002). Nesting density in the Lower Rio Grande Valley was generally lower than in Tamaulipas, with an average of 10–25 nests/ha (4–8 nests/ac) and occasionally higher densities of 75–185 nests/ha (30–75 nests/ac) (Waggerman 2001; Schwertner et al. 2002).

Brush clearance combined with effects of drought and Hurricane Gilbert in 1988 led to a 94% reduction in active nesting colonies in Tamaulipas (Y. Johnson et al. 2009). Overhunting, exposure to pesticides, and the loss of nesting habitat and native plants that provided food led to severe population declines of White-winged Doves in the Lower Rio Grande Valley during the twentieth century (Texas Game, Fish and Oyster Commission 1945; Swanson and Rappole 1992; Tacha et al. 1994; Hayslette, Tacha, and Waggerman 1996; Burkepile et al. 2002; Bautch 2004). By 1939 it was estimated that there were 500,000–600,000 doves in the region and 200,000–300,000 in 1940 (Marsh and Saunders 1942; Texas Game, Fish and Oyster Commission 1945). During 2002 the breeding population was estimated to be 413,351 (Waggerman 2002). Despite population declines in northeastern Mexico and extreme southern Texas, the White-winged Dove has undergone rapid range and population expansions, mostly in Texas, during the past 40 years by taking advantage of nest sites and water and food resources in urban environments (Schwertner et al. 2002; Small, Baccus, and Schwertner 2006; Veech, Small, and Baccus 2011). Christmas Bird Count data indicate a dramatic increase in the Texas winter population beginning in the 1990s, which is partly related to the nonmigratory nature of urban White-winged Doves (Schwertner et al. 2002). In contrast, Arizona breeding populations have remained relatively stable (Schwertner et al. 2002). Little is known about the population status of White-winged Doves in other parts of Mexico, Central America, and the Caribbean (Schwertner et al. 2002).

Specific Habitat Requirements

Natural nesting habitat of White-winged Doves includes thorny woodlands and brush, cacti-paloverde (*Parkinsonia* spp.), oak-juniper (*Quercus*

spp.–*Juniperus* spp.) woodlands, and riparian woodlands (George et al. 1995; Schwertner et al. 2002). White-winged Doves will also nest in citrus orchards, salt cedar (*Tamarix ramosissima*), and urban and suburban shade trees. Thorny woodlands dominated by Texas ebony (*Ebenopsis ebano*), spiny hackberry, anacua, and brasil provided ideal nesting habitat for White-winged Doves in northeastern Mexico and southern Texas; however, agriculture and urbanization led to severe reduction of this habitat, and only isolated patches of thorn forest now remain in the region (Jahrsdoerfer and Leslie 1988; Bautch 2004; Brush 2005). Subclimax plant communities consisting of honey mesquite (*Prosopis glandulosa*), sweet acacia (*Vachellia farnesiana*), sugar hackberry (*Celtis laevigata*), false willow (*Baccharis* spp.), green ash (*Fraxinus pennsylvanica*), soapberry (*Sapindus saponaria*), and cedar elm (*Ulmus crassifolia*) will also be utilized as nesting habitat if they occur near resacas or other water resources (Schwertner et al. 2002). However, White-winged Doves usually avoid nesting in mesquite, possibly because of the more open branching pattern and less-dense foliage (George et al. 1995; Breeden et al. 2008). In urban areas, White-winged Doves prefer to nest in older, taller trees and regularly use live oak (*Quercus virginiana*), Arizona ash (*Fraxinus velutina*), cedar elm, gum bumelia (*Sideroxylon lanuginosum*), pecan (*Carya illinoinensis*), Arizona cypress (*Cupressus arizonica*), and occasionally Mexican fan palm (*Washingtonia robusta*) (Schwertner et al. 2002; Eitniear 2008). Generally, White-winged Doves prefer nesting and roosting habitat interspersed

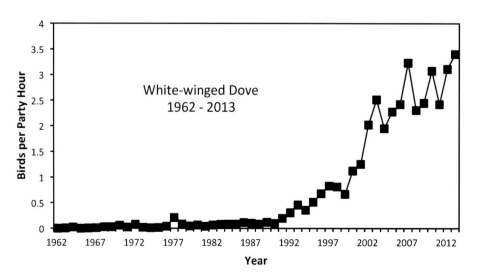

Figure 15.3. Trend in White-winged Dove wintering populations in Texas, based on Christmas Bird Count data. Note the sharp increase beginning in the early 1990s.

Figure 15.4. White-winged Dove habitat on the outskirts of San Antonio. Note dark foliage of live oak tree canopy. Photo credit: Eric Grahmann.

with foraging areas such as agricultural fields and cacti communities (Cottam and Trefethen 1968; Schwertner et al. 2002). Habitat used during migration and winter is similar to breeding habitat.

Habitat management

The loss of woody habitat is the main threat to White-winged Doves in Texas, especially in the Lower Rio Grande Valley. Land acquisition by the US Fish and Wildlife Service (USFWS), TPWD, and nongovernmental organizations such as the National Audubon Society and the Nature Conservancy has led to the preservation of more than 18,000 ha (44,479 ac) of actual or potential White-winged Dove habitat. Many of the privately owned ranches in southern Texas also possess significant amounts of White-winged Dove

habitat. Because of the species' ability to adapt to urban habitats, the loss of native vegetation has not been as devastating to White-winged Doves as it has been to other avian species. Specific habitat management recommendations for White-winged Doves include planting grain food plots that mature prior to or during the arrival of spring migrants, maintaining grain fields near brushy nesting areas, and providing reliable drinking water through the establishment of watering troughs, wildlife guzzlers, artificial ponds, lawn sprinklers, and bird baths (Schacht, Tacha, and Waggerman 1995; George et al. 1995). Given their preference for using mature tall trees as nest sites, White-winged Doves will benefit from landscaping approaches for residential or business areas that include planting species such as live oak and pecan. Multinational cooperation will be required to preserve important White-winged Dove breeding and wintering habitat in Mexico and Central America. Homerstad, Waggerman, and George (1988) presented detailed recommendations for White-winged Dove habitat restoration in the Lower Rio Grande Valley of Texas and reported that cropland could be reforested with native brush at a cost of about $400/ha or $165/ac.

Hunting and Conservation

Texas hunting season length

Dove hunting season varies in timing and length throughout Texas. The TPWD divides Texas into three dove hunting zones: North, Central, and South. The North Zone is that portion of Texas north of a line from Fort Hancock to Texarkana. The South Zone is that portion of Texas south of a line from Del Rio to Orange. The Central Zone is that portion of Texas between the North and South Zones. Hunters should consult the current Texas Parks and Wildlife Outdoor Annual for an exact description of these zones. Each zone has two separate hunting seasons for doves. The first hunting season in the North and Central Zones lasts from early September to late October, and the second starts in late December and ends in early January. The first South Zone hunting season lasts from late September to late October and the second from late December to late January. Hunting can begin one-half hour before sunrise and can continue until sunset.

A special season for White-winged Doves takes place in the western portion of the South Zone, during which Mourning and White-tipped Doves may also be taken. The Special White-winged Dove Area is that portion of the South Zone west of a line from San Antonio to Corpus Christi. Hunters should consult the current Texas Parks and Wildlife Outdoor Annual for an exact description of this area. The Special White-winged Dove Season takes place on the first two weekends of September. Hunting begins at noon and continues until sunset. The TPWD estimates that White-winged Dove harvest has increased from about 2 million birds per year to more than 3.6 million birds per year from 2005 to 2014 (Purvis 2014).

Texas bag limits

Bag limit for the regular dove hunting seasons in all zones is 15 doves composed of Mourning, White-winged, and White-tipped Doves in aggregate, to include not more than two White-tipped Doves. The possession limit for the regular dove hunting season is three times the daily bag limit. During the special season in the Special White-winged Dove Area, the daily bag limit is 15 doves in aggregate, not to include more than two Mourning Doves and two White-tipped Doves.

Geographic restrictions on hunting in Texas

There are no geographic restrictions on hunting in Texas. Dove hunters must complete the Harvest Information Program (HIP) questionnaire when they renew their hunting licenses. Dove hunters must also purchase the Texas Migratory Game Bird Hunting Stamp.

Research Needs and Priorities

Brown et al. (1977), George et al. (1995), and Schwertner et al. (2002) have called for the following research priorities:

1. Increase accuracy in estimating the harvest of White-winged Doves in the United States using the National Migratory Bird Harvest Information Program and encourage the countries of Latin America to implement similar surveys.

2. Develop a method of reliably estimating White-winged Dove populations, survival, and recruitment in each state.

3. Determine the effect of hunting on breeding populations in the United States, Mexico, and Central America.

4. Determine why most of the range expansion and population growth has occurred primarily in urban areas.

5. Determine why the White-winged Dove population in the Lower Rio Grande Valley and northeastern Mexico has not regained its

historical size. Although fragmentation of native thornbrush habitat has contributed to the dove's demise, it does not explain why urban populations in these areas have not achieved the sizes observed in places like San Antonio, Texas.

6. Examine the impact that the invading White-winged Doves are having on other species, especially Mourning Doves. Recent research suggests that increasing numbers of Eurasian Collared-Doves in urban areas have not had negative impacts on White-winged Doves partly because these species are generalists in their selection of nest sites (Ludwick 2008). Little research, however, has focused on interspecific interactions among Mourning and White-winged Doves.

7. Gain better understanding of nesting-habitat requirements, as White-winged Doves appear to be more adaptable than previously believed (Schwertner et al. 2002).

8. Gain better understanding of the ecology and habitat of White-winged Doves in Latin America.

9. Investigate the winter ecology of nonmigratory populations and wintering populations in Mexico and Central America.

10. Determine the nutritional requirements of White-winged Doves.

11. Expand the work of Pruett et al. (2000, 2011) to include the entire range. Range-wide study of natural genetic variation will provide a better understanding of the White-winged Dove's biogeographic and demographic history. Analysis of adaptive genetic variation could provide reasons for why the species has expanded in some areas and not in others.

Literature Cited

American Ornithologists' Union. 2002. Forty-third supplement to the *American Ornithologists' Union Check-List of North American Birds*. *Auk* 119:897–906.

Bautch, K. A. 2004. Historic and current forage area locations and food abundance in relation to nesting sites for White-winged Doves in the Lower Rio Grande Valley of Texas. Master's thesis, Texas A&M University–Kingsville.

Breeden, J. B., F. Hernández, N. J. Silvy, F. E. Smeins, and J. A. Roberson. 2008. Nesting habitat of White-winged Doves in urban environments of South Texas. *Proceedings of the Annual Conference of the Southeastern Association of Fish and Wildlife Agencies* 62:58–63.

Brown, D. E., D. R. Blankinship, P. K. Evans, W. H. Kiel Jr., G. L. Waggerman, and C. K. Winkler. 1977. White-winged Dove (*Zenaida asiatica*). In *Management of Migratory Shore and Upland Game Birds in North America*, edited by G. C. Sanderson, 247–72. Washington, DC: International Association of Fish and Wildlife Agencies.

Brush, T. 2005. *Nesting Birds of a Tropical Frontier: The Lower Rio Grande of Texas*. College Station: Texas A&M University Press.

Burkepile, N. A., D. G. Hewitt, G. L. Waggerman, M. F. Small, and E. C. Hellgren. 2002. Effects of methyl parathion on White-winged Dove productivity and reproductive behavior. *Journal of Wildlife Management* 66:202–11.

Clapp, R. B., M. K. Klimkiewicz, and A. G. Futcher. 1983. Longevity records of North American birds: Columbidae through Paridae. *Journal of Field Ornithology* 54:123–37.

Collier, B. A., S. R. Kremer, C. D. Mason, M. J. Peterson, and K. W. Calhoun. 2012. Survival, fidelity, and recovery rates of White-winged Doves in Texas. *Journal of Wildlife Management* 76:1129–34.

Collier, B. A., S. R. Kremer, C. D. Mason, J. Stone, K. W. Calhoun, and M. J. Peterson. 2013. Immigration and recruitment in an urban White-winged Dove breeding colony. *Journal of Fish and Wildlife Management* 4:33–40.

Cottam, C., and J. B. Trefethen. 1968. *White-Wings: The Life History, Status, and Management of White-winged Dove*. Princeton, NJ: D. Van Nostrand.

Eitniear, J. C. 2008. White-winged Doves nesting in palm trees. *Bulletin of the Texas Ornithological Society* 41:28–29.

Engel-Wilson, R. W., and R. D. Ohmart. 1978. *Assessment of the Vegetation and Terrestrial Vertebrates on the Rio Grande between Ft. Quitman and Haciendita, Texas: March 1977–March 1978*. Tempe, AZ: International Boundary and Water Commission.

George, R. R., R. E. Tomlinson, R. W. Engel-Wilson, G. L. Waggerman, and A. G. Spratt. 1995. White-winged Dove. In *Migratory Shore and Upland Game Bird Management in North America*, edited by T. C. Tacha and C. E. Braun, 29–50. Washington, DC: International Association of Fish and Wildlife Agencies.

George, R. R., G. L. Waggerman, D. M. McCarty, R. E. Tomlinson, D. Blankinship, and J. H. Dunks. 2000. *Migration, Harvest and Population Dynamics of White-winged Doves Banded in Texas and Northeastern Mexico, 1950–1978*. Austin: Texas Parks and Wildlife Department.

Goodwin, D. 1983. *Pigeons and Doves of the World.* Ithaca, NY: Cornell University Press.

Haughey, R. A. 1986. Diet of desert nesting western White-winged Doves. Master's thesis, Arizona State University.

Hayslette, S. E., and B. A. Hayslette. 1999. Late and early season reproduction of urban White-winged Doves in southern Texas. *Texas Journal of Science* 51:173–80.

Hayslette, S. E., T. C. Tacha, and G. L. Waggerman. 1996. Changes in White-winged Dove reproduction in southern Texas, 1954–1993. *Journal of Wildlife Management* 60:298–301.

Homerstad, G. E., G. L. Waggerman, and R. R. George. 1988. The reforestation of cropland in the Lower Rio Grande Valley of Texas with emphasis on White-winged Dove nesting habitat. *Proceedings of the Second Regional Conference of the Rio Grande Border States on Parks and Wildlife.* Saltillo, Coahuila, Mexico.

Jahrsdoerfer, S. E., and D. M. Leslie Jr. 1988. *Tamaulipan Brushland of the Lower Rio Grande Valley of South Texas: Description, Human Impacts, and Management Options.* Biological Report 88(36). Washington, DC: US Fish and Wildlife Service.

Johnson, K. P., and D. H. Clayton. 2000. A molecular phylogeny of the dove genus *Zenaida*: Mitochondrial and nuclear DNA sequences. *Condor* 102:864–70.

Johnson, Y. S., F. Hernández, D. G. Hewitt, E. J. Redeker, G. L. Waggerman, H. O. Meléndez, H. V. Z. Treviño, and J. A. Roberson. 2009. Status of White-winged Dove nesting colonies in Tamaulipas, México. *Wilson Journal of Ornithology* 121:338–46.

Jones, C. G. 1945. Past and present whitewings. *Texas Game and Fish* 3:13.

Lockwood, M. W., and B. Freeman. 2004. *The TOS Handbook of Texas Birds.* College Station: Texas A&M University Press.

Ludwick, T. J. 2008. Assessing the impact of the Eurasian Collared-Dove on the breeding ecology of White-winged Doves and other native columbids. Master's thesis, Texas A&M University–Kingsville.

Marsh, E. G., and G. B. Saunders. 1942. The status of the white-winged dove in Texas. *Wilson Bulletin* 54:145–46.

Oberholser, H. C. 1974. *The Bird Life of Texas.* Austin: University of Texas Press.

Pruett, C. L., S. E. Henke, S. M. Tanksley, M. F. Small, K. M. Hogan, and J. Roberson. 2000. Mitochondrial DNA and morphological variation of White-winged Doves in Texas. *Condor* 102:871–80.

Pruett, C. L., S. M. Tanksley, M. F. Small, J. F. Taylor, and M. R. J. Forstner. 2011. The effects of range expansion on the population genetics of White-winged Doves in Texas. *American Midland Naturalist* 166:415–25.

Purvis, J. 2014. *Small Game Harvest Survey Results 1994–95 thru 2013–14.* Austin: Texas Parks and Wildlife Department.

Rappole, J. H., G. W. Blacklock, and J. Norwine. 2007. Apparent rapid range change in South Texas birds: Response to climate change? In *The Changing Climate of South Texas 1900–2100: Problems and Prospects, Impacts and Implications,* edited by J. Norwine and K. John, 133–45. Kingsville: CREST-RESSACA, Texas A&M University–Kingsville.

Schacht, S. J., T. C. Tacha, and G. L. Waggerman. 1995. Bioenergetics of White-winged Dove reproduction in the Lower Rio Grande Valley of Texas. *Wildlife Monographs* 129.

Schwertner, T. W., H. A. Mathewson, J. A. Roberson, M. Small, and G. L. Waggerman. 2002. White-winged Dove (*Zenaida asiatica*). In *The Birds of North America Online,* edited by A. Poole. Ithaca, NY: Cornell Laboratory of Ornithology http://bna.birds.cornell.edu .bnaproxy.birds.cornell.edu/bna/species/710/articles/ introduction.

Scudday, J. F., T. L. Gallucci, and P. S. West. 1980. *The Status and Ecology of the White-winged Dove of Trans-Pecos Texas.* Final report, US Fish and Wildlife Service Contract 14–16–2096. Alpine, TX: Sul Ross State University.

Small, M. F., J. T. Baccus, and T. W. Schwertner. 2006. Historic and current distribution and abundance of White-winged Doves (*Zenaida asiatica*) in the United States. *Occasional Publication of the Texas Ornithological Society* No. 6.

Small, M. F., C. L. Schaefer, J. T. Baccus, and J. A. Roberson. 2005. Breeding ecology of White-winged Doves in a recently colonized urban environment. *Wilson Bulletin* 117:172–76.

Swanson, D. A., and J. H. Rappole. 1992. Status of White-winged Dove in southern Texas. *Southwestern Naturalist* 37:93–97.

Tacha, T. C., S. J. Schacht, R. R. George, and E. F. Hill. 1994. Anticholinesterase exposure of White-winged Doves breeding in Lower Rio Grande Valley, Texas. *Journal of Wildlife Management* 58:213–17.

Texas Game, Fish and Oyster Commission. 1945. *Principal Game Birds and Mammals of Texas.* Austin: Texas Game, Fish and Oyster Commission.

Texas Parks and Wildlife Department. 2015. *South Texas Wildlife Management: White-winged Doves.* https:// tpwd.texas.gov/landwater/land/habitats/southtx_plain /upland_birds/white_winged_dove.phtml.

Tweit, R. C. 2007. White-winged Dove. *The Texas Breeding Bird Atlas.* College Station: Texas A&M University System. http://txtbba.tamu.edu/species-accounts /white-winged-dove.

Veech, J. A., M. F. Small, and J. T. Baccus. 2011. The effects of habitat on the range expansion of a native and an introduced bird species. *Journal of Biogeography* 38:69–77.

Waggerman, G. L. 1973. *White-winged Dove Harvest Regulations.* Performance report, Federal Aid Project W-30-R-28. Austin: Texas Parks and Wildlife Department.

———. 2001. *White-winged and White-tipped Dove Density, Distribution, and Harvest.* Performance report, Federal Aid Project W-128-R10. Austin: Texas Parks and Wildlife Department.

———. 2002. *White-winged and White-tipped Dove Density, Distribution, and Harvest.* Performance report, Federal Aid Project W-128-R10. Austin: Texas Parks and Wildlife Department.

West, L. M., L. M. Smith, R. S. Lutz, and R. R. George. 1993. Ecology of urban White-winged Doves. *Transactions of the North American Wildlife Natural Resource Conference* 59:70–77.

Wolf, B. O., and C. Martinez del Rio. 2000. Use of saguaro fruit by White-winged Doves: Isotopic evidence of a tight ecological association. *Oecologia* 124:536–43.

16

Ring-necked Pheasant

The cock pheasant is a prize well calculated to delight the heart of a sportsman.—BENT (1932, 320)

Introduction

The Ring-necked Pheasant (*Phasianus colchicus*) is an exotic galliform that was introduced to North America from Asia during the nineteenth century. The translocation of the Ring-necked Pheasant represents one of the most successful wildlife introductions in North America. After the initial introductions over a century ago, self-sustaining populations became established relatively quickly throughout the United States. The Ring-necked Pheasant is now an iconic game bird in parts of the United States where grain farming is a dominant land use. It has also become an important part of the ecological community that it inhabits and is one of the most studied game birds in the world.

Giudice and Ratti (2001) provide a detailed description of Ring-necked Pheasants, and what follows is a summary of their description. Mature males are brilliantly colored, with greenish-blue feathers and red wattles on their head, a white collar on their neck, coppery reddish-brown feathers on their body, and a long, flamboyant tail. Mature females are not as colorful as males, being covered with dull, mottled brown feathers that often have a reddish glimmering sheen, as well as black spots and bars.

Fossil records indicate that Ring-necked Pheasants appeared during the early Pleistocene in China, where the species most likely evolved. Other fossil records from the mid- to late Pleistocene have been documented in Ireland and through continental Europe into Kazakhstan east to Japan (Tyrberg 1998). There is little doubt that wherever pheasants occurred throughout their native range, they were part of the diets of early humans. Because they occur as part of the native fauna in Eurasia and as an exotic transplant, Ring-necked Pheasants have one of the widest distributions of any game bird in the world.

Distribution

The current distribution of the Ring-necked Pheasant in Texas includes 50 counties in the High Plains and Rolling Plains, where grain farming is an important land use. The first recorded Ring-necked Pheasant introduction in Texas occurred along the Texas coast on the Aransas National Wildlife Refuge in the 1930s (Holloran and Howard 1956), but this introduction failed because habitat and climatic conditions on the Coastal Prairie were not conducive to pheasant production (Guthery, Custer, and Owen 1980). The first successful Ring-necked Pheasant introductions in Texas occurred in the Panhandle in the 1950s. However, establishment of the initial self-sustaining populations in the Panhandle likely occurred via dispersal of migrants from neighboring states (Evans 1977). There has been speculation that birds released in Colorado

Figure 16.1. *(Top)*, male Ring-necked Pheasant. Photo credit: Larry Ditto. *(Bottom)*, female Ring-necked Pheasant. Photo credit: Greg Lasley.

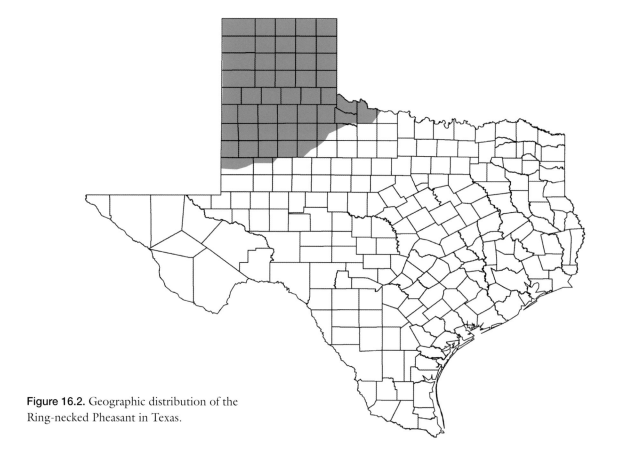

Figure 16.2. Geographic distribution of the Ring-necked Pheasant in Texas.

were the source of Ring-necked Pheasants in Texas, but birds or their descendants from Oklahoma were a far more likely source because the dispersal distance was shorter (Guthery et al. 1984). These early Texas populations were bolstered by periodic and frequent introductions by landowners and civic and youth organizations as well as government agencies, which facilitated the spread of Ring-necked Pheasants through portions of the High Plains and Rolling Plains (Guthery et al. 1984). Farming practices between the 1940s and 1960s created habitat conditions compatible with Ring-necked Pheasant production, which permitted additional range expansion. However, the initiation of modern clean-farming practices about 30 years ago has reduced the amount of usable Ring-necked Pheasant habitat, which has resulted in local population declines and extirpations. Ring-necked pheasants remain common in northern Texas, but their distribution has become more fragmented than it was 40 to 50 years ago.

Breeding Biology

The biology and natural history of Ring-necked Pheasants has been studied throughout their North American distribution, and a good deal of research has been conducted in Texas. Their biology and natural history are fairly consistent regardless of where they occur, with the exception of region-specific variables such as timing of breeding that are influenced by climate, and site-specific variables such as nest losses that are influenced by habitat conditions and/or predator populations.

Migration

Ring-necked Pheasants are basically sedentary and do not display long seasonal migrations. However, movement from summer to fall-winter habitats has been documented for Ring-necked Pheasants in the Panhandle and is apparently dictated by changes in the conditions of croplands (Whiteside and Guthery 1983).

Timing of breeding

Intense and frequent crowing of male Ring-necked Pheasants marks the arrival of the breeding season, which is initiated at the onset of spring when temperatures and day length begin to increase and snow cover disappears. Therefore, the timing of the start of breeding varies among years. Breeding in the Panhandle and Rolling Plains typically occurs from March to June, but it can begin earlier and extend into the summer depending on weather and habitat conditions (Taylor 1980).

Behavior

Giudice and Ratti (2001) provide a comprehensive review of Ring-necked Pheasant behavior in their species account for the *Birds of North America* series. The following summary of notable behaviors by Ring-necked Pheasants is based on their account.

Ring-necked Pheasants spend the majority of their time on the ground and are fast runners. When disturbed or alarmed, they are capable of strong and rapid flight. They are also capable of swimming. Pheasants are social birds, particularly hens, which form harems during the breeding season. They often gather to feed in small groups during nesting and then aggregate in larger groups during the fall and winter; some groups may include males. Males are more solitary than females, particularly during the breeding season, but they will gather in larger groups during cold winter weather. Ring-necked Pheasants appear to have strong breeding-site fidelity in that males generally return to the same breeding territory and hens return to the same nesting area during subsequent years. Ring-necked Pheasants are polygynous in that males mate with numerous hens in the territories they establish. Males advertise that they are in breeding condition by crowing loudly and frequently, primarily during dawn and dusk in spring. They also attract hens by strutting and other display behaviors. They establish territories and aggressively defend them while attempting to attract harems from other males. Aggressive encounters between males are common, although fatalities rarely occur. Hens may display aggressive behaviors within a harem, but encounters that result in physical contact are rare. Hens do not defend a nest from other hens

or predators, nor do they defend or actively protect their broods from potential threats. However, hens do emit specific vocalizations to warn chicks or gather them if threats are present. Daily behavior involves feeding during the morning, moving to heavy cover where they spend the middle of the day, resuming feeding during late afternoon, and finally roosting around dusk. There exists some concern that Ring-necked Pheasants could have a detrimental effect on Lesser Prairie-Chicken populations where the 2 species coexist, because research has documented aggressive Ring-necked Pheasant behavior toward Lesser Prairie-Chickens (Svedarsky, Oehlenschlager, and Tonsager 1982; Vance and Westemeier 1979).

Clutch size and incubation

Clutch size ranges from 6 to 15 eggs and averages 10 to 12 eggs; clutch size tends to be smaller later in the nesting season (Giudice and Ratti 2001). Hens incubate eggs for an average of 23 days and produce 1 clutch per year, unless a nest or brood is depredated, after which renesting is common.

Nest losses

Nest losses vary considerably depending on land-use practices, predator populations, and weather. Taylor (1980) reported that on his Panhandle study sites, crop harvesting, predators, abandonment, and flooding accounted for 32%, 21%, 15%, and 5% of nest losses, respectively. Predation in particular can be a major cause of nest losses in certain areas (Giudice and Ratti 2001) where nesting habitat is limited and diverse and/or abundant predator populations are present.

Phenology

Chicks are precocial. Hens lead chicks away from the nest almost immediately after they hatch, although hens and their broods typically remain about 100–150 m (110–164 yd) from the nest site for about a week (Riley, Clark, and Vohs 1998; Giudice and Ratti 2001). Chicks start developing flight feathers within a few days of hatching, and when they are 2 weeks old they are able to make short flights. When chicks are about a week old, hens move broods up to 1000 m (1,100 yd) from nest sites (Riley, Clark, and Vohs 1998).

Hens care for chicks by leading them on foraging activities and while doing so communicate with them via vocalizations that warn them of potential danger, consolidate them when they scatter, and gather them for brooding at night or during inclement weather. Chicks attain juvenile plumage when they are 6 weeks old and become independent of hens when they are 6–8 weeks old. By 16 weeks, juveniles resemble adults (Iowa Department of Natural Resources 2015).

Diet and foraging

Ring-necked Pheasant diets are very broad. Giudice and Ratti (2001) summarized the seasonal foraging and food preferences of pheasants and reported that seeds, grasses, and roots as well as fruits and nuts are important fall and winter foods. Invertebrates and succulent leaves and shoots of herbaceous plants become more important during spring and summer, especially for hens. Agricultural crops make up the bulk of pheasant diets throughout the year, followed by noncultivated plants and animal matter. Since favored habitats in Texas are croplands, grains such as corn, grain sorghum, and wheat are preferred foods. However, seeds of ragweed (*Ambrosia* spp.), smartweed (*Polygonum* spp.), foxtail (*Setaria* spp.), and sunflower (*Helianthus* spp.) are important seed foods for Ring-necked Pheasants in Texas. Woody vegetation is typically not abundant where Ring-necked Pheasants occur in Texas, but they readily consume the mast produced by shrubs and trees in shelterbelts. Grasshoppers, beetles, ants, caterpillars, snails, and earthworms represent important invertebrates consumed by Ring-necked Pheasants, and they are particularly important to hens during spring and to chicks during their first few weeks of life (Korschgen 1964; Stromborg 1979). Ring-necked Pheasants forage on the ground by using their beaks to pick up food items. Because they have strong legs and feet with prominent toes and claws, they also vigorously scratch the soil surface to access food items. Pheasants also forage aboveground on the lower layers of shrubs and trees to access fruit and nuts (Giudice and Ratti 2001).

Demography and vital rates

The Ring-necked Pheasant is not a long-lived species. Annual survival rates are low and vary by sex, age, and the region of the United States where studies are conducted, because of the effects of habitat conditions, predator populations, and weather. Peterson, Dumke, and Gates (1988) summarized results from 13 states, primarily from the Midwest, and reported an annual survival range of 18%–39% for juvenile females, 16%–45% for adult females, 7%–16% for juvenile males, and 7%–34% for adult males. They also reported that fall-to-spring survival for hens ranged from 43% to 77% and spring-to-fall survival ranged from 36% to 81%. Weather can have a negative impact on hen survival; survival rates of hens during cold winters with deep snow in South Dakota and North Dakota resulted in hen survival of 3% and 4%, respectively (Gabbert et al. 1999; Homan, Linz, and Bleier 2000). Brood survival is also generally low, particularly during a chick's first 2 weeks, although chick survival increases thereafter. In Iowa, Riley, Clark, and Vohs (1998) reported that chick survival ranged from 11% to 46%, although in the Texas Panhandle, Shupe (1984) reported a higher chick survival rate of about 75% for chicks from 0 to 10 weeks of age. Ring-necked Pheasants breed as yearlings (Giudice and Ratti 2001); thus all members of a population are capable of contributing to annual population recruitment, although recruitment is typically poor. Giudice and Ratti (2001) estimated that 1.6 chicks per hen were recruited into fall populations. Thus, pheasant chick mortality is high, and mortality remains high among yearlings and adults, such that a 2-year-old bird is an old bird in a Ring-necked Pheasant population. Approximately 5% of a population is made up of birds older than 3 years, but Giudice and Ratti (2001) indicated that most wild birds suffer mortality by the age of 3; complete population turnover occurs about every 5 years.

Age and sex ratios

Age ratios of Ring-necked Pheasants are dominated by juveniles or yearlings in the fall prior to hunting season; 2-year-old birds are rare in fall populations (Switzer 2009). Sex ratios are generally estimated prior to and after hunting seasons to evaluate the impacts of harvest on breeding season population levels. One study in the Texas Panhandle using harvest data estimated that fall sex ratios were 1.2 hens per rooster, 1.7 hens per rooster, and 1.4 hens per rooster in 1979–80,

1980–81, and 1981–82, respectively (Whiteside and Guthery 1983). The percentage of roosters in a population decreases after the hunting season since almost every state limits harvest to roosters only. In the Texas Panhandle, Whiteside and Guthery (1983) reported that sex ratios increased to 9.4 hens per rooster, 3.7 hens per rooster, and 3.7 hens per rooster in 1979–80, 1980–81, and 1981–82, respectively. Sex ratios can vary tremendously on an annual basis. For example, Switzer (2009) reported that winter sex ratios in South Dakota ranged from 20 to 61 roosters per hen between 1946 and 2009. He indicated that the 10-year range between 1999 and 2008 was 32–47 roosters per hen and the average was 39 roosters per hen.

Population Status and Trends

Ring-necked Pheasants have been present in the Panhandle of Texas since they emigrated from Oklahoma during the 1940s and were released periodically thereafter. Population trend data were not collected until 1958, when the National Audubon Society Christmas Bird Count began. Much of the variation for the first 25 years of the survey can probably be attributed to periodic drought and cold winters, which result in poor food and habitat conditions, and thus poor survival and reproduction. The Ring-necked Pheasant increase that is apparent from the mid-1980s to the early 1990s coincided with the first Conservation Reserve Program (CRP) sign-up period, when

thousands of acres of highly erodible cropland were taken out of production and converted to permanent grass cover, which generally provided pheasants with good habitat conditions. However, with the exception of a few years of pheasant increases during the early 2000s, Ring-necked Pheasant populations have steadily declined since about 1993, and populations reached historic lows during the most recent counts. Trend data from the Texas Parks and Wildlife Department (TPWD) summer-fall roadside pheasant survey from 1977 to 2001 are remarkably similar to the CBC data and mimic the steady decline in Texas Ring-necked Pheasant populations over the past two decades. TPWD biologists attribute the Ring-necked Pheasant decline in Texas to the modern farming practices that have been implemented over the past two to three decades (Cook and Miller 2002). The Ring-necked Pheasant decline is not occurring just in Texas. For example, almost 30 years ago, Dahlgren (1988) lamented the decline of Ring-necked Pheasant populations in the United States that began in the early 1970s and continued through the mid-1980s; he was pessimistic about a reversal of this trend. He attributed the declines to changes in farming practices, which emphasized larger fields, clean-farming practices, and increased use of herbicides and insecticides, all of which reduced important Ring-necked Pheasant foods and habitat. The most recent trend data from Iowa (Rodgers 1999), Missouri (Emmerich, Alleger, and White 2012), South Dakota (Runia 2009), and

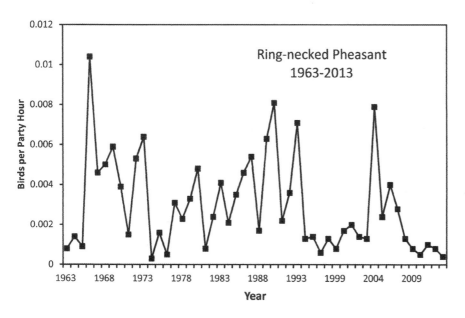

Figure 16.3. Population trend for Ring-necked Pheasants in Texas, based on Christmas Bird Count data.

Pennsylvania (Pabian et al. 2015) generally mirror the Ring-necked Pheasant declines that have been occurring in Texas for the past decade; all of the declines are attributed to the land-use practices that Dahlgren (1988) described. Cook and Miller (2002) believed that the dramatic changes in farming practices that have occurred in the Texas Panhandle over the past 35 years have reduced Ring-necked Pheasant habitat to the extent that the peak Ring-necked Pheasant populations of 40 to 50 years ago will probably not return anytime soon.

Habitat Requirements and Management

Ring-necked Pheasants require habitat components that fulfill their seasonal food and cover requirements. Therefore Ring-necked Pheasant habitat requirements in the Texas Panhandle basically center around cropland and playas (Taylor 1980; Guthery and Bryant 1982). Whiteside and Guthery (1983) summarized seasonal habitat use in the Panhandle, reporting that Ring-necked Pheasants use cropland during the spring for nesting and feeding, although they also use playas for nesting. To some extent cropland is used almost exclusively during summer where grain crops provide abundant foods. Playa basin use increases in frequency during fall; playas are used almost exclusively during winter when cover in crop fields is limited. Important crops include corn, wheat, and grain sorghum (Taylor 1980), as well as soybeans, alfalfa, rye, and oats (Shupe 1984). Grains are an important part of Ring-necked Pheasant diets, particularly during winter (Bolen and Guthery 1982), and the plants provide important escape, thermal, nesting, and brooding cover. Cotton,

Figure 16.5. Ring-necked Pheasant habitat in cornfield. Photo credit: Eric Grahmann.

corn, and the vegetation communities of playas are also a source of invertebrates (Shupe 1984), which are an essential part of Ring-necked Pheasant diets, particularly among nesting hens and their broods during summer. Native grasses and forbs are also important components of Ring-necked Pheasant habitats because in addition to crops, grasses and forbs also provide important cover, as well as important invertebrate habitat. The trees and shrubs that make up shelterbelts and are often found around abandoned farmsteads are important habitat components because the fruits and nuts of woody plants are consumed by Ring-necked Pheasants, and woody cover is very important during cold winter storms. Additionally, undisturbed roadside ditches and fencerows provide nesting and brooding cover, as do abandoned homesteads, which also provide cover during severe winter weather.

Habitat management

Research conducted in the Panhandle has clearly indicated how landscapes should be managed to facilitate Ring-necked Pheasant production. Cropland alone will not support a sustainable Ring-necked Pheasant population. Whiteside and Guthery (1983) indicated that a management unit for Ring-necked Pheasants should include 400 ha (1,000 ac) within about a 1 km (0.62 mi) radius of a playa lake. They recommended two Ring-necked Pheasant management scenarios for the Panhandle: (1) provide a summer crop of either corn or grain sorghum and a winter crop of wheat adjacent to an ungrazed playa, or (2) plant corn, wheat, sorghum, or any other crop adjacent to an ungrazed playa. Management activities should focus on playas larger than 4.0 ha (10 ac). Playas that are modified to collect irrigation tailwater represent better pheasant habitat than unmodified ones because modified playas provide abundant cattail (Typhaceae) and bulrush (Cyperaceae) communities, which serve as important winter cover (Guthery and Stormer 1984). If possible, portions of farm acreages should be left fallow each year and odd areas should be maintained to provide weeds for food seeds and brood cover. Additionally, the vegetation along roadside ditches and fence lines should not be mowed, particularly during spring nesting season, because it provides tall herbaceous cover for nesting hens and their broods. Managing weeds with herbicides reduces Ring-necked Pheasant food supplies; therefore herbicide use should be limited if Ring-necked Pheasant management is a priority.

Hunting and Conservation

Hunting

The first Ring-necked Pheasant hunting season in Texas occurred for a week in mid-December 1958 and bag limits were two roosters per day and four in possession (Guthery, Custer, and Owen 1980). The TPWD has liberalized the hunting season since then.

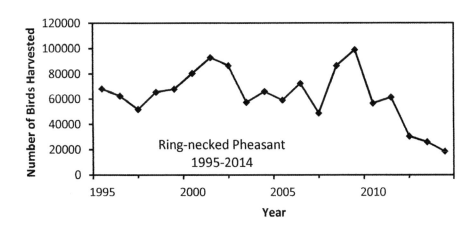

Figure 16.4 Harvest trends of Ring-necked Pheasants in Texas, 1995–2014. Source: Texas Parks and Wildlife Department.

The current hunting season length has been extended to a month, from December 4 to January 3, and the bag limit has increased to three roosters per day and six in possession (Texas Parks and Wildlife Department 2015). Hunting is permitted in 37 Texas counties, and with the exception of Wilbarger County, all of these counties are in the southern High Plains from Lubbock north to the Oklahoma border. Harvest data collection was initiated by the TPWD in 1995 and has been ongoing annually since then. From 1995 to about 2009, the number of Ring-necked Pheasants harvested was relatively stable around an average of about 63,000 birds each year, with the exception of 2000–2001 and 2008–2009, when more than 90,000 birds were harvested. However, since 2008–2009, annual Ring-necked Pheasant harvests have steadily declined, which mirrors the population decline that has evidently been occurring over the past five years. The number of hunters pursuing Ring-necked Pheasants each year has also declined, from more than 28,000 in 2007–2008, the second-highest number recorded over a 20-year period, to an all-time low of about 7,500 hunters in 2013–2014 (Purvis 2014). The reduced harvests of the past seven years are a reflection of hunter difficulty in finding Ring-necked Pheasants and/or a lack of interest among hunters because the birds have become difficult to locate.

Conservation

As indicated earlier in this chapter, Ring-necked Pheasant populations are declining in Texas, a trend that is apparently ongoing throughout their distribution in the United States. The statewide drought that prevailed from 2009 to 2013 undoubtedly contributed to the recent years of decline. It is probably unrealistic to expect that pheasant populations will recover to the peaks seen 40–50 years ago. Profound changes in farming practices have altered landscapes of the Panhandle to the extent that Ring-necked Pheasant habitat has been reduced substantially since the 1970s (Cook and Miller 2002). Modern farming practices emphasize large crop-field sizes to maximize production, which has reduced weedy field edges and limited cover along fence lines. Moreover, clean farming and increased use of herbicides have also reduced the waste grain and forbs that are important Ring-necked

Pheasant foods. Additionally, many farmers have transitioned from row-water irrigation to center-pivot sprinklers, which are more efficient and therefore waste less water. However, the declining use of row-water irrigation has reduced the number of modified playas that capture excess irrigation water, thus reducing the quality of Ring-necked Pheasant habitat in playas. The Ogallala Aquifer, which supplies the irrigation water used by Panhandle farmers, has been receding for at least the past 30 years, and this also poses a threat to Ring-necked Pheasant habitat because corn production requires irrigation and farmers will stop growing corn if they can no longer irrigate it.

The CRP was first implemented in the mid-1980s to establish grass cover on tens of thousands of acres of highly erodible soils in the Texas Panhandle. It was predicted that it would increase the amount of pheasant habitat and thereby improve Ring-necked Pheasant populations. A number of studies conducted within the Ring-necked Pheasant's range in the United States indicate that the establishment of CRP grass cover resulted in population increases (Riley 1995; Haroldson et al. 1996; Nielson et al. 2008). However, Rodgers (1999) indicated that Ring-necked Pheasant populations in western Kansas declined by over 60% between 1966–1975 and 1986–1995 despite the establishment of almost 700,000 ha (1.74 million ac) of CRP acreage in western Kansas since 1985. He believed that whatever benefits the addition of CRP acreage provided Ring-necked Pheasants were insufficient to overcome the habitat loss that occurred as a result of the modern farming practices that prevailed in western Kansas. Similarly, Cook and Miller (2002) and Pabian et al. (2015) indicated that Ring-necked Pheasant habitat improvement efforts have not been sufficient to compensate for the habitat loss resulting from modern farming practices in the Texas Panhandle and Pennsylvania, respectively. Therefore, Ring-necked Pheasant conservation can be improved by reducing field size, limiting the use of herbicides to control weeds and reduce wheat stubble habitats, increasing the use of prescribed burns on field edges to promote forb growth, maintaining cover along ditches and fencerows, suspending mowing activities during spring nesting season, avoiding overgrazing rangelands, suspending grazing of playa lakes, modifying playas so that they capture irrigation water, and providing at least 400 ha (1,000 ac) of summer and winter crops within a 1 km (0.62 mi) radius of a playa. A reduction in Ring-necked Pheasant bag limits and hunting season lengths is not being contemplated by TPWD officials at this time. However, to ensure that pheasant hunting remains a reality, improved pheasant management should be encouraged among agricultural producers in the Texas Panhandle.

Research Priorities

1. Ring-necked Pheasant populations are becoming more fragmented in the Texas Panhandle; therefore research should be conducted on how metapopulation theory can be applied to determine how to arrange habitat corridors and facilitate movement and dispersal among populations.

2. Determine the appropriate components of Conservation Reserve Program vegetation mixtures that would encourage Ring-necked Pheasant use of CRP fields.

3. Determine the appropriate spatial arrangement of important habitat types (CRP fields, cropland, tailwater pits, rangeland, abandoned areas, and shelterbelts) that provide landscapes that maximize Ring-necked Pheasant populations.

4. Conduct research on the impacts of harvest management in counties where Ring-necked Pheasant populations are declining.

5. Conduct research on the impacts of climate change on Ring-necked Pheasant population dynamics.

Literature Cited

Bent, A. C. 1932. *Life Histories of North American Gallinaceous Birds.* US National Museum Bulletin 162. Washington, DC: Smithsonian Institution.

Bolen, E. G., and F. S. Guthery. 1982. Playas, irrigation and wildlife in west Texas. *Transactions of the North American Wildlife and Natural Resources Conference* 47:528–41.

Cook, G. D., and G. T. Miller. 2002. *A Primer: Ring-necked Pheasant Habitat Management in the Texas Panhandle.* Austin: Texas Parks and Wildlife Department.

Dahlgren, R. B. 1988. Pheasant survival and the role of predation. In *Pheasants: Symptoms of Wildlife Problems on Agricultural Lands,* edited by D. L. Hallett, W. R. Edwards, and G. V. Burger, 29–43. Bloomington, IN: North Central Section of the Wildlife Society.

Emmerich, B., M. Alleger, and B. White. 2012. *Missouri Quail and Pheasant Population Status Report.* http://www.mdc.mo.gov/sites/default/files/resources/2010/03/quailpheasantstatus2012.pdf

Evans, P. 1977. History of pheasants in Texas. *Texas Parks and Wildlife* 35:12–14.

Gabbert, A. E., A. P. Leif, J. R. Purvis, and L. D. Flake. 1999. Survival and habitat use by Ring-necked Pheasants during two disparate winters in South Dakota. *Journal of Wildlife Management* 63:711–22.

Giudice, J. H., and J. T. Ratti. 2001. Ring-necked Pheasant (*Phasianus colchicus*). In *The Birds of North America Online,* edited by A. Poole. Ithaca, NY: Cornell Laboratory of Ornithology. http://bna.birds.cornell.edu/bna/species/572. doi:10.2173/bna.572.

Guthery, F. S., and F. C. Bryant. 1982. Status of playas in the southern Great Plains. *Wildlife Society Bulletin* 10:309–17.

Guthery, F. S., J. Custer, and M. Owen. 1980. *Texas Panhandle Pheasants: Their History, Habitat Needs, Habitat Development Opportunities and Future.* USDA Forest Service General Technical Report RM-74. Washington, DC.

Guthery, F. S., and F. A. Stormer. 1984. Wildlife management scenarios for playa vegetation. *Wildlife Society Bulletin* 12:227–34.

Haroldson, K. J., R. O. Kimmel, M. R. Riggs, and A. H. Berner. 2006. Association of Ring-necked Pheasant, Gray Partridge, and Meadowlark abundance to Conservation Reserve Program grasslands. *Journal of Wildlife Management* 70:1276–84.

Holloran, A. F., and J. A. Howard. 1956. Aransas Refuge wildlife introductions. *Journal of Wildlife Management* 20:460–61.

Homan, H. J., G. M. Linz, and W. J. Bleier. 2000. Winter habitat use and survival of female Ring-necked Pheasants (*Phasianus colchicus*) in southeastern North Dakota. *American Midland Naturalist* 143:463–80.

Iowa Department of Natural Resources. 2015. The Ring-necked Pheasant. Life History Accounts. http://www.iowadnr.gov/Hunting/PheasantSmallGame.aspx.

Iowa Upland Game Bird Study Advisory Committee. 2010. *A Review of Iowa's Upland Game Bird Populations.* Report submitted to the governor and General Assembly. Des Moines.

Korschgen, L. J. 1964. Foods and nutrition of Missouri and Midwestern pheasants. *Transactions of the North American Wildlife Conference* 29:159–81.

Nielson, R. M., L. L. McDonald, J. P. Sullivan, C. Burgess, D. S. Johnson, D. H. Johnson, S. Bucholtz, and S. H.

Howlin. 2008. Estimating the response of Ring-necked Pheasants (*Phasianus colchicus*) to the Conservation Reserve Program. *Auk* 125:434–44.

Pabian, S. E., A. M. Wilson, S. R. Klinger, and M. C. Brittingham. 2015. Pennsylvania's Conservation Reserve Program benefits Ring-necked Pheasants but not enough to reverse decline. *Journal of Wildlife Management* 79:641–46.

Peterson, L. R., R. T. Dumke, and J. M. Gates. 1988. Pheasant survival and the role of predation. In *Pheasants: Symptoms of Wildlife Problems on Agricultural Lands*, edited by D. L. Hallett, W. R. Edwards, and G. V. Burger, 165–98. Bloomington, IN: North Central Section of the Wildlife Society.

Purvis, J. 2014. *Small Game Harvest Survey Results 1994–95 thru 2013–14*. Austin: Texas Parks and Wildlife Department.

Riley, T. Z. 1995. Association of the Conservation Reserve Program with Ring-necked Pheasant survey counts in Iowa. *Wildlife Society Bulletin* 23:386–90.

Riley, T. Z., W. R. Clark, and P. A. Vohs. 1998. Survival of Ring-necked Pheasant chicks during brood rearing. *Journal of Wildlife Management* 62:36–44.

Rodgers, R. D. 1999. Why haven't pheasant populations in western Kansas increased with CRP? *Wildlife Society Bulletin* 27:654–65.

Runia, T. J. 2009. Influence of the Conservation Reserve Program and landscape composition on the spatial demographics of prairie grouse in northeastern South Dakota. Master's thesis, South Dakota State University.

Shupe, T. E. 1984. Pheasant brood ecology and effects of irrigation on wildlife on the Texas High Plains. Master's thesis, Texas Tech University.

Stromborg, K. L. 1979. Pheasant food habits in spring and consumption of seed treatment pesticides. *Journal of Wildlife Management* 43:185–89.

Svedarsky, W. D., R. J. Oehlenschlager, and T. D. Tonsager. 1982. A remnant flock of Greater Prairie Chickens in north central Minnesota. *Loon* 54:5–13.

Switzer, C. T. 2009. *Ring-necked Pheasant Management Plan for South Dakota 2009–2014*. Version 09–01. Pierre: South Dakota Department of Game, Fish and Parks.

Taylor, T. T. 1980. Nesting of Ring-necked Pheasants in the Texas Panhandle. Master's thesis, Texas Tech University.

Texas Parks and Wildlife Department. 2015. Outdoor Annual. Austin: Texas Parks and Wildlife Department.

Tyrberg, T. 1998. Pleistocene birds of the Palearctic: A catalogue. Nuttall Ornithological Club Publication No. 27. http://nuttallclub.org/Publications.htm.

Vance, D. R., and R. L. Westemeier. 1979. Interactions of pheasants and prairie chickens in Illinois. *Wildlife Society Bulletin* 7:221–25.

Whiteside, R. W. 1983. Aspects of the ecology and management of pheasants in the High Plains of Texas. PhD diss., Texas Tech University.

Whiteside, R. W., and F. S. Guthery 1983. Ring-necked Pheasant movements, home ranges, and habitat use in west Texas. *Journal of Wildlife Management* 47:1097–104.

17

Lesser Prairie-Chicken

It has disappeared from many sections where it was once abundant; too much grazing on, and extensive cultivation of, the grassy plains have driven it out.—BENT (1932, 280)

Introduction

The Lesser Prairie-Chicken (*Tympanuchus pallidicinctus*) is a small prairie grouse closely related to the Greater Prairie-Chicken (*T. cupido*). It was likely confused with the Greater Prairie-Chicken when it was first encountered by Europeans who settled in the western Great Plains during the 1800s (Taylor and Guthery 1980). It was first described as a distinct species in 1885 (Ridgway 1885). The historical habitat it occupied is distinctly different from that of the Greater Prairie-Chicken, as the only range overlap between the two species occurred in a small portion of western Kansas. Unlike the Greater Prairie-Chicken, which occupies tallgrass prairie communities, Lesser Prairie-Chickens use arid, mid- and short-grass prairie that supports scattered stands of sand sagebrush (*Artemisia filifolia*) and sand shinnery oak (*Quercus havardii*) (Taylor and Guthery 1980). In addition to different habitat preferences, Lesser Prairie-Chicken courtship behavior and vocalizations are distinctly different from those of the Greater Prairie-Chicken (Hagen and Giesen 2005). The Lesser Prairie-Chicken's distinctive courtship behavior made an indelible impression on Native Americans, who imitated the breeding displays and movements of males during traditional ceremonies

(Lehmann, Lehmann-Carssow, and Silvy 2010). Undoubtedly Native Americans utilized them as a source of food as well.

Hagen and Giesen (2005) provide a detailed description of Lesser Prairie-Chickens, which is summarized as follows. They are medium-sized, grayish-brown grouse; sexes are mostly similar in plumage throughout the year. Adults are barred with alternating brown and buffy white bands. Upper portions of the body are darker and more richly colored than lower portions. Tail is short, rounded, and dark. Bright yellow eye combs are evident on adult males, and during the breeding season dull red air sacs are apparent on the side of the neck. Males have a tuft of elongated feathers, or pinnae, on the side of the neck that they erect during courtship displays. Females also have pinnae but they are shorter than those on males. Immature Lesser Prairie-Chickens closely resemble adults but are more richly colored, particularly on the throat.

The recent consideration of the Lesser Prairie-Chicken for listing under the Endangered Species Act has apparently resulted in a flurry of research on nesting and brood rearing (Hagen et al. 2013; Grisham et al. 2014), mating chronology (Behney et al. 2012), lek density modeling (Timmer et al. 2014), and breeding season survival (Grisham and Boal 2015).

Figure 17.1. *(Top)*, male Lesser Prairie-Chicken. Photo credit: Larry Ditto. *(Bottom)*, female Lesser Prairie-Chicken. Photo credit: Larry Ditto.

Distribution

The Lesser Prairie-Chicken was once distributed more broadly through Texas than current distribution indicates. Pleistocene fossils similar to the Lesser Prairie-Chicken have been found in Oregon (Ridgway and Friedman 1946) and southern New Mexico (Wetmore 1932). The extinct species *T. seres* and *T. stirtoni*, which were similar to the Lesser Prairie-Chicken, were found in Newton County, Arkansas (Wetmore 1959), and Bennett County, South Dakota (Miller 1944), respectively. However, the geographic distribution of the Lesser Prairie-Chicken included the southern High Plains from southwestern Colorado to western Kansas south into western Oklahoma, farther south through the Texas Panhandle to perhaps the northern Edwards Plateau, and finally west into the Trans-Pecos and the western fringes of New Mexico (Lehmann, Lehmann-Carssow, and Silvy 2010; Hagen and Giesen 2005). Their present distribution has shrunk considerably because of a combination of conversion of rangelands to farming, livestock overgrazing of rangelands, alteration of fire regimes and the accompanying invasion of woody species, invasion of exotic plants, suburbanization, construction of roads and utility corridors, and fossil fuel exploration (Robb and Schroeder 2005). Fragmented populations now occur in a small portion of western and southwestern Colorado, disjunct portions of western Kansas, extreme northwestern Oklahoma, and along the border of Oklahoma and the Texas Panhandle. Small fragmented populations also occur in the southwestern Texas Panhandle and extend into a few counties in New Mexico. Two populations currently occur in Texas (fig. 17.2). One population occupies five counties and portions of four other counties in the northeastern Texas Panhandle, and the other population occurs in four counties and portions of seven other counties in the extreme southwestern portion of the Panhandle.

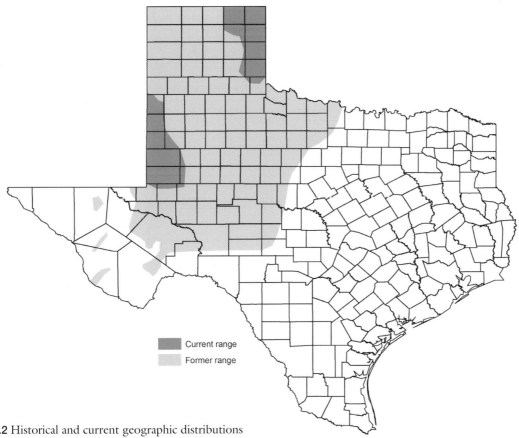

Figure 17.2 Historical and current geographic distributions of the Lesser Prairie-Chicken in Texas.

Breeding Biology

The breeding biology of Lesser Prairie-Chickens is fairly consistent throughout the species' geographic distribution. It is typically influenced by local and annual weather patterns, particularly drought, which suppresses breeding.

Migration

Early observers believed that during the 1800s Lesser Prairie-Chickens were migratory in that the northern portion of their range served as breeding habitat while the southern portion served as wintering habitat (Bent 1932; Sharpe 1968). Taylor and Guthery (1980) disputed this assertion, stating that the movements of the most mobile of grouse species rarely extend about 30 km, which is much shorter than the distance required to move from the northern portion of the Lesser Prairie-Chicken range to the southern portion on an annual basis. Instead, Taylor and Guthery (1980) suspected that birds observed in the southern portion of their range were residents and not migrants because the habitat currently occupied by Lesser Prairie-Chickens was present in the late 1800s. Although Lesser Prairie-Chickens are capable of movements exceeding 30 km (18.6 mi) (Hagen 2003), the majority of extended movements likely represent dispersal of juveniles, movements to winter sources of agricultural crop foods, or responses to severe weather (Taylor and Guthery 1980; Hagen and Giesen 2005). Copelin (1963) reported that most movements between overwinter habitat and leks immediately prior to the breeding season in Oklahoma were less than 2.4 km (1.5 mi). Therefore, it is generally agreed today that Lesser Prairie-Chickens are sedentary rather than migratory.

Timing of breeding

Breeding typically occurs in response to increasing day length and the onset of spring weather. Thus the initiation of breeding activity can vary from year to year but has been reported to occur between January and June (Merchant 1982; Hagen and Giesen 2005). Crawford and Bolen (1976a) reported that Lesser Prairie-Chicken males in the southern Panhandle of Texas were present on leks from early March to late May, but the peak intensity of breeding occurred between the last week of March and the second week of April. They indicated that hens appeared on leks soon after the males during the last week of March and remained there until the third week of May, though over 80% of the hens were present on leks during the first 2 weeks of May and 80% of copulations occurred during this time. Breeding begins to diminish as hens leave leks in late May to nest, and male lek attendance dissipates accordingly until leks are abandoned in early summer.

Behavior

Hagen and Giesen (2005) provide a detailed description of Lesser Prairie-Chicken behavior that is summarized here. Almost all Lesser Prairie-Chicken behavior occurs on the ground, although they are capable of strong flight when alarmed. They will make short flights between feeding and loafing areas; such flights are generally less than 1 km (0.62 mi). They do not swim. Lesser Prairie-Chickens are polygynous and have a lek mating system. Males have strong lek site fidelity; many birds return to the same lek site to breed annually. Breeding behavior is most intense and visible during the spring breeding season, when males engage in elaborate breeding rituals on leks. Peak activity occurs at dawn and continues for about 2 to 3 hours. To attract hens to their small breeding territories on leks and defend territories from other males, males emit a "booming" vocalization by inflating and expelling air through the sacs on their throats. Ritual behavior usually accompanies booming, and males perform this behavior by exposing and enlarging their eye combs, extending the pinnae on their heads, elevating their tails, and simultaneously drooping their wings while spreading primary feathers. At the same time, they extend their necks, stamp their feet on the ground, and move forward. After stamping their feet, males also fan and move their tail retrices in a manner that produces a rustling sound. A "flutter jump" often occurs among males when hens appear on leks, which involves males rising or fluttering up to 3 m (10 ft) above the ground and rotating 180° when they land. The wing beats associated with flutter jumps are noisy and can be heard up to 30 m (100 ft) away. Aggressive encounters between males on leks are common and include many of the behaviors already described. Such encounters often end in chases and fights, especially when hens arrive in the area. Breeding is done primarily by the dominant males. Hens will also emit "booming" sounds when a number of them congregate on a small area of a lek, and the dominant hen generally chases the other hens off the lek, after which she is followed by a male. Hens have strong nest-site fidelity; they often nest in the vicinity of the previous year's nest site. Hens also communicate with their broods using a number of vocalizations that serve as warning, assembling, or brooding signals. Lesser Prairie-Chickens are highly social. Males form flocks that are associated with specific leks, and fall-winter flocks are often large, up to 80 birds.

Behavioral interactions between Lesser Prairie-Chickens and other gallinaceous birds that share their habitat have been recorded in several studies (Sharpe 1968; Vance and Westemeier 1979; Holt et al. 2010). Lesser Prairie-Chickens are subservient in encounters with Ring-necked Pheasants and Greater Prairie-Chickens. In areas where these species co-occur, Lesser Prairie-Chicken populations decline or are extirpated. Nest parasitism by Ring-necked Pheasants is another factor that results in lost Lesser Prairie-Chicken productivity (Westemeier et al. 1998).

Clutch size and incubation

Lesser Prairie-Chickens appear to have strong nest-site fidelity, as the hens tend to nest in the vicinity of the previous year's nest site (Pitman et al. 2006). Nests are bowl-shaped depressions on the soil surface that hens line with dried vegetation and feathers (Bent 1932). Hens lay 1 egg per day and cover eggs with vegetation until the final egg is laid and incubation begins (Hagen and Giesen 2005). Clutch sizes range from 8 to 14 eggs and average 10.4 eggs (Hagen and Giesen 2005). However, Patten et al. (2005) reported that geographic variation occurred in clutch size between New Mexico (8.7 eggs) and Oklahoma (10.8 eggs), and they attributed this difference to life history adaptations to habitat fragmentation and land uses specific to the areas Lesser Prairie-Chickens inhabited. Hens that lose their first nest may renest about 2 weeks later; clutch sizes of second nests are usually smaller (Pitman 2003). Juvenile and adult hens had similar clutch sizes for first nests in Kansas, but juveniles had larger clutch sizes than adults in second nests (Pitman 2003). Incubation requires 24–26 days (Hagen and Giesen 2005).

Nest losses

Lesser Prairie-Chicken nest success is variable and depends on a multitude of site-specific factors such as nesting habitat conditions and drought. For example, Hagen and Giesen (2005) reported that nest success ranged from 0 to 67% and averaged 28% in 10 studies across the species' geographic range. Davis (2009) recorded a nest success rate of 76% in New Mexico, and Lautenbach (2015) reported a nest success rate of 39% in southwestern Kansas. In addition, Lyons et al. (2011) reported that nest success in the northeastern Texas Panhandle (67%) was higher than in the southwestern Texas Panhandle (38%), and that drought apparently had an impact on nesting attempts, nest success, and renesting attempts. Pitman et al. (2006) indicated that nest success in southwestern Kansas was 26% and that nest success was similar for juveniles (31%) and adults (27%). They also found higher nest success for first nests (29%) than second nests (14%), and 95% of all nests completed occurred between May 5 and July 2. Mammalian predators are responsible for most nest losses, although birds and reptiles also prey on nests (Hagen and Giesen 2005; Pitman et al. 2006). Anthropogenic features such as power line transmission towers, wellheads, and buildings can result in hens avoiding what would otherwise be considered good nesting habitat (Pitman et al. 2005; Pitman 2003).

Phenology

Nesting behavior begins in mid-April and extends into May. Hatching peaks in late May–June (Copelin 1963; Merchant 1982; Hagen and Giesen 2005). Hagen and Giesen (2005) and Robb and Schroeder (2005) detailed chick behavior and development, and a summary of their work is provided here. Chicks are precocial; thus hens lead chicks away from the nest within 24 hours of hatching to habitat patches with abundant invertebrates. Hens brood chicks periodically throughout the day and during the night during the first 2 weeks, and otherwise chicks forage on insects throughout the day. Chicks develop rapidly and are capable of flight when they are 2 weeks old. Both male and female chicks reach the expected body mass of yearlings 76–80 days after hatching, which is generally in August, and thus become independent of hens soon thereafter, at about 12–15 weeks of age. Once they reach independence, juveniles form mixed flocks with adults during the fall.

Diet and foraging

Lesser Prairie-Chickens forage on the ground in native rangeland vegetation or in grain fields (Hagen and Giesen 2005). Invertebrates are an important component of the diets of both adults and juveniles, followed by plant material (Van Pelt et al. 2013). Seeds and the new green growth of plants are important foods during spring, and invertebrates become increasingly important as nesting ensues (Van Pelt et al. 2013). Summer diets of adults in New Mexico were composed of over 50% invertebrates, followed by leaves and flowers, and then seeds as well as acorns of shinnery oak (*Quercus harvardii*; C. Davis et al. 1979). Fall and winter diets are dominated by a mixture of seeds and plant material, followed by invertebrates; waste grain in wheat and sorghum fields becomes increasingly important during winter (Crawford and Bolen 1976c; Riley, Davis, and Smith 1993). Brood diets are composed almost entirely of invertebrates during their first few weeks of life. Jones (1963) found that insects made up more than 85% of juvenile diets in Oklahoma, and C. Davis et al. (1979) indicated that long-horned grasshoppers (Tettigoniidae), treehoppers (Membracidae), and beetles (Coleoptera) were the major component of the diets of chicks more than 10 weeks old. Adults forage either alone or in small flocks, generally during early morning or late afternoon, although chicks forage throughout the day (Hagen and Giesen 2005).

Demography and vital rates

Lesser Prairie-Chickens are capable of breeding their first year, and most all females breed. Few yearling males breed because adult males dominate territories on leks (Hagen and Giesen 2005). Hens generally raise only 1 successful brood annually, although some hens will renest if their first nest fails. The earlier a

first nest fails, the more likely it is that a renesting attempt will occur (Pitman 2003). Reproductive success and recruitment into fall populations vary with precipitation and are, as expected, lower during drought. Hagen and Giesen (2005) reported that brood sizes during late summer in New Mexico and Oklahoma ranged from 3.5 to 7.8 and were lower during drought years. D. Davis (2009) indicated that brood success in New Mexico was 50%, and fall hunter bags in New Mexico comprised 53%–55% juveniles (Campbell 1972). The maximum estimated life span of Lesser Prairie-Chickens is 5 years (Campbell 1972), but survival for most birds is probably less than or equal to 2 years (Hagen et al. 2005). Survival varies according to age, sex, season, and location. For example, Campbell (1972) estimated that annual survival in New Mexico was 47%, although Jamison (2000) estimated that annual survival was 74% in southwestern Kansas. In Kansas annual survival for adult hens (37%) was lower than that of yearlings (57%; Hagen 2003), while survival among males in New Mexico was higher among adults (35%–45%) than it was for yearlings (31%–32%; Campbell 1972). Survival rates during the breeding season for both sexes are typically lower than at other times of the year (Jones 2009). Overwinter survival estimates have ranged from 31% to 80% in Texas (Lyons et al. 2009; Kukal 2010; Pirius et al. 2013). Pitman (2003) indicated that overwinter survival rates were similar between adults (63%) and juveniles (64%). Chick survival is lowest during their first 14 days of life (Pitman 2003; Lautenbach 2015), and survival from hatch to 60 days has been reported to be 11% (Pitman 2003) in southwestern Kansas, 39% in another southwestern Kansas study (Lautenbach 2015), and 49% in southwestern New Mexico (Fields et al. 2006). Broods raised by adults had higher survival rates (49%) than broods raised by subadults (5%) (Pitman 2003). Pitman (2003) estimated that overwinter and annual survival of chicks and juveniles was 70% and 12%, respectively. On average, probably about half of a Lesser Prairie-Chicken population turns over each year.

Age and sex ratios

Lesser Prairie-Chicken populations are typically composed of more males than females. Taylor and Guthery

(1980) provided an overall sex ratio of 1.0 male/0.78 female from 4 studies conducted in Oklahoma and New Mexico. Hagen and Giesen (2005) reported an overall adult sex ratio from 3 studies in Oklahoma and New Mexico as 1.72 males/1.0 female. Age ratios generally favor juveniles. Taylor and Guthery (1980) reported an overall age ratio from 3 studies as 1.12 juveniles/1.0 adult.

Population Status and Trends

Lesser Prairie-Chickens were once thought to inhabit about 473,000 km² (182,843 sq mi) of short-grass prairie, although portions along boundaries of this estimated range were likely uninhabitable (Van Pelt et al. 2013). Taylor and Guthery (1980) estimated that they occupied 358,000 km² (138,225 sq mi), which probably accounted for boundary habitat that was unusable. Nevertheless, the historical geographic range of the Lesser Prairie-Chicken was an enormous area, which has been reduced by 83% during the past century to about 80,300 km² (30,900 sq mi; Van Pelt et al. 2013) of very fragmented habitat that supports a number of metapopulations of Lesser Prairie-Chickens. Mote et al. (1999) believed that Lesser Prairie-Chicken populations had declined by 97% rangewide. Garton (2012) estimated that populations increased during the latter part of the 1960s and then suffered a severe decline from about 200,000 birds in the 1970s to about 50,000 to 100,000 birds in the mid-1990s, when the range-wide population stabilized. Between 1999 and 2012, Garton (2012) estimated that 67,473 birds existed across their range. Because of the significant decline of the Lesser Prairie-Chicken throughout its geographic range, the US Fish and Wildlife Service published a final ruling to list it as a threatened species in April 2014 (US Fish and Wildlife Service 2014).

After the late 1800s, Lesser Prairie-Chicken populations in Texas followed a pattern similar to one that occurred throughout their range. Jackson and DeArment (1963) noted that the population in the Texas Panhandle had experienced an alarming decline between 1952 and 1956 because of a severe drought and also noted that the population had not recovered when good rainfall resumed two years after the drought. Sullivan, Hughes, and Lionberger

(2000) indicated that between 1963 and 1980, a large reduction (78%) in Lesser Prairie-Chicken numbers occurred for populations in the southwestern and south-central part of the Texas Panhandle, but that populations in the northeastern part of the Panhandle remained stable. Furthermore, between 1990 and 2000, numbers in the northeastern Panhandle were about 7% lower than the 1942–1989 average, and for the southwestern Panhandle numbers were almost 55% below the 1969–1989 average. Garton (2012) estimated that between 1999 and 2012, about 32,000 birds occurred in the mixed-grass prairie ecoregion of the northeastern Texas Panhandle and western Oklahoma, and about 5,000 birds occurred in the shinnery oak prairie of the southwestern Texas Panhandle and southeastern New Mexico. The most recent population estimates for Texas indicate that the population declined from about 35,000 birds in 2012 to 18,474 birds in 2013 and then increased to 22,415 birds in 2014 (McDonald et al. 2014). The 53% decline between 2012 and 2013 was attributed to severe drought. Although Lesser Prairie-Chicken populations have recently suffered a significant decline since 2012, McDonald et al. (2014) indicated that small range expansions have occurred for populations in both the southwestern and northeastern portions of the Texas Panhandle as a result of landowner incentive programs and cooperative efforts between state and federal agencies and private landowners.

Habitat Requirements and Management

Lesser Prairie-Chicken populations require sufficient breeding, nesting, brood-rearing, summer, and fall-winter habitat to maintain self-sustaining populations (Van Pelt et al. 2013). Lesser Prairie-Chickens prefer short- to mid-grass vegetation communities interspersed with shrubs (Jones 1963). In Texas, populations in the southwestern portion of the Panhandle occupy sand shinnery oak mixed-grassland communities (Hagen et al. 2005) characterized by subordinate sand sagebrush and fragrant sumac (*Rhus aromatica*), as well as sand bluestem (*Andropogon hallii*), little bluestem (*Schizachyrium scoparium*), sand dropseed (*Sporobolus cryptandrus*), and switchgrass (*Panicum virgatum*) (Taylor and Guthery 1980). Populations in

Figure 17.3. Lesser Prairie-Chicken habitat in short-grass prairie. Photo credit: Eric Grahmann.

the northeastern Panhandle occupy a mixture of sand sagebrush and sand shinnery oak grasslands (Hagen et al. 2005) that have subordinate amounts of Chickasaw plum (*Prunus angustifolia*) and fragrant sumac, as well as the same dominant grasses that occur in the southwestern portion of the Panhandle (Taylor and Guthery 1980). However, Cannon and Knopf (1979) emphasized that Lesser Prairie-Chickens respond to the two major plant communities differently, suggesting that in sand sagebrush communities brush is more important, whereas in sand shinnery oak communities midsized to tall perennial grass cover is more important. Crops such as corn, wheat, and grain sorghum are also grown in both regions, and cropland is useful habitat (Applegate and Riley 1998; Hagen et al. 2005), although Crawford and Bolen (1976a) indicated that habitat begins to deteriorate

for Lesser Prairie-Chickens when more than 37% of the landscape is cropland.

Breeding habitats or leks are typically areas with short vegetative cover surrounded by sand sagebrush or shinnery oak (Giesen 1998), where the breeding displays of males are very visible to hens. Leks are often located on high points such as ridges or knolls (Hagen et al. 2004). Abandoned oil pads, heavily grazed areas, infrequently used roads, recently burned areas, areas of herbicide treatments, and cultivated fields next to rangeland are also used as leks as long as vegetation is very short (Hagen et al. 2005). Van Pelt et al. (2013) reported that maintaining a mixture of nesting habitat from April to June and brooding habitat from June to August is critical to Lesser Prairie-Chicken habitat. Nesting habitat is typically within 1.6 km (1 mi) of leks and is composed of a high density of perennial grass clumps about 30 cm (12 in) in height, together with about 30% sand sagebrush or shinnery oak (Applegate and Riley 1998). Visual obstruction is typically higher at nest sites, which provides better concealment for nests and incubating hens. It is evidently important, because higher visual obstruction at nests in the northeastern Panhandle resulted in higher nest success than for nests in the southwestern Panhandle where visual obstruction at nests was lower (Lyons et al. 2011). Tall, dense stands of vegetation appear to be important to nest success (Hagen et al. 2004), and in sand sagebrush communities in Kansas, higher nest success was associated with high shrub densities (Pitman 2003). Brood habitat is provided by plant communities that harbor abundant invertebrates, which are essential components of chick diets. Hagen et al. (2004) indicated that brood habitat in Oklahoma, New Mexico, and Kansas had moderate stands of cover composed of a mixture of forbs, grasses, and shrubs that were about 30 cm tall and provided sufficient bare ground to facilitate brood foraging and rapid escape from potential threats. Applegate and Riley (1998) reported that green wheat fields are good brood habitats because they support abundant invertebrates. During summer, Lesser Prairie-Chickens in the southwestern Panhandle selected sites with high shinnery oak cover and height, together with a high diversity of forbs and grasses (Taylor and Guthery 1980). During fall and winter, cultivated fields that supply waste grains are important Lesser Prairie-Chicken habitats (Kukal 2010), although adjacent rangelands composed of taller grasses remain important as loafing and roosting sites (Hagen and Giesen 2005). Shrub cover is also a requirement of winter habitats, as Pirius et al. (2013) and Kukal (2010) found that Lesser Prairie-Chickens in the southwestern and northeastern Panhandle preferred grasslands with scattered sand shinnery oak and sand sagebrush, respectively.

Habitat management

Lesser Prairie-Chicken habitat management requires careful planning because they are more sensitive to disturbance than many of the other upland game bird species detailed in this book. Many of the traditional management techniques that are employed to improve habitat for turkeys and pheasants, for example, may render prairie-chicken habitat unusable. Since Lesser Prairie-Chickens occupy primarily rangelands, livestock grazing is an important habitat management tool. Excessive grazing coupled with drought have been two of the primary reasons for the dramatic decline that has occurred among Lesser Prairie-Chickens over the years. Maintaining bunchgrasses at a height of about 30 cm (12 in) on rangelands occupied by Lesser Prairie-Chickens is important. Thus, moderate grazing or reducing stocking rates during drought is an important habitat management strategy. Prescribed burning and herbicide application are brush management techniques that have been used to improve grazing on rangelands occupied by Lesser Prairie-Chickens. Prescribed burning in particular can be beneficial because it can create new lek sites (Cannon and Knopf 1979), and the increased forb response of newly burned areas provides good foraging habitat (Boyd and Bidwell 2001). Similarly, Doerr and Guthery (1983) reported that tebuthiuron used to manage shinnery oak at a rate of 0.4–0.6 kg/ha (0.35–0.53 lb/ac) and applied to small areas interspersed throughout a larger area improved habitat by increasing nesting cover and forb production while still leaving untreated areas that provided woody thermal and escape cover. However, prescribed fire and herbicides can in many instances render treated areas unusable by removing too much of the grass and/or woody cover that provides important nesting, brooding, loafing, and winter habitats (Taylor and Guthery 1980; Boyd and Bidwell 2001; Bell 2005). Extensive and continuous prescribed burns or herbicide treatments that impact sand sagebrush or sand shinnery oak communities over hundreds or thousands of hectares essentially destroy Lesser Prairie-Chicken habitat for a substantial amount of time. It is far better to restrict prescribed burns to smaller patches and schedule treatments over a multiyear planning horizon so that habitat management actions occur gradually over time and on a small scale annually. Applying brush management in this manner, coupled with appropriate and flexible livestock grazing, will promote habitat diversity that will improve Lesser Prairie-Chicken habitat conditions.

In addition to active habitat management, reducing long-term anthropogenic disturbance activities, such as road construction and energy exploration, should be considered, because Lesser Prairie-Chickens are sensitive to disturbance (Hagen et al. 2004). Construction activities or other frequent disturbances to an area frequented by Lesser Prairie-Chickens will likely prompt them to abandon important leks (Crawford and Bolen 1976b) or nesting areas (Pitman 2003) that have been used for years. Another anthropogenic action that was anticipated to be of benefit to Lesser Prairie-Chickens was the US Department of Agriculture's Conservation Reserve Program (CRP), which was initiated in the mid-1980s and took millions of acres of highly erodible cropland out of production by paying farmers to plant acreages to permanent grass cover. Sullivan, Hughes, and Lionberger (2000) indicated that reauthorization of the CRP in 1996 may have benefited wildlife in general in the southern Great Plains, but they indicated that CRP implementation in the Texas Panhandle will have to improve in order for Lesser Prairie-Chickens to benefit. However, Fields et al. (2006) indicated that the long-term benefit of the CRP was evident on their southwestern Kansas study area, particularly during the breeding season, and further indicated that the CRP may allow birds to persist during drought. Ripper and VerCauteren (2007) also believed that CRP plantings in Kansas were consistent with the range expansion they observed. CRP plantings that are most beneficial to Lesser Prairie-Chickens are a mixture of native grasses and forbs (Applegate and Riley 1998).

Proper and timely habitat management activities that manipulate or maintain vegetation communities in a manner that is beneficial to Lesser Prairie-Chickens are important to maintaining self-sustaining populations. However, manipulating vegetation communities alone is unlikely to have the desired result of conserving the Lesser Prairie-Chicken. The geographic distribution of this bird has declined by 92% since the 1800s (Taylor and Guthery 1980), and it exists today as isolated populations only where suitable habitat remains. Clearly, habitat fragmentation is one of the major threats to the continued existence of Lesser Prairie-Chickens. For example, Woodward et al. (2001) reported that Oklahoma landscapes where populations had declined had greater rates of landscape change and shrubland loss than landscapes where populations had not declined. Additionally, Fulendorf et al. (2002) found that changes in landscape structure

over several decades had a stronger relationship with Lesser Prairie-Chicken dynamics than did current landscape structure. Woodward et al. (2001) suggested that conservation of Lesser Prairie-Chickens needs to focus on maintaining the stability of vegetation communities and land use. Habitat management therefore needs to not only focus on manipulating vegetation communities to provide better habitat conditions, but should also emphasize preventing additional landscape fragmentation where remaining populations occur. In addition, it should reduce fragmentation by creating habitat corridors that permit dispersal between populations that are separated. Finally, since Lesser Prairie-Chicken productivity is particularly susceptible to drought, habitat management needs to anticipate the impacts of climate change on population persistence. Dunn and Milne (2014) believe that aridity and higher temperatures resulting from climate change would make it more difficult for Lesser Prairie-Chicken populations to persist in New Mexico and the southwestern Texas Panhandle. Similarly, Grisham et al. (2013) modeled the impacts of climate change on Lesser Prairie-Chicken populations and predicted that above-average winter temperatures could have a negative impact on populations because of more frequent drought. Therefore, future habitat management planning should account for the potential impacts of climate change on Lesser Prairie-Chickens. A major effort should be made to conserve and maintain existing nesting and brooding habitats in particular, and appropriately established CRP plantings could contribute to this endeavor.

Hunting and Conservation

Hunting Lesser Prairie-Chickens has been suspended in all five states where populations currently exist, because the bird was recently designated as a threatened species in the United States by the US Fish and Wildlife Service. Hunting prairie-chickens was legal in Texas up until 2009, when it was suspended. Hunters were permitted to harvest two birds and were allowed four in possession. Hagen et al. (2004) provide trend data for Lesser Prairie-Chicken harvests in Texas between the mid-1960s and early 2000s, and with the exception of 1970, when about 3.5 birds were harvested per hunter, Lesser Prairie-Chicken harvests averaged about 1.5 birds per hunter up to the mid- to late 1980s, when harvests began to decline. Prairie-chickens were not harvested through the mid-1990s, but harvests resumed in 1997 and rose to about one bird per hunter before again declining.

Conservation

Because of the current status of the Lesser Prairie-Chicken as a federally threatened species, it has now become a priority among the states that the species inhabits. The game and fish agencies of the five states that support Lesser Prairie-Chicken populations recognized the precarious status of the bird several years before federal listing. Representatives of each state formed an interagency working group whose primary goal was to develop a conservation plan that identified regional threats and outlined a plan of action that would increase the range-wide population and expand distribution (Mote et al. 1999). What has resulted from this initial meeting is a collaborative range-wide conservation plan that was formalized in 2013. It was believed that if the plan was implemented in a timely manner, it would preclude the need for federal listing of the species (Van Pelt et al. 2013). The primary goal of the plan is to conserve Lesser Prairie-Chickens for future generations and to facilitate uninterrupted economic activity throughout the entire five-state range. An important aspect of this plan is to actively engage and provide incentives for private landowners to become involved in Lesser Prairie-Chicken conservation, since almost all of the current populations occur on private land. This plan did not circumvent federal listing of the species, but it does provide a very detailed description of Lesser Prairie-Chicken life history and habitat requirements, and it identifies conservation strategies and planned activities that should be implemented to conserve and expand populations.

The Lesser Prairie-Chicken range-wide conservation plan developed by Van Pelt et al. (2013) describes conservation planning for the bird in great detail. A summary of the plan is provided here. The plan identifies both range-wide and subpopulation goals and establishes a benchmark number of birds across the range that will be attained in 10 years. It also identifies the specific habitat types and the amounts of these habitat types that are needed to attain the range-wide 10-year population goal. In addition, the plan identifies focal areas and connectivity zones where conservation activities are emphasized to yield desired habitats in an effort to mitigate the current fragmentation issue, which is a significant limiting factor. One highlight of the plan is that it emphasizes encouraging private landowners to volunteer in Lesser Prairie-Chicken conservation by giving them genuine incentives to provide better habitat conditions. Energy companies and other land developers are also encouraged to participate in the conservation plan, and this would be accomplished via negotiated agreements that would avoid or minimize disturbance activities, or at least mitigate the impact of these activities. Research needs are identified in the plan and monitoring activities are suggested for implementation. Furthermore, the plan includes an adaptive management framework that incorporates monitoring results and relevant new information into ongoing conservation planning to maximize benefits to Lesser Prairie-Chicken populations. Finally, the conservation plan encourages input from state and federal agencies, private landowners, nongovernmental organizations, industry, and the general public in the Lesser Prairie-Chicken conservation planning process. Lesser Prairie-Chicken conservation will require cooperation and the collaboration of numerous stakeholders in order to achieve the goals of improving and expanding habitat, and ultimately increasing Lesser Prairie-Chicken numbers throughout their historical geographic range.

Research Priorities

1. Habitat fragmentation is a significant threat to Lesser Prairie-Chicken populations. Therefore, developing methods of applying metapopulation theory to Lesser Prairie-Chicken populations should be a research priority.

2. Determine how to maximize reproductive success of Lesser Prairie-Chicken hens.

3. Conduct research on chick ecology, with particular emphasis on chick habitat and survival.

4. Identify the Conservation Reserve Program vegetation mixtures that Lesser Prairie-Chickens prefer.

5. Since the Lesser Prairie-Chicken is now a federally listed species, it is appropriate to begin conducting research on the best techniques for translocation of birds to bolster or start new populations.

Literature Cited

Applegate, R. D., and T. Z. Riley. 1998. Lesser Prairie-Chicken management. *Rangelands* 20:13–15.

Behney, A. C., B. A. Grisham, C. W. Boal, H. A. Whitlaw, and D. A. Haukos. 2012. Sexual selection and mating chronology of Lesser Prairie-Chickens. *Wilson Journal of Ornithology* 124:96–105.

Bell, L. A. 2005. Habitat use and growth and development of juvenile prairie chickens in southeast New Mexico. Master's thesis, Southeastern Oklahoma State University.

Bent, A. C. 1932. *Life Histories of North American Gallinaceous Birds*. US National Museum Bulletin 162. Washington, DC: Smithsonian Institution.

Boyd, C. S., and T. G. Bidwell. 2001. Influence of prescribed fire on Lesser Prairie-Chicken habitat in shinnery oak communities in western Oklahoma. *Wildlife Society Bulletin* 29:938–47.

Campbell, H. 1972. A population study of Lesser Prairie-Chickens in New Mexico. *Journal of Wildlife Management* 36:689–99.

Cannon, R. W., and F. L. Knopf. 1979. Lesser Prairie-Chicken responses to range fires at the booming ground. *Wildlife Society Bulletin* 71:44–46.

Copelin, F. F. 1963. *The Lesser Prairie-Chicken in Oklahoma*. Technical Bulletin 6. Oklahoma City: Oklahoma Wildlife Conservation Department.

Crawford, J. A., and E. G. Bolen. 1976a. Effects of land use on Lesser Prairie-Chickens in Texas. *Journal of Wildlife Management* 40:96–104.

———. 1976b. Effects of lek disturbances on Lesser Prairie-Chickens. *Southwestern Naturalist* 21:238–40.

———. 1976c. Fall diet of Lesser Prairie Chickens in west Texas. *Condor* 78:142–44.

Davis, C. A., T. Z. Riley, R. A. Smith, H. R. Suminski, and M. J. Wisdom. 1979. *Habitat Evaluation of Lesser Prairie-Chickens in Eastern Chaves County, New Mexico*. Las Cruces: New Mexico Agricultural Experiment Station.

Davis, D. M. 2009. Nesting ecology and reproductive success of Lesser Prairie-Chickens in shinnery oak-dominated rangelands. *Wilson Journal of Ornithology* 121:322–27.

Doerr, T. B., and F. S. Guthery. 1983. Effects of tebuthiuron on Lesser Prairie-Chicken habitat and foods. *Journal of Wildlife Management* 47:1138–42.

Dunn, W. C., and B. T. Milne. 2014. Implications of climatic heterogeneity for conservation of the Lesser Prairie-Chicken (*Tympanuchus pallidicinctus*). *Ecosphere* 5:64.

Fields, T. L., G. C. White, W. C. Gilgert, and R. D. Rodgers. 2006. Nest and brood survival of Lesser Prairie-Chickens in west central Kansas. *Journal of Wildlife Management* 70:931–38.

Fuhlendorf, S. D., A. J. Woodward, D. M. Leslie, and J. S. Shackford. 2002. Multi-scale effects of habitat loss and fragmentation on Lesser Prairie-Chicken populations of the US southern Great Plains. *Landscape Ecology* 17:617–28.

Garton, E. O. 2012. An assessment of population dynamics and persistence of Lesser Prairie-Chickens. Unpublished manuscript. Western Association of Fish and Wildlife Agencies.

Giesen, K. M. 1998. Lesser Prairie-Chicken (*Tympanuchus pallidicinctus*). Account No. 364. In *The Birds of North America*, edited by A. Poole and F. Gill. Washington, DC: American Ornithologists' Union.

Grisham, B. A., and C. W. Boal. 2015. Causes of mortality and temporal patterns in breeding season survival of Lesser Prairie-Chickens in shinnery oak prairies. *Wildlife Society Bulletin* 39:536–42.

Grisham, B. A., C. W. Boal, D. A. Haukos, D. M. Davis, and K. K. Boydston. 2013. The predicted influence of climate change on Lesser Prairie-Chicken reproductive parameters. *PLoS One* 8 (7): e68225.

Grisham, B. A., P. K. Borsdorf, C. W. Boal, and K. K. Boydston. 2014. Nesting ecology and nest survival of Lesser Prairie-Chickens on the southern High Plains of Texas. *Journal of Wildlife Management* 78:857–66.

Hagen, C. A. 2003. A demographic analysis of Lesser Prairie-Chicken populations in southwestern Kansas: Survival, population viability and habitat use. PhD diss., Kansas State University.

Hagen, C. A., and K. M. Giesen. 2005. Lesser Prairie-Chicken (*Tympanuchus pallidicinctus*). In *The Birds of North America Online*, edited by A. Poole. Ithaca, NY: Cornell Laboratory of Ornithology. http://bna.birds.cornell.edu/bna/species/364.

Hagen, C. A., B. A. Grisham, C. W. Boal, and D. A. Haukos. 2013. A meta-analysis of Lesser Prairie-Chicken nesting and brood-rearing habitats: Implications for habitat management. *Wildlife Society Bulletin* 37:750–58.

Hagen, C. A., B. E. Jamison, K. M. Giesen, and T. Z. Riley. 2004. Guidelines for managing Lesser Prairie-Chicken populations and their habitats. *Wildlife Society Bulletin* 32:69–82.

Hagen, C. A., J. C. Pitman, B. K. Sandercock, R. J. Robel, and R. D. Applegate. 2005. Age-specific variation in apparent survival rates of male Lesser Prairie-Chickens. *Condor* 107:78–86.

Holt, R. D., M. J. Butler, W. B. Ballard, C. A. Kukal, and H. Whitlaw. 2010. Disturbance of lekking Lesser Prairie-Chickens (*Tympanuchus pallidicinctus*) by Ring-necked Pheasants (*Phasianus colchicus*). *Western North American Naturalist* 70:241–44.

Jackson, A. S., and R. DeArment. 1963. The Lesser Prairie Chicken in the Texas Panhandle. *Journal of Wildlife Management* 27:733–37.

Jamison, B. E. 2000. Lesser Prairie-Chicken chick survival, adult survival and habitat selection and movement of males in fragmented landscapes of southwestern Kansas. Master's thesis, Kansas State University.

Jones, R. E. 1963. Identification and analysis of Lesser and Greater Prairie-Chicken habitat. *Journal of Wildlife Management* 27:757–78.

Kukal, C. A. 2010. The over-winter ecology of Lesser Prairie-Chickens (*Tympanuchus pallidicinctus*) in the northeast Texas Panhandle. PhD diss., Texas Tech University.

Lautenbach, J. M. 2015. Lesser Prairie-Chicken reproductive success, habitat selection and response to trees. PhD diss., Kansas State University.

Lehmann, V. W., N. Lehmann-Carssow, and N. J. Silvy. 2010. Prairie Chickens. *Handbook of Texas Online*. http://www.tshaonline.org/handbook/online/articles/tbp02.

Lyons, E. K., B. A. Collier, N. J. Silvy, R. R. Lopez, B. E. Toole, R. S. Jones, and S. J. DeMaso. 2009. Breeding and non-breeding survival of Lesser Prairie-Chickens *Tympanuchus pallidicinctus* in Texas, USA. *Wildlife Biology* 15:89–96.

Lyons, E. K., R. S. Jones, J. P. Leonard, B. E. Toole, R. A. McCleery, R. R. Lopez, M. J. Peterson, and N. J. Silvy. 2011. Regional variation in nesting success of Lesser Prairie-Chickens. In *Ecology, Conservation, and Management of Grouse*, edited by B. K. Sandercock, K. Martin, and G. Segelbacher, 223–32. *Studies in Avian Biology* 39.

McDonald, L., G. Beauprez, G. Gardner, J. Griswold, C. Hagen, F. Hornsby, D. Klute, et al. 2014. Range-wide population size of the Lesser Prairie-Chicken: 2012 and 2013. *Wildlife Society Bulletin* 38:536–46.

Merchant, S. S. 1982. Habitat use, reproductive success and survival of female Lesser Prairie-Chickens in two years of contrasting weather. Master's thesis, New Mexico State University.

Miller, A. H. 1944. An avifauna from the lower Miocene of South Dakota. *Bulletin of the Department of Geological Sciences, University of California, Berkeley* 27:85–100.

Mote, K. D., R. D. Applegate, J. A. Bailey, K. E. Giesen, R. Horton, and J. L. Sheppard. 1999. Assessment and conservation strategy for the Lesser Prairie-Chicken (*Tympanuchus pallidicinctus*). Emporia: Kansas Department of Wildlife and Parks.

Patten, M. A., D. H. Wolfe, E. Shochat, and S. K. Sherrod. 2005. Habitat fragmentation, rapid evolution and population persistence. *Evolutionary Ecology Research* 7:235–49.

Pirius, N. E., C. W. Boal, D. A. Haukos, and M. C. Wallace. 2013. Winter habitat use and survival of Lesser Prairie-Chickens in West Texas. *Wildlife Society Bulletin* 37:759–65.

Pitman, J. C. 2003. Lesser Prairie-Chicken nest site selection and nest success, juvenile gender determination and growth, and juvenile survival and dispersal in southwestern Kansas. Master's thesis, Kansas State University.

Pitman, J. C., C. A. Hagen, B. E. Jamison, R. J. Robel, T. M. Loughin, and R. D. Applegate. 2006. Nesting ecology of Lesser Prairie-Chickens in sand sagebrush prairie of southwestern Kansas. *Wilson Journal of Ornithology* 118:23–35.

Pitman, J. C., C. A. Hagen, R. J. Robel, T. M. Loughin, and R. D. Applegate. 2005. Location and success of Lesser Prairie-Chicken nests in relation to vegetation and human disturbance. *Journal of Wildlife Management* 69:1259–69.

Ridgway, R. 1885. A new variety of prairie chicken. *Bulletin, Essex Institute* 5:199.

Ridgway, R., and H. Friedman. 1946. *The Birds of North and Middle America, Part 10*. US National Museum Bulletin 50. Washington, DC: Smithsonian Institution.

Riley, T. Z., C. A. Davis, M. Ortiz, and M. J. Wisdom. 1992. Vegetative characteristics of successful and unsuccessful nests of Lesser Prairie-Chickens. *Journal of Wildlife Management* 56:383–87.

Riley, T. Z., C. A. Davis, and R. A. Smith. 1993. Autumn and winter foods of the Lesser Prairie-Chicken (*Tympanuchus pallidicinctus*) (Galliformes: Tetraonidae). *Great Basin Naturalist* 53:186–89.

Ripper, D., and T. VerCauteren. 2007. *Assessment of CRP Fields within Current Lesser Prairie-Chicken Range*. Technical Report PPR-LEPC-ED07–01. Brighton, CO: Rocky Mountain Bird Observatory.

Robb, L. A., and M. A. Schroeder. 2005. *Lesser Prairie-Chicken* (Tympanuchus pallidicinctus): *A Technical Conservation Assessment*. USDA Forest Service, Rocky Mountain Region. http://www.fs.fed.us/r2/projects/scp/assessments/lesserprairiechicken.pdf.

Sharpe, R. S. 1968. The evolutionary relationships and comparative behavior of prairie chickens. PhD diss., University of Nebraska.

Sullivan, R. M., J. P. Hughes, and J. E. Lionberger. 2000. Review of the historical and present status of the Lesser Prairie-Chicken in Texas. *Prairie Naturalist* 32:177–88.

Taylor, M. A., and F. S. Guthery. 1980. *Status, Ecology and Management of Lesser Prairie-Chicken*. USDA Forest Service General Technical Report RM-77. Fort Collins, CO: Rocky Mountain Forest and Range Experiment Station.

Timmer, J. M, M. J. Butler, W. B. Ballard, C. W. Boal, and H. A. Whitlaw. 2014. Spatially explicit modeling of Lesser Prairie-Chicken lek density in Texas. *Journal of Wildlife Management* 78:142–52.

US Fish and Wildlife Service. 2014. Endangered and threatened wildlife and plants: Determination of threatened status for the Lesser Prairie-Chicken; final rule. *Federal Register* 50 CFR 17:19973–20071. https://federalregis ter.gov/a/2014-07302.

Van Pelt, W. E., S. Kyle, J. Pitman, D. Klute, G. Beauprez, D. Schoeling, A. Janus, and J. Haufler. 2013. *The Lesser Prairie-Chicken Range-Wide Conservation Plan.* Cheyenne, WY: Western Association of Fish and Wildlife Agencies.

Vance, D. R., and R. L. Westemeier. 1979. Interactions of pheasants and prairie chickens in Illinois. *Wildlife Society Bulletin* 7:221–25.

Westemeier, R. L., J. E. Buhnerkempe, W. R. Edwards, J. D. Brawn, and S. A. Simpson. 1998. Parasitism of Greater Prairie-Chicken nests by Ring-Necked Pheasants. *Journal of Wildlife Management* 62:854–63.

Wetmore, A. 1932. Additional records of birds from cavern deposits in New Mexico. *Condor* 34:141–42.

———. 1959. Notes on certain grouse of the Pleistocene. *Wilson Bulletin* 71:178–82.

Woodward, A. J., S. D. Fulendorf, D. M. Leslie Jr., and J. Shackford. 2001. Influence of landscape composition and change on Lesser Prairie-Chicken (*Tympanuchus pallidicinctus*) populations. *American Midland Naturalist* 145:261–74.

Gambel's Quail

Dawn on the delta was whistled in by Gambel quail, which roosted in the mesquites overhanging camp.—LEOPOLD (1949)

Introduction

The Gambel's Quail (*Callipepla gambelii*) is an iconic species of the Desert Southwest. This species is distributed primarily throughout the Sonoran and western Chihuahuan Deserts and is widely hunted throughout Arizona and southern New Mexico. It is hunted to a much lesser extent in Texas. Gambel's Quail weigh between 160 and 180 g (5.6 to 6.3 oz; Gorsuch 1934). Both male and female Gambel's Quail exhibit black comma-shaped topknots, or plumes, by which this species is best recognized. The male's plume is distinctively larger and darker than the female's plume. Both the male and female have bluish-gray upper parts, buff-colored bellies and rear underparts, and maroon side patches streaked with white. Despite these similarities in plumage, male and female Gambel's Quail are dimorphic, meaning that the sexes differ in both coloration and size. Males and females can be easily distinguished from one another, as the males sport a cinnamon-brown crown, a black face and bib outlined by white stripes, and a distinct black patch on the belly, among other characteristics. In addition to these dissimilarities, female Gambel's Quail appear drabber in color and have browner feathers. This species is represented in Texas by the subspecies *C. g. ignoscens*, which is found in southern

New Mexico and West Texas. Because this subspecies has a limited distribution in the state, little published information exists on it in Texas. Therefore, information throughout this chapter is largely synthesized from other states where the majority of research has been conducted on the other subspecies of Gambel's Quail. However, several recent unpublished theses from Sul Ross State University have provided notable contributions to our understanding of Gambel's Quail ecology in Texas (Gray 2005; Ortega-Sánchez 2006; Sullins 2006; Thornton 2007; Temple 2014).

Distribution in Texas

Gambel's Quail are distributed across West Texas below 1350 m (4,400 ft) in elevation within intermountain basins. Specifically they are found in El Paso and Hudspeth Counties, the western edge of Culberson County, and along the Rio Grande and the southern extent of its major tributaries (e.g., Alamito and Terlingua Creeks) in southern and western Jeff Davis, Presidio, and Brewster Counties (Sullins 2006). The easternmost portion of their range extends along the Rio Grande to Boquillos Canyon on the eastern side of Brewster County (Sullins 2006). Historically, Gambel's Quail reportedly ranged across these areas in addition to more eastern reaches of the Rio Grande

Figure 18.1. *(Top)*, male Gambel's Quail. Photo credit: Larry Ditto. *(Bottom)*, female Gambel's Quail. Photo credit: Larry Ditto.

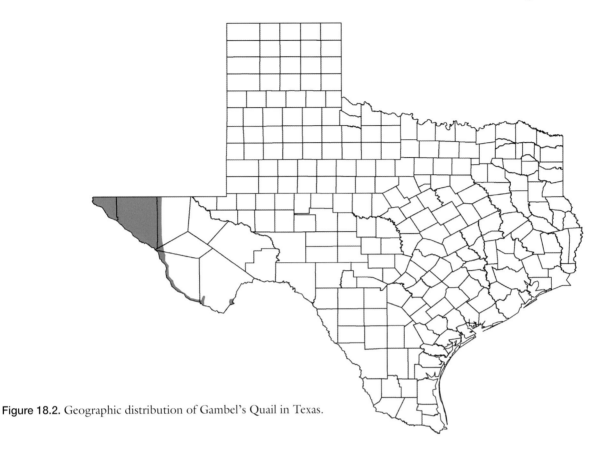

Figure 18.2. Geographic distribution of Gambel's Quail in Texas.

to Terrell County (Texas Game, Fish and Oyster Commission 1945).

The current geographic range of Gambel's Quail is thought to be the result of a post-Pleistocene northward expansion in response to postglacial warming and drying climatic trends (Williford et al. 2014).

Biology

The life history and ecology of Gambel's Quail are known mostly from studies across Arizona and New Mexico. Gorsuch (1934), Edminster (1954), Brown (1989), and Kuvlesky, DeMaso, and Hobson (2007) give detailed information regarding the biology, behavior, and annual life cycle of this bird. Much of the information here is summarized from these publications.

Migratory routes and timing

Gambel's Quail are a resident, nonmigratory species.

Timing of breeding

Gambel's Quail breeding phenology in Texas has not been thoroughly studied but is thought to be variable, ranging from March through October with a peak in activity from May through July. As with other quail species, the onset of breeding condition is determined primarily by photoperiod, which results in increased gonadal development. However, the actual commencement and duration of this breeding season can be determined by temperature, precipitation, and/or the occurrence of green herbaceous vegetation (Hungerford 1964; Heffelfinger et al. 1999). In Arizona, the breeding season ranges from early March to July, although most hatching occurs from late April to May (Raitt and Ohmart 1966).

Behavior

Gambel's Quail are a mobile ground species, preferring to run into dense cover rather than fly when pursued by a ground predator. Throughout their range, Gambel's Quail are mostly gregarious, being found in social units called coveys during fall, winter, and dry periods (Gullion 1962). In New Mexico and Arizona, coveys of Gambel's Quail range from 5 to 22 birds (Gullion 1962). However, after reproductively profitable years, covey sizes have been documented from 30 to a reported several hundred birds (Gorsuch 1934; Brown 1989). Brown (1989) reported that most coveys maintain home ranges of between 19 and 95 ha (47 to 235 ac); however, Gullion (1962) reported home ranges averaging only 14 ha (34 ac). These home ranges are probably biased low, since they were calculated by sightings rather than by radiotelemetry. Most coveys exhibit high site fidelity, shifting only 100 m (310 ft) on average each day, while there is a tendency for increasing movement as the winter progresses (Gullion 1962; Brown 1989). Gullion (1962) documented coveys increasing movement to 1000 m (1,093 yd) by March. Gray (2005) documented a single covey dispersal of 9.6 km (6 mi) from the original capture site in Texas. It is likely that estimates of home range size and movements may improve with the advent of measurements from radiotelemetry methods.

Coveys can disband and birds can pair as early as late February. Gambel's Quail have been previously described as having a monogamous mating system, and presumably some birds begin pair formation while still within the covey (Brown et al. 1998). However, Hagelin (2003) found that the occurrence of social monogamy instead ranged from 30% to 86%, while polygamy (sequential, long-term pairings) was common. Adult females are equally likely to exhibit social monogamy or polygamy each season.

Home ranges and core areas during the breeding season in West Texas averaged 156 and 33 ha (385 and 82 ac), respectively (Temple 2014). These estimates are substantially greater than reports of home ranges estimated farther west because these data were collected using radiotelemetry as opposed to sightings. Within their home ranges, Gambel's Quail construct nests on the ground by scratching out a well-concealed crude depression under a small dense-canopied shrub, cactus, or senesced plant material. Although the vast majority of nests are constructed on the ground, Gambel's Quail have occasionally been documented nesting in stumps, woodpiles, hay bales, packrat (*Neotoma* spp.) middens, and shrubs up to 150 cm (59 in) (Bent 1932; Walsberg and Zerba 1986; Thompson 1993). After nest construction, the female incubates the clutch while the male often remains close by, although the male may incubate the nest should misfortune strike the hen (Brown 1989). Interestingly, the ability of Gambel's Quail to survive and reproduce tends to be greater for heavier birds and those that nest earlier in the season (Hagelin 2003). Gambel's Quail chicks hatch synchronously and follow their parents shortly after hatching. As with all New World quail species, Gambel's Quail chicks are precocial, meaning they are able to feed themselves almost immediately after hatching.

Gambel's Quail inhabit a hot environment. Even in the shade, temperatures often soar toward the upper limits of their thermoneutrality (4°C above body temperature) throughout much of the day. At these temperatures, the birds maintain a body temperature (37.3°C–41.5°C or 99.1°F–106.7°F, depending on activity) that is close to their upper lethal limit (Bartholomew and Dawson 1958; Goldstein 1984). It is therefore no surprise that the activity pattern of Gambel's Quail on hot summer days is bimodal, with morning and late afternoon foraging periods being separated by a long quiescent stint during midday (Goldstein 1984). Gambel's Quail remain relatively inactive, resting, preening, and dust bathing in shaded areas throughout most of the day (Goldstein and Nagy 1985; Guthery et al. 2001). During morning and evening, they are more vigorous, spending time foraging and socializing.

Gambel's Quail calls vary widely (Ellis and Stokes 1966) but can be divided into 5 main groups in response to various stimuli. These calls, in order of the most prominent and common, are tooks, chips, kaas, wits, and squeals.

Tooks—Continuous low chatter given throughout the day, especially during feeding.

Chips—Alarm calls given in response to strange objects, terrestrial predators, or stressful situations.

Kaas—Used for locating other quail during pair or covey aggregation and during the breeding season by males. The "kaa-AA-aa" is usually given by a lone male from an elevated perch.

Wits—Made during antagonistic situations.

Squeals—Distress calls upon capture.

Clutch size and incubation

Gambel's Quail eggs are a light cream color and are covered in irregular dark brown blotches. Clutch sizes typically average between 10 and 14 eggs (Gorsuch 1934; Brown 1989), although they can range between 5 and 20 eggs (Bent 1932; Gorsuch 1934). Incubation lasts for 21–23 days.

Nest losses

A comprehensive study focusing exclusively on nest losses for Gambel's Quail has not been conducted. Temple (2014) recorded nest success at 89% in West Texas. This hatch rate is exceptionally high for any species of quail; it is thought that nest success averages between 30% and 60% in most cases. In addition to the usual mammalian nest predators such as coyotes (*Canis latrans*), rodents including ground squirrels (*Spermophilus* spp.) have been described as major nest predators in Arizona and California (Leopold 1977; Brown 1989).

Diet and foraging

Diets of Gambel's Quail vary considerably by region, plant community, season, and plant phenology. They are primarily a ground-foraging species that spends crepuscular and cloudy daytime periods searching for food. Although these birds forage almost exclusively on the ground, Gambel's Quail occasionally forage in shrubs (Parker 1986), especially when these plants produce mast in the form of fruits and seeds (Campbell 1957).

Gambel's Quail food items vary widely. In the month of August alone, Gorsuch (1934) found 114 species of plant and animal foods in the digestive tracts of only 30 Gambel's Quail in Arizona. This range in dietary selection may be an adaptation for life in a challenging environment. Overall, seeds, green leaf material, mast, and insects are the primary food items (Brown 1989). Plant material, mainly seeds and greens (when available), is the most frequent food item, accounting for more than 90% of adult diets (Gorsuch 1934). Along the Rio Grande watershed north of Las Cruces, New Mexico, 91% percent of the food items consumed by Gambel's Quail consisted of seeds and fruits, 7% green leaf material, and 2% insects (Campbell 1957). Across the various studies that have been conducted on Gambel's Quail food habits, several plant genera recur in diets across their range. These species include locoweeds (*Astragalus* spp.), deer vetches (*Lotus* spp.), filaree (*Erodium* spp.), lupines (*Lupinus* spp.), tumbleweeds (*Salsola kali*), tallow weeds (*Plantago* spp.), tansy mustard (*Descurainia pinnata*), mesquites (*Prosopis* spp.), and acacias (*Acacia* spp.) (Campbell 1957; Gullion 1960; Hungerford 1962; Brown 1989). In Texas, 20 foods constituted 91% of the total volume of all items consumed. Seeds and green vegetation included species such as tumbleweed, desert willow (*Chilopsis linearis*), cowpen daisy (*Verbesina encelioides*), blazing star (*Mentzelia multiflora*), plains bristlegrass (*Setaria leucopila*), Virginia pepperweed (*Lepidium virginicum*), mesquite (*Prosopis glandulosa*), whitethorn acacia (*Acacia constricta*), catclaw acacia (*Acacia greggii*), bluebonnet (*Lupinus* spp.), ragweed (*Ambrosia* spp.), lineleaf whitepuff (*Oligomeris linifolia*), and bladderpods (*Lesquerella* spp.) (Sullins 2006). Fruits of Berlandier's wolfberry (*Lycium berlandieri*), littleleaf sumac (*Rhus microphylla*), Warnock's condalia (*Condalia warnockii*), and netleaf hackberry (*Celtis reticulata*) were consumed. Insect matter in Gambel's Quail diets rarely exceeds 15%, although insects are a seasonally important food source. They are especially important to chicks, as young birds depend on invertebrate forage during their first few weeks of life. Invertebrates in the orders Arachnida, Diptera, Coleoptera, Hemiptera, Homoptera, Hymenoptera, Isoptera, Orthoptera, Mallophaga, and Lepidoptera have been recorded as food items for Gambel's Quail (Gorsuch 1934; Campbell 1957; Brown 1989).

Along with food, the provision of free (standing) water has been a source of contention among Gambel's Quail enthusiasts for decades (Kuvlesky, DeMaso, and Hobson 2007). Gambel's Quail use free water when available, but like other New World quail species, they are able to meet their water needs from their foods and metabolic water produced during digestion (Gorsuch 1934; Brown 1989).

Demography and vital rates

In Arizona, Gambel's Quail densities have been reported at 28 birds/km² or about 11/sq mi (Parker 1986). Annual survival and reproduction are known to fluctuate closely with precipitation patterns, and adult breeding season survival ranges between 16% and 78%, although mortality rates have been reported to exceed 90% during an exceptionally dry year in southern Nevada (Gullion 1960; Sowls 1960; Gray 2005; Temple 2014). In West Texas, annual survival ranged from 16% to 40% (Gray 2005). Depredation by raptors accounted for the majority of Gambel's Quail mortality in West Texas (Temple 2014). They have been found to avoid congregating around watering areas during times of peak raptor use (Beck, Engen, and Gelfand 1973). For chicks, mortality is usually high, as more than 50% of a given brood typically do not survive to experience their first winter (Sowls 1960). Predators are known to be the largest source of mortality for Gambel's Quail, but depredation has not been thoroughly studied for this species.

Age at first reproduction

Gambel's Quail do not reproduce until the spring following the year in which they were hatched. Subadult birds appear to breed later than adults during the breeding season (Brown 1989).

Age and sex ratios

In West Texas, age ratios range from 0.33 to 6 juveniles per adult depending on the output of the previous breeding season (Gray 2005). For Gambel's Quail, reproduction can be almost nil during drought; however, in fall juveniles can account for 80% of the population when precipitation in winter, spring, and/or summer is plentiful (Brown 1989).

During the breeding season, Gambel's Quail sex ratios are skewed toward males, presumably because females experience greater mortality while incubating. Sex ratios have been reported in the range of 51%–60% male to 40%–49% female (Gorsuch 1934; Campbell and Lee 1956; Sowls 1960) across their range. In Texas, Gambel's Quail sex ratios have ranged from 0.73 to 2.14 males per female (Gray 2005). At hatching, sex ratios of Gambel's Quail are thought to be equal.

Population Status and Trends

Sampling Gambel's Quail populations in Texas is difficult because the majority of their limited geographic range lies mostly on private property. However, their populations are thought to be stable excluding annual variability because of precipitation. Data collected during Christmas Bird Counts indicate that Gambel's

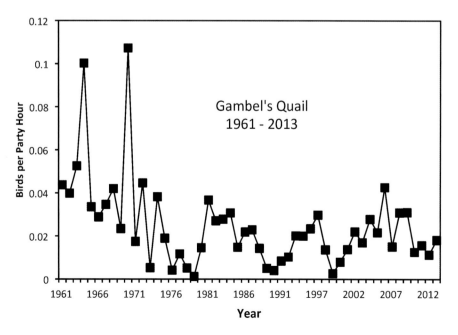

Figure 18.3. Population trend of Gambel's Quail in Texas based on Christmas Bird Count data from 1961 to 2013. While numbers are variable, populations appear to be stable in Texas.

Quail populations decreased during the 1960s but have since stabilized. The reason for this decline is unknown. This species is no longer found along swaths of historically occupied stretches of the Rio Grande along the eastern edge of Brewster County.

Specific Habitat Requirements

In the Trans-Pecos region of Texas, Gambel's Quail are most commonly associated with relatively densely vegetated desert riparian drainages that run through sparsely vegetated desert (Gray 2005; Ortega-Sánchez 2006; Ortega-Sánchez et al. 2009). Gray (2005) reported that of 811 Gambel's Quail locations taken using radiotelemetry in West Texas, 92% were within riparian corridors. Similarly, Ortega-Sánchez (2006) reported a high amount of habitat use (86% and 91% of all observations) in desert riparian communities.

Riparian areas amenable to Gambel's Quail in Texas harbor a variety of dense-canopied woody and succulent species such as littleleaf sumac, catclaw acacia, Torrey mesquite (*Prosopis glandulosa* var. *torreyana*), prickly pear (*Opuntia* spp.), desert willow, whitethorn acacia, desert hackberry (*Celtis pallida*), and whitebrush (*Aloysia gratissima*); however, drainages dominated by giant sacaton (*Sporobolus wrightii*) and salt cedar (*Tamarix pentandra*) are also used. Gray (2005) reported that Gambel's Quail show preference for native riparian vegetation rather than salt cedar thickets, although Ortega-Sánchez (2006) found no difference in use between these community types. Along the Rio Grande, Gambel's Quail can be found in association with irrigated agricultural operations if sufficient desert thornscrub is available to them nearby. Because midday temperatures often exceed 40°C (104°F) through spring, summer, and fall in

Figure 18.4. Gambel's Quail habitat along the upper Rio Grande in Texas. Photo credit: Eric Grahmann.

West Texas, dense-canopied shrubs are likely to be essential for avoiding heat stress (Guthery et al. 2001). Goldstein and Nagy (1985) recorded ground surface temperatures exceeding 60°C (140°F) in the Mojave Desert where Gambel's Quail occur.

Shrubs are also important to Gambel's Quail for another reason. Unlike our other species of quail in Texas, Gambel's Quail prefer to roost above ground level (Brown et al. 1998). Roosting shrubs such as hackberry and littleleaf sumac are ideal because of their dense canopy structure. Roosts are typically used night after night unless disturbance persuades the birds to roost elsewhere.

Bare ground and forbs are important components of Gambel's Quail habitat. Gambel's Quail used sites that had greater proportions of bare ground than two other sympatric quail species in southern Arizona (Guthery et al. 2001). It is essential for travel, especially for a bird that prefers to walk or run rather than fly. In addition, when precipitation occurs, bare ground gives rise to the various annual forbs that Gambel's Quail depend on for food, and, as a beneficial by-product of forb presence, insects. Years in which forbs abound are tied to the greatest production in Gambel's Quail populations (Gorsuch 1934; Brown 1989).

Nest sites are typically not limiting to Gambel's Quail, as nests are simply a crude depression scratched out under a low-growing shrub, subshrub, cacti, or residual plant debris (Brown 1989). However, Temple (2014) found that Texas sotol (*Dasylirion texanum*) was the nesting substrate of choice. Such nest sites abound across the habitat of Gambel's Quail.

Habitat management

The most popular management practice implemented to benefit Gambel's Quail is the development of water resources for drinking, mostly in the form of gallinaceous guzzlers (Brown 1989). The effort and money that is expended for these supplemental water units to provide drinking water is intriguing since Gambel's Quail do not require artificial water sources for their survival (Campbell 1960; Hungerford 1960). Furthermore, the unintended consequences of providing free water (e.g., a potential increase in mesocarnivore distribution) have not been studied. However, water sources that result in moist soil oases may hold merit

in arid-land quail management, since these areas could indirectly benefit quail by providing patches of green herbaceous vegetation, seeds, and insects that would otherwise be absent during drier seasons. Water trough overflows and spreader dams allow water to slowly soak into the soil and create these robust patches. Although spreader dams and moist-soil sites are touted as positive management strategies for quail in West Texas, they have not yet been found to conclusively benefit the sympatric Scaled Quail (*Callipepla squamata*) (Lerich 2002). Furthermore, Landgrebe et al. (2007) found that the occurrence of parasites in Scaled Quail was greater in an area with spreader dams in West Texas. Along with the lack of decisive evidence supporting the benefits of such practices, the intensity at which these practices must be implemented to benefit Gambel's Quail is unknown.

Land management techniques to improve sites for Gambel's Quail include dike and levee construction, the installation of diversion dams and berms, gully shaping to hold rainfall, and winter disking of hardpan soils to increase infiltration. The idea behind these practices is that should any rainfall occur, such areas would result in productive patches with forbs and insects by capturing water and sediment where it would normally run into stream channels. It should be noted that where Gambel's Quail occur in Texas, some sites may not lend themselves to soil disturbance methods and cultivation because of rocks and erosion concerns on slopes and along desert drainages.

Another common practice implemented for Gambel's Quail is the provision of supplemental feed in the form of grain. Campbell (1959) suggested that if Gambel's Quail benefited from the provision of grain, their population increase, if any, was too small to justify the expense. Some land managers in West Texas are convinced that providing supplemental feed in this arid environment enhances quail survival and carryover to more favorable years, but these positive benefits have not been scientifically documented.

In Arizona, overgrazing is thought to have deleterious impacts on Gambel's Quail (Gorsuch 1934). Guthery et al. (2001) provided slightly conflicting data regarding this observation, as Gambel's Quail preferred using habitat with greater amounts of bare ground, even in proximity to more productive range.

In Texas, Gambel's Quail show a strong affinity for arid and sparse herbaceous plant communities even in proximity to more productive desert shrublands and grasslands.

Nonnative, invasive plant species are a concern for Gambel's Quail in Texas. Ortega-Sánchez (2006) suggested that salt cedar could reach a threshold at which usable space for Gambel's Quail would decrease. Gambel's Quail use salt cedar for cover, but how they make use of large monotypic stands of this species is unknown. Regardless, conserving diverse desert riparian shrublands should be paramount since such communities provide for all needs of Gambel's Quail.

When discussing management for Gambel's Quail, Gorsuch (1934) stated, "Gambel's Quail can best be increased by preserving and rehabilitating their habitat." As in 1934, this statement remains true today. Since Gambel's Quail inhabit a challenging arid environment that recovers exceptionally slowly after major disturbances (e.g., bulldozed riparian zones or mining), management strategies should focus on the preservation and restoration of their habitat. In a study conducted near Tucson, Arizona, Gambel's Quail were more common on uncleared mesquite-dominated rangeland than on areas where mesquite had been completely cleared (Germano, Hungerford, and Martin 1983). In West Texas, woody plant communities along the Rio Grande and its tributaries are extremely important for this species. Restoring dense woody plant canopies in desert riparian areas and associated uplands in conjunction with the various forbs that Gambel's Quail depend on for food are commendable acts of management. Gullion (1960) stated that shrubs suitable for roosting can be limiting to Gambel's Quail. Typically, these shrubs can be found in acceptable densities in undisturbed riparian communities. Along with conserving remnant undisturbed habitats, maintaining desert scrub communities along agricultural fencerows and in nearby landholdings can positively benefit Gambel's Quail in agricultural and urban landscapes. As with other quail species, maintaining large habitat patches and connectivity between them is likely important. The greatest threat to this and other quail species is habitat loss.

Hunting and Conservation

Gambel's Quail hold game bird status, with seasons and bag limits equivalent to those of other quail species in the state, excluding the Montezuma Quail (*Cyrtonyx montezumae*).

Texas hunting season length, 2013–2014

The 2013–2014 hunting season was 121 days (October 26, 2013–February 23, 2014).

Texas bag limits

The daily bag limit (per person) for Gambel's Quail in Texas is 15 in the aggregate with the Northern Bobwhite (*Colinus virginianus*) and Scaled Quail. The possession limit for these species is 45 per person.

Geographic restrictions on hunting in Texas

There are no geographic restrictions on Gambel's Quail hunting in Texas as long as they are hunted within their native geographic range.

Research Needs and Priorities

Most research on this species has been conducted in other states and on other Gambel's Quail subspecies. In addition, almost all comprehensive studies on this species are more than 20 years old and were conducted before the widespread use of radiotelemetry in quail research. The recent flurry of research on Gambel's Quail from Sul Ross State University (Gray 2005; Ortega-Sánchez 2006; Sullins 2006; Thornton 2007; Temple 2014) is a welcome infusion of new knowledge of this species in Texas.

Because so little research has been conducted on Gambel's Quail in Texas, virtually any study focusing on their distribution, general life history, population ecology, harvest, and habitat will yield valuable information. Furthermore, additional information is needed to determine the impacts of agricultural and urban expansion and invasion by nonnative plant species on their habitat and populations.

Literature Cited

Bartholomew, G. A., and W. R. Dawson. 1958. Body temperatures in California and Gambel's Quail. *Auk* 75 (2): 150–56.

Beck, B. B., C. W. Engen, and P. W. Gelfand. 1973. Behavior and activity cycles of Gambel's Quail and raptorial birds at a Sonoran Desert waterhole. *Condor* 75 (4): 466–70.

Bent, A. C. 1932. *Life Histories of North American Gallinaceous Birds.* US National Museum Bulletin 162. Washington, DC: Smithsonian Institution.

Brown, D. E. 1989. *Arizona Game Birds.* Tucson: University of Arizona Press.

Brown, D. E., J. C. Hagelin, M. Taylor, and J. Galloway. 1998. Gambel's Quail (*Callipepla squamata*). No. 321. In *The Birds of North America*, edited by A. Poole and F. Gill. Washington, DC: American Ornithologists' Union.

Campbell, H. 1957. Fall foods of Gambel's Quail (*Lophortyx gambelii*) in New Mexico. *Southwestern Naturalist* 3:122–28.

———. 1959. Experimental feeding of wild quail in New Mexico. *Southwestern Naturalist* 4:169–75.

———. 1960. An evaluation of gallinaceous guzzlers for quail in New Mexico. *Journal of Wildlife Management* 24:21–26.

Campbell, H., and L. Lee. 1956. Notes on the sex ratio of Gambel's and Scaled Quail in New Mexico. *Journal of Wildlife Management* 20:93–94.

Edminster, F. C. 1954. *American Game Birds of Field and Forest.* New York: Charles Scribner's Sons.

Ellis, C. R., Jr., and A. W. Stokes. 1966. Vocalizations and behavior in captive Gambel Quail. *Condor* 68:72–80.

Germano, D. J., R. Hungerford, and S. C. Martin. 1983. Responses of selected wildlife species to the removal of mesquite from desert grassland. *Journal of Range Management* 36:309–11.

Goldstein, D. L. 1984. The thermal environment and its constraints on activity of desert quail in summer. *Auk* 101:542–50.

Goldstein, D. L., and K. A. Nagy. 1985. Resource utilization by desert quail: Time and energy, food and water. *Ecology* 66:378–87.

Gorsuch, D. 1934. Life history of the Gambel Quail in Arizona. *Biological Science Bulletin* 5:1–89.

Gray, M. T. 2005. Population demographics and spatial characteristics of Gambel's Quail in the Chihuahuan Desert, Texas. Master's thesis, Sul Ross State University.

Gullion, G. W. 1960. The ecology of Gambel's Quail in Nevada and the arid southwest. *Ecology* 41:518–36.

———. 1962. Organization and movements of coveys of a Gambel Quail population. *Condor* 64:402–15.

Guthery, F. S., N. M. King, W. P. Kuvlesky Jr., S. DeStefano, S. A. Gall, and N. J. Silvy. 2001. Comparative habitat use by three quails in desert grassland. *Journal of Wildlife Management* 65 (4): 850–60.

Hagelin, J. C. 2003. A field study of ornaments, body size, and mating behavior of the Gambel's Quail. *Wilson Bulletin* 115:246–57.

Harveson, L. A., P. M. Harveson, and C. Richardson, eds. *Proceedings of the Trans-Pecos Wildlife Conference.* Alpine, TX: Sul Ross State University.

Heffelfinger, J. R., F. S. Guthery, R. J. Olding, C. L. Cochran Jr., and C. M. McMullen. 1999. Influence of precipitation timing and summer temperatures on reproduction of Gambel's Quail. *Journal of Wildlife Management* 63:154–61.

Hensley, M. M. 1954. Ecological relations of the breeding bird population of the desert biome in Arizona. *Ecological Monographs* 24:185–207.

Hungerford, C. R. 1960. Water requirements of Gambel's Quail. *Transactions of the North American Wildlife and Natural Resources Conference* 25:231–40.

———. 1962. Adaptations shown in selection of food by Gambel's Quail. *Condor* 64:213–19.

———. 1964. Vitamin A and productivity in Gambel's Quail. *Journal of Wildlife Management* 28:141–47.

Kuvlesky, W. P., Jr., S. J. DeMaso, and M. D. Hobson. 2007. Gambel's Quail ecology and life history. In *Texas Quails: Ecology and Management*, edited by L. A. Brennan, 6–22. College Station: Texas A&M University Press.

Landgrebe, J. N., B. Vasquez, R. G. Bradley, A. M. Fedynich, S. P. Lerich, and J. M. Kinsella. 2007. Helminth community of Scaled Quail (*Callipepla squamata*) from western Texas. *Journal of Parasitology* 93:204–8.

Leopold, A. 1949. *A Sand County Almanac.* Oxford: Oxford University Press.

———. 1977. *The California Quail.* Berkeley: University of California Press.

Lerich, S. P. 2002. Nesting ecology of Scaled Quail at Elephant Mountain Wildlife Management Area, Brewster County, Texas. Master's thesis, Sul Ross State University.

Ortega-Sánchez, A. 2006. Delineation of habitats and a comparison of density estimators for Gambel's Quail in the Trans-Pecos, Texas. Master's thesis, Sul Ross State University.

Ortega-Sánchez, A., L. A. Harveson, R. R. Lopez, and M. R. Sullins. 2009. Delineation of Gambel's Quail habitat in the Trans-Pecos, Texas. *Proceedings of the National Quail Symposium* 6:190–94.

Parker, K. C. 1986. Partitioning of forage space and nest sites in a desert shrubland bird community. *American Midland Naturalist* 115:255–67.

Raitt, R. J., and R. D. Ohmart. 1966. Annual cycle of reproduction and molt in Gambel's Quail of the Rio Grande Valley, southern New Mexico. *Condor* 68:541–61.

Sowls, L. K., 1960. Results of a banding study of Gambel's Quail in southern Arizona. *Journal of Wildlife Management* 24:185–90.

Sullins, M. R. 2006. Status, distribution, and principal foods of Gambel's Quail in Trans-Pecos, Texas. Master's thesis, Sul Ross State University.

Temple, R. A., Jr. 2014. Breeding season dynamics and spatial characteristics of Scaled and Gambel's Quail in a desert shrubland, Trans-Pecos, Texas. Master's thesis, Sul Ross State University.

Texas Game, Fish and Oyster Commission. 1945. *Principal Game Birds and Mammals of Texas.* Austin: Texas Game, Fish and Oyster Commission.

Thompson, B. C. 1993. A successful, elevated Gambel's Quail nest in a suburban area. *Southwestern Naturalist* 38:174–75.

Thornton, M. G. 2007. Reproductive physiology of Gambel's Quail in Trans-Pecos Texas. Master's thesis, Sul Ross State University.

Walsberg, G. E., and E. Zerba. 1986. Use of a *Neotoma* nest for breeding by Gambel's Quail. *Southwestern Naturalist* 31:256.

Williford, D., R. W. DeYoung, R. L. Honeycutt, L. A. Brennan, F. Hernandez, J. R. Heffelfinger, and L. A. Harveson. 2014. Phylogeography of the Gambel's Quail (*Callipepla gambelii*) of western North America. *Wilson Journal of Ornithology* 126:218–35.

19

Scaled Quail

You will not be able to walk them up, for they will outrun you. If you chase after them, you will still be hard pressed to catch up to the nucleus of the covey.—BROWN (1989)

Introduction

The Scaled Quail (*Callipepla squamata*) is a species of the short grasslands and shrublands of the Chihuahuan Desert and Tamaulipan Biotic Province. It is hunted throughout its geographic range in the United States, most commonly in southeastern Arizona, southern New Mexico, and West Texas, and to a lesser extent in South Texas. Most South Texas quail hunters bypass it for the more popular Northern Bobwhite (*Colinus virginianus*).

The Scaled Quail is the largest quail species in Texas, weighing between 177 and 205 g (6.2–7.2 oz) (Johnsgard 1973). Its appearance can be partially described by three other common names used for this species in Texas: blue quail, scalies, and cottontops, in order of popularity. Males and females are mostly monomorphic, as their sex is difficult to distinguish without the bird in hand. Plumage characteristics overlap even more between juvenile males and females.

Scaled Quail are best recognized by their bluish-gray plumage with black feather margins, giving them a "blue-scaled" appearance. This plumage extends from their neck, breast, and upper belly and then fades to a buff color on their undersides. Both males and females exhibit white cotton-like plumes. Feathers on the wings, tail, face, and flanks are brownish gray,

Figure 19.1. Male Scaled Quail. Note the dark-colored patch on the belly, indicating this bird is the Chestnut-bellied subspecies. Female plumage is similar, but with a lighter bluish tint on the upper neck and breast and a lighter-colored chestnut patch on the belly. Photo credit: Greg Lasley.

although the flanks are streaked with white. Despite the similarities between the sexes of Scaled Quail, males and females can be distinguished mainly by their throat plumage. Males sport a solid buff cream-colored patch, while females have feathers that are lightly streaked with brown. Males are also slightly more colorful, as they are somewhat bluer in appearance, exhibit more prevalent and whiter side streaking, and have whiter head plumes than females. These differences are most evident when a mated pair is seen side by side during the breeding season. Males occasionally sport a maroon patch on the belly that tends to be darker than that infrequently seen on females (Bent 1932).

There are two subspecies of Scaled Quail that range in Texas: the Arizona Scaled Quail (*C. s. pallida*), which occurs in West Texas, the western Edwards Plateau and Rolling Plains, and Texas Panhandle; and the Chestnut-bellied Scaled Quail (*C. s. castanogastris*), which ranges across the Tamaulipan Biotic Province of South Texas. The indeterminate boundary of these subspecies overlaps somewhere in the vicinity of Del Rio and Comstock, Texas. The Arizona Scaled Quail is the larger and paler colored of the two subspecies

found in the state, while the Chestnut-bellied Scaled Quail is the smallest and darkest of Scaled Quail subspecies. The Chestnut-bellied Scaled Quail is best known for the russet-chestnut patch on the male's belly.

Most literature on the Scaled Quail discusses the Arizona subspecies, and the Chestnut-bellied Scaled Quail has not been widely studied. Information throughout this chapter is synthesized largely from data collected on the Arizona subspecies.

Distribution in Texas

Scaled Quail are distributed in South Texas roughly south and west of Highway 281 and south of Highway 90 to Uvalde, then northward, roughly west of the 100th meridian (fig. 19.2). They are found in unfragmented landscapes of semiarid and arid shrubland and short grassland from close to sea level to about 1700 m (5,600 ft); however, birds have been located up to 2377 m (7,800 ft) in elevation (Oberholser 1974). On the periphery of this distribution, they are found irregularly in small, isolated, remnant metapopulations.

Figure 19.2. Historical and current geographic distribution of the Scaled Quail in Texas. Its range has been contracting southward and westward over the past three decades.

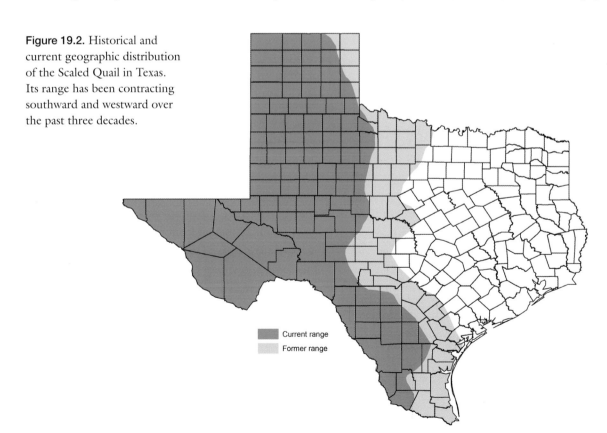

Scaled Quail were once known to range to the Gulf Coast in South Texas and about 75–100 km (47–62 mi) north and east of their current distribution across the state (Texas Game, Fish and Oyster Commission 1945). The range of Scaled Quail in Texas has been contracting, moving progressively westward with time. The species is no longer detected on the easternmost survey routes in southern Texas (Hernández et al. 2012). Molecular genetic data indicate that this species has undergone northward and perhaps westward population expansion from a Pleistocene refugium. Compared to the other Scaled Quail subspecies, the Chestnut-bellied subspecies contains greater genetic diversity, which may indicate that this refugium was in South Texas (Williford et al. 2014).

Biology

The life history and ecology of the Arizona Scaled Quail are known mostly across southeastern Arizona, New Mexico, and Oklahoma. Schemnitz (1961), Brown (1989), and Silvy, Rollins, and Whisenant (2007) give detailed information regarding the biology, behavior, and annual life cycle of this bird. Detailed life history information is generally meager for the Chestnut-bellied Scaled Quail.

Migratory routes and timing

The Scaled Quail is a resident, nonmigratory species, although occasional seasonal movements have been documented (Campbell and Harris 1965).

Timing of breeding

The Scaled Quail breeding season in Texas ranges from late March through late September, with a peak in activity from May through July. The onset of breeding condition is determined primarily by photoperiod, which results in increased gonadal development. However, the actual commencement and duration of the breeding season can be determined by temperature, precipitation, and/or the occurrence of green herbaceous vegetation. Most birds are found in breeding pairs by mid-April. Typically, the earliest eggs are laid in mid-April, while earliest incubation initiates in early May. Nests of Scaled Quail have been found as early

as April 7 and as late as September 22 (Jensen 1925; Lerich 2002).

Behavior

Similar to the other New World quail species, Scaled Quail are a ground-dwelling species, preferring to walk or run rather than fly when pursued by a ground predator. This is especially true across sparsely vegetated rangeland, on which these birds are known to send bird dogs and hunters alike on cross-country treks in their pursuit. However, when pressured onto a hill or mesa or into dense cover, or when separated from their covey, Scaled Quail hold and flush, contrary to popular hunting lore that suggests otherwise. In the open country of West Texas, Scaled Quail typically fly about 45 to 180 m (50 to 200 yd) to dense cover or to the slope of a hill or mesa when flushed (Schemnitz 1961).

Scaled Quail live their lives almost exclusively on the ground, where they feed, nest, rest, and roost, among other activities; the exception is occasional perching on vantage points atop fence posts or in woody vegetation. Scaled Quail occasionally forage in shrubs for fruit, although this behavior is uncommon (Bardwell et al. 2011). Just as with other New World quail species, Scaled Quail are gregarious, spending time in coveys during fall, winter, and dry periods. For Arizona Scaled Quail, coveys average around 25 and range from 3 to 50 birds (Schemnitz 1961; Anderson 1978). In South Texas, Chestnut-bellied Scaled Quail covey sizes average about 15 and usually do not exceed 20 birds (Lehmann 1984). However, after reproductively profitable years in large parcels of habitat, covey aggregations have been documented exceeding 100 birds (Wallmo 1956; Schemnitz 1961). Most coveys, pairs, and single birds are thought to be relatively sedentary, inhabiting home ranges averaging about 21 ha (52 ac) and ranging from 10 to 40 ha (25–100 ac) (Schemnitz 1961). However, despite their affinity for a given area, Scaled Quail have occasionally been documented moving up to 40 km (28 mi), and even 96 km (60 mi), in New Mexico and West Texas (Campbell and Harris 1965).

Coveys can disband and birds can pair as early as late February. Scaled Quail, like other quail species, are thought to be mostly monogamous (Wallmo 1956), but they likely partake in at least some polygamous mating. Breeding season home ranges and core areas average 145 and 31 ha (145 and 76 ac) in West Texas, respectively (Temple 2014). Typically, within their core area of use, Scaled Quail construct nests on the ground, creating a well-concealed, crude depression. Typically, these nests are scratched out under a prickly pear, yucca (*Yucca* spp.), sotol (*Dasylirion* spp.), lechuguilla (*Agave* spp.), short, dense-canopied shrub, bunchgrass, or senesced plant material. After nest construction, the female incubates the clutch while the male often remains close by. The male may incubate the nest should the hen be killed (Schemnitz 1961). Scaled Quail chicks hatch synchronously, are precocial, and follow their parents shortly after hatching. Brood sizes upon hatching average about 10 birds (Schemnitz 1961).

Scaled Quail usually spend morning and late evening foraging and socializing, and at midday they rest, preen, and dust bathe under shade (Schemnitz 1961). However, on relatively cool and cloudy days, they will actively feed and move around throughout the day.

Scaled Quail calls vary widely (Anderson 1978). Calls commonly given include the chip-chur, shriek, tsing, ti-chunk, cuts, and squeal (Anderson 1978).

Chip-Chur—Given by either sex when separated from other quail or by males from an elevated perch advertising single status (may be given in combination with the "shriek"). These calls are given at both high and low volumes depending on the situation. The head and tail are pumped with each syllable.

Shriek—Given by single males, usually from an elevated perch advertising single status (may be given in combination with the "chip-chur"). This call may be used irregularly as a covey call before sunrise.

Tsing—An alarm call given in response to strange objects, terrestrial predators, or stressful situations.

Ti-chunk—Loud call used as an alarm in response to an extreme threat or during social conflict. The head and tail are pumped in an exaggerated manner with each syllable.

Cuts—Continuous low chatter given throughout the day, especially during feeding.

Squeal—Distress call upon capture.

Clutch size and incubation

Scaled Quail eggs are a light cream color and are covered in irregular light brown specks. Clutch sizes typically average about 13 eggs but can range from 5 to 22 eggs (Schemnitz 1961; Pleasant, Dabbert, and Mitchell 2006). Clutch sizes tend to be smaller with poor weather conditions (high temperatures and little rainfall), but large with good weather conditions. Incubation lasts for 21–23 days.

Nest losses

Scaled Quail nest success is highly variable, ranging from 14% to 90%. In the southern High Plains of Texas, nest success averaged 54% during a 2-year study (Pleasant, Dabbert, and Mitchell 2006). In the Trans-Pecos region, estimated nest success ranged from 36% (Lerich 2002) to 73% (Temple 2014). Hens have been documented renesting up to 3 times in a single nesting season in both the Panhandle (Pleasant, Dabbert, and Mitchell 2006) and South Texas Plains when conditions remained favorable. The amount and timing of precipitation ultimately influence overall nesting success and annual production. However, Scaled Quail typically raise at least some broods even in the worst years. In Schemnitz's (1961) study conducted in the southern High Plains where only 14% nest success was observed, 39% of nest failure was caused by human disturbance related to farming activities.

Diet and foraging

Compared to the partially sympatric Northern Bobwhite, which inhabit more mesic regions, Scaled Quail exhibit a wider dietary spectrum (Schemnitz 1964; Campbell-Kissock, Blankenship, and Stewart 1985) and are generally less affected by macronutrient deficiencies (Giuliano, Lutz, and Patino 1996). In addition, Scaled Quail are more capable in adjusting digestive organs to extract energy and accumulate lipid reserves when seed availability is restricted (Leif and Smith 1993). These characteristics are likely to be adaptations for living in an arid environment where food resources may occasionally be limited.

Similar to other quail species, Scaled Quail have diets that vary considerably by region, plant community, season, and plant phenology; however, seeds and fruits from forbs and woody plants are more widely used compared to the Northern Bobwhite (Lehmann and Ward 1941; Campbell-Kissock, Blankenship, and Stewart 1985; Hammerquist-Wilson and Crawford 1987). Overall, and in order of occurrence, seeds, green leaf material, mast, and insects are the primary food items. Plant material, mainly seeds, fruits, and greens (when available), is the most frequent food item, accounting for more than 90% of adult diets (Schemnitz 1961). Across their range, seeds that recur in the diets of Scaled Quail include those of honey mesquite (*Prosopis glandulosa*), various sunflowers (*Helianthus* spp.), cultivated sorghum (*Sorghum* spp.), several species of croton (*Croton* spp.), Russian thistle (*Salsola kali*), multiple species of acacia (*Acacia* spp.), broom snakeweed (*Gutierrezia sarothrae*), spurges (*Euphorbia* spp.), several species of bristlegrass (*Setaria* spp.), bluebonnets (*Lupinus* spp.), locoweeds (*Astragalus* spp.), caltrops (*Kallstroemia* spp.), sidas (*Sida* spp.), and pigweeds (*Amaranthus* spp.). In the southern High Plains, other major seeds consumed by Scaled Quail include those of cowpen daisy (*Verbesina encelioides*), western ragweed (*Ambrosia psilostachya*), gumweed (*Grindelia* spp.), sand lily (*Leucocrinum* spp.), few-flowered psoralea (*Psoralidium tenuiflorum*), white ratany (*Krameria grayi*), and sand sagebush (*Artemisia filifolia*) (Schemnitz 1961; Davis, Barkley, and Haussamen 1975; Griffing and Davis 1976; Ault and Stormer 1983). In the Trans-Pecos, seeds of fiddleneck (*Amsinckia intermedia*), green carpetweed (*Mollugo verticillata*), copperleaf (*Acalypha ostryifolia*), verbenas (*Verbena* spp.), and sumpweed (*Iva* spp.) were consumed frequently (Bardwell et al. 2011). In South Texas, other important seed and fruit sources include bearded dalea (*Dalea lasiathera*), creeping bundleflower (*Desmanthus virgatus*), desert yaupon (*Schaefferia cuneifolia*), granjeno (*Celtis pallida*), low menodora (*Menodora heterophylla*), ponyleaf oxalis (*Oxalis dichondrifolia*), Hall's panicum

(*Panicum hallii*), narrowleaf forestiera (*Forestiera angustifolia*), sensitive briar (*Neptunia pubescens*), wild beans (*Phaseolus* spp.), and fruit from various cacti (Lehmann and Ward 1941; Campbell-Kissock, Blankenship, and Stewart 1985; Hammerquist-Wilson and Crawford 1987). The seeds of various woody plants constituted 68% of the diets of Chestnut-bellied Scaled Quail in a study conducted by Lehmann and Ward (1941). Aside from more typical foraging, Scaled Quail have been documented feeding on undigested seeds in cattle manure (Campbell 1959). In South Texas, Scaled Quail were often found feeding on the seeds of mesquite and various acacias that passed through the digestive systems of cattle. This behavior was especially common during drought.

In addition to seeds and fruits, a diverse array of green herbaceous vegetation is also widely eaten in times of availability. Green vegetation is consumed primarily during winter and spring and ranges from 7% to 52% of Scaled Quail diets (Lehmann and Ward 1941; Campbell-Kissock, Blankenship, and Stewart 1985; Medina 1988). Plants such as trailing ratany (*Krameria lanceolata*), woolly locoweed (*Astragalus mollissimus*), primrose (*Oenothera* spp.), white milkwort (*Polygala alba*), tansy mustard (*Descurainia pinnata*), telegraph plant (*Heterotheca villosa*), scarlet globemallow (*Sphaeralcea coccinea*), bladderpods (*Lesquerella* spp.), cryptantha (*Cryptantha minima*), wild buckwheat (*Eriogonum* spp.), and woolly plantain (*Plantago patagonica*) are consumed in the southern High Plains. Wild carrot (*Chaerophyllum* spp.) was a major source of green vegetation for Scaled Quail in South Texas, accounting for 7% of the total crop content during winter (Lehmann and Ward 1941).

Insect matter in Scaled Quail diets rarely exceeds 10%, although insects are a seasonally important food source. They are especially important to hens at the onset of breeding and to chicks and juveniles, as young birds depend on invertebrate forage for their first few weeks of life (Cain et al. 1982; Ault and Stormer 1983). Insects in the orders Hemiptera, Orthoptera, Coleoptera, Hymenoptera, Isoptera, Lepidoptera, and Cicadellidae have been recorded as major food items for Scaled Quail, although insects in other orders are eaten (Schemnitz 1961; Ault and Stormer 1983; Bardwell et al. 2011). Desert termites were especially prevalent in the diets of Chestnut-bellied Scaled Quail during fall in South Texas (Campbell-Kissock, Blankenship, and Stewart 1985) and may be an important food source during drought when other insects are less abundant.

A comparison of the diets of adults and juveniles in the Trans-Pecos showed that adults consumed more forbs (35.8% to 58.8%) by volume, whereas juveniles consumed a greater percentage of woody plant seeds (6.5% to 35.8%) and insects (14.7% to 17.2%) by volume.

Scaled Quail use free (standing) water when available, but it is not required for their survival. Instead, they are able to meet water needs from sources derived from their food and metabolic water produced during digestion. In a study that examined water deprivation for both Gambel's and Scaled Quail under controlled conditions, it was found that Scaled Quail lost less water while attempting to remain cool in temperatures in excess of 40°C (Henderson 1971).

Demography and vital rates

Scaled Quail covey density has been reported in West Texas at 1 covey/2.4 km², or about 0.3 covey/sq mi (Gage 2011). While variable, densities of Scaled Quail average 16 birds/km² (6.2 birds/sq mi) and range from 2 to 33 birds/km² (about 0.8 to 12.7 birds/sq mi) on the southern High Plains (Schemnitz 1961; Ault and Stormer 1983; Saiwana et al. 1998). Annual survival and reproduction fluctuate with precipitation patterns, but survival and nest success do not vary as widely as in other quail species (Campbell 1968; Campbell et al. 1973; Brown 1989; Bridges et al. 2001). Breeding season survival ranges from 50% to 75% (Lerich 2002; Temple 2014). Hawks were the greatest predators of adult Scaled Quail in Temple's (2014) study. In the Oklahoma Panhandle, the Northern Harrier (*Circus cyaneus*) and Cooper's Hawk (*Accipiter cooperii*) were the main species observed harassing Scaled Quail (Schemnitz 1961). In Lerich's (2002) study, mammals and raptors accounted for 43% and 13% of mortalities, respectively, while 9% of mortalities resulted from drownings in water troughs. Cold, wet weather has been hypothesized to decrease

chick survival in the Texas Panhandle when it occurs within a week after hatching (Pleasant, Dabbert, and Mitchell 2006).

Age at first reproduction

Scaled Quail do not reproduce until the spring following the year in which they were hatched.

Age and sex ratios

Scaled Quail juvenile-to-adult ratios average 2.3 juveniles per adult and have been reported ranging from 0.6 in poor years to almost 5 juveniles per adult in the best years (Schemnitz 1961; Campbell and Harris 1965). These ratios are a function of both juveniles entering the population and adult survival. Typically, good reproductive years are represented by high juvenile-to-adult ratios, while low juvenile production is common in years with low amounts of rainfall.

Sex ratios for Scaled Quail are about equal for juveniles but are skewed toward males for adult birds. For adults, sex ratios have been reported from 59%–70% male to 30%–41% female (Campbell and Lee 1956; Schemnitz 1961). Similar to the sex ratios of other quail species, those of Scaled Quail are thought to be skewed toward males because females may experience greater nesting season mortality while incubating.

Population Status and Trends

Excluding variation in annual production related to precipitation, data collected during the Breeding Bird Survey indicate that Scaled Quail populations have been declining precipitously since at least the 1970s. The Chestnut-bellied Scaled Quail has declined at a rate of 5% per year in the Tamaulipan Biotic Province, the greatest of any region surveyed in the Scaled Quail's geographic range (Hernández et al. 2012). Quail detections in the core of the Scaled Quail's range in the Tamaulipan Biotic Province were 80 Scaled Quail for every 20 Northern Bobwhite during the 1960s, but this ratio is currently about 5 Scaled Quail for every 95 Northern Bobwhite.

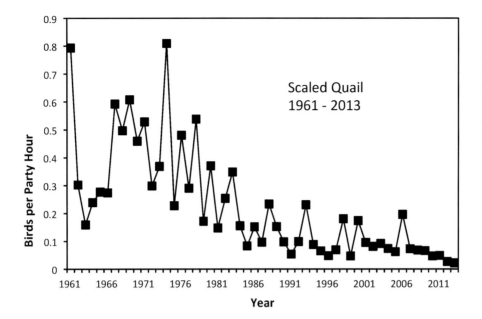

Figure 19.3. Population trend of Scaled Quail in Texas based on Christmas Bird Count data. While numbers vary with rainfall patterns, populations of Scaled Quail have been declining in Texas since at least the 1970s.

Specific Habitat Requirements

Texas's two subspecies of Scaled Quail inhabit different vegetation regions within the state. The more widespread Arizona subspecies uses relatively open semidesert grass and scrubland in West Texas compared to the Chestnut-bellied subspecies, which uses the relatively dense Tamaulipan thornscrub habitat of South Texas. More specifically, habitat for the Arizona subspecies of Scaled Quail can be described as short-grass prairie dominated by tobosagrass (*Pleuraphis mutica*), gramas (*Bouteloua* spp.), and muhlygrasses (*Muhlenbergia* spp.) with interspersed cacti such as cholla (*Cylindropuntia* spp.) and prickly pear, and short-statured shrubs or mesquite. Arizona Scaled Quail also frequent creosotebush (*Larrea tridentata*) and tarbush (*Flourensia cernua*) scrublands with patches of annual and perennial grasses and forbs. To a lesser extent, they are found in sand sage (*Artemisia filifolia*) grasslands. In South Texas, the Chestnut-bellied subspecies inhabits mainly blackbrush (*Acacia rigidula*) and guajillo (*Acacia berlandieri*) caliche and gravel ridges, saline clay flats dominated by honey mesquite (*Prosopis glandulosa*) and Texas prickly pear (*Opuntia engelmannii* var. *lindheimeri*), and other, similar shrub communities that have sparse herbaceous structure on the ground. In these South Texas scrublands, short-grasses such as gramas, dropseeds

(*Sporobolus* spp.), bristlegrasses, and curly mesquite-grass (*Hilaria belangeri*), in addition to a wide variety of annual and perennial forbs, are common.

Aside from the presence of desert shrubs, sub-shrubs, and succulents, a shared feature in the habitat of the two subspecies lies within herbaceous plant communities. Generally, Scaled Quail prefer communities with moderately dense shrub and grass patches separated by large areas of bare ground. The presence of ample bare ground is essential to Scaled Quail (Hammerquist-Wilson and Crawford 1987). In far West Texas, which receives less precipitation than other areas of the state, good Scaled Quail habitat has a high degree of herbaceous structure compared to surrounding rangeland. By contrast, in South Texas where greater precipitation is received, Scaled Quail habitat is usually sparse in nature compared to surrounding vegetation communities (Hall 1998). This illustrates how quail tend to be associated with areas of greater site productivity as one moves on a precipitation gradient from east to west, as highlighted by Spears et al. (1993) for Northern Bobwhites. Although relative herbaceous cover may vary across the range of the Scaled Quail, overall standing crop and interspersion of herbaceous vegetation and bare ground are similar.

Scaled Quail tend to avoid dense vegetation since this cover might impede their travel on the ground

Figure 19.4. *(Top)*, Chestnut-bellied Scaled Quail habitat; *(bottom)*, Arizona Scaled Quail habitat in Texas. Although there are some commonalities, the habitat associated with these two subspecies varies considerably in Texas. Photo credits: Eric Grahmann.

(Medina 1988; Schemnitz 1964). Furthermore, Scaled Quail habitat is patchy, with interspersed patches of bare ground, shrubs, and forbs in a mosaic of short-to mid-grass. Conflicting information exists concerning the herbaceous communities most favorable for Arizona Scaled Quail. Bristow and Ockenfels (2006) found that Scaled Quail use areas with grass canopy cover exceeding 26%. In contrast, Medina (1988) found higher Scaled Quail densities in areas with low perennial grass and high forb cover. It is possible that Arizona Scaled Quail exhibit enough habitat plasticity to inhabit a variety of range conditions. Arizona Scaled Quail habitat is open and more or less free of dense shrub communities. Bristow and Ockenfels (2006) found that Scaled Quail avoided areas with more than 10% tree canopy cover and preferred areas with greater grass species richness than that randomly available on the landscape. Guthery et al. (2001) described Arizona Scaled Quail habitat as having low shrub cover and moderate amounts of grass compared to sympatric Gambel's and Masked Bobwhite Quails (*Colinus virginianus* var. *ridgwayi*) in Arizona. At sites with contrasting range conditions, more Scaled Quail were found in midsuccessional grassland sporting intermediate coverages of grasses and shrubs, when compared to late-successional (dense grass, few shrubs) and heavily grazed range (little grass, dense shrubs) (Smith, Holechek, and Cardenas 1996; Nelson et al. 1997; Nelson, Holechek, and Valdez 1999). This is similar to the findings of Saiwana et al. (1998), who found greater Scaled Quail abundance in a grass-shrubland mosaic than in wide-open late-successional grassland. Arizona Scaled Quail use sites with greater visual obstruction and lower temperatures in a matrix of open desert grassland.

In a study conducted in South Texas, Hammerquist-Wilson and Crawford (1987) found that Chestnut-bellied Scaled Quail used sparse rangeland with a thornscrub overstory and that they preferred areas with more than 35% woody cover. Moreover, Texas prickly pear and bare ground most accurately described core areas used. Lehmann and Ward (1941) and Hall (1998) described large numbers of Scaled Quail where prickly pear, tasajillo (*Cylindropuntia leptocaulis*), and tornillo (*Prosopis reptans*) were found. Both studies suggested that heavy cactus cover may be essential for

the welfare of the Chestnut-bellied Scaled Quail in South Texas. Although woody cover is widely used and preferred by Scaled Quail in South Texas, monotypic thickets of woody plants such as whitebrush (*Aloysia gratissima*) tend to be avoided (Hall 1998).

Throughout the range of the Scaled Quail, temperatures often exceed 40°C (104°F) through late spring, summer, and early fall, and temperatures above 45°C (113°F) can have adverse effects on their survival (Henderson 1971). Therefore, dense-canopied shrubs, cacti, and artificial structures that provide shady understory are crucial during midday. In the southern High Plains, vegetation widely used for shade and resting includes skunkbush sumac (*Rhus trilobata*), cholla, lotebush (*Ziziphus obtusifolia*), yuccas, and sandplum (*Prunus angustifolia*) (Schemnitz 1961; Rollins 2000). Artificial structures such as livestock pens, buildings, farm machinery, and junk piles are also readily used if they have the appropriate structure. In the Trans-Pecos of Texas, shrubs such as Torrey mesquite (*Prosopis glandulosa* var. *torreyana*), littleleaf sumac (*Rhus microphylla*), catclaw acacia (*Acacia greggii*), and tarbush are widely used for shade. Although loafing cover is more abundant and widespread in South Texas, Chestnut-bellied Scaled Quail are partial to dense-canopied shrubs and cacti such as coma (*Sideroxylon celastrinum*), Texas persimmon (*Diospyros texana*), knifeleaf condalia (*Condalia spathulata*), blackbrush acacia, honey mesquite, and Texas prickly pear.

Because of their flexibility in the use of different substrates for nesting cover, this artifact of habitat is usually not limiting to Arizona Scaled Quail. Pleasant, Dabbert, and Mitchell (2006) found that Arizona Scaled Quail did not appear to select any particular plant species near which to associate their nests in the southern High Plains. Most quail tend to respond to the structure of the substrate rather than the species of plant for nesting (Guthery 1999). However, plant species providing this favorable structure and those often used by Scaled Quail for nests in West Texas include sotol, Russian thistle, yuccas, threeawns (*Aristida* spp.), tobosagrass, mesquite, javelinabush (*Condalia ericoides*), and catclaw acacia (Schemnitz 1961; Lerich 2002; Pleasant, Dabbert, and Mitchell 2006; Temple 2014). On sandy soils in West Texas, shin oak (*Quercus havardii*), sand sagebrush, and weeping lovegrass (*Eragrostis curvula*) are used. In the Trans-Pecos region, Texas sotol (*Dasylirion texanum*) was the preferred nesting substrate for both Scaled and Gambel's Quail (Temple 2014). The Chestnut-bellied Scaled Quail, on the other hand, is very partial to Texas prickly pear for nesting, and the removal of this plant could have adverse effects on its welfare. In a study conducted in South Texas from 2009 to 2014, roughly 80% of Scaled Quail nests were found in prickly pear. Other nests were found at the base of shrubs such as mesquite and guayacan (*Guaiacum angustifolium*) and grasses such as purple threeawn (*Aristida purpurea*) and Texas bristlegrass (*Setaria texana*).

Roost sites for Arizona Scaled Quail are in grassland with short shrubs or yuccas nearby. These areas are usually located on, but are not limited to, ridgetops or hillsides where the quail roost in small groups of 2–5 birds (Brown 1989). A patch for roosting should support grasses (0.1–0.4 m tall, or 4–16 in) having about 45% cover. A 0.3 ha (0.7 ac) unit of roosting cover for every 23 ha (57 ac) was recommended by Stormer (1984).

Habitat management

Habitat loss, fragmentation, incompatible livestock grazing, and invasion by woody plants and nonnative grasses are considered predominant factors influencing the long-term decline of Scaled Quail in Texas. In general, large parcels of unaltered native plant communities still support robust populations of Scaled Quail. Conservation of large, contiguous parcels of habitat is of utmost importance for the conservation of this species. Unfortunately, much effort is expended toward other practices to benefit Scaled Quail, often with neutral or sometimes unintended negative results.

In Texas, most management practices for Scaled Quail are focused on supplementation, particularly through the provision of supplemental water or grain. As with Gambel's Quail, gallinaceous guzzlers have been widely developed to benefit Scaled Quail throughout the arid Southwest. Scaled Quail readily use guzzlers and other sources of "free" standing water; however, this practice cannot be justified on a biological basis, as Scaled Quail do not require standing water.

Food has not been found to be a limiting factor for adult Scaled Quail (Schemnitz 1961), although many managers and biologists suggest that it can be limiting in times of severe drought. Campbell (1959) found no conclusive evidence of the value of providing Scaled Quail supplemental feed in New Mexico. He suggested that if feeding did result in increased quail density, the magnitude of such effects was not large enough to justify the expense. Studies are needed to assess the effectiveness of this exercise during drought conditions, especially within the most arid reaches of Scaled Quail range. The establishment of water and feeders may be of value if the objectives are to view and/or concentrate quail (Campbell 1960); however, their use has not been validated on a biological basis of increasing usable space and productivity.

In West Texas, the installation of spreader dams and runoff catchments is a popular practice for Scaled Quail management. Spreader dams are designed to slow rainfall runoff, giving moisture a chance to soak into the ground rather than be lost as runoff into drainages (Lerich 2002). Spreader dams retain standing water for hours to days, depending on a variety of factors. Where water and nutrients are collected, relatively mesic patches of plant growth and arthropod production form. Such oases have the potential to benefit Scaled Quail. Lerich (2002) compared adult and nest survival of Scaled Quail between pastures with and without spreader dams, but he found no differences between the two sites. On the same study area, Landgrebe et al. (2007) found that the occurrence of parasites was greater in the area with spreader dams, but it was unclear whether the mere presence of spreader dams had a causal effect on parasites and/or their transmission to quail. The effects of spreader dams on Scaled Quail remain under investigation.

On wide-open landscapes in West Texas, woody cover for protection from predators and unsuitable thermal conditions can limit usable space. Scaled Quail prefer low-growing, dense-canopied shrubs for cover, but they tend to avoid areas with tree cover exceeding 6% in semiarid grasslands (Bristow and Ockenfels 2006). Schemnitz (1961) found that Scaled Quail primarily used areas where there was suitable dense-canopied shrub cover or other similar structured features (e.g., cattle pens) on the southern High

Plains, as 83% of 2,048 observations were made in conjunction with this type of cover. The use of these features was especially prevalent when quail were faced with adverse conditions during winter. Schemnitz (1961) suggested that the addition of dense-canopied shrubs or artificial structures could be meaningful in increasing usable space for Scaled Quail where these features are lacking on the landscape.

Areas without woody cover tend to be more of an exception throughout the range of Scaled Quail in Texas. Often, woody cover is common and its encroachment is considered a problem on West Texas rangelands. Generally, woody plant treatments are applied on large areas without consideration of the potential unintended effects on Scaled Quail. In the Trans-Pecos region of West Texas, widespread applications of tebuthiuron herbicides are often used to control woody species. Scaled Quail were found to avoid large areas formerly treated with the herbicide Spike 20P, even when grass cover was increased in areas with nearly barren ground (Gage 2011). Forb species richness and woody cover were decreased in treated areas, even up to five years after treatment. Gage (2011) suggested that insufficient brush cover in combination with the dense grassland produced via the Spike 20P application resulted in insufficient habitat for Scaled Quail. If the use of this herbicide is planned, he recommended leaving patches of untreated brush across the rangeland interface, especially along drainages and hillsides.

In South Texas, Scaled Quail habitat (Tamaulipan shrubland) is often manipulated via root plowing, roller chopping, and herbicide applications with the goal of increasing grass cover, aesthetics, and huntability. An unfortunate side effect of some treatments is the loss of Scaled Quail habitat, although the direct effects of some treatments on Scaled Quail are unknown. Lehmann and Ward (1941) recommended that where the Chestnut-bellied Scaled Quail is desired, plots of cacti approximately 0.4 ha (1 ac) in extent should be left at intervals of 100 m (109 yd).

Perhaps the most helpful habitat management tool that can be used throughout the range of the Scaled Quail is grazing. Grazing can be positive, negative, or neutral depending on the situation and the amount of residual cover left by livestock. Since the Arizona subspecies inhabits the more xeric regions across the Scaled Quail range, it can be sensitive to extended periods of overgrazing. Grazing recommendations compatible with Scaled Quail in West Texas suggest that perennial grassland be grazed lightly to moderately (less than 30% of the annual standing crop of forage), or sometimes not at all. Bristow and Ockenfels (2006) suggested that land management practices that reduce grass species richness and cover while increasing tree coverage may reduce Arizona Scaled Quail habitat. They recommended that more than 25% grass canopy cover of 20 cm (about 8 in) in height be left to provide optimum cover. Pleasant, Dabbert, and Mitchell (2006) and Schemnitz (1961) made similar recommendations in the southern High Plains of Texas. Not only was overgrazing detrimental to herbaceous cover, but livestock also restricted the growth of shrubby woody species. Woody plants were frequently browsed to the point they were of little value to Scaled Quail (Schemnitz 1961). It should be noted that the detriment or virtue of grazing for the Arizona Scaled Quail may depend on site productivity and precipitation. Joseph et al. (2003) found that Scaled Quail densities were lower in areas with poor perennial grass cover during drought, but densities were greater in these areas during times of plentiful rainfall. Rangelands that provide grassy and relatively sparse patches are favorable because patch use by Scaled Quail varies with precipitation and its influence on the herbaceous standing crop. In wet years, some patches may become too thick, while in dry years, these same patches may be those that harbor sufficient cover.

Patch heterogeneity is also important to the Chestnut-bellied Scaled Quail, but in contrast to the situation with the Arizona subspecies, undergrazing tends to cause greater concern in its more mesic range. This is true mostly in areas that have been manipulated to increase forage for livestock through brush clearing and planting of productive grass species. In South Texas, Scaled Quail tend to prefer xeric habitats and are better adapted to exploiting habitats created by drought and/or overgrazing than the sympatrically occurring Northern Bobwhite (Campbell-Kissock, Blankenship, and Stewart 1985). Some of the most thriving populations of Scaled Quail in South Texas are present on naturally sparse rangeland and/or large, heavily grazed ranches.

Across the range of the Scaled Quail, habitat is decreasing as a result of invasions by nonnative grasses (Medina 1988). Former strongholds for Scaled Quail in South Texas and the Permian Basin support fewer Scaled Quail because of nonnative grass invasions. Specifically, pervasive grasses such as Lehmann lovegrass (*Eragrostis lehmanniana*), buffelgrass (*Pennisetum ciliare*), and Old World bluestems (e.g., *Dichanthium annulatum* and *Bothriochloa ischaemum*) simplify vegetation communities and render habitat unusable when they form monotypic stands (Medina 1988; Bristow and Ockenfels 2006). Medina (1988) found that Lehmann lovegrass stands supported fewer (1% of observations) Scaled Quail than any other habitat type surveyed in southeastern Arizona. Forbs, which are important to Scaled Quail for seeds, greens, insects, and cover, are reduced in communities dominated by Lehmann lovegrass (Medina 1988) and buffelgrass (Sands et al. 2009). Furthermore, areas planted to or invaded by these grasses can become dispersal barriers to Scaled Quail, further fragmenting their habitat. In South Texas, sustained grazing pressure from cattle can be used to reduce grass standing crop and increase bare ground and annual forbs for Scaled Quail. This practice has been used successfully to remediate habitat for Scaled Quail in shrublands fragmented by the planting of buffelgrass.

In Texas, Scaled Quail habitat continues to be lost at a high rate, often under the guise of good range stewardship. So often, rangeland is erroneously categorized as degraded if shrubs are abundant or if grass cover is any less than what is preferred by the cattle baron. Philosophically, range and wildlife managers must ask, if current range conditions do not represent those seen historically, at least in part, how is it that the Scaled Quail (a sparse grassland–shrubland obligate species) was once more abundant than the Northern Bobwhite in the western two-thirds of the state and ranged nearly 160 km (about 100 mi) east of its current distribution? Davis, Barkley, and Haussamen (1975) debated this very issue as ranchers waged war against mesquite and broom snakeweed in New Mexico to the dereliction of Scaled Quail. Thousands of hectares of western grass-scrubland are being treated with tebuthiuron herbicides to increase grasses at the expense of the forbs, shrubs, and subshrubs that are critical components of Scaled Quail habitat. In South Texas, extensive hectares of Tamaulipan thornscrub have been, and continue to be, converted to unnatural grasslands via root plowing, roller chopping, and the application of brush-killing herbicides. With this continued combination of habitat loss and land fragmentation in Texas, one must wonder what the future holds for Scaled Quail in the state. Scaled Quail are sensitive to fragmentation and the overall loss of their habitat (Rho 2003).

Hunting and Conservation

Scaled Quail hold game bird status, with seasons and bag limits equivalent to those of other quail species in the state, excluding the Montezuma Quail (*Cyrtonyx montezumae*), which is not hunted. Generally, hunting these birds is challenging because of their ability to outpace hunters on open ground. Scaled Quail hunters usually bag fewer than 3 birds/hunter/day, averaging 0.9 bird/hunter/day, and harvest an average of 11.3 birds/year (Campbell and Harris 1965). Regardless of these relatively low bags, Scaled Quail have a cult following of hunters in West Texas, and to a lesser degree in South Texas. With the exception of hunter success, which typically ranges from about 60% to about 80%, every other metric related to Scaled Quail hunting in Texas has been eroding more or less steadily during the past 20 years. Annual estimated harvest fell from more than 500,000 birds in 1994 to about 27,000 birds in 2011; 2014 showed a major rebound in Scaled Quail harvest to just over 100,000 birds. The number of hunters who pursue Scaled Quail in Texas has fallen from about 47,000 in 1994 to a little more than 10,000 in 2014. The hunter-days spent afield in pursuit of Scaled Quail have fallen from more than 191,000 in 1994 to just over 47,000 in 2014 (Purvis 2014).

Texas hunting season length, 2013–2014

The 2013–2014 hunting season was 121 days (October 26, 2013–February 23, 2014).

Texas bag limits

The daily bag limit (per person) for Scaled Quail in Texas is 15 in the aggregate with Northern Bobwhite and Gambel's Quail. The possession limit for these species is 45 per person.

Geographic restrictions on hunting in Texas

There are no geographic restrictions on quail hunting in Texas. However, Scaled Quail hunting is restricted to their geographic range within the state.

Research Needs and Priorities

Most published studies on Scaled Quail have been conducted with means other than radiotelemetry. Furthermore, most studies have focused on the Arizona Scaled Quail rather than on the Chestnut-bellied Scaled Quail. Because the Chestnut-bellied subspecies occupies very different plant communities compared to the Arizona subspecies, almost any research on aspects of Chestnut-bellied life history should be considered a priority in Texas.

Very little research has been conducted on the life history and habitat use of Scaled Quail using newer and more technologically advanced methods such as radiotelemetry. Any study using these methods will likely yield updated information on the species. Studies focused on fragmentation effects as well as studies attempting to discern minimum population and habitat patch size are badly needed as this species continues to decline.

Literature Cited

Anderson, W. L. 1978. Vocalizations of Scaled Quail. *Condor* 80:49–63.

Ault, S. C., and F. A. Stormer. 1983. Seasonal food selection by Scaled Quail in northwest Texas. *Journal of Wildlife Management* 47:222–28.

Bardwell, J. H., C. M. Ritzi, S. P. Lerich, and A. M. Fedynich. 2011. Late summer dietary survey of Scaled Quail (*Callipepla squamata*). *Bulletin of the Texas Ornithological Society* 44:1–2.

Bent, A. C. 1932. *Life Histories of North American Gallinaceous Birds*. US National Museum Bulletin 162. Washington, DC: Smithsonian Institution.

Bridges, A. S., M. J. Peterson, N. J. Silvy, F. E. Smeins, and X. B. Wu. 2001. Differential influence of weather on regional quail abundance in Texas. *Journal of Wildlife Management* 65:10–18.

Bristow, K. D., and R. A. Ockenfels. 2006. Fall and winter habitat use by Scaled Quail in southeastern Arizona. *Rangeland Ecology and Management* 59:308–13.

Brown, D. E. 1989. *Arizona Game Birds*. Tucson: University of Arizona Press.

Cain, J. R., D. S. Smith, R. J. Lien, and J. W. Lee. 1982. Protein requirements of growing Scaled Quail. *Poultry Science* 60:16–32.

Campbell, H. 1959. Experimental feeding of wild quail in New Mexico. *Southwestern Naturalist* 4:169–75.

———. 1960. An evaluation of gallinaceous guzzlers for quail in New Mexico. *Journal of Wildlife Management* 24:21–26.

———. 1968. Seasonal precipitation and Scaled Quail in eastern New Mexico. *Journal of Wildlife Management* 32:641–44.

Campbell, H., and B. K. Harris. 1965. Mass population dispersal and long-distance movements in Scaled Quail. *Journal of Wildlife Management* 29:801–5.

Campbell, H., and L. Lee. 1956. Notes on the sex ratio of Gambel's and Scaled Quail in New Mexico. *Journal of Wildlife Management* 20:93–94.

Campbell, H., D. K. Martin, P. E. Ferkovich, and B. K. Harris. 1973. *Effects of Hunting and Some Other Environmental Factors on Scaled Quail in New Mexico*. Wildlife Monographs 34.

Campbell-Kissock, L., L. H. Blankenship, and J. W. Stewart. 1985. Plant and animal foods of Bobwhite and Scaled Quail in southwest Texas. *Southwestern Naturalist* 30:543–53.

Davis, C. A., R. C. Barkley, and W. C. Haussamen. 1975. Scaled Quail foods in southeastern New Mexico. *Journal of Wildlife Management* 39:496–502.

Gage, R. T. 2011. Effects of Spike 20P on habitat use and movements of mule deer and other wildlife in Trans-Pecos, Texas. Master's thesis, Sul Ross State University.

Giuliano, W. M., R. S. Lutz, and R. Patino. 1996. Reproductive responses of adult female Northern Bobwhite and Scaled Quail to nutritional stress. *Journal of Wildlife Management* 60:302–9.

Griffing, J. P., and C. A. Davis. 1976. Comparative foods of sympatric Scaled Quail and Mourning Doves. *Southwestern Naturalist* 21:248–49.

Guthery, F. S. 1999. Slack in the configuration of habitat patches for Northern Bobwhites. *Journal of Wildlife Management* 63:245–50.

Guthery, F. S., N. M. King, W. P. Kuvlesky Jr., S. DeStefano, S. A. Gall, and N. J. Silvy. 2001. Comparative habitat use by three quails in desert grassland. *Journal of Wildlife Management* 65:850–60.

Hall, B. W. 1998. Habitat use by sympatric Northern Bobwhites and Scaled Quail in the western Rio Grande plains. Master's thesis, Texas A&M University–Kingsville.

Hammerquist-Wilson, M., and J. A. Crawford. 1987. Habitat selection by Texas Bobwhites and Chestnut-Bellied Scaled Quail in south Texas. *Journal of Wildlife Management* 51:575–82.

Henderson, C. W. 1971. Comparative temperature and moisture responses in Gambel and Scaled Quail. *Condor* 73:430–36.

Hernández, F., C. J. Parent, I. C. Trewella, and E. D. Grahmann. 2012. The forgotten quail decline: The plight of Scaled Quail in Texas. *Proceedings of the National Quail Symposium* 7:365.

Jensen, J. K. 1925. Late nesting of the Scaled Quail (*Callipepla squamata squamata*). *Auk* 42:129–30.

Johnsgard, P. A. 1973. *Grouse and Quails of North America.* Lincoln: University of Nebraska Press.

Joseph, J., J. L. Holechek, R. Valdez, M. Collins, and M. Thomas. 2003. Effects of rangeland ecological condition on Scaled Quail sightings. *Journal of Range Management* 56:314–18.

Landgrebe, J. N., B. Vasquez, R. G. Bradley, A. M. Fedynich, S. P. Lerich, and J. M. Kinsella. 2007. Helminth community of Scaled Quail (*Callipepla squamata*) from western Texas. *Journal of Parasitology* 93:204–8.

Lehmann, V. W. 1984. *Bobwhites in the Rio Grande Plain of Texas.* College Station: Texas A&M University Press.

Lehmann, V. W., and H. Ward. 1941. Some plants valuable to quail in southwestern Texas. *Journal of Wildlife Management* 5:131–35.

Leif, A. P., and L. M. Smith. 1993. Winter diet quality, gut morphology and condition of Northern Bobwhite and Scaled Quail. *Journal of Field Ornithology* 64:527–38.

Lerich, S. P. 2002. Nesting ecology of Scaled Quail at Elephant Mountain Wildlife Management Area, Brewster County, Texas. Master's thesis, Sul Ross State University.

Medina, A. L. 1988. Diets of Scaled Quail in southern Arizona. *Journal of Wildlife Management* 52:753–57.

Nelson, T., J. Holechek, and R. Valdez. 1999. Wildlife plant community preference in the Chihuahuan Desert. *Rangelands* 21:9–11.

Nelson, T., J. L. Holechek, R. Valdez, and M. Cardenas. 1997. Wildlife numbers on late and mid-seral Chihuahuan Desert rangelands. *Journal of Range Management* 50 (6): 593–99.

Oberholser, H. C. 1974. *The Bird Life of Texas.* Austin: University of Texas Press.

Pleasant, G. D., C. B. Dabbert, and R. B. Mitchell. 2006. Nesting ecology and survival of Scaled Quail in the southern High Plains of Texas. *Journal of Wildlife Management* 70:632–40.

Purvis, J. 2014. *Small Game Harvest Survey Results 1994–95 thru 2013–14.* Austin: Texas Parks and Wildlife Department.

Rho, P. 2003. GIS-based multiple-scale study on Scaled Quail. PhD diss., Texas A&M University.

Rollins, D. 2000. Status, ecology, and management of Scaled Quail in west Texas. *Proceedings of the National Quail Symposium* 4:165–72.

Saiwana, L., J. L. Holechek, A. Tembo, R. Valdez, and M. Cardenas. 1998. Scaled Quail use of different seral stages in the Chihuahuan Desert. *Journal of Wildlife Management* 62:550–56.

Sands, J. P., L. A. Brennan, F. Hernandez, W. P. Kuvlesky Jr., J. F. Gallagher, D. C. Ruthven III, and J. E. Pittman III. 2009. Impacts of Buffelgrass (*Pennisetum ciliare*) on a forb community in south Texas. *Invasive Plant Science and Management* 2:130–40.

Schemnitz, S. D. 1961. *Ecology of the Scaled Quail in the Oklahoma Panhandle.* Wildlife Monographs 8.

———. 1964. Comparative ecology of Bobwhite and Scaled Quail in the Oklahoma Panhandle. *American Midland Naturalist* 71:429–33.

Silvy, N. J., D. Rollins, and S. W. Whisenant. 2007. Scaled Quail ecology and life history. In *Texas Quails: Ecology and Management*, edited by L. A. Brennan, 65–88. College Station: Texas A&M University Press.

Smith, G., J. L. Holechek, and M. Cardenas. 1996. Wildlife numbers on excellent and good condition Chihuahuan Desert rangelands: An observation. *Journal of Range Management* 49:489–93.

Spears, G. S., F. S. Guthery, S. M. Rice, S. J. DeMaso, and B. Zaiglin. 1993. Optimum seral stages for Northern Bobwhites as influenced by site productivity. *Journal of Wildlife Management* 57:805–11.

Stormer, F. A. 1984. Night-roosting habitat of Scaled Quail. *Journal of Wildlife Management* 48 (1): 191–97.

Temple, R. A., Jr. 2014. Breeding season dynamics and spatial characteristics of Scaled and Gambel's Quail in a desert shrubland, Trans-Pecos, Texas. Master's thesis, Sul Ross State University.

Texas Game, Fish and Oyster Commission. 1945. *The Principal Game Birds and Mammals of Texas.* Austin: Texas Game, Fish and Oyster Commission.

Wallmo, O. C. 1956. *Ecology of the Scaled Quail in West Texas.* Austin: Texas Game, Fish and Oyster Commission.

Williford, D., R. W. DeYoung, R. L. Honeycutt, L. A. Brennan, and F. Hernandez. 2014. Phylogeography of the scaled quail in the American Southwest. *Western North American Naturalist* 74:18–32.

20

Northern Bobwhite

Loss of habitat undoubtedly remains the key cause of the quail decline.—GUTHERY (2000)

Introduction

The Northern Bobwhite (*Colinus virginianus*) is the most widespread of all North American quail. It once inhabited nearly all grasslands, shrublands, and open forest savannahs across the eastern United States east of the 105th meridian and south of latitude 45°N; however, populations have declined precipitously over the past century. Fortunately, huntable populations of this species are still found in several regions of Texas.

Bobwhites in Texas weigh between 125 g (4.4 oz) and 210 g (7.4 oz); average body weights are around 165 g (5.8 oz). Both males and females are generally brown, with small dark brown, black, and white markings on their necks and backs. Brown feathers transition to a rusty brown on their flanks, where a few rows of white and black feathers run the bird's length. Undersides of both sexes are cream to white, with small zigzag dark brown lines running horizontally across the breast and belly. Tails of both sexes are grayish brown. Males and females can be distinguished by facial coloration. Males sport a conspicuous white throat and broad white stripe over the eye, whereas these areas are a light brown on females. Males also have a black and dark brown crest and stripe running from their beak to below the eye, and to their nape. These areas are generally a lighter brown on females.

Northern Bobwhites are represented by three subspecies in Texas, including the Eastern (*C. v. mexicanus*), Great Plains (*C. v. taylori*), and Texas Bobwhites (*C. v. texanus*). Although the line of demarcation between these subspecies is more or less continuous, the Eastern Bobwhite generally inhabits the pine savannahs and grasslands of East Texas into the southeastern states, while the Great Plains Bobwhite is found in North Texas and the Panhandle, north through the Great Plains states. The Texas Bobwhite is the most common of these three subspecies in Texas and ranges throughout the remainder of the state (Williford et al. 2014).

Distribution in Texas

Northern Bobwhites historically ranged statewide from East Texas to the 102nd meridian. Today, bobwhites are nearly extinct in the Piney Woods region of East Texas and large parts of the Post Oak Savannah, Blackland Prairie, and eastern Edwards Plateau. Huntable populations (more than 1 bird/4 ha or 9.9 ac) can be found in all other regions with suitable habitat except for the Trans-Pecos and High Plains ecoregions. Bobwhites have reportedly expanded their range slightly westward in some areas with irrigation farming and more conservative grazing management practices. The

Figure 20.1. *(Top)*, male; *(bottom)*, female Northern Bobwhites. Photo credits: Larry Ditto.

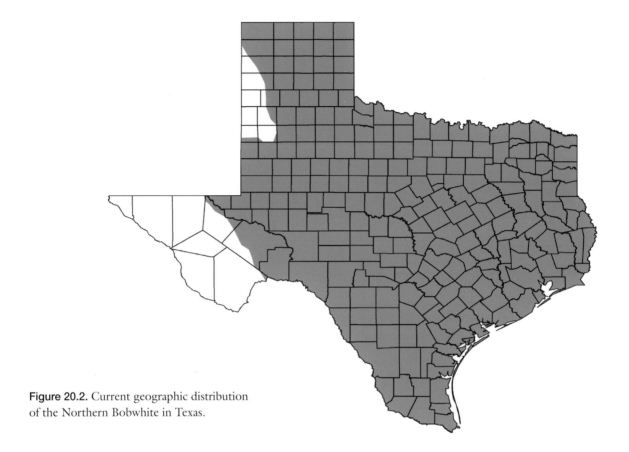

Figure 20.2. Current geographic distribution of the Northern Bobwhite in Texas.

current distribution of Northern Bobwhites in central and North Texas is most likely the result of a post-Pleistocene northward range expansion from South Texas and Mexico (Williford et al. 2016).

Biology

The Northern Bobwhite is one of the most studied wildlife species in the world. Thousands of articles have been published regarding its ecology, habitat, and management. For detailed information on the biology, behavior, and annual life cycle of this bird, see Stoddard (1931), Rosene (1969), Lehmann (1984), Roseberry and Klimstra (1984), Brennan (1999, 2007), Guthery (2000, 2002), Hernández and Peterson (2007), and Brennan, Williford, and Hernández (2014).

Migratory routes and timing

The Northern Bobwhite is a resident, nonmigratory species.

Timing of breeding

In Texas, the Northern Bobwhite breeding season ranges mostly from March through October, although evidence of egg laying has been observed during every month of the year in South Texas (Lehmann 1984). Within this breeding season, most clutches are laid from late April through early July, with birds initiating nests slightly later and ending earlier in more northern and western reaches of the state. Across the state, nest initiations typically occur within days of one another if sufficient rainfall has occurred. Aside from photoperiod, which physiologically prepares the birds for reproduction (by enlarging the gonads and initiating breeding behavior), the actual onset of the nesting season is also influenced by weather and the occurrence of green vegetation. Specifically, factors such as extreme temperatures and dry conditions with little green vegetation are associated with slightly later initiation of nesting, or sometimes little or no nesting at all. Conversely, mild spring temperatures with plentiful

NORTHERN BOBWHITE | 195

rainfall stimulate Northern Bobwhites to nest slightly earlier in the year. Toward the end of the nesting period, cooler than normal summer temperatures and abundant rainfall and associated green vegetation may influence hens to nest into late summer and fall. Late hatches (October to early December) occur most often after a hot and/or dry spring and summer is followed with abundant rain in late summer to early fall. Late hatches are most common in South Texas.

Behavior

Northern Bobwhites are a species of primarily grass and shrubland environments, and thus their behavior is a reflection of these habitats. Most of their life is spent on the ground, where they primarily walk and periodically run on open ground near herbaceous or low-growing woody vegetation. However, bobwhites often fly short distances to reach desired areas or perch aboveground. With the perceived threat of predation, bobwhites usually freeze while emitting a soft, almost inaudible call, holding still in dense cover such as grass until the threat approaches too closely. When this happens, they flush in dramatic fashion, often startling the unsuspecting traveler. Perch sites, often on top of fence posts and in small trees and shrubs, are used primarily during spring and summer by single males advertising their presence via their mating call. Occasionally, groups of birds will collectively perch on low vantage points.

Throughout the year, bobwhites inhabit home ranges of about 30 ha (74 ac), but these vary from 6 ha (15 ac) to 90 ha (222 ac). Within home ranges, bobwhites spend the majority of their time in smaller areas. These sites are called core areas. Core areas in Texas average 5 ha (12 ac) and range from 0.5 ha (1.2 ac) to 22 ha (54 ac). Home range and core area sizes for bobwhites vary by locale, season, and individual.

Bobwhites are social birds and can be found in coveys during fall, winter, and dry periods. Covey sizes average between 10 and 12 birds but can range from extremes of 4 to around 30 birds. Most often, smaller covey sizes are found at the beginning of the breeding season as birds begin to pair, or at the end of hot, dry summers in which little reproduction occurred. Conversely, exceptionally large coveys are found during and after productive breeding seasons. However,

bobwhite coveys are observed most often with around an average of 11 individuals. Williams, Lutz, and Applegate (2003) found that coveys on the extreme ends of the size spectrum had low group persistence and survival compared to coveys that were closer to average in size. Large coveys (15–22 birds) had greater group movement and individual mass loss. Optimal covey size in their study was suggested to be about 11 birds. Contrary to conventional thought, bobwhite coveys are not static, as birds frequently transfer to other coveys throughout the fall and winter (Lehmann 1984, appendix E).

Coveys begin to disband into pairs during late February and early March, and nearly all birds are in pairs by mid-April. Males and females exhibit a variety of breeding behaviors during this time (Stokes 1967). Bobwhites were once thought to have a monogamous mating system (Stoddard 1931; Rosene 1969), as some pairs remain together throughout the breeding season; however, it is now known that bobwhites exhibit a more polygamous-type mating system called rapid asynchronous multiclutch polygamy (Curtis et al. 1993; Burger et al. 1995).

Bobwhite pairs construct well-concealed nests on the ground, typically at the base of bunchgrasses, but forbs, subshrubs, cacti, and shrubs are also used. Although certain types of plants (e.g., bunchgrasses) are used more than others for nests, plant structure seems to be a predominant factor in determining nest site selection. For instance, a forb or shrub with a structure similar to that of a suitably sized bunchgrass may be used as a nest site just as readily. Nests typically consist of a scratched-out depression about 12 cm (5 in) wide and 6 cm (2.4 in) deep, which is lined with residual plant material (e.g., senesced grass leaves) to form a bowl, and the nest may contain a roof. After nest construction, the female incubates the clutch while the male often remains close by, although males occasionally incubate clutches. Northern Bobwhite chicks hatch synchronously and leave the nest, following their parents shortly after hatching. Bobwhite chicks are precocial and are able to feed themselves almost immediately after hatching. The growth of chicks is rapid, as primary feathers begin to show at about 3 days. Chicks are capable of short flight at 14 days and are capable of living without parental care at 5 weeks of age. Chicks resemble adults in size and plumage at 15 weeks of age.

Northern Bobwhites use a variety of calls (Stokes 1967) in response to various stimuli, and these calls can be divided into 5 main groups. In order of the most prominent and common, these calls are pur-ee, bob-white, clucks, toil-ick, and squeal.

> Pur-ee—Also pronounced "koi-lee" or "hoyee," this call is used for locating other quail during pair or covey aggregation. It is given by 1 or more members of a covey during fall and winter prior to sunrise.

> Bob-white—Used by single males during the breeding season to advertise their position and attract females. This call is usually given from an elevated perch, and more calls are given during peak nesting season. In proximity to a calling bird, it is typically heard as 3 syllables ("ah, bob-white").

> Clucks—Continuous low chatter given throughout the day, especially during feeding.

> Toil-ick—An alarm call given in response to strange objects, terrestrial predators, or stressful situations.

> Squeal—Distress call upon capture.

Clutch size and incubation

Northern Bobwhite eggs are a solid chalky white. Hens lay about 1 egg per day, and once the clutch is complete, they begin incubation. Clutch sizes are large and typically average about 12–15 eggs and range from 5 to 22 eggs. Clutch size tends to be larger for initial nests and smaller for renesting attempts after an initial nest is lost. Incubation lasts for 21–23 days and is carried out primarily by the hen; however, males have been documented incubating about 20% of the time (Burger et al. 1995). Incubation by males is most common when the female has been killed.

Nest losses

Nest success for bobwhites is low and ranges from 15% to a high of more than 60%. However, nest success most often averages around 30%. Generally, nest success is lower with poor conditions (e.g., hot, dry summers) and greater when conditions are favorable (e.g., cool, moist summers). Bobwhites are able to cope with such high nest failure by renesting if conditions remain advantageous, and many hens will attempt to renest if their initial nest is depredated. Burger et al. (1995) estimated that the time from when a clutch is lost to a following nest attempt is 19.5 days. In exceptionally good nesting years, bobwhites have been recorded renesting up to 4 times in a single nesting season, and occasionally hens successfully incubate and raise 2 broods in 1 year. This occurrence is the exception rather than the rule, but it gives some insight into the reproductive capacity of bobwhites when conditions are favorable. On average, about 70% of nest losses are caused by predation (Lehmann 1984; Roseberry and Klimstra 1984). Primary nest predators vary by region but generally include coyotes (*Canis latrans*), raccoons (*Procyon lotor*), striped skunk (*Mephitis mephitis*), and snakes. However, the list of Northern Bobwhite predators is long and includes unlikely culprits such as white-tailed deer (*Odocoileus virginianus*), nine-banded armadillos (*Dasypus novemcinctus*), and ground squirrels (*Spermophilus* spp.), among many others. Other causes of nest failure include human activities (16%), abandonment (9%), and weather (5%) (Lehmann 1984; Roseberry and Klimstra 1984).

Diet and foraging

Larson et al. (2010) provide a thorough overview of Texas bobwhite diets; general information on diet and foraging is provided below.

Diets of Northern Bobwhites vary considerably by region, plant community, season, and plant phenology. They forage primarily on open ground and between herbaceous plants where seeds, green leaf material, mast (fruits of trees and shrubs), and insects are consumed. However, the vast majority of the foods eaten are hard-coated seeds produced by forbs and grasses. Throughout the year, about 60%–80% of food items consumed are seeds (Larson et al. 2010), while green vegetation and insect matter largely make up the remainder. Specifically, about 70% of the diet is seeds and mast, 12% insects, 10% green vegetation, and 8% miscellaneous items (Lehmann 1984).

Diet composition varies widely in space and time. Seeds are consumed more widely during late summer, fall, and winter. As spring approaches and succulent green vegetation becomes available, insects and green leaf material are consumed more frequently. Insects are consumed the most by laying hens and chicks. Chicks require a diet high in proteins and fats, which insects provide, for their first few weeks of life. The diet of chicks typically consists of about 80% insects. Succulent green leaves can be consumed in vast amounts at times (72% in southwestern Texas), especially during moist fall-spring periods. Mast is consumed upon availability, as fruits and seeds from woody plants are usually produced episodically depending on the species.

Bobwhites are known to consume seeds and parts of more than 1,000 different types of plants. However, a few notable species typically make up the bulk of seeds consumed in a given area. For example, Lehmann (1984) found that crotons (*Croton* spp.) and panicums (*Panicum* spp.) made up about 20% and 30% of the diets of 565 bobwhites in South Texas, respectively. In the Rolling Plains of Texas, Jackson (1969) found that 7 forb species contributed 40% of the food volume of 963 crops examined. Important seeds repeatedly found in bobwhite crops include crotons, sunflowers (*Helianthus* spp.), ragweeds (*Ambrosia* spp.), panicums, bristlegrasses (*Setaria* spp.), paspalums (*Paspalum* spp.), rosettegrasses (*Dichanthelium* spp.), signalgrasses (*Urochloa* spp.), prickly poppies (*Argemone* spp.), bundleflowers (*Desmanthus* spp.), common broomweed (*Amphiachyris dracunculoides*), partridgepeas (*Chamaecrista* spp.), buffalobur (*Solanum rostratum*), erect dayflower (*Commelina erecta*), tallow weeds (*Plantago* spp.), vetches (*Vicia* spp.), snoutbeans (*Rhynchosia* spp.), and milkpeas (*Galactia* spp.). Domestic crop seeds commonly found in the crops of bobwhites in agricultural landscapes or with access to feeding sites include milo (*Sorghum bicolor*), corn (*Zea mays*), and wheat (*Triticum aestivum*), among others. Although many dietary items are similar to those eaten by the sympatric Scaled Quail (*Callipepla squamata*), bobwhites generally have a narrower diet and consume more seeds from grasses and fewer seeds and fruits from woody plants (Campbell-Kissock, Blankenship, and Stewart 1985; Hammerquist-Wilson and Crawford 1987).

The relative number of seeds from woody plants can be high in bobwhite diets; the commonly eaten seeds from woody plants in Texas include those of mesquite (*Prosopis glandulosa*), gum bumelia (*Sideroxylon lanuginosum*), hackberry (*Celtis* spp.), and agarito (*Mahonia trifoliolata*). Fruits from plants such as prickly pears (*Opuntia* spp.), bumelias (*Sideroxylon* spp.), hackberries, agarito, dewberries (*Rubus* spp.), American beautyberry (*Callicarpa americana*), and brasil (*Condalia hookeri*) are consumed, among many others.

Of the portion of the diet composed of insects, bobwhites are particularly fond of grasshoppers (order Orthoptera). However, a wide suite of insects are consumed, particularly those in the orders Coleoptera, Hymenoptera, Blattodea, and Arachnida, among others. In southwest Texas, desert termites can be important in drier periods when other insects are not available, as termites remain active during the morning even when rainfall is lacking (Campbell-Kissock, Blankenship, and Stewart 1985).

Northern Bobwhites use free water when available, but they are able to meet their water needs from their foods and metabolic water produced during digestion.

Demography and vital rates

Through nearly a century of research, bobwhite demography and population dynamics are better understood than those of many other wildlife species in the United States, but there is still much to be learned. High numbers of bobwhites in nearly fully usable habitat under advantageous conditions reach densities of around 247 birds/km² (0.39 sq mi, or 1 bird or more/ac). However, bobwhite densities more often range between 25 and 50 birds/km² (0.39 sq mi, or 1 bird/4–5 ac). In periods of extreme and prolonged drought or in landscapes with low amounts of usable space, densities of around 10 birds/km² (0.39 sq mi, or 1 bird/10–20 ac) are approached.

Bobwhites are generally short-lived and have an average life span of about 6 months. Rarely, bobwhites can live up to 5 years in the wild. Annual mortality of adult birds is around 70%–80%, and fewer than 40% of chicks survive 3 weeks after hatching (DeMaso et al. 1997). Female survival is generally lower than that of males. Presumably, hens survive at lower rates because of higher mortality associated with the dangers of nesting.

Factors known to kill bobwhites include catastrophic weather events such as extreme temperatures, high winds (leading to accidents during flight), deluges associated with hurricanes (especially for preflight birds; Hernández et al. 2002), prolonged snow coverage (leading to hypothermia and starvation), and freezing rain. Other causes of death include high parasite loads, diseases, and starvation, but also accidents (e.g., flight into a barbed wire fence), vehicle collisions, and predators. Overall, predation is the greatest source of mortality for bobwhites. Cause-specific mortality is largely unknown for bobwhite chicks, although predation by native and introduced fire ants (*Solenopsis* spp.) has been documented, particularly during or shortly after hatching. Aside from humans, common mammalian predators of adult bobwhites include bobcats (*Lynx rufus*), coyotes, and raccoons, but most predations by these species are unlikely to occur at a scale significant enough to limit populations in areas with abundant habitat such as South Texas. Several species of snakes occasionally prey on bobwhites, including the western diamondback rattlesnake (*Crotalus atrox*). However, a significant source of bobwhite mortality comes at the talons of raptors. Several species of hawks, including the Northern Harrier (*Circus cyaneus*) and Sharp-shinned (*Accipiter striatus*), Cooper's (*Accipiter cooperii*), Red-tailed (*Buteo jamaicensis*), Swainson's (*Buteo swainsoni*), and Harris's Hawks (*Parabuteo unicinctus*), as well as large owls, including the Great Horned (*Bubo virginianus*) and Barn Owl (*Tyto alba*), kill bobwhites in Texas.

Age at first reproduction

Contrary to what some people think, bobwhites hatched early in a breeding season have not been documented nesting during that same breeding season. Juvenile bobwhites do not reproduce until the following spring, when almost all birds will attempt to breed.

Age and sex ratios

Age ratios range from nearly no juveniles per adult during years of abnormally poor production to 5 or more juveniles per adult in very good years. However, year in and year out, ratios average around 3.4 juveniles per adult across the state. These ratios also vary across Texas, averaging 2.7 juveniles per adult in South Texas (Lehmann 1984), 3.5 juveniles per adult in the Piney Woods (Rosene 1969), and 3.9 juveniles per adult in the Rolling Plains (Jackson 1969).

Bobwhite reproductive success can vary closely with precipitation. Tri et al. (2013) found that 94% of the annual variation in juvenile-to-adult ratios is correlated with annual precipitation in semiarid environments. In more mesic environments, this relationship deteriorates. In coastal environments generally prone to flooding, production may be suppressed with increasing rainfall.

Northern Bobwhite sex ratios are skewed toward males, presumably because females experience greater mortality while incubating. Sex ratios range from 53%–56% male to 44%–47% female. At hatching, sex ratios of Northern Bobwhites are nearly equal (Brennan, Williford, and Hernández 2014).

Population Status and Trends

The Northern Bobwhite has been declining across its geographical range for at least a century. Data collected during the Christmas Bird Counts, in addition to other sources, indicate that Northern Bobwhite populations have been decreasing in Texas since at least the 1970s. Wild Northern Bobwhites are locally extinct in the East Texas Piney Woods ecoregion; they are typically found in and around areas on national forest lands managed for the endangered Red-cockaded Woodpecker (*Picoides borealis*) that are maintained as open, parklike pine stands with frequent prescribed fire. They are also found in small, isolated pockets in the Post Oak Savannah, Blackland Prairie, and Cross Timbers and Prairies ecoregions, especially in areas where native grasses and forbs are present and coastal Bermuda grass is scarce. Although they go through dramatic boom-and-bust dynamics in relation to drought and rainfall, populations appear to be relatively stable (i.e., with no long-term declines) in the South Texas Plains, Coastal Sand Sheet, Gulf Coastal Plains, and Rolling Plains ecoregions.

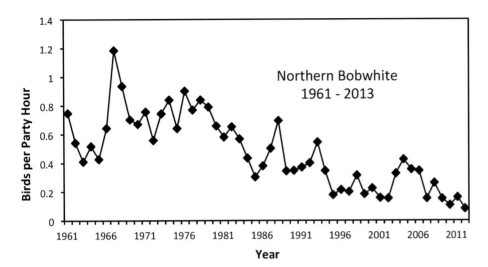

Figure 20.3. Population trend of the Northern Bobwhite in Texas based on Christmas Bird Count data, 1961–2013. While numbers vary with rainfall patterns, populations have declined in Texas, especially since the 1970s.

Specific Habitat Requirements

Hernández and Guthery (2012) and Larson et al. (2010) give detailed information on the specific habitat requirements and management of bobwhites in Texas. Much of the following section is based on these works.

Bobwhite habitat varies substantially in appearance, plant species composition, and configuration across their range; however, the structural composition and juxtaposition of habitat attributes to which bobwhites respond are generally similar (Guthery 1999). For example, bobwhites can be found from the nearly treeless and shrubless grasslands of the Texas barrier islands to the semiforested grassland savannahs of eastern and central Texas, the Tamaulipan shrublands of South Texas, and the semiarid rangelands and drainages of West Texas. They can even be found in agricultural landscapes as long as some natural refuge is afforded. However, in all of these landscapes, necessary habitat components are interspersed.

Northern Bobwhite habitat is generally patchy and harbors a diverse array of plants. This diversity in plant communities provides the structure needed for the birds' day-to-day activities. Such features include interspersed low-growing woody plants for shade (loafing cover) and protection from predators (escape cover), bunchgrasses for nesting and screening cover, forbs (broad-leaved herbaceous plants) for screening cover, brooding cover, and seeds and insects, and bare ground between and under plants for travel and

food searching. Kopp et al. (1998) estimated the ideal amounts of habitat components for bobwhites in South Texas to be around 50% woody cover, 30% herbaceous cover, and from 20% to 68% bare ground. However, such bounds of habitat components surely vary across years and among the different habitat configurations that sustain bobwhites. Regardless, all of these Northern Bobwhite habitat characteristics must be interspersed across the countryside so that they are readily accessible within the home range and across an area large enough to support a viable population.

Bobwhites are found across Texas in landscapes with nearly 0 (open prairies and barrier islands) to more than 60% woody cover. The importance of this cover is suspected to be inversely proportional to the amount of tall herbaceous vegetation present on the landscape. Bobwhites use woody cover mostly for loafing, where they rest and dust bathe while avoiding harmful temperatures during midday. In habitat where woody plants are not available, structurally comparable components are used in their place. For instance, on the Coastal Prairies of Texas, bobwhites can use tall-statured forbs and grasses such as sunflowers, crotons, camphorweed (*Heterotheca subaxillaris*), rattlepods (*Sesbania* spp.), and bluestem grasses, or human-made items such as old car bodies and cattle pens. Typically, woody plants used for loafing cover are low growing and have dense canopies and relatively open understories with lateral screening cover. A few examples of species that are commonly used where there are respectable populations of bobwhites in Texas include honey mesquite, lotebush (*Ziziphus obtusifolia*), McCartney's rose (*Rosa bracteata*), granjeno (*Celtis pallida*), brasil, coma (*Sideroxylon celastrinum*), Texas persimmon (*Diospyros texana*), and shin oak (*Quercus sinuata*). Woody cover is also critical for long-term persistence of Northern Bobwhite populations and may be a crucial resource that allows a population to persist through bottleneck conditions during a drought (DeMaso et al. 2014).

Northern Bobwhites roost on the ground. Roost sites are typically found in open grassland away from tall obstructions in case the birds must flush after dark to escape predation. However, bobwhites have been found to use taller and brushier areas for roosting. Hernández and Peterson (2007) noted that bobwhites with chicks, especially chicks hatched later in the year, were inclined to roost on the ground in areas with generally tall vegetation and brush cover when compared to groups with broods hatched earlier in the year. In a study on the southern Edwards Plateau, bobwhites were found to roost in thickets of shin oak and in shrubby growth at the base of live oaks (*Quercus virginiana*). It has not been determined why these particular birds found it advantageous to roost in these unconventional areas.

Although bobwhites will use a variety of substrates for nesting including low shrubs, subshrubs, forbs, and cacti, the vast majority of bobwhite nest sites are in perennial bunchgrasses about the size and shape of a basketball. Specifically, bunchgrasses measuring more than 22.4 cm (8.8 in) in width and height are selected (Arredondo et al. 2007).

In Texas, several grass species and genera provide this structure and are repeatedly used. These include, but are not limited to, native bluestems (little bluestem, *Schizachyrium scoparium*; silver bluestem, *Bothriochloa saccharoides*, and others in the *Andropogon* genus), nonnative bluestems (yellow bluestem, *Bothriochloa ischaemum*, and others in the *Dichanthium* genus), threeawns (*Aristida* spp.), panicums (*Panicum* spp.), paspalums (*Paspalum* spp.), lovegrasses (*Eragrostis* spp.), bristlegrasses (*Setaria* spp.), pappusgrasses (*Pappophorum* spp.), balsamscales (*Elyonurus* spp.), tanglehead (*Heteropogon contortus*), and buffelgrass (*Pennisetum ciliare*). It is recommended that suitably sized bunches for nesting be available in densities of at least 730/ha (about 340/ac) in areas with about 37% herbaceous cover (Arredondo et al. 2007). On rangelands with abundant prickly pear (*Opuntia* spp.), sparse herbaceous cover, and/or heavy grazing, prickly pear is readily used for nesting (Carter, Rollins, and Scott 2002; Hernández et al. 2003). In two studies, 57% (Carter, Rollins, and Scott 2002) and 37% (Hernández et al. 1999), respectively, of bobwhite nests were located within prickly pear even when adequate bunchgrass cover was available.

After chicks hatch, they must have access to areas with abundant insects. Such areas, termed "brooding habitat," are critical to chick survival. These sites may be localized in patches or nearly ubiquitous across the landscape. But overall, they are characterized as having the following components: (1) shade, (2) open ground under herbaceous cover, and (3) succulent green vegetation (Lehmann 1984). Shade is important to chicks, as prolonged exposure to the sun can cause overexposure to their thermal limits (Taylor and Guthery 1994). Vegetation must be open at the ground level so that chicks can travel unimpeded. Finally, green, growing vegetation provides habitat for the abundant insects that are critical to chicks during their first weeks of life. Taylor, Church, and Rusch (1999) found that broods preferred patches with greater amounts of bare ground (15%), forb cover (30%), and generally tall vegetation (40 cm or 15 in) compared to random sites. Taylor and Guthery (1994) found that the moisture content of vegetation (140 g/m^2 or 1.4 oz/sq yd) was 180% greater at brooding sites than in areas used for loafing and roosting.

Overall, natural grasslands, savannahs, and shrublands, in addition to suitable agricultural landscapes, provide habitat components needed for bobwhites. If the conservation of bobwhites and associated wildlife is a land management goal, conserving and restoring large landscapes containing these community types should be of greatest priority.

Habitat management

Many factors have received blame for widespread bobwhite population declines, including red imported fire ants, drought, disease, and increased predator densities, among others. Some of these factors may impact bobwhite populations on a local scale, but

Figure 20.4. Northern Bobwhite habitat in Texas. Bobwhites persist in a variety of vegetation types in Texas including *(top)*, mesic prairie; *(middle)*, savannah; and *(bottom)*, shrubby drainages. Photo credits: Eric Grahmann.

the proximate cause that has unequivocally led to population declines is habitat loss, or the loss of usable space to bobwhites across the landscape (Hernández et al. 2013). According to Guthery (1997), for an area "to be fully usable, a point must by definition be associated with habitat compatible with the physical, behavioral, and physiological adaptations of bobwhites in a time-unlimited sense." In other words, bobwhites must have access to all habitat features necessary for survival and reproduction across the landscape 365 days a year to sustain a population. In areas that cease to provide this simple requirement, bobwhites disappear. Such is the case in parts of Texas where urban sprawl and simplified agricultural landscapes have eliminated bobwhites. Bobwhite numbers are reduced with decreasing usable space, but fortunately, populations can be restored or enhanced with the addition of usable space.

Landscapes that provide all necessary requirements of bobwhite habitat contain adequate food and water (provided through a diverse array of plant and animal foods), shelter (provided by vegetation of appropriate structure and composition), and space (all needs provided in an area large enough to sustain a population). Overall, land management practices focused on the increase of usable space and habitat patch connectivity are most likely to yield returns in bobwhites year in and year out.

First and foremost, habitat management techniques should be purposeful (Larson et al. 2010); that is, they should address limiting factors that suppress usable space. For example, if a habitat component meets at least the minimum food requirements for survival and reproduction, it is unlikely that the provision of extra food via supplementation or fallow disking will result in more bobwhites. An example of the purposeful use of fallow disking would be in an area with low usable space dominated by a monotypic stand of nonnative grass (e.g., limiting bare ground, cover, and brooding habitat).

For years, bobwhites have been classified as an early successional species that depends on early seral stage vegetation communities (Stoddard 1931; Rosene 1969), and most management techniques have been recommended (e.g., disking and prescribed fire) to set back plant succession. Although many practices have

been proven in relatively mesic systems, disturbance-based management for bobwhites may be inappropriate in more arid environments (Spears et al. 1993). This is partially because (1) bobwhites are associated with late-successional perennial grasses in more arid regions, and (2) drought, a disturbance in and of itself, typically overrides the potential value of human-induced disturbances in semiarid environments. The optimum seral stage of plant communities for bobwhites varies inversely with site productivity (Spears et al. 1993), and thus bobwhites are more associated with areas that have abundant bare ground and forbs in mesic ranges compared to drier ones.

Regarding habitat management, the conservation of native grasslands, shrublands, grassland savannahs, and other landscapes usable to bobwhites must be of highest priority. In these landscapes, management should be focused on the maintenance of usable bobwhite habitat rather than misleading manipulative strategies (e.g., serial disking on diverse native grassland). In most cases little can be done to make these systems more habitable to quail.

Management in landscapes where significant alteration has taken place (e.g., farmland and root-plowed rangeland) is a different matter entirely. In these systems, natural disturbance and hydrologic cycles can be altered, leading to scenarios (e.g., dense monotypic brushland) in which management is needed to maintain respectable densities of bobwhites.

The most widely available and important management tools for bobwhite habitat in Texas include grazing, disking, prescribed fire, brush manipulation, and overall habitat and travel corridor restoration. The two most popular habitat management techniques in Texas are briefly described here.

Cattle grazing and associated land management practices are collectively the most important factors influencing bobwhite populations on Texas rangelands. Much rangeland across the state has been rendered unusable because overstocked cattle have denuded the landscape of critical bunchgrasses needed for nesting and forbs important for food and cover. Along with overgrazing itself, the cultural and aesthetic phenomenon of "clean pasture ranching" (e.g., using nonnative forage grasses, fertilizer, and weed killer; mowing; total brush clearing; and tree trimming) has been counterproductive for bobwhites on these ranges. Interestingly, it is difficult to pay for such practices from cattle revenue alone. Lusk et al. (2002) found that the mean number of livestock in a given area of rangeland was an important determinant of bobwhite abundance in six Texas ecoregions.

However, along with the negative aspects associated with overgrazing, grazing itself can have neutral and even positive impacts on bobwhites. For example, grazing within the capacity of available forage is practiced on many ranches that maintain good populations of bobwhites. In some cases, grazing can be a rejuvenating disturbance on rangelands, especially those in more mesic regions. In areas where grass tends to become too thick for bobwhites, grazing can be a beneficial management strategy by reducing grass cover and enhancing bare ground, forbs, and plant species richness. Grazing is most helpful on mesic grasslands and landscapes dominated by dense invasive grasses (e.g., guinea grass [*Megathyrsus maximus*], tanglehead, and buffelgrass). Overall, conservative grazing (up to 25% annual standing crop removal) is recommended on native rangelands where bobwhite management is a priority. On rangeland dominated by dense stands of invasive grasses, more liberal (25%–50% annual standing crop removal) and sustained grazing is recommended to keep aggressive grasses in check.

Disking is a popular management practice typically carried out during winter. Winter disking is used to stimulate warm-season annual forbs. The annual forbs produced with this disturbance method are generally prolific seed and insect producers, and these seeds can easily be found in the turned-up soil created by the disks. However, the value of this method hinges on whether usable space is increased by enhancing screening cover, travel pathways, and insects for chicks. Since food has not been found to be limiting to adult bobwhites in the wild, it is unlikely that usable space is enhanced by the provision of food. However, this practice is valuable in areas where grass becomes too thick and limits usable space. For example, near-monotypic stands of invasive grasses such as tanglehead, Old World bluestems, and buffelgrass are prime candidates to receive disk strips. Where these grasses proliferate, usable space is decreased because bare ground and forbs are less abundant (Sands et al. 2009, 2012). In these situations, bobwhite populations can be suppressed (Flanders et al. 2006). In subtropical regions of Texas, disking across diverse native plant communities should be discouraged, as this practice can spread noxious nonnative grasses that degrade bobwhite habitat (Johnson and Fulbright 2008).

Overall, habitat management must be purposeful and focused on increasing usable space if gains are to be made in bobwhite numbers. On fully usable habitat such as diverse native grasslands, maintenance strategies to sustain the integrity of these communities are most appropriate. Recovery across ecoregions where bobwhite populations have declined must focus on the conservation of remaining habitat and the restoration of native plant communities and landscape corridors if bobwhites are to recover on these landscapes.

Hunting and Conservation

Northern Bobwhites hold game bird status, with seasons and bag limits equivalent to those of other native quail species in the state, excluding the Montezuma Quail (*Cyrtonyx montezumae*). Except for a hunter success rate that ranges from about 70% to 80%, every other aspect of Northern Bobwhite hunting has been declining in Texas. From 1994 to 2014, the total estimated annual harvest declined from about 2 million birds to about 220,000 birds. Over this same 20-year period, the number of Northern Bobwhite hunters fell from nearly 150,000 to about 31,500, and the hunter days spend afield declined from more than 686,000 to just under 110,000 (Purvis 2014).

Texas hunting season length, 2013–2014

The 2013–2014 hunting season was 121 days (October 26, 2013–February 23, 2014).

Texas bag limits

The daily bag limit (per person) for Northern Bobwhite in Texas is 15 in the aggregate with Scaled and Gambel's Quails (*Callipepla gambelii*). The possession limit for these species is 45 per person.

Geographic restrictions on hunting in Texas

There are no geographic restrictions on quail hunting in Texas.

Research Needs and Priorities

Bobwhites are the most widely studied wildlife species in the world. Surprisingly, there is still much to learn about this iconic bird. Because we live in a dynamic ecological and sociological environment, new challenges to bobwhites are constantly arising. For instance, increasing urbanization and cleaner farming techniques continue to test bobwhite populations, and understanding how bobwhite populations may be affected is important. Furthermore, better habitat and population restoration techniques must be developed to ensure that this species remains populous for future generations. Fortunately, new technologies to come (e.g., areal drones and Global Positioning System transmitters) may allow researchers to learn more and propel our understanding of this species, and these technologies should be evaluated and used if they are determined to hold merit in wildlife research.

Moving forward, studies focusing on metapopulation dynamics, density dependence and independence, fragmentation, and habitat patch connectivity will be important in the future. In addition, furthering our knowledge of habitat and population restoration will be critical if this species continues to decline.

Literature Cited

Arredondo, J. A., F. Hernández, F. C. Bryant, R. L. Bingham, and R. Howard. 2007. Habitat suitability bounds for nesting cover of Northern Bobwhites on semiarid rangelands. *Journal of Wildlife Management* 71 (8): 2592–99.

Brennan, L. A. 1999. Northern Bobwhite (*Colinus virginianus*). In *The Birds of North America*, edited by A. Poole and F. Gill. Washington DC: American Ornithologists' Union.

———, ed. 2007. *Texas Quails: Ecology and Management.* College Station: Texas A&M University Press.

Brennan, L. A., D. L. Williford, and F. Hernández. 2014. Northern Bobwhite (*Colinus virginianus*). In *The Birds of North America Online*, edited by A. Poole. Ithaca, NY: Cornell Laboratory of Ornithology. http://bna .birds.cornell.edu.bnaproxy.birds.cornell.edu/bna /species/397/articles/introduction.

Burger, L. W., Jr., M. R. Ryan, T. V. Dailey, and E. W. Kurzejeski. 1995. Reproductive strategies, success, and mating systems of Northern Bobwhite in Missouri. *Journal of Wildlife Management* 59:417–26.

Campbell-Kissock, L., L. H. Blankenship, and J. W. Stewart. 1985. Plant and animal foods of Bobwhite and Scaled Quail in southwest Texas. *Southwestern Naturalist* 30:543–53.

Carter, P. S., D. Rollins, and C. Scott. 2002. Initial effects of prescribed burning on survival and nesting success of Northern Bobwhites in west-central Texas. *Proceedings of the National Quail Symposium* 5:129–34.

Curtis, P. D., B. S. Mueller, P. D. Doerr, C. R. Robinette, and T. DeVos. 1993. Potential polygamous breeding behavior in Northern Bobwhite. *Proceedings of the National Quail Symposium* 3:55–63.

DeMaso, S. J., F. Hernández, L. A. Brennan, N. J. Silvy, W. E. Grant, X. B. Wu, and F. C. Bryant. 2014. Short- and long-term influence of brush canopy cover on Northern Bobwhite demography in southern Texas. *Rangeland Ecology and Management* 67:99–106.

DeMaso, S. J., A. D. Peoples, S. A. Cox, and E. S. Parry. 1997. Survival of Northern Bobwhite chicks in western Oklahoma. *Journal of Wildlife Management* 61:846–53.

Flanders, A. A., W. P. Kuvlesky, D. C. Ruthven, R. E. Zaiglin, R. L. Bingham, T. E. Fulbright, F. Hernández, and L. A. Brennan. 2006. Effects of invasive exotic grasses on south Texas rangeland breeding birds. *Auk* 123:171–82.

Guthery, F. S. 1997. A philosophy of habitat management for Northern Bobwhites. *Journal of Wildlife Management* 61:291–301.

———. 1999. Slack in the configuration of habitat patches for Northern Bobwhites. *Journal of Wildlife Management* 63:245–50.

———. 2000. *On Bobwhites.* College Station: Texas A&M University Press.

———. 2002. *The Technology of Bobwhite Management: The Theory behind the Practice.* Ames: Iowa State University Press.

Hammerquist-Wilson, M., and J. A. Crawford. 1987. Habitat selection by Texas bobwhites and Chestnut-Bellied Scaled Quail in south Texas. *Journal of Wildlife Management* 51:575–82.

Hernández, F., L. A. Brennan, S. J. DeMaso, J. P. Sands, and D. B. Wester. 2013. On reversing the Northern Bobwhite decline: 20 years later. *Wildlife Society Bulletin* 37:177–88.

Hernández, F., and F. S. Guthery. 2012. *Beef, Brush, and Bobwhites: Quail Management in Cattle Country.* 2nd ed. College Station: Texas A&M University Press.

Hernández, F., S. E. Henke, N. J. Silvy, and D. Rollins. 2003. The use of prickly pear cactus as nesting cover for Northern Bobwhite. *Journal of Wildlife Management* 67:417–23.

Hernández, F., and M. J. Peterson. 2007. Northern Bobwhite ecology and life history. In *Texas Quails: Ecology and Management*, edited by L. A. Brennan, 40–64. College Station: Texas A&M University Press.

Hernández, F., J. D. Vasquez, F. C. Bryant, A. A. Radomski, and R. Howard. 2002. Effects of Hurricane Brett on Northern Bobwhite survival in south Texas. *National Quail Symposium Proceedings* 5:87–90.

Jackson, A. S. 1969. *A Handbook for Bobwhite Quail Management in the West Texas Rolling Plains.* Bulletin 48. Austin: Texas Parks and Wildlife Department.

Johnson, M. V. V., and T. E. Fulbright. 2008. Is exotic plant invasion enhanced by a traditional wildlife habitat management technique? *Journal of Arid Environments* 72:1911–17.

Kopp, S. D., F. S. Guthery, N. D. Forrester, and W. E. Cohen. 1998. Habitat selection modeling for Northern Bobwhites on subtropical rangeland. *Journal of Wildlife Management* 62:884–95.

Larson, J. A., T. E. Fulbright, L. A. Brennan, F. Hernández, and F. C. Bryant. 2010. *Texas Bobwhites: A Guide to Their Foods and Habitat Management.* Austin: University of Texas Press.

Lehmann, V. W. 1984. *Bobwhites in the Rio Grande Plains of Texas.* College Station: Texas A&M University Press.

Lusk, J. M., F. S. Guthery, R. R. George, M. J. Peterson, and S. J. Demaso. 2002. Relative abundance of bobwhites in relation to weather and land use. *Journal of Wildlife Management* 66:1040–51.

Purvis, J. 2014. *Small Game Harvest Survey Results 1994–95 thru 2013–14.* Austin: Texas Parks and Wildlife Department.

Roseberry, J. L., and W. D. Klimstra. 1984. *Population Ecology of the Bobwhite.* Carbondale: Southern Illinois University Press.

Rosene, W. 1969. *The Bobwhite Quail: Its Life and Management.* New Brunswick, NJ: Rutgers University Press.

Sands, J. P., L. A. Brennan, F. Hernández, W. P. Kuvlesky Jr., J. F. Gallagher, D. C. Ruthven III, and J. E. Pittman III. 2009. Impacts of buffelgrass (*Pennisetum ciliare*) on a forb community in south Texas. *Invasive Plant Science and Management* 2:130–40.

———. 2012. Impacts of introduced grasses on breeding season habitat use by Northern Bobwhite in the south Texas plains. *Journal of Wildlife Management* 76:608–18.

Spears, G. S., F. S. Guthery, S. M. Rice, S. J. DeMaso, and B. Zaiglin. 1993. Optimum seral stage for Northern Bobwhites as influenced by site productivity. *Journal of Wildlife Management* 57:805–11.

Stoddard, H. L. 1931. *The Bobwhite Quail: Its Habits, Preservation, and Increase.* New York: Charles Scribner's Sons.

Stokes, A. W. 1967. Behavior of the bobwhite, *Colinus virginianus. Auk* 84:1–33.

Taylor, J. S., K. E. Church, and D. H. Rusch. 1999. Micro-habitat selection by nesting and brood-rearing Northern Bobwhites in Kansas. *Journal of Wildlife Management* 63:686–94.

Taylor, J. S., and F. S. Guthery. 1994. Components of Northern Bobwhite brood habitat in southern Texas. *Southwestern Naturalist* 39:73–77.

Tri, A. N., J. P. Sands, M. C. Buelow, D. Williford, E. M. Wehland, J. A. Larson, K. Brazil, J. B. Hardin, F. Hernandez, and L. A. Brennan. 2013. Impacts of weather on Northern Bobwhite sex ratios, body mass, and annual [roduction in south Texas. *Journal of Wildlife Management* 77:579–86.

Williams, C. K., R. S. Lutz, and R. D. Applegate. 2003. Optimal group size of Northern Bobwhite coveys. *Animal Behaviour* 66:377–87.

Williford, D., R. W. DeYoung, R. L. Honeycutt, L. A. Brennan, and F. Hernández. 2016. *Phylogeography of the Bobwhite (Colinus) Quails.* Wildlife Monographs 193.

Williford, D., R. W. DeYoung, R. L. Honeycutt, L. A. Brennan, F. Hernández, E. M. Wehland, J. P. Sands, S. J. DeMaso, K. S. Miller, and R. M. Perez. 2014. Contemporary genetic structure of the Northern Bobwhite west of the Mississippi River. *Journal of Wildlife Management* 78:914–29.

21

Montezuma Quail

Open the crop of a fat little Mearns' quail and you find an herbarium of subsurface foods scratched from the rocky ground you thought barren.—LEOPOLD (1949)

Introduction

The Montezuma Quail (*Cyrtonyx montezumae*) is a strikingly beautiful and secretive quail species of the oak-juniper-pine hills and mountains of the southwestern United States and the Sierra Madre of Mexico. Of our four species of quail in Texas, this particular species has the widest assortment of common names, including Mearns's quail, harlequin quail, fool's quail, crazy quail, black quail (codorniz negra), Messena's quail, and codorniz pinta, among others. The names "fool's quail" and "crazy quail" are derived from this bird's behavior of holding still in grassy cover, only to either seemingly disappear or burst into flight when nearly stepped on.

Montezuma Quail are the largest of Texas's quail species. Their weight averages 184–189 g (6.5–6.7 oz) for females, and 202 g (7.1 oz) for males (Leopold and McCabe 1957; Stromberg 1990). In West Texas, weights range between 190 and 250 g (6.7–8.8 oz) and average 220 g (7.8 oz) (Hernández 2004). Fall juvenile weights average 151 g (5.3 oz) (Stromberg 1990).

Male and female Montezuma Quail are dimorphic, meaning that the sexes differ in both coloration and size (fig. 21.1). Males are easily distinguished from females by their black-and-white harlequin-marked heads with a rusty to buff helmet-like head cap, and a black and pale blue beak. They have brown- and black-checkered backs with white pointed streaks oriented from head to tail. The breast is a mahogany or maroon that fades into dark underparts, while the flanks are a dark charcoal gray with white spots. Females, on the other hand, are relatively drab in coloration but generally sport cinnamon-brown to tan plumage with darker markings and sharp white streaks on the back. The legs of both males and females are grayish blue and terminate in long claws used for digging subterranean foods.

This species is represented in Texas by the *C. m. mearnsi* subspecies, which is found from northern Mexico into southeastern Arizona, southern New Mexico, and South and West Texas. Because of this species' secretive behavior, coupled with its relatively low population densities (compared to other quails) and restricted distribution in the state, little published information exists on Montezuma Quail in Texas or across other portions of its range.

Distribution in Texas

Montezuma Quail are distributed west of the Pecos River in most oak-juniper-pine vegetation associations above 1219 m (4,000 ft) on mountains, hills,

Figure 21.1. Male (*background*) and female (*foreground*) Montezuma Quail. Photo credit: Larry Ditto.

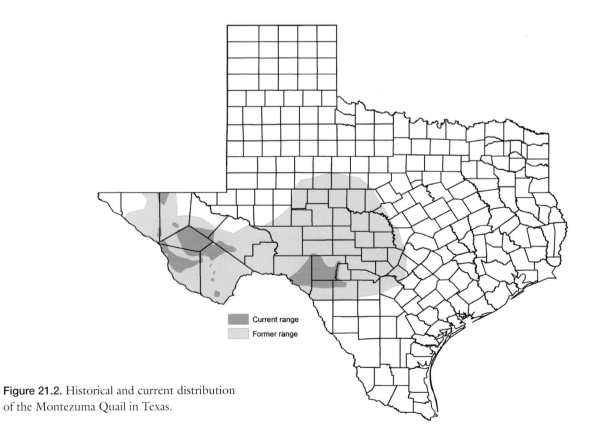

Current range
Former range

Figure 21.2. Historical and current distribution of the Montezuma Quail in Texas.

and otherwise rugged terrain with good herbaceous cover. On the southern Edwards Plateau, Montezuma Quail are found primarily above 450 m (1,476 ft) in elevation in Edwards and Val Verde Counties. They are also found on the eastern side of Real County and the northern sides of Uvalde and Kinney Counties in suitable habitat. On the Edwards Plateau, Montezuma Quail are found in association with oak-juniper-piñon savannahs on hills and rugged terrain. Occasionally, Montezuma Quail are reported on steep, high-elevation areas on private ranches between the Sky Islands of the Trans-Pecos and the southern Edwards Plateau. Across their range in Texas, populations tend to be localized. Historically, Montezuma Quail were thought to have occurred in nearly every county in the Trans-Pecos and Edwards Plateau (Texas Game, Fish and Oyster Commission 1945).

Biology

The life history and ecology of the Montezuma Quail have been described mostly in Arizona and Mexico. Leopold and McCabe (1957), D. Brown (1989), and Harveson et al. (2007) give detailed information regarding the biology, behavior, and annual life cycle of this bird. Much of the following section is summarized from these sources.

Migratory routes and timing
Montezuma Quail are a resident, nonmigratory species.

Timing of breeding
Montezuma Quail breeding condition is likely determined by photoperiod. Generally, males begin to call and quail are paired by late March, and the breeding season can last until October (Leopold and McCabe 1957). Although they exhibit a prolonged breeding season, most nesting takes place from June through August. This is typically the case in the Trans-Pecos of Texas, where nesting can occur from April through October but most often from June through August, when the majority of rainfall occurs via monsoonal storms. Interestingly, populations between the Trans-Pecos and Edwards Plateau regions of Texas may exhibit slightly contrasting nesting

seasons because of differences in rainfall regimes. On the Edwards Plateau, where rainfall regimes are typically bimodal (peaking in April–June and again in September–October), Montezuma Quail are thought to nest earlier than their western counterparts. Sorola (1986) recorded 7 observations of broods on the Edwards Plateau during June and 5 observations in September. In 2014, Grahmann and Moore (2014) found a brood with chicks of different ages (estimated at 2 and 3–4 weeks of age) on June 6. The oldest of these chicks were likely hatched around the second week of May. Similarly, Albers and Gehlbach (1990) found hatchlings on a nearby ranch on June 15 on the Edwards Plateau. They also found "half grown" birds on September 18, suggesting that Montezuma Quail in this area nest at least into July. Because of their late nesting season in association with monsoonal rains, renesting is thought to be more uncommon than for other quail species (Leopold and McCabe 1957).

Behavior
Montezuma Quail are remarkably secretive birds that spend almost all their time on the ground in association with dense herbaceous cover on hilltops and slopes. This is likely a behavioral strategy aimed at avoiding predators, as Montezuma Quail lie motionless until the predator approaches within a couple of meters, at which point the birds often flush uphill. This behavioral mechanism is so ingrained that Montezuma Quail have even been witnessed "freezing" on wide-open ground in response to a predator. Although Montezuma Quail tend to hold tight in dense cover, they are sneaky and can slip through vegetation unnoticed upon their escape. In sparser habitat, Montezuma Quail tend to run and flush more readily, but these instances are mostly exceptions. Most flight distances are between 16 and 30 m (51–100 ft), after which this bird runs a short distance and then hides (Leopold and McCabe 1957).

Montezuma Quail are found in coveys during fall and winter, as well as after chicks hatch during summer. Within family units and aggregate coveys, birds are often observed in proximity to one another. Covey sizes for Montezuma Quail are generally small compared to those of other New World quail and average around 7.6 birds. On the Edwards Plateau, covey size averaged 7.8 birds (Sorola 1986). Covey sizes have been reported from 3 to 30 birds. Coveys in West Texas were observed with between 3 and 9 birds (Hernández 2004), while coveys were seen ranging from 3 to 11 birds on the Edwards Plateau (Grahmann and Moore 2014).

Compared to other quail species, Montezuma Quail are relatively sedentary, as individuals frequent the same areas, ranging from 1 to 5 ha (2.5–12.4 ac) each day during fall and winter and 50 ha (124 ac) during spring (Stromberg 1990). However, movements tend to increase as coveys disband into breeding pairs. Stromberg (1990) reported that most Montezuma Quail frequented small ranges from 0.09 to 6 ha (0.2–14.8 ac) during midwinter. During late winter and spring, the birds spent 3–10 days on nonoverlapping areas as large as 50 ha (123.5 ac). Daily movements were small (15–60 m, 49–197 ft), and birds typically did not move more than 100 m (328 ft) per day (Stromberg 1990). However, in the Davis Mountains of West Texas, Montezuma Quail have been documented traveling 8–11 km (5–7 mi) in a 2-to 3-week period (Greene and Harveson 2014).

Coveys begin to disband in February and pairing is complete by May. Montezuma Quail are thought to be monogamous, but detailed studies on social interactions in the wild have not been conducted. During the nesting season, Montezuma Quail construct nests by scratching out a depression under a bunchgrass and then create a nest dome by lining the sides and nest roof with threaded grasses and forbs. Both the female and male may collectively partake in nest construction, after which the female incubates the clutch while the male often remains close by. Males may occasionally incubate nests. Montezuma Quail chicks hatch synchronously and follow their parents shortly after hatching. The chicks are precocial and are able to feed themselves almost immediately after hatching. However, compared to parents of other New World quail species, Montezuma Quail parents are particularly attentive to their young (Leopold and McCabe 1957).

Montezuma Quail live almost exclusively on the ground. Although the daily activity pattern of Montezuma Quail is bimodal, with most activity taking place in the mornings and evenings, they tend to be late risers from the roost (D. Brown 1989) and tend to feed more often during midday compared to other quail species. This is especially true during cold winter days. Bishop and Hungerford (1965) found that Montezuma Quail did not have full crops until about 1500 hours (3:00 p.m. PDT). At night, Montezuma Quail roost on the ground in a circle with their heads facing outward in a grassy area (D. Brown 1989).

Compared to other quails, Montezuma Quail do little advertisement calling (Sorola 1986). Calls are heard primarily during morning and evening hours. Sorola (1986) reported that 79% of calls were heard before 1030 hours (10:30 a.m. CST) and 27% were heard during the afternoon. Montezuma calls can be divided into 5 groups: descending whistles, buzzes, growls, clucks, and squeals. The volume and frequency of calls for this species tend to be subtle, and some calls may incorporate frequencies inaudible to humans. Even when calls are heard, they are ventriloquial in nature and pinpointing these quail based on calls is difficult.

> Descending whistles—Described as an owl-like call, typically 7–11 descending notes. Given by adults and chicks of both sexes for locating other quail. This call is given most often in the morning, evening, or after rainfall.
>
> Buzzes—Used during the breeding season by the male to locate females. This call is given most often in the morning, evening, or after rainfall. Unlike males of other quail species, Montezuma males almost never give this call from a perch higher than the surrounding herbaceous cover.
>
> Growls—Close communication by males with other quail.
>
> Clucks—Barely audible chatter between quail, especially when feeding.
>
> Squeals—Distress calls upon capture or in defense of chicks.

Clutch size and incubation

Montezuma Quail eggs are chalky white, similar to those of the Northern Bobwhite (*Colinus virginianus*). However, Montezuma eggs have a more rounded apex. Clutch sizes typically average around

11 and range from 6 to 16 eggs. Incubation lasts from 25 to 26 days. Although clutch sizes are large, brood sizes are typically smaller and average 6.6. to 8.4 chicks (Leopold and McCabe 1957).

Nest losses

A comprehensive study focusing exclusively on nest losses of Montezuma Quail has not been conducted. In Mexico and West Texas, major nest predators are thought to be coatimundi (*Nasua narica*), peccary (*Pecari tajacu*), raccoon (*Procyon lotor*), and skunks in the genera *Mephitis*, *Spilogale*, and *Conepatus* (Leopold and McCabe 1957). If nests are depredated early in the nesting season, hens may attempt to renest under favorable conditions (D. Brown 1989).

Diet and foraging

Montezuma Quail are primarily a ground-foraging species and use their stout legs, long toes, and elongated claws to scratch or dig for subterranean plant material, seeds, and insects. They scratch using one foot at a time and take frequent breaks to peer into their diggings for food items. Digging sites usually cover several square meters in which numerous conical depressions are scratched out of crumbly soil. Depressions where Montezuma Quail find bulbs are littered with the outside husks of these plant parts. Montezuma Quail forage most often along hillsides and small draws in organically rich and crumbly soil with ample grass for screening cover. Feeding areas in Texas are described as open grassy patches, as Montezuma Quail tend to avoid foraging for subterranean plants under tree canopies (Albers and Gehlbach 1990). However, in Arizona, foraging areas are often located under trees and shrubs in addition to open areas (Bishop and Hungerford 1965).

Overall, Montezuma Quail consume a variety of dietary items including seeds, mast, insects, and green leaf material. The relative percentage of these items in their diet depends on rainfall, food availability, and grazing management. Montezuma Quail apparently require greater amounts of fats and proteins and likely depend on a widely varied diet consisting of important subterranean foods, as they are not found in areas lacking these critical food items.

Seventy-one percent of fall and winter diets consists of vegetable matter, and most of these items are subterranean plant organs (Leopold and McCabe 1957). Important subterranean foods consumed by Montezuma Quail include corms of violet woodsorrels (*Oxalis* spp.), bulbs from wild onions (*Allium* spp.), and tubers from sedges (*Cyperus* spp.), morning glory (*Ipomoea* spp.), and nightshade (*Solanum* spp.). These plants are fed upon mostly from fall to early spring and during droughty periods. Their presence is critical to the Montezuma Quail. Violet woodsorrels occurred in 39% of crops and were 32% by volume of crops in Arizona when averaged across years and seasons in a study conducted by Bishop and Hungerford (1965). However, bulbs from violet woodsorrels alone made up 64% of Montezuma Quail diets during winter months. Bulbs from *Oxalis amplifolia* and tubers from *Cyperus rusbyi* made up 77% of Montezuma Quail diets in Arizona during R. Brown's (1982) study. Drummond's woodsorrel (*Oxalis drummondii*) is the woodsorrel species and food plant of most importance to Montezuma Quail in the Edwards Plateau and Trans-Pecos regions of Texas. These plant foods are reduced in summer diets, as food preference switches to insects upon their availability (Leopold and McCabe 1957).

Seeds are consumed in greatest abundance during spring and summer and to a lesser extent during fall and winter. Seeds that are widely consumed include those from panicums (*Panicum* spp.), dayflowers (*Commelina* spp.), morning glories, mountainbeans (*Phaseolus* spp.), bristlegrasses (*Setaria* spp.), piñon ricegrass (*Piptochaetium fimbriatum*), toothed spurge (*Euphorbia dentata*), paspalums (*Paspalum* spp.), rough buttonweed (*Diodia teres*), caltrops (*Kallstroemia* spp.), prickly pears (*Opuntia* spp.), velvetpod mimosa (*Mimosa dysocarpa*), acacias (*Acacia* spp.), piñons (*Pinus* sp.), sunflowers (*Helianthus* spp.), century plants (*Agave* spp.), and acorns from live oak species (*Quercus* spp.). Fruits of ground cherry (*Physalis* spp.), prickly pear, sumacs (*Rhus* spp.), junipers (*Juniperus* spp.), and madrone (*Arbutus* spp.) are eaten as well.

Insects are consumed in great quantity by Montezuma Quail during the summer and to a lesser extent during spring and fall (Bishop and Hungerford 1965). Montezuma Quail diets in spring in Arizona consisted of 50% insects, although insects were nearly absent from diets during winter. As with other species of quail, the importance of insects is most pronounced for laying hens and chicks (Leopold and McCabe 1957). Young birds depend on invertebrate forage their first few weeks of life. Invertebrates in the orders Orthoptera, Hemiptera, Homoptera, Coleoptera, Hymenoptera, Arachnida, Diptera, Lepidoptera, Isoptera, and Chilopoda are most often consumed.

Montezuma Quail occasionally use free water when available, but they are able to meet their water needs from their water-rich foods (primarily corms, bulbs, roots, and tubers) and metabolic water produced during digestion.

Demography and vital rates

Densities of Montezuma Quail coveys have been reported from 8.1 to 10.3 coveys/km² (247 ac) and from 10 to 42.6 birds/km² (1 bird/25 to 5.8 ac) (Leopold and McCabe 1957; R. Brown 1982). On the Edwards Plateau, densities of Montezuma Quail have been reported from 8 to 10 birds/km² (1 bird/31 to 25 ac) (Albers and Gehlbach 1990).

Montezuma Quail are largely dependent on monsoonal rainfall in the Sky Islands of the Desert Southwest. In Arizona, the percentage of juvenile Montezuma Quail in hunter bags, as well as hunter success, was correlated mostly with June–August rainfall (D. Brown 1979). Presumably, Montezuma Quail survival and nest success are greater because of increased cover and food resources during summers of high rainfall. Leopold and McCabe (1957) estimated that losses of adults, chicks, and eggs cumulatively reach 40% during the breeding season. These cumulative breeding season losses are less than what is generally reported for other quail species. As with other quails inhabiting arid lands, annual survival and reproduction fluctuate closely with precipitation patterns, as drought precludes successful nesting and influences survival. D. Brown (1979) estimated yearly adult survival rates of between 18% and 59%.

Inclement weather can also result in high quail mortality, as deep snows are reported to result in high death rates of Montezuma Quail (Leopold and McCabe 1957). It is thought that periodic deep snow accumulations limit this species at its northernmost range. However, prolonged periods with accumulated snow are uncommon in Texas, with the exception of the highest elevations in the Guadalupe, Davis, and Chisos Mountains. Most predations on adult Montezuma Quail are likely by raptors (Hernández 2004; Hernández et al. 2009). R. Brown (1982) and Stromberg (1990) witnessed predation of Montezuma Quail by Sharp-Shinned (*Accipiter striatus*) and Cooper's Hawks (*Accipiter cooperii*). Stromberg (1990) also reported a single Cooper's Hawk focusing on the area where a covey resided. This single bird killed 6 Montezuma Quail apparently from the same covey. Otherwise, little is known about predators and predation rates of Montezuma Quail.

Age at first reproduction

Montezuma Quail do not reproduce until the spring following the year in which they were hatched.

Age and sex ratios

Age ratios of Montezuma Quail have been documented at 1.6 juveniles per adult (Leopold and McCabe 1957).

Although sex ratios are even for most quail species at hatching, Montezuma Quail sex ratios are skewed toward males. Sex ratios have been reported ranging from 53% to 63% male and 37% to 44% female (Leopold and McCabe 1957; Stromberg 1990).

Population Status and Trends

Sampling Montezuma Quail populations is difficult because of their secretive nature coupled with their distribution, which lies mostly on rugged and remote private ranches. Excluding variation related to weather, their populations are thought to be at least stable and possibly increasing because of better grazing management practices and the limited clearing of monotypic juniper stands on the Edwards Plateau. Montezuma Quail range was once thought to be retracted to suitable habitat in the Davis Mountains of West Texas and in Edwards County, where refuge from overgrazing (steep hillsides and canyons) existed in small pockets (Oberholser 1974; Sorola 1986); however, they are now known to occupy nearly every Madrean Sky

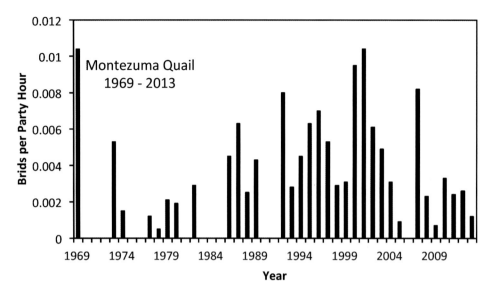

Figure 21.3. Population indices of Montezuma Quail in Texas based on Christmas Bird Count data. Note that gaps in data indicate that Montezuma Quail were not detected during those count years.

Island west of the Pecos and to have a larger distribution than previously described (Oberholser 1974) on the southern Edwards Plateau (Sorola 1986; Grahmann and Moore 2014).

Specific Habitat Requirements

Montezuma Quail inhabit mostly mountainous and hilly terrain in open evergreen and oak woodlands, savannahs, and grasslands. In the Trans-Pecos region of Texas, they are most commonly associated with evergreen mountainous Madrean Sky Islands and grasslands. On the Edwards Plateau they are found in association with hilly oak-juniper savannahs and grassy mesas. On grasslands, Montezuma Quail densities are typically lower in areas without tree cover (Bristow and Ockenfels 2004).

In the Trans-Pecos of Texas, mountains and hills from 1219 m (4,000 ft) harbor Montezumas; however, higher elevations starting from 1600 m (5,249 ft) most often support these quail where suitable habitat is found. In these areas, typical habitat is signified by plant communities including gray oak (*Quercus grisea*), Alligator juniper (*Juniperus deppeana*), red-berry juniper (*Juniperus pinchotii*), Mexican piñon (*Pinus cembroides*), fragrant sumac (*Rhus aromatica*), Texas mountain laurel (*Sophora secundiflora*), and mountain mahogany (*Cercocarpus montanus*). Montezuma Quail are also found in association with ponderosa pine woodlands (*Pinus ponderosa*) at high elevations and

in desert grasslands at lower elevations. Grass assemblages in montane Montezuma Quail habitat include gramas (*Bouteloua* spp.), muhlies (*Muhlenbergia* spp.), threeawns (*Aristida* spp.), tanglehead (*Heteropogon contortus*), plains lovegrass (*Eragrostis intermedia*), green sprangletop (*Leptochloa dubia*), cane bluestem (*Bothriochloa barbinodis*), hooded windmillgrass (*Chloris cucullata*), and Hall's panicum (*Panicum hallii*), among others.

Montezuma Quail prefer sloped (20%–30%), woodland-forested areas with dense herbaceous screening cover at least 10 cm (4 in) in height in the Trans-Pecos (Garza 2007; Greene and Harveson 2014). The percentages of grass cover and food plant density were greater on sites with high habitat suitability for Montezuma Quail in West Texas (Gonzalez-Sanders 2012). Montezuma Quail were found in areas with at least 6.5% forb cover and 2.7 food plants/m² (10.7 sq ft) (Gonzalez-Sanders 2012). Hernández et al. (2006) found that foraging habitat in West Texas had 12.1 wild onion plants/m² (10.7 sq ft), compared to only 0.8 onion plants/m² (10.7 sq ft) in areas not used for foraging. High onion densities were associated mostly with rocky soils and outcrops. In addition, foraging sites were located in areas with an average 22.6% slope, compared to an average 8% slope in nonforaging areas. In the Sky Islands of Arizona, Stromberg (1990) suggested that Montezuma Quail preferred north-facing slopes for general site use.

Figure 21.4. Montezuma Quail habitat in *(top)*, the Trans-Pecos; and *(bottom)*, Edwards Plateau regions of Texas. Photo credits: Eric Grahmann.

On the Edwards Plateau (generally above 450 m in elevation, 1,476 ft), hilly savannahs of Ashe juniper (*Juniperus ashei*), escarpment live oak (*Quercus fusiformis*), Texas persimmon (*Diospyros texana*), Texas mountain laurel, agarito (*Berberis trifoliolata*), evergreen sumac (*Rhus virens*), Texas piñon (*Pinus remota*), and Texas sotol (*Dasylirion texanum*) represent typical habitat in areas with sufficient topography and herbaceous cover. Sorola (1986) found Montezuma Quail in savannahs with 20%–25% woody cover. Albers and Gehlbach (1990) found that occupied patches of habitat averaged 62% cover of grasses taller than 0.3 m (1 ft), compared to 25% in unoccupied habitat. Common grasses providing suitable cover on the southern Edwards Plateau include various grama grasses (*Bouteloua* spp.) and threeawns, green sprangletop, Hall's panicum, slim tridens (*Tridens muticus*), and little bluestem (*Schizachyrium scoparium*). Common and significant forbs for Montezuma Quail on the southern Edwards Plateau include Drummond's woodsorrel, Drummond's wild onion, and one-seed croton (*Croton monanthogynus*). Less typical but occasionally occupied habitat on the Edwards Plateau is found where this region transitions to Tamaulipan shrubland and Chihuahuan Desert grassland. Along with vegetational features, sites most occupied tend to be on hilltops and hillsides, rather than in valley flats. On the southern Edwards Plateau, Montezuma Quail forage primarily on hillsides (Albers and Gehlbach 1990), and Sorola (1986) found them primarily on hillsides with 25%–45% slope.

Montezuma foraging habitat varies among seasons and land use. Overall, foraging sites had grass taller than 0.3 m (1 ft), and deeper soils with less soil moisture than sites where foraging did not occur (Albers and Gehlbach 1990). In addition, quail exhibited greater selection of grassy feeding sites on the grazed compared to the ungrazed treatment. Across their range, Montezuma Quail depend on subterranean food plants for survival. Sites harboring Montezuma Quail contain 10.9 kg/ha (9.7 lb/ac) or more of food (R. Brown 1982).

Breeding season habitat for Montezuma Quail had greater plant diversity and grass and tree cover than randomly sampled sites in Arizona (Bristow and Ockenfels 2004). Overall, areas with tree cover between 26% and 50% and grass canopy from 51% to 75% at 20 cm (8 in) height were recommended.

Montezuma Quail most often construct a nest by scratching out a depression under suitably structured grasses on hillsides (Wallmo 1954). These quail then weave leaves of grasses and parts of forbs into a dome (or chamber) about 13–15 cm (5–6 in) wide by 10 cm (4 in) tall (Wallmo 1954; Leopold and McCabe 1957). Documented nesting plants for Montezuma Quail include bull muhly (*Muhlenbergia emersleyi*), piñon ricegrass, plains lovegrass, curly mesquite (*Hilaria belangeri*), hairy grama (*Bouteloua hirsuta*), blue grama (*Bouteloua gracilis*), bulb panicgrass (*Panicum bulbosum*), bedstraw (*Galium* spp.), and yellow bluestem (*Bothriochloa ischaemum*). Nests have also been described as simple depressions in leaves on the ground under or at the base of trees or boulders (Wallmo 1954).

Roosting habitat is described as an area with abundant tall grass (e.g., tanglehead and sideoats grama) with interspersed short shrubs on a hillside. Most roosting sites were located on southeast-facing slopes, although most daytime habitat use was on north-facing slopes (Stromberg 1990). In these areas, Montezumas typically roosted side by side next to a boulder with overhanging tall grass. During winter, roosts may be associated with rocks that may radiate heat well into the nighttime hours. Roosts are thought to receive repeated use.

Overall, habitat structure near ground level may be more important than overstory habitat structure or species composition for determining habitat suitability for the Montezuma Quail, given that the basic needs of the species are met (Gonzalez-Sanders 2012).

Habitat management

Montezuma Quail inhabit rocky and sloped terrain, and thus many habitat management techniques used for other quail species (e.g., rangeland reseeding via drill) cannot be used. Overall, two forms of habitat management are most often used to manage and restore habitat for Montezuma Quail. These include (1) compatible grazing and (2) woody plant management.

Across their geographic range, overgrazing is recognized as the single most important factor influencing the occurrence of Montezuma Quail (Miller 1943; Texas Game, Fish and Oyster Commission 1945; Leopold and McCabe 1957; Bishop and Hungerford 1965; R. Brown 1982; Albers and Gehlbach 1990), and in Texas, overgrazing has been identified as the predominant contributor to widespread declines and local extinctions (Texas Game, Fish and Oyster Commission 1945; Oberholser 1974). For example, on a formerly occupied ranch on the Edwards Plateau, Montezuma Quail were thought to be extirpated because of overgrazing (40%–50% grass removal by livestock; Albers and Gehlbach 1990). In Arizona, pairs of Montezuma Quail avoided areas with less than 25% grass canopy cover (Bristow and Ockenfels 2004). As in Texas, heavy grazing does not appear to be compatible with Montezuma Quail conservation.

Overgrazing can affect Montezuma Quail in three primary ways: it can (1) eliminate herbaceous screening cover, (2) eliminate critical food plants, and (3) reduce connectivity of habitat patches, making remaining patches too small to support populations. The process by which Montezuma Quail disappear with cover removal has not been documented, but it is believed that the birds are depredated shortly after their screening cover is removed. Because of their secretive nature and their behavior of remaining motionless at the threat of predation, tall grass or similarly structured cover is critical to the survival of these birds. Accordingly, R. Brown (1982) found that forage utilization levels accounted for the majority of variation in Montezuma pair density, as greater utilization rates were associated with decreasing density.

Leopold and McCabe (1957) found that overgrazing resulted in the elimination of bulb-bearing forbs and sedges in Mexico. Once this food supply and associated tall grass cover were removed, the quail were no longer found. Overgrazing by sheep and goats most likely eliminates these food plants, as these herbivores are physiologically better able to graze low-growing food plants such as woodsorrels than are cattle.

Despite reports of Montezuma Quail disappearances associated with grazing, they apparently can tolerate some grazing as long as enough grass cover is left.

Leaving residual grass cover greater than 50% at 20 cm (8 in) in height was recommended by Bristow and Ockenfels (2004). Furthermore, R. Brown (1982) suggested that subterranean food plants can actually be increased by suppressing grass cover when it becomes too thick. In a study conducted on the Edwards Plateau, population densities of Montezuma Quail were similar on moderately grazed and ungrazed ranches, although characteristics of foraging habitat differed. Greater grass cover and shrub density were selected for on a moderately grazed ranch, and on an ungrazed ranch, aspects of soil moisture and slope were most selected for at foraging sites (Albers and Gehlbach 1990). Although Montezuma Quail tolerated grazing, their foraging behavior was altered on moderately grazed range.

Suggestions for grazing vary from leaving a minimum of 25% grass cover to grazing no less than 50% of the annual standing crop (R. Brown 1982; Albers and Gehlbach 1990; Bristow and Ockenfels 2004). Regardless of differing recommendations, land managers interested in Montezuma Quail should consider using forage conservatively (less than 25% use of annual production). Even if the conservation of Montezuma Quail is not a priority, use of native forages over this limit would not be advised, since areas where Montezuma Quail occur usually exhibit large degrees of topographic relief and thus are more prone to soil erosion. Overall, the abundance of this quail species tends to be inversely proportional to the abundance of livestock and the amount of grass cover removed (Leopold and McCabe 1957).

Nearly two centuries of overgrazing and fire suppression have resulted in woody plant invasions on Texas rangelands. Throughout West Texas and especially on the Edwards Plateau, juniper densities have increased dramatically. Juniper is found throughout most areas Montezuma Quail occupy, and these plants can be valuable when found in a savannah-like scattering. However, Montezuma Quail avoid large areas dominated by closed-canopy juniper stands (Sorola 1986). In these communities, plant diversity and herbaceous cover are lacking because of shading and resource competition from the juniper. The result is herbaceous communities unsuitable for Montezuma

Quail and a woody canopy not amenable to escape by flight. Woody stands are avoided not only locally on the Edwards Plateau; large tracts of monotypic juniper may serve as a barrier to this species' eastward expansion. Patches of habitat restored via juniper removal, coupled with proper livestock grazing, have resulted in the colonization of Montezuma Quail on some ranches. Landowners aiming to partake in juniper clearing should sculpt areas into savannahs rather than remove all juniper plants. Some juniper cover should be left along steep slopes, in riparian zones, and around other desirable tree species susceptible to wind damage. It is further advised that large, mature junipers not be removed.

Hunting and Conservation

Leopold and McCabe (1957) stated that the "Montezuma Quail is a fine game bird and its hunting, where it is reasonably numerous, should be encouraged." The problem for biologists and hunters is in determining what is "reasonably numerous." For years, biologists have attempted a variety of methods to survey the quail's populations and relative abundances to no avail. The secretive nature of this bird precludes the standard sampling of populations typically used for other quail species. Partly because of this, the Montezuma Quail is classified as a game bird with an indefinitely closed hunting season in Texas.

Research Needs and Priorities

Most studies on this species have been conducted in Arizona and Mexico. Even fewer studies have been conducted away from the Sky Islands east of the Pecos River. In addition, almost all comprehensive studies on this species are more than 20 years old, and only one published study has used modern radiotelemetry.

Because so little research has been conducted on the Montezuma Quail in Texas, virtually any study focusing on its distribution, general life history, population ecology, habitat use, and censusing techniques will yield valuable information. Furthermore, additional information is needed to determine the effects of habitat restoration practices through relaxed livestock grazing and excess juniper removal.

Literature Cited

Albers, R. P., and F. R. Gehlbach. 1990. Choices of feeding habitat by relict Montezuma Quail in central Texas. *Wilson Bulletin* 102:300–308.

Bishop, R. A., and C. R. Hungerford. 1965. Seasonal food selection of Arizona Mearns Quail. *Journal of Wildlife Management* 29:813–19.

Bristow, K. D., and R. A. Ockenfels. 2004. Pairing season habitat selection by Montezuma Quail in southeastern Arizona. *Journal of Range Management* 57:532–38.

Brown, D. E. 1979. Factors influencing reproductive success and population densities in Montezuma Quail. *Journal of Wildlife Management* 43:522–26.

———. 1989. *Arizona Game Birds.* Tucson: University of Arizona Press.

Brown, R. L. 1982. Effects of livestock grazing on Mearns Quail in southeastern Arizona. *Journal of Range Management* 35:727–32.

Garza, E. P. 2007. A multi-scale analysis of Montezuma Quail habitat in the Davis Mountains of Texas. Master's thesis, Sul Ross State University.

Gonzalez-Sanders, C. 2012. An evaluation of a presence-absence survey to monitor Montezuma Quail in western Texas. Master's thesis, Texas A&M University–Kingsville.

Grahmann, E. D., and J. M. Moore. 2014. An exploratory survey of Montezuma Quail in the southern Edwards Plateau. Unpublished data.

Greene, C., and L. A. Harveson. 2014. A quail of many names: The mysterious Montezuma. *Desert Tracks*, Spring, 7 (1). Borderlands Research Institute. Alpine, TX: Sul Ross State University.

Harveson, L. A., T. H. Allen, F. Hernández, D. A. Holdermann, J. M. Mueller, and M. Shawn Whitley. 2007. Montezuma Quail ecology and life history. In *Texas Quails: Ecology and Management*, edited by L. A. Brennan, 23–39. College Station: Texas A&M University Press.

Hernández, F. 2004. Characteristics of Montezuma Quail populations and habitats at Elephant Mountain Wildlife Management Area, Texas. Master's thesis, Sul Ross State University.

Hernández, F., E. Garza, L. A. Harveson, and C. E. Brewer. 2009. Fate and survival of radio-marked Montezuma Quail. *Proceedings of the National Quail Symposium* 6:426–31.

Hernández, F., L. A. Harveson, F. Hernández, and C. E. Brewer. 2006. Habitat characteristics of Montezuma Quail foraging areas in west Texas. *Wildlife Society Bulletin* 34:856–60.

Leopold, A. 1949. *A Sand County Almanac.* Oxford: Oxford University Press.

Leopold, A. S., and R. A. McCabe. 1957. Natural history of the Montezuma Quail in Mexico. *Condor* 59:3–26.

Miller, L. 1943. Notes on the Mearns Quail. *Condor* 45:104–9.

Oberholser, H. C. 1974. *The Bird Life of Texas.* Austin: University of Texas Press.

Sorola, S. H. 1986. *Investigation of Mearns' Quail Distribution.* Federal Aid Project No. W-108-R-9. Austin: Texas Parks and Wildlife Department.

Stromberg, M. R. 1990. Habitat, movements, and roost characteristics of Montezuma Quail in southeastern Arizona. *Condor* 92:229–36.

Texas Game, Fish and Oyster Commission. 1945. *Principal Game Birds and Mammals of Texas.* Austin: Texas Game, Fish and Oyster Commission.

Wallmo, O. C. 1954. Nesting of Mearns Quail in southeastern Arizona. *Condor* 56:125–28.

22

Wild Turkey

The turkey is considered the most wary of all upland game species and ranks as the choicest table fare.
—LEOPOLD, GUTIÉRREZ, AND BRONSON (1981, 55)

Introduction

The Wild Turkey is an important component of the wildlife resources in Texas. There are three subspecies in Texas: the Rio Grande Wild Turkey (*Meleagris gallopavo intermedia*), the Eastern Wild Turkey (*M. g. silvestris*), and Merriam's Wild Turkey (*M. g. merriami*). Wild Turkeys are native to North America. They are thought to have evolved from pheasants about 11 million years ago (Helm-Bychowski and Wilson 1986). The oldest fossils of Wild Turkeys were found in Pliocene deposits (2–3 million years old) in Texas and Kansas (Steadman 1980), but where Wild Turkeys originated is not clear. It has been suggested that Merriam's Wild Turkey originated from the feral Large Indian domestic turkey in New Mexico, which may have appeared as early as AD 500 (McKusick 1980). Regardless of where they originated, they have been an integral part of the flora and fauna of North America for millennia and were used by Native Americans as food, as well as for clothing and ornaments for many generations (Kennamer, Kennamer, and Brenneman 1992). In Texas the Tonkawa and Lipan commonly ate Wild Turkeys (Schorger 1966). Europeans who explored and settled Texas 150–300 years ago also consumed Wild Turkeys because hunting them was easy. Unregulated hunting, particularly by European settlers (Sawyer 2013), almost extirpated Wild Turkeys in Texas during the late nineteenth and early twentieth centuries.

Mature males, or gobblers, are about 100 cm (40 in) tall, whereas adult females are about 76 cm (30 in) tall (Pelham and Dickson 1992). The largest subspecies is the Eastern Wild Turkey, with a maximum recorded weight of 18 kg (31 lb), followed by the Rio Grande and Merriam's subspecies, both with maximum recorded weights of about 12 kg (26 lb). Males typically possess more iridescent feathers, particularly on their chests, than do females, which appear duller in color. Plumage characteristics vary with individual subspecies. The tips of tail feathers and the feathers at the base of the tail can be used to differentiate the three subspecies of turkey found in Texas. The Eastern subspecies has dark brown tips on its tail feathers, whereas the Rio Grande subspecies has buff or tan tips (Alldredge et al. 2014), and the Merriam's subspecies has white tips. Wild Turkeys have few feathers on their head and neck, which instead have protuberances of bare skin called caruncles. The head and neck of gobblers are bright red and blue during the breeding season. Males also possess beards, which are specialized feathers hanging from their chests that begin growing during their first year and become longer as the bird becomes older. Hens occasionally have beards,

Figure 22.1. Male (*left*) and female (*right*) Rio Grande Wild Turkeys. Photo credit: Larry Ditto.

Figure 22.2. Distribution of Eastern, Rio Grande, Merriam's, and Rio Grande–Merriam's Wild Turkey hybrids in Texas.

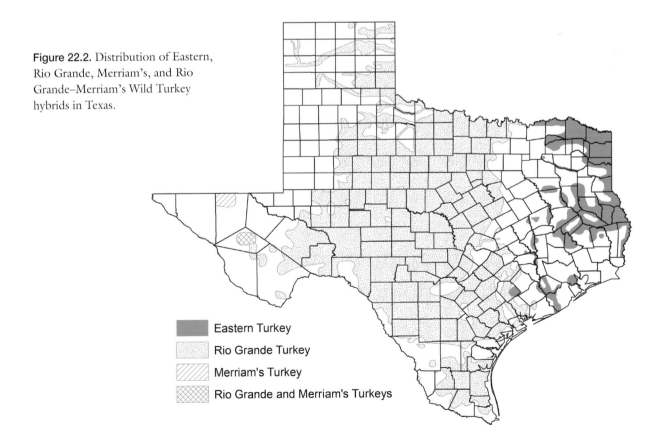

but this is rare, and beards on hens are shorter than those on males. The legs of Wild Turkeys do not have feathers, and males have protuberances on their lower legs called spurs that grow longer as the males mature.

Distribution

The three subspecies of Wild Turkey inhabit distinct portions of Texas. The Rio Grande Wild Turkey once occurred from Mexico north throughout the savannahs and southern Coastal Prairies through the rangelands of the Edwards Plateau, Rolling Plains, and riparian habitats in the prairies of the Panhandle and was estimated to number almost 2 million birds in Texas (Beasom and Wilson 1992). More recently the Rio Grande subspecies has been utilizing riparian areas to colonize the Trans-Pecos and is now present in some of the mountain ranges. As with the other turkey subspecies, unregulated hunting during the late 1800s and early 1900s almost extirpated the Rio Grande Wild Turkey, reducing numbers to perhaps 100,000 birds and restricting them to isolated areas of their historical range (Alldredge et al. 2014). Fortunately, during the early part of the nineteenth century, conservationists like the King Ranch's Caesar Kleberg implemented hunting restrictions and prevailed upon politicians to enact game laws that imposed hunting and bag limits and enabled Wild Turkey populations to recover. In addition, aggressive trapping and translocation efforts between the 1930s and 1990s carried out by the Texas Game, Fish and Oyster Commission and later by its predecessors, including the Texas Parks and Wildlife Department (TPWD), resulted in the reestablishment of almost 23,000 Rio Grande Wild Turkeys to numerous locations in their former historical range (Beasom and Wilson 1992). Today Rio Grande Wild Turkeys occur throughout most of their historical range in Texas, which extends from the Rio Grande north through the central third of the state into the eastern Panhandle.

The Eastern Wild Turkey is a forest bird. Its historical range included almost 12 million ha (30 million ac) of pine-hardwood forests in the Piney Woods of East Texas and small portions of the Post Oak Savannah (Alldredge et al. 2014). The western limit of its range was the Trinity River; it is now thought to be restricted by limited annual rainfall in the Post Oak Savannah (Campo and Dickson 1990). Like the Rio Grande subspecies, Eastern Wild Turkeys were basically extirpated from East Texas by 1900 by unregulated hunting and forest clearing (Campo and Dickson 1990). Efforts to restore Eastern Wild Turkeys to their historical range using pen-reared birds were initiated by the Texas Game, Fish and Oyster Commission during the 1940s, but these efforts failed. Attempts to reestablish turkeys in East Texas by translocating the Rio Grande subspecies were also unsuccessful (Alldredge et al. 2014). Therefore, in the late 1980s biologists initiated a 20-year effort to restore populations of Eastern Wild Turkeys by translocating them from other states to suitable habitat in East Texas. By the mid-1990s 7,000 wild birds had been translocated to more than 80 areas in more than 30 East Texas counties (Campo and Dickson 1990; Conway et al. 2010). Wild Turkeys have been reestablished in East Texas, but success has been limited because Eastern Wild Turkeys occur in only relatively isolated areas (Conway et al. 2010). Recently, a new restoration strategy that involves releasing a much larger number of birds, including a larger ratio of gobblers to hens, together with a new habitat evaluation technique that ensures that turkeys are released in the best available habitat (Lopez et al. 2000), has renewed optimism that restoring self-sustaining populations will eventually occur.

The Merriam's Wild Turkey inhabits the steep mountain terrain of the western United States. A small population currently exists in the Guadalupe Mountains of West Texas (Shaw and Mollohan 1992). It is believed that the Merriam's Wild Turkey distribution has always been restricted to the Guadalupe and Franklin Mountains (Shaw and Mollohan 1992), the Davis Mountains, and a few smaller mountain ranges in West Texas (Cathey et al. 2008). Today the only Merriam's Wild Turkey population in Texas inhabits the Guadalupe Mountains, where hybridization with Rio Grande Wild Turkeys is probably occurring, as it almost certainly is among populations in the Davis Mountains (Cathey et al. 2008). Presumably the Guadalupe Mountain population is self-sustaining and probably not hunted, because most if not all Merriam's Wild Turkeys occur in Guadalupe Mountains National Park where hunting is prohibited.

Breeding Biology

Although 3 subspecies of Wild Turkey occur in Texas, the breeding biology of these subspecies is very similar. The relatively subtle differences among the 3 subspecies are largely due to the climate of the regions each subspecies inhabits as well as the annual weather patterns that occur in specific locales. The annual life cycles of Wild Turkeys can be divided into 3 distinct seasons: (1) a spring breeding season; (2) a late spring–summer nesting and poult-rearing season; and (3) a fall-winter season. Generally the breeding season for Wild Turkeys begins in March and extends into early summer in the Panhandle, where spring climatic conditions begin later in the year. Initiation of breeding activity is dictated by day length and habitat conditions. Breeding behavior begins when day length begins to increase but can be suppressed or delayed if drought conditions are prevalent in a specific area or region. For example, Beasom and Pattee (1980) reported that rainfall during the late summer and fall prior to the breeding season had a greater impact on Rio Grande Wild Turkey productivity the following spring than spring rainfall did during the breeding season. Thus, accumulated soil moisture several months prior to the breeding season appears to impact productivity by influencing food quality and abundance during the breeding season. Consequently, Wild Turkeys may begin breeding as early as February in South Texas when day length begins to increase, if rainfall during the previous late summer and fall was adequate. This influence of rainfall on Wild Turkey breeding probably prevails throughout Texas, although the impact is not as pronounced for Eastern Wild Turkeys because East Texas typically receives more annual rainfall than the rangelands and mountains occupied by Rio Grande and Merriam's Wild Turkeys, respectively.

Breeding behavior begins when Wild Turkeys are in their large winter flocks. Mature males begin gobbling and strutting and hens become disassociated from other hens that were members of their large winter flocks, although hens may remain in small groups of 4–5 individuals. As breeding activity accelerates, male gobbling and strutting behavior intensifies as gobblers attempt to attract hens. Hens become progressively more solitary and eventually completely avoid other turkeys after they have mated and dispersed in search of a nesting site. Generally, a higher percentage of adult hens in a population are bred than juveniles, and they disperse a shorter distance from their winter home ranges to nest than juveniles. Peak nesting activity typically occurs from April through late May for all 3 subspecies of Wild Turkey in Texas. Clutch sizes range from 7 to 14 eggs but average about 11 eggs. Hens produce 1 egg per day until a full clutch is completed, and then they begin incubating eggs for most of the day, leaving the nest for a few hours to forage and find water. Most poults hatch during late spring and early summer after an incubation period of about 28 days. Poults respond to vocalizations of hens and begin following hens within a day of hatching. Poults grow rapidly and replace down with pin feathers at about 2 to 3 weeks of age. After 3 months, or typically by August or September, poults resemble adults, though they are smaller.

Wild Turkey hens and their broods begin to associate with other family groups during late summer. By early fall, the large winter flocks of hens and juveniles begin to assemble. These flocks can number 100 birds or more for the Rio Grande subspecies. Mature gobblers and 2-year-old males form smaller bachelor groups that generally isolate themselves from the large hen-juvenile flocks during fall and winter. This social behavior continues throughout the winter until breeding activity resumes, generally in March the following spring.

Demography

Like the populations of any other species of wildlife, those of Wild Turkeys are ultimately determined by the number of young that are produced each year, the age and sex survival rates, and the dispersal of birds into and out of populations. Juvenile males do not breed during their first year. Although juvenile hens are capable of breeding and producing poults, most of the breeding and poult production is accomplished by adult hens. Annual survival rates vary depending on myriad factors, such as predation, weather, and hunting, and these can be specific to a given region or locale. Annual survival ranges from 58% to 70% (Campo, Swank, and Hopkins 1984; Vangilder 1992;

Cathey et al. 2008) and generally varies annually. Typically about half of a Wild Turkey population turns over every year. However, a Wild Turkey's life span can extend over multiple years. There are reports of Rio Grande Wild Turkeys living for as long as a decade (Ronnie Howard, personal communication). Survival is lowest during spring. Indeed, the highest mortality rates among turkey hens typically occur during the spring nesting season because hens are more vulnerable to predators when they are incubating eggs on ground nests. Nesting rates for hens are typically high, ranging from 96% to 100%, and renesting does occur. Rates of renesting range from 45% to 67% (Campo, Swank, and Hopkins 1984; Vangilder 1992). Nest success and hen success (meaning poults are produced) are also variable, ranging from 35% to 92% and 25% to 82%, respectively (Campo, Swank, and Hopkins 1984; Vangilder 1992). Locales or regions with diverse and abundant predator populations often have low hen success and poult production through high rates of nesting hen mortality or elevated rates of nest predation. High rates of hen mortality and nest predation were the likely reason for poor production of Rio Grande Wild Turkeys in South Texas (Reyes-Ramirez et. al. 2012). Evidently, nest predation among Eastern Wild Turkeys has been significant enough to suppress poult production, which has been a major factor in the limited success of restoration efforts (Conway et al. 2010). Hen survival begins to improve as hens hatch poults in late spring and summer and remains high until the next spring nesting season.

Poult survival is variable, ranging from 12% to 52% (Spears et al. 2007) depending on the region where populations occur, but probably averages about 25%. Most poult mortality occurs during the first 2 weeks after hatching, when they are incapable of flight, have difficulty eluding predators, and cannot yet roost in trees. However, poult survival begins to stabilize after their first month, and most poults that survive throughout the summer and reach 3 to 4 months of age survive and enter the fall population when they are much less vulnerable to mortality events.

Like hen survival, gobbler survival is lowest during the spring because gobblers trying to attract hens are more vulnerable to predators. In the Texas Panhandle, adult and juvenile gobblers experienced the lowest survival rates of the year during spring. Adult gobblers, who do virtually all of the breeding, experience lower survival than juvenile males. Most of the male Wild Turkey mortality that occurred in one study was attributed to mammalian predators (Holdstock et al. 2006). Additional mortality occurs among gobblers during spring when they are attracted to hunters who call them within shotgun range. Gobbler survival is much higher during the summer, fall, and winter, although turkey hunting does occur in some Texas counties during the fall and winter hunting seasons. However, hunting mortality during the general hunting season generally has an inconsequential effect on Rio Grande Wild Turkey populations; the majority of Texas counties have multiple bird limits on Rio Grande Wild Turkeys during the fall season. Fall hunting is not permitted for Eastern Wild Turkeys, and spring bag limits are restricted to 1 gobbler in East Texas because TPWD officials fear that hunting mortality among gobblers could have a negative impact on restoration efforts. Moreover, a 1-gobbler bag limit is in effect for 8 counties surrounding La Grange because of concerns that Rio Grande Wild Turkey populations are limited in that area. As stated earlier, hunting has no effect on the Merriam's subspecies because hunting is not permitted in Guadalupe Mountains National Park.

Populations can also be bolstered or reduced via dispersal, because Wild Turkeys moving from one area to another can increase one population and decrease another depending on dispersal rates. However, it appears that dispersal generally occurs among hens, and specifically among juveniles that move from their natal ranges in an effort to locate areas or locales with fewer turkeys. Research in the Panhandle indicated that juvenile Rio Grande hens were responsible for most of the dispersal and that dispersing juveniles were likely responsible for colonizing new areas (R. Phillips et al. 2007). Similarly, a study conducted on translocated Eastern Wild Turkeys in East Texas found that dispersing hens were responsible for most of the colonization of new areas that occurred (Hopkins et al. 1982).

Population Status and Trends

Wild Turkey harvest trends from 1995 to 2014, obtained from the Texas Parks and Wildlife Department (2014a), include all three subspecies as well as Rio Grande–Merriam's hybrids. With the exception of

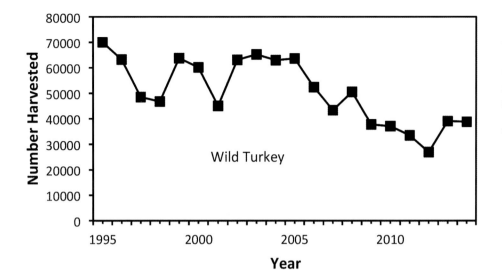

Figure 22.3. Wild Turkey harvest trends, 1995–2014. Data from the Texas Parks and Wildlife Department include aggregate data for all three subspecies and Rio Grande–Merriam's Wild Turkey hybrids.

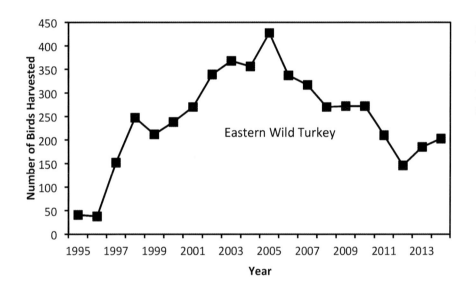

Figure 22.4 Eastern Wild Turkey harvest trends, 1995–2014. Data from Texas Parks and Wildlife Department from 28 counties.

three years of harvest decreases, Wild Turkey harvests were stable at about 62,000 birds between 1995 and 2005. Thereafter, Wild Turkey harvests steadily declined on a statewide basis to a low of about 30,000 birds in 2013.

Because TPWD biologists have expended considerable effort to restore Eastern Wild Turkey populations to East Texas, annual harvest records have been maintained for this subspecies because successful hunters are required to bring their harvested gobbler to a TPWD check station. Eastern Wild Turkey hunting was resumed in Texas in 1995 and has continued for the last 20 years. Initially, fewer than 50 birds were harvested during the first two seasons, but then harvests increased substantially to a high of almost

450 birds in 2005. Thereafter Eastern Wild Turkey harvests steadily declined to about 200 for the 28 East Texas counties where hunting is permitted.

Wild Turkey population trend data from the Christmas Bird Count, compiled annually by the National Audubon Society (2015), represent results for all three subspecies; thus it is not possible to discuss trends for individual subspecies. The statewide population declined slightly between the mid-1970s and early 2000s and then began a significant increase until 2009, when the statewide population again declined. Since the majority of these data reflect numbers for the Rio Grande subspecies, variation in abundance is likely attributable to variable range conditions, which can often be attributed to variable annual rainfall.

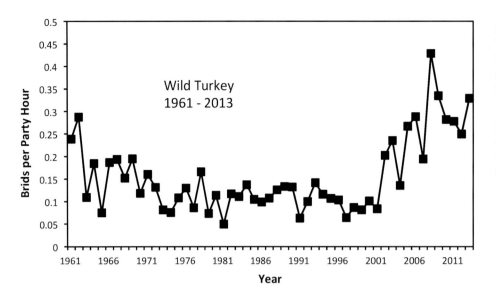

Figure 22.5. Trend in Wild Turkey populations in Texas, based on Christmas Bird Count data compiled by the National Audubon Society, 1961–2013. Data include Rio Grande, Eastern, and Merriam's subspecies. Note the apparent recent increase in numbers.

Specific Habitat Requirements

Habitats for Wild Turkeys in Texas differ according to subspecies. However, the presence of woody vegetation is a critical habitat component for all three subspecies. For example, the savannahs of South Texas almost certainly did not support as many Rio Grande Wild Turkeys as are present today because turkeys were likely restricted to the vicinity of creeks and rivers where the large trees they require for roosting were present (Beasom and Wilson 1992). Wild Turkeys have a number of important habitat requirements, but roosting habitat is absolutely critical because Wild Turkeys must roost aboveground at night. Indeed, daily movements are dictated largely by the proximity of roosts and may not exceed 0.4 km (0.25 mi) from the nearest roost (Beasom and Wilson 1992). Large mature trees with spreading crowns and numerous large horizontal branches are favored roosts for all three subspecies of Wild Turkey. More than 30 tree species in Texas have been documented as being used by Wild Turkeys for roosts (Beasom and Wilson 1992; C. Phillips et al. 2011). Some of the preferred species for Rio Grande Wild Turkeys throughout their range in Texas are oak (*Quercus* spp.), hackberry (*Celtis* spp.), pecan (*Carya* spp.), sweetgum (*Liquidambar* spp.), and juniper (*Juniperus* spp.), along with elm (*Ulmus* spp.), cottonwood (*Populus* spp.), and hickory (*Carya* spp.). If large trees are not abundant, Rio Grande Wild Turkeys often roost in large mesquite

(*Prosopis* spp.) trees and will also roost on power lines, utility transmission towers, and windmills. In South Texas and perhaps other regions, Wild Turkeys will also readily use roosts constructed specifically for them if the roosts are erected in the proper location. Adequate roosting habitat is rarely a problem for Eastern Wild Turkeys because of the abundance of large pine (*Pinus* spp.) trees and the diversity of large hardwood species that occur throughout East Texas. Merriam's Wild Turkeys will roost in large evergreen trees such as ponderosa pine (*Pinus ponderosa*), as well as deciduous species like oak and cottonwood that occur in Guadalupe Mountains National Park.

In addition to roosting habitat, Wild Turkeys require a diversity of woody species that provide food and cover. Oak, hackberry, juniper, pecan, elm, and hickory are important tree species that, in addition to roosts, produce nuts and fruits that are readily consumed by Wild Turkeys (Beasom and Wilson 1992; Hurst 1992; Cathey et al. 2008). Important shrubs and vines that provide food as well as escape and loafing cover are sumac (*Rhus* spp.), persimmon (*Diospyros* spp.), grape (*Vitis* spp.), granjeno (*Celtis pallida*), lime prickly ash (*Zanthoxylum fagara*), agarito (*Mahonia trifoliolata*), mesquite (*Prosopis* spp.), prickly pear (*Opuntia* spp.), tasajillo (*Cylindropuntia leptocaulis*), juniper (*Juniperus* spp.), and dewberry (*Rubus* spp.). In East Texas, American beautyberry (*Callicarpa americana*), sassafrass (*Sassafrass* spp.), dogwood (*Cornus* spp.), plum (*Prunus* spp.), grape, and blackberry are important

Figure 22.6. *(Top)*, Eastern Wild Turkey habitat. Photo credit: Katherine Miller. *(Bottom)*, Rio Grande Wild Turkey habitat in South Texas. Photo credit: Eric Grahmann.

food-producing shrubs that also provide cover (Hurst 1992; Alldredge et al. 2014).

Though woody species are important in habitats for Wild Turkeys, open areas dominated by herbaceous vegetation are equally important. Generally the ratio of woody to open areas should be about 50:50 to meet the annual habitat requirements of Wild Turkeys. Openings of about 12–20 ha (30–50 ac) should be dispersed throughout forests or rangelands occupied by Wild Turkey populations. Herbaceous vegetation communities ideally should be composed of a diversity of grass and forb species, because Wild Turkeys consume a tremendous variety of herbaceous foods. The seeds, leaves, stems, roots, and tubers of a variety of grass and forb species represent important foods for Wild Turkeys. Bristlegrass (*Setaria* spp.), dropseeds (*Sporobolus* spp.), paspalums (*Paspalum* spp.), and panic grasses (*Panicum* spp.) represent a few of the grass species favored by turkeys. Several of the many forb species consumed by Wild Turkeys include flatsedge (*Cyperus* spp.), smartweed (*Polygonum* spp.), false dandelion (*Hypochaeris* spp.), croton (*Croton* spp.), beggartick (*Bidens* spp.), broomweed (*Amphiachyris dracunculoides*), wild onion (*Allium* spp.), sheep sorrel (*Rumex acetosella*), ragweed (*Ambrosia* spp.), and clover (*Trifolium* spp.). However, a diverse herbaceous community provides not only important plant foods but also important microhabitat for invertebrates, which also are very important Wild Turkey foods. Wild Turkeys eat a wide variety of insects and other invertebrates throughout the year depending on availability. Herbaceous openings also provide critical nesting and brooding habitat, particularly on the rangelands occupied by Rio Grande Wild Turkeys. Wild Turkeys generally do not construct a bowl-like structure as a nest. Instead they seek a structure that provides good overhead cover that will conceal a hen while she is on a nest. Openings or pastures that provide about 60 cm (24 inches) of cover represent good turkey habitat, although large clumps of ragweed or old man's beard (*Usnea* spp.) provide good nesting sites. Eastern Wild Turkeys often nest under dense shrubs or vines if herbaceous nesting cover is limited, although herbaceous openings such as pastures or power line corridors seem to be favored by nesting hens. Openings dominated by grasses and forbs also serve as important brood habitat for all three subspecies of Wild Turkey in Texas. Herbaceous cover about 60 cm (24 in) in height provided by a diversity of native grasses and forbs is also very good poult habitat because it not only provides abundant plant food and cover but also abundant and diverse invertebrates, which are important foods. Short shrubs scattered throughout an open area or along the edges provide additional cover used by poults. Eastern Wild Turkey hens and poults will also use forests with an open understory where they can move freely among grasses, forbs, and shrubs.

Water is an integral component of Wild Turkey habitat. Turkeys can obtain water from the foods they consume, but they also make use of free water that occurs in rivers, creeks, ponds, and livestock watering devices. During drought, water is particularly important because foods that provide water are often not as abundant as they are during years of normal rainfall. The availability of free water is therefore particularly important to the Rio Grande and Merriam's subspecies, which occupy more arid habitats than do Eastern Wild Turkeys in East Texas, where annual rainfall is about 125 cm (50 in).

Habitat Management

Managing habitat for Wild Turkeys involves managing sufficient space on a landscape in a manner that provides all the habitat components required to sustain a Wild Turkey population. A large amount of space is required to maintain self-sustaining Wild Turkey populations; therefore habitat should be managed in a manner that provides all the elements a turkey population requires on an annual basis. Wild Turkeys are nomadic and move frequently throughout fairly large areas. For instance, Wild Turkey hens in South Texas can have large annual home ranges that vary from 200 ha (500 ac) for adult hens to 4000 ha (10,000 ac) for juveniles. Consequently, it is important to consider the spatial needs of a Wild Turkey population when planning habitat management activities. Habitat management should ensure that a landscape has the proper ratio of woody plant and herbaceous communities, and that these communities provide sufficient food, cover, and structure for a Wild Turkey population.

Habitat management can be accomplished in a number of ways. For example, mechanical methods such as disking and roller chopping can be used to manage brush for Rio Grande Wild Turkeys to ensure that sufficient herbaceous openings are maintained for nesting, brooding, and foraging. However, when removing woody vegetation it is essential to conserve large trees to maintain roosting habitat because the daily movements of Wild Turkeys are generally dictated by the proximity of roosts. Thinning forests in East Texas, particularly commercial pine plantations that are about 20 years old, on a rotation of about 5 years will provide an open understory habitat needed by nesting hens and their broods. Herbicides can also be used to manage woody vegetation and have the added advantage of selecting specific species of woody plants to target for suppression, thereby maintaining plants that provide better habitat conditions. However, some herbicides used to manage woody vegetation also suppress forbs for up to two years after treatment, which will reduce important turkey foods. Prescribed burning can be used in conjunction with mechanical and chemical habitat management to improve and maintain Wild Turkey habitat conditions. Herbicides will kill woody plants outright or top-kill them, opening up the canopy and allowing the reestablishment of herbaceous vegetation. Prescribed fire is generally applied two or three years after herbicide treatments or a thinning operation in an East Texas forest to allow enough herbaceous vegetation, or fine fuel, to accumulate. Fire is then used to improve Wild Turkey habitat conditions by rejuvenating grass and forb communities and removing standing dead woody material. Grazing can also be used to manage the grass and forb components of Wild Turkey habitat if proper stocking rates allow sufficient cover to be available during the nesting and brooding seasons. In fact, the timing of any habitat management operation is critical because habitat management should not be applied when turkeys are vulnerable or when important habitats are needed. For instance, prescribed fire, grazing, or mowing should not be conducted during spring and summer when hens are nesting and raising broods. Winter fires are generally better for Wild Turkeys because cool fires stimulate forb production during the late spring and summer and therefore encourage the production of important turkey foods.

Landowners and land managers should carefully plan habitat management activities over a multiyear planning horizon. Habitat management should focus on maximizing plant community improvement during a time of year that does not harm Wild Turkeys. Moreover, creating or improving habitat diversity is an important goal that can best be accomplished by assigning management operations to specific parts of the landscape on a specific schedule. For example, brush management or forest thinning could be restricted to specific 200 ha (500 ac) sites on a 4000 ha (10,000 ac) property on a five-year schedule, followed by prescribed burning three to five years after the initial clearing or thinning operation. Herbicide treatments could also be included in the management plan as long as treatments followed a specific schedule in designated areas where targeted plants were abundant and suppression would benefit Wild Turkeys. Cattle grazing could even be part of the habitat management plan too as long as stocking rates were closely monitored and grazing was suspended during the nesting season in important nesting and brooding habitats. A Wild Turkey management plan should promote both woody and herbaceous plant species diversity so that the critical habitat components that Wild Turkeys require are provided in adequate quantities on an annual basis.

Conservation

Turkey hunting seasons in Texas are regulated within North and South Zones, and special regulations occur in specific counties (Texas Parks and Wildlife Department 2014b). There are currently four Wild Turkey hunting seasons in Texas: (1) a fall archery-only hunting season; (2) three fall and two spring youth hunting seasons that are zone specific; (3) a general statewide fall-winter hunting season; and (4) two general spring hunting seasons that are zone specific, with an Eastern Wild Turkey hunting season in East Texas. Hunting season lengths vary according to season. Fall archery season is four days during the last week of September; youth-only seasons occur for about a day in the fall and spring; the general fall-winter hunting season occurs for two months to 80 days from November to January; and the spring season occurs for a month to six weeks from March through May. Wild Turkey hunting bag limits in Texas are generally four birds in the aggregate, of which only one bird can be the Eastern subspecies, and most counties permit harvest of either sex during fall, while gobblers and bearded hens can be harvested during spring. Exceptions are in an eight-county area centered around La Grange and 28 East Texas counties where there is only a spring season with a bag limit of one gobbler.

According to a recent Texas Parks and Wildlife Department document (2014a), Wild Turkeys remain one of the most popular game birds among hunters, but the number of hunters has steadily declined over the past decade because of perceived lack of Wild Turkeys. TPWD officials are concerned that the reduced harvests that have occurred over the past 10 years are a reflection of reduced Wild Turkey abundance. The disappointing results of recent restocking efforts in East Texas have prompted TPWD officials to considered closing the spring Eastern Wild Turkey hunting season, although this has not yet occurred. Nevertheless, both harvest and population trend data suggest that Wild Turkey populations in Texas are declining. The TPWD is addressing this situation by funding research to examine whether harvest rates indicate that a population decline is occurring, and officials are optimistic that new restocking methodology will gradually result in an increase in the Eastern Wild Turkey population. Private landowners can contribute to the TPWD's efforts to conserve Wild Turkey populations by cooperating with research efforts, initiating habitat improvements recommended in this chapter, or obtaining assistance from TPWD biologists, Natural Resources Conservation Service Range Conservationists, or Texas AgriLife Extension personnel.

Research Priorities

1. Apply metapopulation theory to Wild Turkey population management to develop a scientifically based strategy to effectively deal with habitat fragmentation issues, especially for Eastern Wild Turkey populations.

2. Develop an accurate and precise technique to estimate Wild Turkey populations.

3. Determine where to locate constructed (anthropogenic) roosts on rangelands where natural roosting habitat is limited.

4. Conduct research on poult population and ecology for Eastern and Rio Grande Wild Turkey populations, particularly in the Edwards Plateau, Rolling Plains, and South Texas.

5. Conduct research on the ecology of Merriam's Wild Turkey in Guadalupe Mountains National Park.

6. Conduct research on the impacts of climate change on Wild Turkey population dynamics.

Literature Cited

Alldredge, B. E., J. B. Hardin, J. Whiteside, J. L. Isabelle, S. Parsons, W. C. Conway, and J. C. Cathey. 2014. *Eastern Wild Turkeys in Texas: Biology and Management.* College Station: Texas AgriLife Extension.

Beasom, S. L., and O. H. Pattee. 1980. The effect of selected climatic variables on Wild Turkey productivity. *Proceedings of the National Wild Turkey Symposium* 4:127–35.

Beasom, S. L., and D. Wilson. 1992. Rio Grande turkey. In *The Wild Turkey: Biology and Management*, edited by J. G. Dickson, 306–30. Mechanicsburg, PA: Stackpole Books.

Campo, J. J., and J. G. Dickson. 1990. *The Eastern Wild Turkey in Texas.* Texas Parks and Wildlife Department Report PWD-8R-7100–137B-2/90.

Campo, J. J., W. G. Swank, and C. R. Hopkins. 1984. Brood habitat use by eastern Wild Turkeys in eastern Texas. *Journal of Wildlife Management* 53:479–82.

Cathey, J. C., K. Melton, J. Dreibelbis, B. Cavney, S. L. Locke, S. J. DeMaso, T. W. Schwertner, and B. Collier. 2008. *Rio Grande Wild Turkey in Texas: Biology and Management.* College Station: Texas AgriLife Extension.

Conway, W. C., C. E. Comer, G. H. Calkins, and J. Isabelle. 2010. *Restoring Wild Turkey to East Texas: Past and Present.* Stephen F. Austin State University Faculty Publications Paper 376.

Helm-Bychowski, K. M., and A. C. Wilson. 1986. Rates of nuclear DNA evolution in pheasant-like birds: Evidence from restriction maps. *Proceedings of the National Academy of Sciences* 83:688–92.

Holdstock, D. P., M. C. Wallace, W. B. Ballard, J. H. Brunjes, R. S. Phillips, B. L. Spears, S. J. DeMaso, J. D. Jernigan, R. D. Applegate, and P. S. Gipson. 2006. Male Rio Grande turkey survival and movements in the Texas Panhandle and southwestern Kansas. *Journal of Wildlife Management* 70:904–13.

Hopkins, C. R., J. J. Campo, W. G. Swank, and D. J. Martin.1982. Dispersal of Eastern Wild Turkeys in east Texas. *Proceedings of the Annual Conference of the Southeastern Association of Fish and Wildlife Agencies* 36:578–85.

Hurst, G. A. 1992. Foods and feeding. In *The Wild Turkey: Biology and Management*, edited by J. G. Dickson, 66–83. Mechanicsburg, PA: Stackpole Books.

Kennamer, J. E., M. C. Kennamer, and R. Brenneman. 1992. History. In *The Wild Turkey: Biology and Management*, edited by J. G. Dickson, 6–17. Mechanicsburg, PA: Stackpole Books.

Leopold, A. S., R. J. Gutiérrez, and M. T. Bronson. 1981. *North American Game Birds and Mammals.* New York: Charles Scribner's Sons.

Lopez, R. R., W. E. Grant, N. J. Silvy, M. J. Peterson, C. K. Feuerbacher, and M. S. Corson. 2000. Restoration of the Wild Turkey in east Texas: Simulation of alternative restocking strategies. *Ecological Modelling* 132:275–85.

McKusick, C. R. 1980. Three groups of turkeys from southwestern archaeological sites. In *Papers in Avian Biology Honoring Hildegard Howard*, edited by K. E. Campbell Jr., 225–35. Los Angeles: Natural History Museum.

National Audubon Society. 2015. Wild Turkey results: Texas. http://netapp.audubon.org/CBCObservation /Historical/ResultsBySpecies.aspx?1.

Pelham, P. H., and J. G. Dickson. 1992. In *The Wild Turkey: Biology and Management*, edited by J. G. Dickson, 32–45. Mechanicsburg, PA: Stackpole Books.

Phillips, C. E., W. P. Kuvlesky Jr., S. J. DeMaso, L. A. Brennan, and D. G. Hewitt. 2011. Landscape metrics related to Rio Grande Wild Turkey winter roosts in south Texas. *Proceedings of the National Wild Turkey Symposium* 10:213–35.

Phillips, R. S., M. C. Wallace, B. L. Spears, J. H. Brunjes, W. B. Ballard, D. P. Holdstock, M. S. Miller, and S. J. DeMaso. 2007. Movement, fidelity and dispersal of Rio Grande Wild Turkeys in the Texas Panhandle. *Proceedings of the National Wild Turkey Symposium* 9:149–57.

Reyes Ramirez, E., M. C. Clayton, C. W. Lawson, S. M. Burns, R. Guarneros-Altimirano, S. J. DeMaso, W. P. Kuvlesky Jr., D. G. Hewitt, J. A. Ortega-Santos, and T. A. Campbell. 2012. Home ranges of female Rio Grande turkeys (*Meleagris gallopavo intermedia*) in southern Texas. *Southwestern Naturalist* 52:198–201.

Sawyer, R. K. 2013. Texas market hunting: Stories of waterfowl, game laws and outlaws. College Station: Texas A&M University Press.

Schorger, A. W. 1966. *The Wild Turkey: Its History and Domestication*. Norman: University of Oklahoma Press.

Shaw, H. G., and C. Mollohan 1992. Merriam's turkey. In *The Wild Turkey: Biology and Management*, edited by J. G. Dickson, 331–49. Mechanicsburg, PA: Stackpole Books.

Spears, B. L., M. C. Wallace, W. B. Ballard, R. S. Phillips, D. P. Holdstock, J. H. Brunjes, R. Applegate, M. S. Miller, and P. S. Gipson. 2007. Habitat use and survival of preflight Wild Turkey broods. *Journal of Wildlife Management* 71:69–81.

Steadman, D. W. 1980. A review of the osteology and paleontology of turkeys (Aves: Meleagridinae). *Contributions of the Science and Natural History Museum of Los Angeles County, California* 330:131–207.

Texas AgriLife Extension Wildlife and Fisheries. 2015. Rio Grande Wild Turkey. http://wildlife.tamu.edu /wildlifemanagement/turkeys/.

Texas Parks and Wildlife Department. 2014a. *Effect of Variable Harvest Regimes on Survival and Recovery of Texas Wild Turkeys.* Request for proposal. Austin, TX.

———. 2014b. *Small Game Harvest Survey Results 1994–1995 through 2013–2104.* PWD-RP-W700–719a. Austin, TX.

Vangilder, L. D. 1992. Population dynamics. In *The Wild Turkey: Biology and Management*, edited by J. G. Dickson, 165–87. Mechanicsburg, PA: Stackpole Books.

23

Plain Chachalaca

[A] . . . glaring problem is the paucity of ecological data for this species throughout most of its range.
—PETERSON (2000)

Introduction

The Plain Chachalaca (*Ortalis vetula*) is a game bird native to South Texas. It is the only member of the family Cracidae found in the United States (Marion 1974b). Although it resembles the Ring-necked Pheasant (*Phasianus colchicus*) and is therefore often referred to as the "Mexican tree pheasant," it is more closely related to the guans and curassows of Central and South America (Peterson 2000). The sexes are alike in appearance, with plumage that is brownish olive on the upper parts fading to gray on the neck and head. Underparts are olive brown or ashy olive, paler than the back, and brighter on the sides of the body. Tail is long and a dark olive with a greenish gloss and white tip. Orbital skin is bare and gray, and bill, legs, and toes are a pale bluish gray. The throat is bare and has a strip of black bristly feathers down the center. Skin on the throat is black until breeding commences, when it turns bright red.

The Plain Chachalaca evolved in North America (Peterson 2000). Fossils of ancestral cracids were found in Oligocene and Miocene formations (Brodkorb 1964; Vuilleumier 1965). Wetmore (1923, 1933) and Miller (1944) indicated that fossil specimens have been found from Miocene and Pliocene deposits in Nebraska and South Dakota, respectively. The Plain Chachalaca is a subtropical and tropical species that is somewhat obscure because the Lower Rio Grande Valley of Texas is a relatively isolated region and many people are unaware that the bird exists. Moreover, though it is frequently heard, because of its wary and secretive behavior and the thick brush it inhabits, the Plain Chachalaca is difficult to observe in the wild. Nevertheless, it is a valued member of Texas' bird community to both birders and hunters because it is such a challenging species to pursue with either binoculars or shotgun.

Chachalacas are largely an enigma to the scientific community. Except for the comprehensive study conducted by Marion (1974a) in the early 1970s in the Lower Rio Grande Valley, very little research has been conducted on the species. Therefore, knowledge of Plain Chachalaca ecology and management is extremely limited. Significant gaps remain in the information required to conserve populations in Texas. Consequently, the work by Marion and the life history account produced by Peterson (2000) have been drawn on heavily for this chapter. One thing that is clear is that Plain Chachalacas in Texas inhabit thick tracts of remnant native brush in a few counties adjacent to the Rio Grande in the Lower Rio Grande Valley. Texas Parks and Wildlife Department officials have made several attempts to establish additional

Figure 23.1. Plain Chachalaca adult (*left*) and partially grown chick (*right*). Photo credit: Larry Ditto.

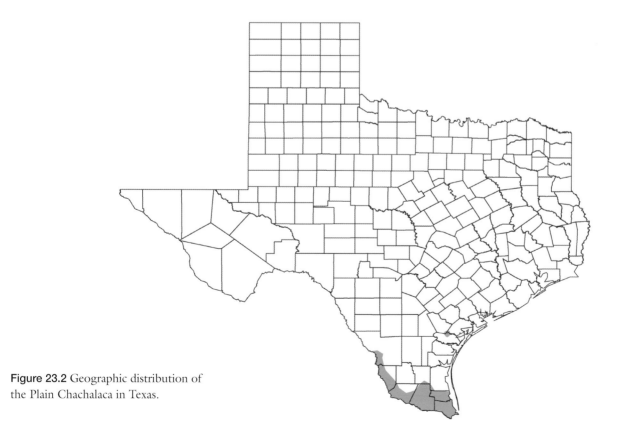

Figure 23.2 Geographic distribution of
the Plain Chachalaca in Texas.

populations in several counties in the northern part of South Texas, one of which was apparently a success. Populations seem to be sustainable, so the Texas Parks and Wildlife Department continues to administer a hunting season on the species. Continued suburban growth and agricultural production in the Lower Rio Grande Valley threaten the last remaining tracts of native brush that represent essential chachalaca habitat.

Distribution

The Plain Chachalaca is distributed from the Lower Rio Grande Valley south along the Gulf Coast into Mexico through the Yucatán Peninsula into northern and central Guatemala, Belize, northern Honduras, and north-central Nicaragua (Peterson 2000). The species has also been successfully introduced to several small islands off the coast of Georgia (Hopkins 1982). In Texas the primary range of the Plain Chachalaca is in the Lower Rio Grande Valley in Cameron, Hidalgo, Starr, and Willacy Counties, though a reintroduced, self-sustaining population occurs in San Patricio County (Peterson 2000). Moreover, several sightings of the species have been recorded in Zapata and Webb Counties, northwest of Starr County along the Rio Grande (Eitniear and Rueckle 1996). Plain Chachalacas were more widely distributed throughout most of the counties in the Lower Rio Grande Valley until about the early 1900s, when widespread areas of native brushland were cleared for agricultural production (Marion 1974b) and the urban centers of the Lower Rio Grande Valley began to grow. Plain Chachalacas were gradually restricted to remnant areas of native brush where they remain in fragmented populations today that continue to be threatened by the enormous population growth of the Lower Rio Grande Valley.

Breeding Biology

Migration

Plain Chachalacas are permanent residents of the areas they occupy and do not migrate (Peterson 2000).

Timing of breeding

Plain Chachalacas are monogamous. Breeding pairs remain together from the time pair bonds are established during late winter until foraging groups form during fall (Marion and Fleetwood 1978; Peterson 2000). Marion and Fleetwood (1978) reported that active breeding behavior begins during February in the Lower Rio Grande Valley after pairs have initiated territory formation and males have begun intense calling. They indicated that most breeding typically occurred between March and April when peak weights and sizes of male testes and female ovaries, respectively, were reached. Nesting began in March and extended into August, although nests in September and October were observed. Peterson (2000) reported that all adults are presumed to breed, and juvenile or sub-adult females are capable of breeding, but the extent to which they contribute to breeding is unknown. Similarly, it is unknown whether juvenile males breed during their first year.

Behavior

Peterson (2000) provided a comprehensive description of chachalaca behavior, which unless otherwise indicated will be summarized here. Plain Chachalacas are largely arboreal and therefore spend the majority of their day in the foliage and branches of trees and shrubs. Most behavior occurs above the ground including calling, preening, sunbathing, roosting, and most foraging activities. Birds walk or run along branches and frequently hop from branch to branch. They are capable of short, powerful flights and display great dexterity in gliding through narrow openings between branches of trees and shrubs. Plain Chachalacas will forage on the ground surface and are powerful runners when disturbed. They are not known to swim and can apparently fly across aquatic impediments when necessary (Gandaria 2009). Plain Chachalacas are extremely vocal, and indeed their name is a result of the "cha-cha-lac" or "cha-ca-lac" calls that emanate from areas they inhabit. This call is used to establish pair bonds as males call to attract females, who will answer a male before he has completed a call so that both calls overlap. Frequently, other Plain Chachalacas will respond to the initial calling of a male and female so that a patch of brush will quickly erupt with a multitude of these calls. Calling is most frequent during the first 3 hours of the day as well as at dusk. Annual peaks of calling occur during the breeding season.

Plain Chachalacas also emit a purr-mutter that is evidently used for communication between pairs, hens and chicks, and family groups during winter and as a warning call (Sutton and Pettingill 1942; Oberholser 1974). Cackles and squawk-squeals are emitted by birds that are alarmed, apparently as warning to other chachalacas in the vicinity (Pearson 1921; Marion 1974a). Hens communicate with chicks using a soft clucking cackle, which the chicks answer with soft peeps (Marion 1974a).

Peterson (2000) summarized behavior associated with breeding as follows. Courtship is simple and involves primarily mutual preening of the head, neck, and base of the tail. Courtship displays also sometimes involve mates providing food items to one another by transferring a berry or seed from one bill to another. Breeding pairs establish a territory in which a nest is built in the branches or forks of trees and shrubs. Plain Chachalacas may also use nests constructed by other bird species. Hens incubate clutches, while males defend a small territory of 10–20 m (30–60 ft) in diameter centered on the nest. When confronted by an intruding male, or when battling for a female, a male makes a threat posture. If another male displays a threat posture, a fight occurs. Fighting typically consists of attempts to grab adversaries with the feet, pecking, and jumping with wings spread to maintain balance. Fights are brief and terminate when one of the antagonists retreats and is closely followed by the other male for a short distance. Little aggression is displayed toward females, and aggressive encounters between males peak during the breeding season. Pairs and family groups of 3–5 individuals make up the basic Plain Chachalaca social unit, although small flocks of 10–20 birds have been observed during the fall and winter months (Teale 1965). These flocks may be a concentration of family groups that are attracted to areas where food is available (Marion 1974a). Family groups remain together until pair bonds begin to form again during late winter.

Clutch size and incubation

Peterson (2000) considered average clutch size to be 3 eggs. Marion and Fleetwood (1978) reported that of 158 clutches they examined in the Lower Rio Grande Valley, clutch size ranged from 2 to 4 eggs and averaged 2.88 eggs. Occasionally more than 1 hen will lay eggs in dump nests, resulting in up to 9 eggs in 1 nest that are not incubated (Marion and Fleetwood 1978). Typically a clutch is produced over a period of 5 days and eggs are incubated by a hen for 20 to 25 days (Peterson 2000).

Nest losses

Nest success in the Lower Rio Grande Valley was reported to be 36% for more than 900 nests that were initiated and 65% for almost 140 nests that were incubated (Marion 1974a; Waggerman and Frye 1974; Peterson 2000). Egg hatchability is high. Hobson and Neikirk (1970) and Marion and Fleetwood (1978) reported that about 90% of almost 300 eggs hatched in their Lower Rio Grande Valley study areas. Most nest losses are the result of predation by raccoons (*Procyon lotor*), opossums (*Didelphis virginiana*), and snakes (Marion and Fleetwood 1978; Peterson 2000).

Phenology

Plain Chachalaca chicks are precocial and are capable of climbing and moving around the nest almost immediately after hatching (Bent 1932; Marion 1976; Peterson 2000). Hens lead chicks to the ground within 2 hours of hatching and chicks follow the hen by leaping and clinging to vines and branches until they reach the ground (Peterson 2000). Since remiges are developed at hatching, chicks are capable of short flights when they are about 5 days old, and a few days afterward chicks are agile fliers and are able to negotiate the tangled branches of thick brush (Delacour and Amadon 1973; Marion 1977). Chicks are brooded by both parents, who show them food and make it available but do not feed them (Peterson 2000). Chicks actively pursue food items such as insects. They grow rapidly, almost doubling their size and tripling their weight during their first month (Marion 1977; Peterson 2000). Plain Chachalaca chicks reach adult size by 3–4 months and adult weight by 5 months (Marion 1977). Parents cooperate in raising broods through summer and into fall, when they form family foraging groups. Individual family groups may coalesce into larger foraging groups during winter. Subadults and juveniles leave the family group and become independent during late winter.

Diet and foraging

Plain Chachalacas are primarily herbivorous and frugivorous, although invertebrates are also part of their diets (Peterson 2000). Plant materials make up more than 70% of Plain Chachalaca diets (Marion 1976), including leaves, flowers, berries, fruits, seeds, and stamens (Leopold 1959; Marion 1976; Peterson 2000). Marion (1976) also indicated that Plain Chachalacas consume food provided by humans such as corn, milo, millet, and wheat (Kenner and Tewes 1994). Marion (1976) reported that seasonal dietary preferences were evident among Plain Chachalacas in the Lower Rio Grande Valley although leaves, buds, berries, and seeds dominated their diets. Ratios of leaves and buds to berries and seeds varied from 39% to 61% during spring to 1% to 99% during fall. Snails (*Gastropoda*) and caterpillars (*Lepidoptera*) were the most common invertebrates eaten, though they made up less than 10% of spring and summer diets. Important woody species were coyotillo (*Karwinskia humboldtiana*), Mexican ash (*Fraxinus berlandieriana*), anaqua (*Ehretia anacua*), pigeonberry (*Rivinia humilis*), cedar elm (*Ulmus crassifolia*), and sugar hackberry (*Celtis laevigata*), while important herbaceous species were lazy daisies (*Aphanostephus* spp.) and thoroughworts (*Eupatorium* spp.). Dietary proportions of specific plant species vary depending on food availability. Plain Chachalacas forage primarily in the branches of trees and shrubs but will also forage on the ground, although they do not scratch the ground surface as many gallinaceous bird species do (Peterson 2000).

Demography and Vital Rates

Plain Chachalacas are capable of breeding during their first year of life, but the limited data available indicate that some subadult females participate in breeding activity, whereas others do not (Marion and Fleetwood 1978; Peterson 2000). It is not known whether subadult males participate in breeding during their first year. The few reproductive success studies that have been conducted for Plain Chachalacas indicate that approximately 0.9 chicks were hatched in nests that were initiated and 2.6 chicks were hatched in nests that were successful (Hobson and Neikirk 1970;

Marion 1974a; Waggerman and Frye 1974). Chick survival is poor. On Marion's (1974a) Lower Rio Grande Valley study area, 2.6 chicks were produced per successful nest, but the ratio of juveniles to adults was 1.03 between May and July and further declined to 0.25 between August and October. This may have been an underestimate because Marion observed 0.73 subadults per adult during the following spring. As with many important aspects of Plain Chachalaca demography, little is known about adult survival. However, the one study that Gandaria (2009) recently conducted in the Lower Rio Grande Valley revealed that the 8-month survival rate of females (40%) was similar to that of males (36%). Gandaria (2009) also indicated that adult survival during the nesting season (41%) was lower than survival during the breeding season (92%). Therefore, population turnover in the Lower Rio Grande Valley may be less than 50% each year. Nevertheless, Plain Chachalacas appear to be relatively long-lived birds compared to most other North American galliforms. Recapture data from Marion and Fleetwood (1978) revealed that 1 male was more than 8 years old, 3 females were more than 7 years old, and 5 individuals were more than 5 years old.

Nest predation, adult survival during the nesting season, and chick survival are clearly important factors that limit the annual growth of Plain Chachalaca populations. Nevertheless, because Plain Chachalacas have long life spans, the reproductive potential of an individual is probably high enough each year to offset nest destruction and abandonment, as well as low nesting season and chick survival rates, at least during an average year. However, like any other wildlife species, Plain Chachalacas are susceptible to catastrophic events that reduce population levels. For example, extremely cold temperatures and snow that occurred over several days in February 1898 supposedly resulted in the deaths of thousands of Plain Chachalacas in the Lower Rio Grande Valley (Smith 1910; Peterson 2000).

Age and sex ratios

Sex ratios do not deviate much from 1:1 (Peterson 2000). Marion and Fleetwood (1978) reported a male-to-female sex ratio of 66:78 and 35:43 during their 2-year study in the Lower Rio Grande Valley. Little information exists for age ratios, but given the

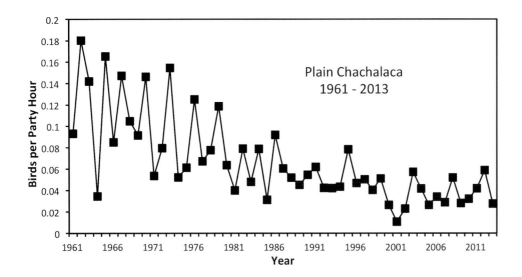

Figure 23.3 Population trend for the Plain Chachalaca in Texas, based on Audubon Society Christmas Bird Count data.

poor survival of chicks and juveniles through the summer (Marion 1974a), age ratios may not exceed 1 juvenile to 1 adult.

Population Status and Trends

Chachalaca trends

Plain Chachalaca trend data from Christmas Bird Count surveys (National Audubon Society 2015) indicate that populations have been steadily declining in Texas for the past 40 years. This trend corresponds inversely to the human population growth of the Lower Rio Grande Valley and the increased agricultural production that was alluded to earlier in this chapter. This decline has been ongoing since at least 1939 and almost certainly earlier because hundreds of thousands of acres of native brushland were destroyed in the Lower Rio Grande Valley during the early twentieth century (Cottam and Trefethen 1968). Marion (1974a) and Marion, O'Meara, and Maehr (1981) surveyed Plain Chachalacas in the Lower Rio Grande Valley in 1972 using prerecorded calls and calculated a density of 2.5 birds/ha (0.93 bird/ac) of occupied habitat, which extrapolated to 18,000 to 21,000 individuals for the Lower Rio Grande Valley. They speculated that populations had increased slightly during the 1960s. More recently, Brush and Cantu (1998) reported that densities on the Santa Ana National Wildlife Refuge (NWR) increased from 1.3 birds/ha (0.53 bird/ac) in the mid-1970s to 2.7 birds/ha (1.0 bird/ac) in the mid-1990s. Plain

Chachalaca numbers fluctuated dramatically between 1965 and 1980 (fig. 23.3), but a negative trend is still evident; thus it is possible that Marion, O'Meara, and Maehr (1981) captured a year or two of population increase or that populations were increasing on the study areas they surveyed. Similarly, the Santa Ana NWR population mentioned by Brush and Cantu (1998) may also have increased from the 1970s to the 1990s, but this increase does not mirror the trend for the entire Lower Rio Grande Valley. A substantial amount of the native brush that Plain Chachalacas require to sustain populations has been lost as a consequence of the tremendous human population growth that the Lower Rio Grande Valley has experienced over the past 25 years. Yet the fragmented populations restricted to these brush remnants remain self-sustaining today; otherwise the Texas Parks and Wildlife Department would not permit hunting. Nonetheless, since Plain Chachalacas are not very mobile and few corridors of suitable habitat link existing populations, the threat of inbreeding and catastrophic events that could extirpate localized populations remains a genuine concern. The self-sustaining status of Plain Chachalaca populations in the Lower Rio Grande Valley is likely precarious if habitat loss continues.

Habitat Requirements and Management

Specific habitat requirements

Plain Chachalaca habitat in the Lower Rio Grande Valley is tall, thorny brushland or thickets (Peterson

Figure 23.4 Plain Chachalaca habitat in South Texas. Photo credit: Damon Williford.

2000). These vegetation communities occur along resacas (creeks), irrigation canals, the Arroyo Colorado, and the Rio Grande. Plain Chachalaca habitat is fragmented and often made up of isolated remnant brush communities scattered throughout the Lower Rio Grande Valley. Some of the best remaining Plain Chachalaca habitat occurs on various national wildlife refuges and Texas Parks and Wildlife Department State Wildlife Management Areas. Marion (1974b) described suitable habitat as dense, brushy woodland on mesic sites. A wide variety of woody species that occur in the Lower Rio Grande Valley brushlands and riparian areas represent chachalaca habitat. Marion (1974b) reported that common woody species that occur in these vegetation communities are granjeno (*Celtis pallida*), Texas sugarberry or sugar hackberry (*C. laevigata*), guayacan (*Porlieria angustifolia*),

huisache (*Acacia farnesiana*), Texas ebony (*Pithecellobium flexicaule*), cedar elm, honey mesquite (*Prosopis glandulosa*), and coma (*Bumelia lanuginosa*). Gandaria (2009) indicated that habitat on his study area consisted of sugar hackberry, cedar elm, and Mexican ash mixed within a honey mesquite–granjeno association. Herbaceous species that occur in chachalaca habitat and are part of their diet include pink mint (*Stachys drummondii*), Texas nightshade (*Solanum triquetrum*), western ragweed (*Ambrosia psilostachya*), common sunflower (*Helianthus annuus*), and white clover (*Trifolium repens*). Since much of the habitat is now fragmented and surrounded by agricultural fields, the edges of crop fields that contain grain sorghum or milo are also utilized as foraging habitat by Plain Chachalacas (Marion 1974b). Water is also an important habitat requirement but is not limiting because of the abundance of waterways and irrigation canals that exist near the vegetation communities that Plain Chachalacas occupy.

The amount of habitat required to maintain self-sustaining Plain Chachalaca populations remains unknown, but clearly self-sustaining populations remain in the fragmented habitats that currently exist in the Lower Rio Grande Valley. The most secure habitats occur on federal refuges and state wildlife management areas. For example, certainly portions of the 39,254 ha (97,000 ac) Laguna Atascosa NWR, the 845 ha (2,088 ac) Santa Ana NWR, and the larger portion of the Las Palomas Wildlife Management Area provide sufficient area to support Plain Chachalaca populations. Nonetheless, the minimum acreage required to do so is unknown. However, home ranges have been calculated in two studies. Balda (1989) reported that male and female home ranges for Plain Chachalacas introduced in San Patricio County were 6.4 ha (15.8 ac) and 4.0 ha (9.88 ac), respectively. Gandaria (2009) reported substantially larger home ranges for the population he studied in the Lower Rio Grande Valley, where the mean home ranges for females and males during the nesting season were 117 ha (289 ac) and 41 ha (101 ac), respectively. Mean breeding-season home ranges for females were 59 ha (146 ac), and for males, 48 ha (119 ac).

Habitat management

Habitat management for Plain Chachalacas involves maintaining or creating the dense stands of brush that are required to sustain populations. Therefore, simply conserving what remains in the Lower Rio Grande Valley is an important but difficult task in the face of continued suburban development and agricultural production. Fortunately, Plain Chachalacas readily utilize secondary growth created when native subtropical and tropical shrublands and woodlands are removed (Peterson 2000). The dense woody vegetation that colonizes sites formerly occupied by these woodlands and forests is readily utilized by Plain Chachalacas after the shrubs and small trees reach a height and density suitable for these birds. The reestablishment efforts of the Texas Parks and Wildlife Department also indicate that Plain Chachalacas can be successfully reestablished or even reintroduced to areas where suitable dense

brushy habitat exists. Generally, allowing brush to invade disturbed sites may eventually result in habitats suitable for chachalacas, especially on mesic sites along creeks and rivers. The Plain Chachalacas recently discovered along the Rio Grande on the outskirts of Zapata and Laredo may represent expansion of the species range; these observations were from mesic areas with dense brush communities. Plain Chachalaca habitat can also be created by planting native shrubs. Over the past 20–30 years, Texas Parks and Wildlife Department officials have planted native shrubs in selected areas of the Lower Rio Grande Valley largely to provide nesting habitat for White-winged Doves, but these plantings also serve as Plain Chachalaca habitat (Waggerman and Frye 1974). Unfortunately, preserving native tracts of brush or reestablishing brush runs counter to what the majority of South Texas landowners want to accomplish because managing land for bobwhites and cattle is often a landowner priority. Bobwhites are grassland-shrubland birds, and cattle of course also require grasslands. Thus, landowner priorities are to clear brush and manage its reinvasion, which generally leaves little habitat for Plain Chachalacas. However, preserving the woody vegetation in the mesic soils of riparian areas would maintain habitat that is required by Plain Chachalacas.

Hunting and Conservation

Hunting

The Plain Chachalaca is considered a game species in Texas and can be legally harvested annually during a hunting season that extends from early November through mid-February in Starr, Hidalgo, Cameron, and Willacy Counties (Texas Parks and Wildlife Department 2015). The daily bag limit is 5 birds, with 10 birds in possession. Harvest trend data are unavailable.

Conservation

Clearly habitat that exists in the Lower Rio Grande Valley today is adequate on some level because self-sustaining populations of Plain Chachalacas remain. Unfortunately, most of the existing habitat is fragmented and occurs as islands in a matrix of human development and agricultural land, making Plain Chachalaca populations that exist in these islands of habitat potentially vulnerable to extinction. We do not know the minimum amount of habitat that is required to maintain a Plain Chachalaca population because we do not know what the minimum viable population size is for Plain Chachalacas. Without this knowledge we cannot determine how much habitat is needed to maintain a minimum viable population of Plain Chachalacas. However, Soule et al. (1988) indicated that 200 individuals are often suitable to maintain bird populations for up to 75 years. Therefore, if we assume that 200 individuals is a suitable minimum population size for Plain Chachalacas and we use Brush and Cantu's (1998) density estimate for the mid-1990s of 2.7 birds/ha (1.01 birds/ac), then more than 81 ha (200 ac) of habitat would be required to maintain a viable population of Plain Chachalacas.

Creating additional Plain Chachalaca habitat should be a priority, particularly creating habitat corridors that link existing populations. Reestablishing native brush as Texas Parks and Wildlife Department officials have done in the past for White-winged Doves can be accomplished if land can be purchased by the state or by enlisting the cooperation of landowners. Moreover, another conservation priority should be to maintain existing habitats by doing whatever is possible to halt the development and agricultural activities that threaten these habitats. The Texas Parks and Wildlife Department and nongovernmental organizations such as the Nature Conservancy, Valley Land Trust, and Las Huellas could purchase property that represents important habitat and designate these properties as Plain Chachalaca Management Areas.

Reestablishing populations in areas where habitat is suitable but where Plain Chachalacas are absent should also be a conservation priority. The Texas Parks and Wildlife Department attempted to reestablish Plain Chachalacas throughout the species' historical range between 1959 and 1999 by releasing more than 1,000 birds on 22 release sites, and these releases were very successful (Peterson 2000). During this same period the Texas Parks and Wildlife Department also released more than 1,500 birds on a few areas in South Texas outside their historical range (Peterson 2000). A new population was established on one of these release sites in San Patricio County, and this population continues to expand (Peterson 2000). Plain Chachalaca sightings are still occasionally recorded where birds were

translocated in Webb, Zapata, and Jim Wells Counties (Eitniear and Rueckle 1996; R. Fugate, personal communication), though the Zapata sightings could represent range expansion along the Rio Grande from existing populations in Starr County. Apparently Plain Chachalacas are very tolerant of being translocated to new areas to establish new populations as long as enough suitable habitat exists at release sites.

Research Needs

The Plain Chachalaca is arguably the least studied upland game bird in Texas. A comprehensive ecological study has not been conducted for Plain Chachalacas in the Lower Rio Grande Valley since Marion conducted his research there in the early 1970s. We simply do not know enough about the species' basic ecology to conserve and manage it properly, although the Texas Parks and Wildlife Department does the best it can with the limited knowledge that is available. Therefore Plain Chachalaca research needs are substantial, but they need to be prioritized in a logical manner so that results generated have the greatest impact on conservation. Peterson (2000) identified several important research needs 15 years ago that remain relevant today. With the exception of Gandaria's (2009) study of a single population at the Santa Ana NWR, no additional research has been completed since Marion's study. The following research priorities should be addressed:

1. Conduct a spatially explicit study of where Plain Chachalacas occur throughout the species' geographic range. A smaller-scale study focusing on the Lower Rio Grande Valley would be more relevant for management of Plain Chachalacas in Texas.

2. Carry out a comprehensive ecological study similar to what Marion accomplished in the early 1970s using modern spatial and telemetry technology that was unavailable to Marion. There is a critical need to understand

   Habitat requirements by life-history stage.

   Seasonal movements and dispersal.

   Food habits and energetics.

   Basic demography and vital rates such as sex- and age-specific survival rates, seasonal survival rates, weekly and monthly chick survival rates, and reproductive potential.

3. Develop a reliable technique to survey Plain Chachalaca populations that will yield precise and reasonably accurate density estimates.

4. Conduct manipulative field experiments.

5. Survey South Texas for additional release sites to either reestablish Plain Chachalacas in parts of their former range or reintroduce them to suitable areas outside their former range in South Texas.

Literature Cited

Balda, W. E. 1989. Evaluation of success of Plain Chachalaca (*Ortalis vetula*) transplants in south Texas. Master's thesis, New Mexico State University.

Bent, A. C. 1932. *Life Histories of North American Gallinaceous Birds*. US National Museum Bulletin 162. Washington, DC: Smithsonian Institution.

Brodkorb, P. 1954. A chachalaca from the Miocene of Florida. *Wilson Bulletin* 66:180–83.

Brush, T., and A. Cantu. 1998. Changes in the breeding bird community of subtropical evergreen forest in the Lower Rio Grande Valley of Texas, 1970s–1990s. *Texas Journal of Science* 50:123–32.

Cottam, C. C., and J. B. Trefethen. 1968. *Whitewings*. Princeton, NJ: D. Van Nostrand.

Delacour, J., and D. Amadon. 1973. *Curassows and Related Birds*. New York: American Museum of Natural History.

Eitniear, J. C., and T. Rueckle. 1996. Noteworthy avian breeding records from Zapata County, Texas. *Bulletin of the Texas Ornithological Society* 29:43–44.

Gandaria, A. G., 2009. Population dynamics of Plain Chachalacas in the Lower Rio Grande Valley. Master's thesis, Texas A&M University.

Hobson, M. S., and J. A. Neikirk. 1970. Reestablishing the Mexican pheasant. *Texas Parks and Wildlife* 28:2–5.

Hopkins, M., Jr. 1982. Plain Chachalaca on Little St. Simons Island. *Oriole* 47:40.

Kenner, J. M., and M. E. Tewes. 1994. Seed preferences of nongame birds in the Rio Grande Valley. *Proceedings of the Annual Conference of the Southeastern Association of Fish and Wildlife Agencies* 48:302–9.

Leopold, A. S. 1959. *Wildlife of Mexico: The Game Birds and Mammals*. Berkeley: University of California Press.

Marion, W. R. 1974a. Ecology of the Plain Chachalaca in the Lower Rio Grande Valley of Texas. PhD diss., Texas A&M University.

———. 1974b. Status of the Plain Chachalaca in south Texas. *Wilson Bulletin* 86:200–205.

———. 1975. Cacklers along the Rio Grande. *Texas Parks and Wildlife* 33 (12): 16–18.

———. 1976. Plain Chachalaca food habits in south Texas. *Auk* 93:376–79.

———. 1977. Growth and development of the Plain Chachalaca in south Texas. *Wilson Bulletin* 89:47–56.

Marion, W. R., and R. J. Fleetwood. 1978. Nesting ecology of the Plain Chachalaca in south Texas. *Wilson Bulletin* 90:386–95.

Marion, W. R., T. E. O'Meara, and D. S. Maehr. 1981. Use of playback recordings in sampling elusive or secretive birds. *Studies in Avian Biology* 6:81–85.

Miller, A. H. 1944. An avifauna from the lower Miocene of South Dakota. *University of California Public Bulletin Department of Geological Sciences* 27:85–100.

National Audubon Society. 2015. Christmas bird count results for Plain Chachalaca. http://netapp.audubon .org/CBCObservation/Historical/ResultsBySpecies .aspx?1.

Oberholser, H. C. 1974. *The Bird Life of Texas*. Austin: University of Texas Press.

Pearson, T. G. 1921. Notes on the bird-life of southeastern Texas. *Auk* 38:513–23.

Peterson, M. J. 2000. Plain Chachalaca (*Ortalis vetula*). In *Birds of North America Online*, edited by A. Poole. Ithaca, NY: Cornell Lab of Ornithology: http://bna .birds.cornell.edu.bnaproxy.birds.cornell.edu/bna /species/550/articles/introduction.

Smith, A. P. 1910. Miscellaneous bird notes from the Lower Rio Grande. *Condor* 12:93–103.

Soule, M. E., D. T. Bolger, A. C. Alberts, J. Wright, M. Sorice, and S. Hill. 1988. Reconstructed dynamics of rapid extinctions of chaparral-requiring birds in urban habitat islands. *Conservation Biology* 2:75–92.

Sutton, G. M., and O. S. Pettingill Jr. 1942. Birds of the Gomez Farias region, southwestern Tamaulipas. *Auk* 59:1–34.

Teale, E. W. 1965. *Wandering through Winter*. New York: Dodd, Mead.

Texas Parks and Wildlife Department. 2015. Outdoor Annual. Austin: Texas Parks and Wildlife Department. http://tpwd.texas.gov/regulations/outdoor-annual/.

Vuilleumier, F. 1965. Relationships and evolution within the Cracidae. *Bulletin of the Museum of Comparative Zoology* 134:1–27.

Waggerman, G. L., and R. G. Frye. 1974. *Chachalaca Life History*. Final report, Federal Aid Project Number W81R17, Job no. 9. Austin: Texas Parks and Wildlife Department.

Wetmore, A. 1923. Avian fossils from the Miocene and Pliocene of Nebraska. *Bulletin of the American Museum of Natural History* 48:483–507.

———. 1933. A fossil gallinaceous bird from the lower Miocene of Nebraska. *Condor* 35:64–65.

24

Resident and Webless Migratory Game Bird Conservation in Texas and the Surrounding Region

Joint Ventures and Landscape Conservation Cooperatives

The principles of landscape ecology and ecosystem management, which lie at the heart of integrated bird conservation, will remain largely esoteric abstractions until we demonstrate the power of conceptual models and geospatial data in multi-scale assessment and planning.—BAXTER (2002)

Introduction

During the past few decades, debates over philosophical opinions and ideological leanings based in the traditional game versus nongame paradigms (Baxter 2002) have pitted traditional wildlife professionals, who typically represented hunters, against a new generation of conservation biologists. However, and fortunately, some people on each side of the debate realized that resources (i.e., funding and personnel) were limited and that landscapes important for the species they cared about were changing drastically, and for the worst for most species.

This dilemma delivered a challenge for conservation, and it required a new way of doing business. This was especially pertinent in light of the emergence of the North American Waterfowl Management Plan in the late 1980s and the fact that the Accelerated Research Program for webless migratory game birds had been terminated in 1982.

The new way of doing business in the bird conservation world centered on partnerships. Successful landscape-level conservation requires cooperation and coordination of efforts among individual conservation entities (Giocomo et al. 2012). A key principle is that no single entity can effectively address the complex landscape-level conservation issues and sustain populations and their supporting habitats in perpetuity. Conservation partnerships are often self-directed initiatives made up of governmental entities and nongovernmental agencies and organizations, as well as corporations and individual landowners. Partners work across administrative boundaries to deliver landscape-level planning and science-based conservation, which results in linking on-the-ground management with established conservation goals.

In Texas there are two types of organizations that use this partnership-based approach toward conservation. The first is Joint Ventures, which use a partnership-based approach to deliver specific bird conservation objectives. The second is Landscape Conservation Cooperatives, which provide science and technical expertise to support conservation planning at landscape scales for many taxa, including some bird species. In

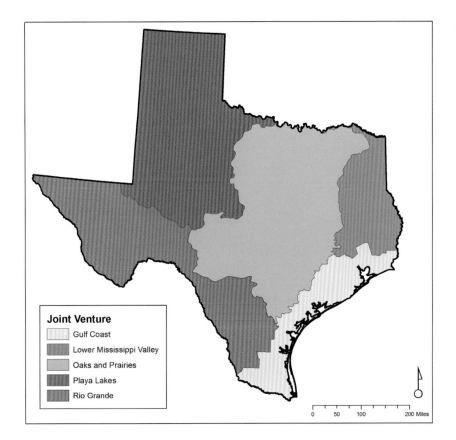

Figure 24.1. Distribution of Joint Ventures across Texas. Photo credit: Mark Parr, USFWS.

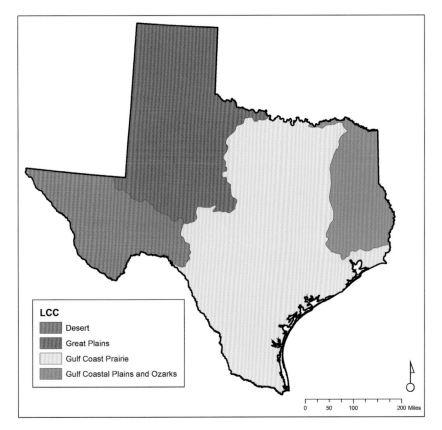

Figure 24.2. Distribution of Landscape Conservation Cooperatives across Texas. Photo credit: Mark Parr, USFWS.

Table 24.1. Priority or focal bird species for joint ventures (JVs) and landscape conservation cooperatives (LCCs) in Texas.

Organization	Species
Gulf Coast JV	Northern Bobwhite Wintering and breeding waterfowl King Rail
Lower Mississippi Valley JV	Northern Bobwhite Purple Gallinule Wintering waterfowl
Oaks and Prairies JV	Northern Bobwhite
Playa Lakes JV	Ring-necked Pheasant Greater and Lesser Prairie-Chickens Scaled Quail Sandhill Crane Wintering waterfowl
Rio Grande JV	Northern Bobwhite Gambel's Quail Montezuma Quail Plain Chachalaca Scaled Quail Wintering waterfowl
Desert LCC	Unknown
Great Plains LCC	Northern Pintail Sandhill Crane Lesser Prairie-Chicken
Gulf Coast Prairie LCC	Mottled Duck Northern Bobwhite Northern Pintail
Gulf Coastal Plains and Ozarks LCC	Northern Bobwhite Eastern Wild Turkey American Woodcock

Texas there are five Joint Ventures and four Landscape Conservation Cooperatives. Many of these partnerships have an interest in game birds and their habitats (table 24.1).

Joint Ventures

Joint Ventures implement national and international bird conservation plans (e.g., for waterfowl [North American Waterfowl Management Plan 2004], land birds [Rich et al. 2004], waterbirds [Kushlan et al. 2002], and shorebirds [Brown et al. 2001]) by "stepping down" the population goals of these larger plans to regional or landscape habitat goals, while feeding local information (known as "rolling up") to the national and international planning groups (Giocomo et al. 2012). This process helps bridge the gap between continental-level planning and local-level management actions by integrating continental priorities throughout the planning process to address local-level conservation activities. This process ensures that local-level information is incorporated into national and international policy making (Giocomo et al. 2012). Joint Ventures document proposed plans of action in an implementation plan that provides guidance for partners on needed conservation actions and outcomes to further bird conservation within the region. Implementation plans are updated periodically to incorporate the best available knowledge and reflect the dynamic nature of interactions between human land use and the environment (Giocomo et al. 2012).

Joint Ventures focus on a broad spectrum of bird conservation activities including biological planning; conservation design; conservation delivery; communication, education, and outreach; research and outcome-based monitoring projects; decision support tools; and fund-raising for these activities through partner contributions and grants.

Although partnerships are common in wildlife conservation, a key distinction in Joint Venture partnerships is that partners are invested in activities and share the risks and costs, as well as the rewards. Joint Venture partners are expected to bring resources (personnel and funding) to help identify and attain shared goals. Goals are broad enough to span the missions of the individual partners and are based on managing bird populations and habitats at the landscape level. Goals do not depend on a single partner or program for success or failure (Giocomo et al. 2012). This partnership model creates motivation to continue to pursue shared goals even if one partner's circumstances change. The result of this process is continuity of conservation regardless of political or administrative changes. The partnership brings together the different abilities of various partners to pursue common goals that some may be unwilling or unable to do alone. For example, one partner may lobby government officials for support, another may provide legal or tax expertise, while a third may provide scientific, technical, fund-raising, or educational and outreach abilities (Graziano 1993).

Landscape Conservation Cooperatives

The US Department of the Interior Secretarial Order No. 3289 established Landscape Conservation Cooperatives as a network of public-private partnerships that provide shared science to ensure the sustainability of America's land, water, wildlife, and cultural resources (LCC Network 2015). Landscape Conservation Cooperatives are self-directed partnerships between federal agencies, states, tribes, nongovernmental organizations, universities, and other entities to collaboratively define science needs and jointly address broad-scale conservation issues, such as climate change and large-scale habitat fragmentation, in a defined geographic area.

The conservation challenges of the twenty-first century are more complex than ever before. In addition to those previously confronted at local scales, widespread threats such as drought, climate change, and large-scale habitat fragmentation are complicating efforts to plan and conduct conservation. Complex threats do not impact just isolated places or individual species, but entire landscapes and multiple resources simultaneously.

These challenges are too large for any single conservation organization to address alone. Partnerships involving many public and private organizations are needed to address landscape-scale issues facing the natural systems we care about. Landscape Conservation Cooperatives provide a forum for states, tribes, federal agencies, nongovernmental organizations, universities, and other groups to work together. Each brings a particular expertise, point of view, or needed resource to leverage in addressing a specific issue (LCC Network 2015).

Landscape Conservation Cooperatives are applied conservation science partnerships with two main purposes. The first, providing the science and technical expertise needed to support conservation planning at landscape scales, is beyond the vision or resources of any one organization (USFWS 2015). Through the efforts of Landscape Conservation Cooperative staff and science-oriented partners, Landscape Conservation Cooperatives generate tools, methods, and data management needed to design and deliver conservation using the Strategic Habitat Conservation approach (USFWS 2015). The second function of Landscape Conservation Cooperatives is to promote collaboration among members in defining shared conservation goals. With these goals in mind, partners can identify where and how they will take action, within their own authorities and organizational priorities, to best contribute to the larger conservation effort (USFWS 2015).

The Strategic Habitat Conservation Approach to Conservation

Strategic Habitat Conservation uses adaptive management through a series of processes: biological planning, conservation design, habitat delivery, monitoring, and research (USFWS 2008). Strategic Habitat Conservation is based on four principles:

1. Start with ecologically meaningful scales.

   Addressing conservation challenges that cross jurisdictional boundaries, such as habitat fragmentation, wildlife disease, and climate change, requires conservation planning at an ecologically appropriate scale (e.g., watersheds, ecoregions) rather than smaller scales (e.g., single land-management units) that coincide with jurisdictional boundaries. By starting at larger versus smaller scales, we are better able to address conservation challenges (e.g., climate change, disease) that cross arbitrary boundaries (USFWS 2015).

2. Work in partnership to maximize effectiveness and efficiency.

   To be successful with conservation at landscape scales, it is important to involve a diversity of partners, both public and private, that have an interest in the geography. Broad conservation

partnerships such as Joint Ventures and Landscape Conservation Cooperatives provide forums for the identification of conservation priorities and common science needs, leveraging funding and capacity, and implementing conservation actions. Also, public support is critical for the implementation of conservation actions at large scales (USFWS 2015).

3. Incorporate elements of an adaptive management framework (fig. 24.3).

   Biological Planning—Biological Planning builds a shared foundation for future conservation efforts by identifying conservation targets, describing current and desired future conditions and defining the conservation deficit, and refining species-habitat relationships (USFWS 2015). Priority or focal species are tools to help focus our biological planning efforts in a way that benefits multiple species on the landscape (Crosby et al. 2015). Population and habitat objectives (e.g., numbers, range, trends) are set for the species to help gauge progress toward achieving the desired conservation outcomes (USFWS 2015).

   Conservation Design—Conservation Design involves using the tools and information available to bring together the products of biological planning to identify strategies for achieving population and habitat objectives (USFWS 2015). Through improved understanding of the relationship between populations and habitats, we assess the ability of landscapes to support a given population and determine the best strategies for attaining the desired conservation outcomes. Landscape Conservation Design is both a partnership-driven process and a product that results in a science-based, spatially explicit representation of the desired future condition of that landscape needed to meet population objectives (USFWS 2015).

   Monitoring and Research—Monitoring and Research are prominent and fundamental elements of Strategic Habitat Conservation that inform the iterative process whereby managers learn and improve conservation outcomes (USFWS 2015). Through targeted and purposeful monitoring we evaluate the effectiveness of our conservation delivery as well as gauge

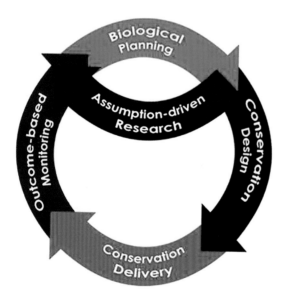

Figure 24.3. Conceptual model of Strategic Habitat Conservation.

progress and the success of our actions. Research validates assumptions used in conservation design and incorporates learning into future conservation planning and decision making.

4. Use appropriate science and tools.

To facilitate achievement of desired biological outcomes, our decisions must be made using the best science and tools available. Each of these components is based on science, including biological, ecological, social, and physical (USFWS 2015). A critical part of the Strategic Habitat Conservation process is identifying gaps in knowledge, generating information and tools to answer questions, and then using that information to inform and refine the decision making.

More Information about Specific Joint Ventures and Landscape Conservation Cooperatives in Texas

Some of the best places to find out more about specific Joint Ventures and Landscape Conservation Cooperatives in Texas are their websites (see links below). Websites contain information on various conservation plans, habitat delivery efforts, funding opportunities, science needs, staff, and more.

Gulf Coast Joint Venture
http://www.gcjv.org/

Lower Mississippi Valley Joint Venture
http://www.lmvjv.org/

Oaks and Prairies Joint Venture
http://www.opjv.org/

Playa Lakes Joint Venture
http://pljv.org/about

Rio Grande Joint Venture
http://www.rgjv.org/

Desert Landscape Conservation Cooperative
http://www.usbr.gov/dlcc/

Great Plains Landscape Conservation Cooperative
http://www.greatplainslcc.org/

Gulf Coast Prairie Landscape Conservation Cooperative
http://gulfcoastprairielcc.org/

Gulf Coastal Plains and Ozarks Landscape Conservation Cooperative
http://gcpolcc.org/

Conclusion

Today, the bird conservation world, at least in North America, is more integrated and cooperative than ever. It has to be. There is no other choice in how to operate when it comes to conserving populations of wild birds and the habitat required to sustain them. While the distinction between game and nongame birds will always remain, it will also continue to change over time, as noted in chapter 1 of this volume. The emergence of cooperative initiatives such as Joint Ventures and Landscape Conservation Cooperatives has been an important step toward overcoming the balkanization of the hunting versus conservation biology worldviews. This is a good thing. We hope it continues. It has to.

Literature Cited

Baxter, C. K. 2002. Defining the demands and meeting the challenges of integrated bird conservation. *Proceedings of the International Partners in Flight Conference* 3:7–12.

Brown, S., C. Hickey, B. Harrington, and R. Gill, eds. 2001. *The U.S. Shorebird Conservation Plan*. 2nd ed. Manomet, MA: Manomet Center for Conservation Sciences.

Crosby, A. D., R. D. Elmore, D. M. Leslie Jr., and R. E. Will. 2015. Looking beyond rare species as umbrella species: Northern Bobwhite (*Colinus virginianus*) and conservation of grassland and shrubland birds. *Biological Conservation* 186:233–40.

Giocomo, J. J., M. Gustafson, J. N. Duberstein, and C. Boyd. 2012. The role of joint ventures in bridging the gap between research and management. In *Wildlife Science: Connecting Research with Management*, edited by J. P. Sands, S. J. DeMaso, M. J. Schnupp, and L. A. Brennan, 239–51. Boca Raton, FL: CRC Press, Taylor and Francis Group.

Graziano, A. 1993. Preserving wildlife habitat: The U.S. Fish and Wildlife Service and the North American Waterfowl Management Plan. In *Land Conservation through Public-Private Partnerships*, edited by E. Endicott, 85–103. Washington, DC: Island Press.

Kushlan, J. A., M. J. Steinkamp, K. C. Parsons, J. Capp, M. A. Cruz, M. Coulter, I. Davidson, et al. 2002. *Waterbird Conservation for the Americas: The North American Waterbird Conservation Plan*. Version 1. Washington, DC: Waterbird Conservation for the Americas.

LCC (Landscape Conservation Cooperatives) Network. 2015. About Landscape Conservation Cooperatives. http://lccnetwork.org/about.

North American Waterfowl Management Plan. 2004. Canadian Wildlife Service, US Fish and Wildlife Service, Secretaría de Medio Ambiente y Recursos Naturales.

Rich, T. D., C. J. Beardmore, H. Berlanga, P. J. Blancher, M. S. W. Bradstreet, G. S. Butcher, D. W. Demarest, et al. 2004. *Partners in Flight North American Landbird Conservation Plan*. Ithaca, NY: Cornell Laboratory of Ornithology.

USFWS (US Fish and Wildlife Service). 2008. *Strategic Habitat Conservation Handbook: A Guide to Implementing the Technical Elements of Strategic Habitat Conservation*. Version 1.0. http://www.fws.gov/Science/doc/SHCTechnicalHandbook.pdf.

USFWS (US Fish and Wildlife Service). 2015. Strategic Habitat Conservation homepage. http://www.fws.gov/landscape-conservation/lcc.html.

Index

Other Books in the Perspectives on South Texas Series

African Americans in South Texas History
Bruce A. Glasrud

Beef, Brush, and Bobwhites: Quail Management in Cattle Country
Fidel Hernández and Fred S. Guthery

Ecología y Manejo de Venado Cola Blanca
Timothy E. Fulbright and J. Alfonso Ortega-Santos

Nesting Birds of a Tropical Frontier: The Lower Rio Grande Valley of Texas
Timothy Brush

Petra's Legacy: The South Texas Ranching Empire of Petra Vela and Mifflin Kenedy
Jane Clements Monday and Francis Brannen Vick

Plants of Deep South Texas: A Field Guide to the Woody and Flowering Species
Alfred Richardson

Racial Borders: Black Soldiers along the Rio Grande
James N. Leiker

Texas Quails: Ecology and Management
Leonard A. Brennan

White-Tailed Deer Habitat: Ecology and Management on Rangelands
Timothy E. Fulbright and J. Alfonso Ortega-Santos